KREGEL POPULAR
COMMENTARY SERIES

STUDIES IN ROMANS

H.C.G. MOULE

STUDIES
IN
ROMANS

STUDIES IN ROMANS

by

H. C. G. Moule

KREGEL PUBLICATIONS
Grand Rapids, Michigan 49501

STUDIES IN ROMANS, published in 1977, by Kregel
Publications, a division of Kregel, Inc. All rights reserved.

Library of Congress Cataloging in Publication Data

Moule, Handley Carr Glyn, Bp. of Durham, 1841-1920.
  Studies in Romans.

  (Kregel Popular Commentary Series)
  Reprint of the 1892 ed. published at the University
Press, Cambridge, Eng., under title The Epistle of Paul
the Apostle to the Romans, and issued in series: The
Cambridge Bible for schools and colleges.
  Includes index.
  1. Bible. N.T. Romans — Commentaries. I. Moule,
Handley Carr Glyn, Bp. of Durham, 1841-1920. II. Title.
BS2663.M68   1977   227'.1'07   77-79180
ISBN 0-8254-3215-4

Printed in the United States of America

CONTENTS

_{*} The Text adopted in this Edition is that of Dr Scrivener's *Cambridge Paragraph Bible.* A few variations from the ordinary Text, chiefly in the spelling of certain words, and in the use of italics, will be noticed. For the principles adopted by Dr Scrivener as regards the printing of the Text see his Introduction to the *Paragraph Bible,* published by the Cambridge University Press.

_{*} In the notes on the Text, among other abbreviations, the following are used:

q. v., *(quod vide,)* = "*to which the reader is referred.*"

q. d., *(quasi dicat,)* = "*as much as to say.*"

_{*} THE AORIST TENSE.

As this tense of the Greek verb is very frequently mentioned in the Notes, we here explain that its ordinary use, as a past tense, is to denote a single and completed past act, or whatever in the past is viewed as such. It thus differs from the Imperfect, which denotes past continuity; and from the Perfect, which denotes continuity between the past and the present.

INTRODUCTION

Chapter 1

SKETCH OF THE LIFE OF ST PAUL

1. "SAUL, who is also called Paul," was born at Tarsus, the capital of the province of Cilicia, and one of the three great Academies (Athens, Alexandria, Tarsus,) of the classic world. His father was a Jew, a Benjamite; one of the great orthodox-patriotic party of the Pharisees; a "Hebrew," in the special sense of a maintainer of Hebrew customs and of the use (within his own household) of the Aramaic language; and, finally, a Roman citizen. This citizenship was no result of the

"freedom" of Tarsus ; for civic "freedom," under the Empire, implied no more at the most than municipal self-government and exemption from public taxation. Saul's father may have been the freedman of a Roman noble; or he may have received citizenship in reward for political services during the great Civil Wars ; or, just possibly, he may have bought the privilege.

His name, as that of his wife, is unknown to us. We gather (2 Tim. i. 3) that they were sincerely pious. They had, besides Saul, at least one child, a daughter. (Acts xxiii. 16.)

2. Saul's circumcision-name was perhaps common in his tribe, in memory of the First King. His other and to us far more familiar name, PAUL, (PAULUS[1]), was probably given him also in infancy, for use in the Gentile world ; just as Jewish children in England now have a Hebrew home-name as well as an English (or otherwise European) name for exterior use. If his father was in any sense a dependent of the Æmilian family, the choice of *Paulus* is easily explained ; for Paulus was a common *cognomen* of the Æmilii. But it was used also by the Sergii and other families.

The name first occurs, Acts xiii. 9. The marked mention of it there is sufficiently explained by the fact that the Gentile name was, just then, in the Apostle's life, necessarily coming to be the more usual name of the two, and that the first distinguished Gentile before whom he spoke for Christ was himself, by a coincidence, a Paulus.

3. The exact date of Saul's birth is quite uncertain ; but it must lie within the few years before and the few years after the common (or Dionysian[2]) date of the Birth of Christ. When Stephen died Saul was still a "young man;" that is (in the then recognized sense of the words) he was not more than forty years old. And the date of Stephen's death must probably be placed in, or very near, A.D. 36[3].

---

[1] So spelt, and not *Paullus*, in the Imperial age.

[2] So called from Dionysius Exiguus, (cent. vi,) framer of the received reckoning. He dated the Incarnation 4 years too late.

[3] Mr Lewin (*Fasti Sacri*) gives much curious evidence in favour of A.D. 37. We incline to place Saul's birth *after* the Era; for, though men up to the age of forty were, as a class, called "young men,"

4. Quite early, perhaps as early as his ninth or tenth year, Saul was transferred, as a student of the Law, to Jerusalem ; where the great Pharisaic Teacher of the day was Gamaliel[1], grandson of Hillel. Gamaliel was an orthodox " Hebrew," but also a student of Gentile literature : and Saul under his influence not only matured into the best Rabbinist of his generation (Gal. i. 14), but also gained an acquaintance, traceable in his Epistles and Discourses, with at least a few Greek authors and with the then prevalent Greek philosophies[2].

Under Gamaliel, too, he would not be discouraged from using (along with the Original Scriptures) the "Septuagint" (LXX.) Greek Version[3]. His quotations from the Old Testament indicate an equal familiarity, or nearly so, with the Original and the Version. He quotes in Greek much as an English Hebraist, with the Authorized Version in his memory, might quote in English.

Whether Saul dwelt continuously at Jerusalem till his first recorded public acts, is uncertain. Acts xxvi. 4, 5, suggests a residence continuous on the whole ; but on the other hand St Paul's silence is sufficient proof that our Lord, during His earthly Life, was unknown to him by sight. This suggests a *break* of residence ; an absence (in Cilicia, or at Alexandria ?) during about the period of our Lord's Ministry ; after which, perhaps, a return to Jerusalem was prompted by the sudden prominence of the *Nazarene heresy*.

5. At the date of Stephen's work Saul was perhaps a member (as a Scribe) of the Great Sanhedrim. But more pro-

there is still some emphasis in the mention of the "youth" of an *individual* of that class.

[1] Cp. Conybeare and Howson, Vol. I. p. 69—71.

[2] This was hardly acquired at Tarsus (unless indeed during his residence there after conversion), for a Pharisee's young son would be carefully guarded from the influence of Gentile schools.

[3] Jewish tradition indeed makes Gamaliel to have been far from favourable to translations of the Sacred Hebrew. J. Lightfoot, (*Horæ Hebr.*, Addenda to 1 Cor. xiv.), quotes from the Talmud that Rabban Gamaliel ordered a Targum (Chaldee paraphrase-version) of Job to be buried under a heap of stones ! But Onkelos, the author of a renowned Targum of the O. T., was Gamaliel's devoted pupil. The Talmudic story must be an invention or distortion.

bably his election into it (which seems to be proved by Acts xxvi. 10, " I gave my *vote* against them,") was due to his display at that great crisis (for such it was both for the Church and the Synagogue,) of intense and energetic zeal.

6. He now became a regularly delegated inquisitor for the Sanhedrim, and (amongst other places, Acts xxvi. 11,) visited Damascus ; of whose 50000 Jews, as of all the Jews of the Dispersion, the High Priest (under certain imperial grants) was not only the spiritual head but also in some respects the civil *patronus.* His delegate thus carried the power of arrest. Under king Aretas of Petra, (a vassal of the Empire), who was just then[1] lord of Damascus, the Jews there had a governor (*ethnarch*, 2 Cor. xi. 32,) of their own ; to whom Saul would shew his commission, but who was soon to set guards at the city-gates to bar the Renegade's escape.

7. On the ever-memorable Conversion we only remark here that the Appearance then granted was, in the Convert's own life-long belief, radically different from what is commonly called a Vision. It was truly, though mysteriously, *corporeal;* for St Paul (1 Cor. xv. 8) bases upon it his claim to count among the witnesses of our Lord's corporeal Resurrection.

We do not dwell on the absolute and perfectly permanent change in the intense purpose of Saul's life which then and there took place ; it is best read in the Scripture pages. We only suggest the study of its two contrasted yet harmonious aspects—the *supernatural* aspect, in that it was wrought by an objective Divine act, which was the issue of a Divine purpose, (Gal. i. 15,) and the first step in a life-long experience of Divine inspiration ; and the *natural* aspect, in that it left the framework of character unchanged ; preserved unimpaired the balance of intellectual judgment—or rather gave a vastly greater expansion to its legitimate use ; and far from leading Saul impatiently to reject old beliefs as such, left him quite as fixedly as ever, and far more deeply than ever, sure of the entire and eternal truth of the prophetic Scriptures, and of the Divine

---

[1] During the reigns of Caligula and Claudius, or nearly so.

meaning of the very Ritual which had once seemed to him irre-
concilably to contradict the teaching of the Nazarenes.

8. After baptism, and some intercourse with the Damas-
cene disciples (Acts ix. 19), and then a withdrawal from the
city (Gal. i. 17) for some weeks or months, Saul began at
Damascus the new work of his life. His withdrawal had secured
for him, probably, the mysterious preparation of supernatural
intercourse with his Master, in the solitudes of Arabia—perhaps
in the peculiarly congenial solitudes of " Sinai in Arabia[1]."

9. After three years (at most) he left Damascus, to avoid
arrest or murder, and made his way to Jerusalem, where Barnabas, his friend and perhaps old fellow-student, introduced
him to the still hesitating Apostles. He became St Peter's
guest ; but after a fortnight of discussions with the Hellenists
of Jerusalem he was again compelled, by plots of assassination,
to retire to the coast of Syria, and thence to his native Tarsus
—A.D. 38 or 39.

10. From Tarsus, no doubt, he now worked as the evan-
gelist of Cilicia, and so spent at least three years. At length he
was summoned by Barnabas to the Syrian Antioch, the scene
of wholly new developements ; for in it first[2] the " Greeks," or
heathen Gentiles, (Acts xi. 20,) had now been freely welcomed
to the covenant of Messiah. At Antioch he laboured with
Barnabas for "a whole year ;"—about A.D. 43, probably ;—a year
memorable as the birth-time of the CHRISTIAN name (Acts xi.
26) ; and then visited Jerusalem, to carry relief there during (or
just before) one of the great dearths which marked the reign
(A.D. 41—54) of Claudius. The martyrdom of St James the son
of Zebedee, and the seizure and deliverance of St Peter, occurred
while Saul and Barnabas were in or near Jerusalem. This brief
and troubled visit is scarcely (it would appear from the words of
Gal. ii. 1) to be reckoned as a visit to the Apostles at all.

11. Now followed, at Antioch, another period of work for

[1] Arabia, however, was then a largely inclusive term. Some have
explained St Paul's absence in Arabia as if it were a first missionary
effort ; but the context in Gal. i. points rather to an occasion of Divine
intercourse and revelations.

[2] Unless indeed Saul in Cilicia had already done the same.

Saul and Barnabas.   It is a period not easy to date : some
reckonings close it A.D. 45, some as late as A.D. 49.   It lasted,
however, till a Divine oracle called Saul and Barnabas to em-
bark on their great Missionary Tour.   They began with Cyprus,
where at Paphos the Proconsul Paulus became, we may hope,
a true convert to the Gospel through the work and word of the
Tarsian Jew who bore his name.   They then passed to the
Pamphylian shore, and thence to the inner uplands of Pisidia
and Lycaonia, including the Isaurian fastnesses where Derbe
stood.   At length they approached, from the West, the Cilician
border, and then returned on their footsteps to the port of
Attalia, and so by sea to the Syrian Antioch.   We attempt no
details of this memorable circuit—crowded as its story is both
with Divine instruction and with innumerable notes of historic
accuracy and reality.

At Antioch they remained "a long time"—probably till A.D.
50 or 51.

12.   And now a disturbance of extreme gravity broke in
upon the work in this great centre of Gentile Christianity.   The
Judaic party in the Christian Church, retaining and intensifying
the exclusive views which had once clouded even St Peter's
mind (Acts x. 34), and which degenerated afterwards into manifold heretical divergences, now intruded on the field of St Paul.
Jerusalem, where by this time the Lord's Brother was what we
may fairly call the Bishop, was recognized as the Metropolis of
the Gospel, and the dispute was referred thither ;—a Divine
oracle (Gal. ii. 2) concurring with, or prompting, the resolve
of the Church.   The result was in some sort a compromise,
though it was a compromise divinely sanctioned (Acts xv. 28) ;
but it was at least so solemn a statement of the covenant-
equality of Gentile Christians, and thus so real a victory for
St Paul, that it secured to him for life the bitter and restless
opposition of the Judaic party—an opposition curiously developed in somewhat later days in the heretical literature falsely
inscribed with the name of Clement of Rome, and in which
St Paul is covertly assailed as the grand corrupter of the *primeval Gospel.*

The undiminished energy of the Judaists, even just after the decision at Jerusalem against their main principle, appears from the successful pressure they put upon St Peter himself, and that too at Antioch (to which he appears to have followed St Paul), to act for the moment as a separatist (Gal. ii. 11—21).

From this crisis, then, St Paul came forth as more than ever a recognized Apostle, co-ordinate with the Twelve, and also more than ever the object of intense hatred with a powerful party.

13. He had returned to Antioch with Barnabas, and accompanied by the new-comers from Jerusalem, Judas and Silas (Silvanus) ; and now, after a residence there of "some days," he proposed to Barnabas a second circuit. But a personal difference[1] led to their separation, and St Paul set out with Silas (say A.D. 51) on an independent track.

This time he went by land ; revisited his plantings in Syria, Cilicia, and Lycaonia ; joined the young Timotheus to his company in what proved to be a life-long connexion ; broke new ground in Phrygia and the "Galatian Region," where (it seems from Gal. iv. 13) he was detained among the Celtic inhabitants by illness—a detention overruled to a large and enthusiastic acceptance of the Gospel, soon however to be marred by Judaic intruders ; and then attempted other districts of Asia Minor.

14. But Divine commands, perhaps in the form of "prophesyings[2]," closed all avenues, and at last guided St Paul across the Ægæan to EUROPE. Here he landed in Macedonia, perhaps A.D. 52 ; made his first converts, now in peace, now amidst cruelties and terrors, at Philippi ; passed southward to Thessalonica, a Jewish centre and a busy trading-place, where he planted a vigorous Church ; then southward still, to Berœa, still followed by Jewish violence but also by Divine blessing ; and at last, for safety's sake, to Athens. Silas and Timotheus were left at Berœa, with orders to follow in due time.

[1] Afterwards healed. Cp. e.g. 1 Cor. ix. 6.
[2] The genuine supernatural phenomena which in later ages were perhaps in some few instances repeated, but in countless other instances unconsciously travestied; e.g. among the French "Prophets of the Cevennes."

15. At Athens he took advantage of the ways of the place, and opened discussion with the students and *dilettanti* who frequented the walks of the Agora; and at length (whether formally or informally, seriously or in irony, who shall say?) he was brought up to answer for his strange doctrine before (or at least in) the sacred Court of Areopagus. His address indicates familiarity with Stoicism.

16. Before long he left Athens for Corinth, the seat of the Roman government of Achaia (i.e. the Southern Greek Province). Here a scene of mingled activity and vice made both peculiar difficulties and peculiar opportunities for St Paul.

17. Early in A.D. 52 Claudius, by a severe but soon cancelled edict, banished from ROME its multitude of Jews. Of these one married pair, Aquila and Prisca (or Priscilla,) settled or rested at Corinth. They were workpeople, hair-cloth workers, and thus plied the trade which long before, (according to Rabbinic precepts, by which every Rabbi was to learn a handicraft against a time of need,) had been taught to the boy Saul. And this trade was now standing St Paul, the Christian Rabbi, in good stead; and thus, perhaps at first in the way of business, he fell in with Aquila and Priscilla. Whether he found them Christians, or (under God) made them such, we shall never know; but it is more *probable* that they were already believers —for otherwise we should certainly expect some distinct allusion in the Acts or the Epistles to so important a conversion. But doubtless they owed their first direct apostolic teaching to St Paul; to whom now they were bound for life in a holy friendship.

We have thus in Aquila and Priscilla, very probably, an example of what is antecedently likely—the arrival already of the Gospel at ROME. The first facts and doctrines may have reached the City soon after the Pentecostal preaching, (see Acts ii. 10), and there they would find rather easy audience than otherwise. At Rome a peculiar weariness of paganism was manifest in many directions; the East was, in a certain sense, in fashion; Judaism had attracted abundant notice; and the prophecies must have been at least superficially known to a multitude of proselytes or semi-proselytes. But no organized Church seems as yet to have arisen at Rome. Indeed there is no clear token of any Christian organization west of the Ægæan, before St Paul's arrival at Philippi.

18. At Corinth St Paul spent eighteen months. This time was marked by the writing of his earliest apostolic Letters—the two *Epistles to the Thessalonians.* These must be dated in, or near, A.D. 53—certainly not earlier.

Great opposition and great success marked the beginnings of the great Corinthian Church, with the "out-stations" (in modern missionary language) which doubtless then sprung up at the port of Cenchreæ and other neighbour-towns. Probably the assistants of St Paul carried the Gospel through the whole Achaian province at this time, or very soon after (2 Cor. i. 1).

About this stage of St Paul's life Nero succeeded Claudius; October, A.D. 54.

19. After scenes of outrage which the proconsul Gallio treated with impartial indifference, St Paul at last left Corinth for Syria; say some time in A.D. 54. He touched at Ephesus; left Aquila there with his wife, perhaps to be the organizer of a regular community; and himself departed for Cæsarea and Jerusalem. There he was perhaps in time to keep, as he had intended, one of the great Festivals; but all that is certain is that he "saluted the Church" of St James, and then soon left for Antioch, where again he spent "some time." (Acts xviii.)

20. Now followed a missionary tour in the "upper coasts," i.e. the inland regions, of Asia Minor. It must have been long and laborious; but it is dismissed by St Luke with a brief allusion. At length St Paul reached the shore, at Ephesus, some time (say) in A.D. 55.

Here an eminent Alexandrian Hellenist convert, Apollos, had meanwhile arrived; had held intercourse with the more advanced and instructed Aquila and Priscilla, and had crossed to Corinth; there to do much good, (Acts xviii. 27, 28,) but also, probably, by his more ornate and philosophically-worded preaching, to raise prejudices, unwittingly, against St Paul.

The Apostle spent about three years at Ephesus in ceaseless

Christian labours; and during this time his assistants travelled, it seems, to Colossæ, and Laodicea, and other places in proconsular Asia which he could not reach (Col. ii. 1). At length the tumult of Demetrius, perhaps at the festival of the *Ephesia,* hastened St Paul's already-planned departure for the European side.

21. Very shortly before this departure, (Spring, A.D. 57,) he had written and sent the *First Epistle to the Corinthians*— occasioned by distressing reports from Corinth as well as by questions raised by the Church there. To give the Epistle time to do its work, he resolved to reach Corinth by a long circuit round the head of the Ægæan, and so southward through Macedonia. Titus went before, to ascertain the state of the Corinthians, and to report to St Paul, if possible, in Asia Minor; but this proved impracticable, and St Paul's intense anxiety was not relieved by the longed-for tidings until he entered Macedonia (2 Cor. ii. 12, 13). Thence he wrote the *Second Epistle to the Corinthians*—a wonderful mosaic of serene revelations of eternal truth and outpourings of personal anxiety and affection.

22. He was now free to visit the Macedonian churches, and to evangelize new districts. Here we may probably place his westward tour (Rom. xv. 19,) as far as the Adriatic seaboard. Now also he effected throughout Macedonia (i.e., in the then sense of that term, the Northern Grecian Province,) the ingathering of a fund, already organized, for the poor Christians at Jerusalem (Rom. xv. 25, 26; 2 Cor. viii. 1—4, ix. 1, 2); —a task which was not only a tangible proof of deep sympathy with the work of St James, but also an expression of St Paul's own heart's love for his fellow Jews. (See Rom. xv. 27.)

But the most lastingly important effort of this period (for to this period it surely belongs[1]) was the *Epistle to the Galatians,* —the result of news of the inroads of Judaic propaganda in that well-loved, but already troubled, scene of his earlier labours. At length he reached Corinth; there found (as we have good

---

[1] Bp Lightfoot's argument seems conclusive for a date falling within this visit to Macedonia and Achaia, and probably very soon after the date of 2 Cor. (See his *Galatians,* pp. 36, &c.)

cause to think) happy results of his two Messages of warning and instruction; and there also collected the Achaian gifts for the Jerusalem Fund, which he now (Rom. xv. 25) prepared to carry to St James.

23. This stay at Corinth lasted only three months. But it was made memorable for ever by the writing of our great Epistle—the EPISTLE TO THE ROMANS. Let us examine the occasion of this Work at some little length.

It is not easy to conjecture the *precise motive* which led to the writing. The Epistle says nothing of *serious* disquiet or disorder among the Roman Christians. It indicates that they were, in a large majority, Gentile converts, and that the Judaic party proper, if present at Rome at all, had very small influence there. Evidently St Paul's informants from Rome told him rather of spiritual maturity and prosperity than of organic difficulty or really anxious controversy.

Nevertheless there was much just now to draw his thoughts specially to the City. The Apostle of the Nations would be sure, at any time, to think with profound interest of Rome; and, in fact, he had long desired to visit it (Rom. xv. 23). But now his beloved and trusted Aquila was once more there, possibly having returned from the Levant to Italy as St Paul's delegate, to form an organized Christian community[1]. And there were other Christian city-residents with whom St Paul had ties of kinship or friendship (Rom. xvi.). Thus through private information, (besides such news of the Roman brotherhood as would naturally permeate everywhere, and especially through the Greek provinces, from the centre of the Empire,) St Paul knew enough of the evangelical affairs of Rome to quicken his interest to a special degree.

His relations with the Church at Rome, if we have sketched them rightly, were thus exactly such as to account for the tone of our Epistle—a tone on the one hand of affectionate acquaintance, and of personal interest in the details of work and

[1] The silence of our Epistle, and of the Epistles afterwards written from Rome, is itself sufficient evidence against the legend (recorded and accepted by St Jerome) of St Peter's Episcopate at Rome.

life, and of consciousness of a *special* warrant to instruct the Roman believers; and yet on the other hand a tone marked by a certain distance and deference, as to those who did not, as a Church, owe their illumination to St Paul's immediate teaching, and who moreover by their metropolitan position stood on a height of influence which would specially appeal alike to his farseeing wisdom and to his noble courtesy.

24. And now not only his thoughts but his movements tended towards Rome. He had traversed with the Gospel message the East of Roman Europe, and his path lay westward. Probably a Divine intimation (see the phrase, Acts xix. 21,) had pointed him to the City; and moreover he was now bent upon a mission to Spain, where his usual *points d'appui*, the Synagogues, were frequent along the eastern shores. Thus, after one necessary visit to Jerusalem, he would take Italy on the road to Spain, and spend some while among the mature and spiritually-minded groups of disciples in the City.

25. Meantime, an opportunity offered for the previous greetings and instructions of an Epistle. A ministrant Christian woman from one of the ports of Corinth was about to sail for Rome; and by her he could send. And what he wrote for Phœbe's care proved to be that profound and magnificent exposition of fundamental principles, and that solution of the great problem of Jewish unbelief, and those abundant precepts of holy practical wisdom, which are now in our hands as the Epistle to the Romans—this Work of which one[1] who had a right to speak has said, (in view only of its intellectual grandeur,) "I think the Epistle to the Romans the most profound work in existence."

26. Looking now into the Epistle, and especially into the more properly dogmatic chapters (i—xi.), we cannot help the question, what determined its actual scale and form? Was it aimed at purely local, or incidental, needs and problems? Or was it, on the contrary, an abstract Treatise on the whole range of Christian truth, written as such, and merely by accident (so to speak) addressed to Rome? Such questions will be pursued

[1] S. T. Coleridge, *Table Talk*, p. 252.

by Christian students under full recollection of the mysterious reality (whatever were the varying methods) of *Inspiration*— that definite and unique influence of the Eternal Spirit on the Scripture-writers which made their writings the Oracles of God. But we are none the less for this—rather the more—entitled to ask what were the circumstances amidst which the Inspirer was pleased to work, or rather which He used as a part of His means —not merely *finding*, but *ordaining*, the conditions and idiosyncrasies of His messengers. Looking thus at our Epistle, taking into account the state of things at Rome, and St Paul's relations with Rome, we venture to account as follows for what we find.

(*A.*) The crisis in Galatia which had so very recently occasioned the Galatian Epistle (see ante, p. 16,) had forced into supreme prominence in St Paul's thought the true doctrine of JUSTIFICATION, as a matter preeminently calling for final and full exposition. It was for him, at that time above all others, the truth of truths; as indeed in its nature, on the whole, it must ever be for the human soul as guilty before God. For though it is not, by any means, the whole of the Gospel, yet such is its position in the Gospel—which is before all things a message to *sinners*—that it holds a direct and vital connexion with every other distinctive doctrine, and (from the point of view of sinful man) dominates the whole.

(*B.*) The problem of JEWISH UNBELIEF was at this time more than ever forced on the Apostle, not only by the fierceness of unbelieving Judaism, but by the misguided energy of Judaic error within the Church. And, moreover, the large Jewish population at Rome, and the remarkable influence[1] of Jewish thought and usages on pagan society there, would also be present in St Paul's thoughts when once he looked towards the City.

(*C.*) Certain minor but pressing questions of ceremonialism, involving principles of toleration, had been recently very prominent at Corinth, where St Paul now was ; and these same questions were said to be in some measure apparent also at Rome.

Thus when he addressed himself, just at that place and time,

---

[1] Fully attested by the Roman satirists.

to an Epistle to the Romans, (a) the mighty Truth of Justification lay providentially uppermost in his thoughts; and he
resolved to state and explain it in all its main bearings, not as in
an abstract treatise merely, but as to *this* community which had
already learned its outline, and which would have a world-wide
influence in its maintenance. And he then further (β) set himself to deal, in unexampled fulness, with the Jewish Problem—
his soul, perhaps, being the more animated to the effort, and the
more prompt to reveal the better Future of Israel, just because
of his own sufferings from unbelieving Rabbinism and from
the malice of the Judaic party. And to these doctrinal passages
he added (γ) the counsels and greetings occasioned by his
knowledge of minuter circumstances at Rome.

The Epistle was evidently written not under pressure of
anxiety, but with calm deliberation.

It was composed, apparently, in the house of a Corinthian
Christian, Gaius or Caius; dictated by St Paul, and written
down by one Tertius. Would that we could call up the scene in
the Corinthian chamber!

27. We have thus dwelt at length on the occasion of the
Epistle[1]. Let us now follow St Paul's life, in simplest outline, to
the close.

The three months at Corinth over, he left Achaia for Macedonia; spent Passover at Philippi; crossed to Asia Minor;
addressed the Ephesian presbyters at Miletus; sailed to Tyre,
and at length (amidst prophecies of danger) reached Jerusalem,
perhaps in May, A.D. 58;—not long after an Egyptian impostor,
at the head of a huge gang of the zealot *Sicarii*, (Assassins,)
had seriously threatened the Roman authorities of Palestine.
In the act of a last effort to conciliate the Judaic party, St Paul
was almost murdered in the Temple by the Jews; rescued by
the Roman commandant, but under the belief that the victim of
the mob was the Egyptian rebel; allowed to defend himself on
the spot before the multitude, and the next day before the Sanhedrim; and then, for safety, conveyed as a prisoner to Cæsarea.

---

[1] A few points, such as evidence of date, genuineness, &c. are treated
below, pp. 25—27.

There, within a fortnight of his arrival at Jerusalem, he was heard before the Procurator Felix; who lingered however over the case, and at last, two years after, when recalled on a serious charge (Summer, A. D. 60,) left St Paul a prisoner still.

Of these two years of St Paul's life we know almost nothing. Some critics assign to them the writing of the Epistles to the Ephesians, Colossians, and Philemon. But these are certainly to be dated later, and from Rome.

28. At length, before Porcius Festus, the Apostle was heard again; but even this far better judge hesitated to do him full justice, and he appealed in due form, as a citizen, to the Emperor's own hearing. He was ere long shipped for Italy; but off the Cretan coast, perhaps early in October, a typhoon struck the ship, which soon was a drifting wreck and was at last run aground at Malta. There the rescued company wintered, and not till the early spring of A. D. 61 (the year of Boadicea's revolt in Britain) did St Paul at last see Rome. At some distance from the City, in detached parties, at two different spots, the representatives of the Church (now for nearly three years in possession of the great Epistle) met the captive Saint, and cheered his anxious and weary spirit by their loyal sympathy.

29. In the City, he was permitted to occupy a hired lodging, perhaps a storey of one of the lofty Roman *tabernæ*. Here, a few days after his arrival, he made a last long effort to convince the leaders of the Roman Jews[1] of the Messiahship of Jesus; and here, under military custody but otherwise unmolested, he spent "two whole years," full no doubt of immense mental and spiritual labour and holy influence, and marked for ever by the writing of the four Epistles, (perhaps in this order[2],) *Philippians, Colossians, Philemon, Ephesians.*

---

[1] The cautious language of these Jews to St Paul (Acts xxviii. 21, 22) does not prove, as some have said, that they knew nothing of any Christian Church at Rome. They spoke diplomatically, with the wish to hear St Paul's own account of the "Nazarenes."

[2] Or nearly so. Setting aside *Philemon* (which, as a personal message, is an appendage to *Colossians*), we may certainly place *Colossians* and *Ephesians* in that order, and may assume that they (with *Philemon*) were written at one time. *Philippians* bears traces of a distinct time of writing. See our edition of *Philippians*, pp. 14—19.

30. This Roman residence closed in the course of A.D. 62, probably in the summer. The question *how* it closed—whether with condemnation to death, or acquittal—is a famous one. Its discussion would be out of place here ; but our undoubting conviction is that the result was St Paul's acquittal; that he was set free [1], and once more undertook missionary labours ; that he visited Western and Eastern Europe, and Asia Minor ; and that, late in this last stage of his life, he wrote the *Pastoral Epistles*—in the order 1 *Timothy, Titus,* 2 *Timothy.* This last most affecting Letter is dated once more from a prison, and from Rome. It is our only relic of St Paul's *second* Roman captivity, which ended in his martyrdom—probably A.D. 66, the year of the Great Fire and of the Neronian Persecution ; though perhaps the date of the martyrdom must be placed one or two years later [2].

Probably soon before St Paul's execution, and probably also at Rome, St Peter had suffered his predicted death. And (if A.D. 66 is the true date) the Jewish War had already begun a few months when St Paul died—to close four years later with the Fall of Jerusalem.

31. The one question within our scope here, connected with this last period of St Paul's life, is the question of a visit to Spain. Was the hope of Rom. xv. 24, 28, at length fulfilled?

There seems to be good evidence that it was. In the Epistle to the Corinthians written by St Paul's own follower, St Clement of Rome, we find it stated (ch. v.) as a familiar fact that St Paul, before his " departure from this world to the holy place," "went to the end of the West [3]." It has been pleaded, against the

---

[1] If the *Epistle to the Hebrews* is St Paul's, it must probably be dated between this release and his departure from Italy. But this is not the place for so large a question.

[2] But the main reason for the later date seems to be the supposed necessity for a long interval between *Philippians* and the *Pastorals,* to explain the change of surroundings and especially of *style.* But at St Paul's age, and after his sufferings and extreme *vicissitudes,* an alteration of style was at least as likely to be sudden as gradual.— Timothy is still addressed as a "young man."—The genuineness of the *Pastorals* is, in our view, a certain fact.

[3] "The end (or limit) of the West" is the only unforced rendering of the Greek of Clement.

theory of a Spanish journey, that this may mean only *Italy*, as viewed from the locality of St Clement's correspondents at *Corinth*. But the then Centre of the World could not possibly be so described, and above all not by a writer dating from Rome, however he might care to put himself in his readers' geographical position. And there is direct evidence besides that such a phrase as "the end of the West" would have a familiar connexion, at that time, with Spain. (See Bp Lightfoot's *S. Clement of Rome*, pp. 49—51.)

This witness, certainly genuine and quite contemporary, is fairly conclusive. St Clement cannot have been mistaken or ignorant on so leading a fact of his great Master's latest labours as the westward limit of those labours.

The only serious difficulty in the theory of the Spanish visit (once granting the theory, necessary to the genuineness of the *Pastorals*, of St Paul's release and second Roman imprisonment) is that there is no traditional trace whatever of any work of St Paul's in Spain[1]. But this is equally true of other districts (as Illyricum), in which however we have St Paul's own word for his labours.

We take it then for certain that St Paul, some time after the spring or summer of A.D. 62, and probably before the spring of A.D. 66, visited the Western Peninsula—whose present name, España, is said[2] to be an aboriginal word, meaning "The Land's End."

The belief that he landed in Britain possesses, in Bp Lightfoot's words (*S. Clement of Rome*, quoted above), "neither evidence nor probability."

32. It is impossible not to wish to know something of St Paul's personal appearance. Mr Lewin (in his *Life and Epistles of St Paul*, Vol. II. ch. xi.) has collected all that ap-

[1] Mr Lewin (*Life*, &c., Vol. II. p. 363, note) quotes an inscription found in Spain, of Nero's time, which commemorates the riddance out of the Province of "robbers, *and of those who sought to instil a new superstition into mankind.*" This probably refers to Christianity, and possibly to the results of St Paul's labours.

[2] By W. von Humboldt, quoted in Smith's *Dict. Class. Geogr.*

proaches to information in this matter; and in this one case at least tradition appears to be something better than mere fancy. It seems to be certain that St Paul's stature was short, if not diminutive; that his head was bald and his face bearded; and that his expression, even if deformed in some measure by *ophthalmia* (which is one of the many conjectural explanations of the "thorn in the flesh"), yet reflected something of his soul. A medallion, dating perhaps from the generation next to St Paul's own, is engraved by Mr Lewin (Vol. II. p. 411) : it gives the profiles of St Paul and St Peter; and that of St Paul expresses, or seems to do so, all the elevation and intensity both of thought and feeling which still, as we read the Epistles, touch us with the touch of life.

33. The character and labours of St Paul have been so often eulogized, and are so inimitably described in a thousand unconscious touches by his own pen, that it would be vain in this brief summary to attempt another portrait. We will only quote the words of a very few of the many existing delineations.

Amidst the circumstances of his apostolic work he developed a force and play of spirit, a keenness, depth, clearness, and cogency of thought, a purity and firmness of purpose, an intensity of feeling, a holy audacity of effort, a wisdom of deportment, a precision and delicacy of practical skill, a strength and liberty of faith, a fire and mastery of eloquence, a heroism in danger, a love, and self-forgetfulness, and patience, and humility, and altogether a sublime power and richness of endowment, which have secured for this chosen Implement[1]of Christ the reverence and wonder of all time.

MEYER: *Brief an die Römer, Einleitung,* p. 7.

I dream'd that with a passionate complaint
I wish'd me born amid God's deeds of might;
And envied those who had the presence bright
Of gifted Prophet and strong-hearted Saint,
Whom my heart loves, and Fancy strives to paint.
I turn'd, when straight a stranger met my sight,
Came as my guest, and did awhile unite
His lot with mine, and lived without restraint.
Courteous he was, and grave,—so meek in mien,

[1] *Rüstzeug:* the word used by Luther in Acts ix. 15, where our Version uses *vessel.*

It seemed untrue, or told a purpose weak;
Yet, in the mood, he could with aptness speak,
Or with stern force, or show of feelings keen,
Marking deep craft, methought, or hidden pride:
Then came a voice, "St Paul is at thy side."[1]

J. H. NEWMAN, 1833: *Verses on Various Occasions*, p. 159.

Imagine the world without St Paul: it would mean the detention of the Gospel, perhaps for centuries, on the borders of Asia, far from this Europe of ours, which Paul (after JESUS CHRIST) has made the centre of the conversion and civilization of the world. Imagine the Bible without St Paul: it would mean Christian truth only half revealed, Christian life only half understood, Christian charity only half known, Christian faith only half victorious.

ADOLPHE MONOD: *Saint Paul, Cinq Discours*, 1.

YET NOT I, BUT THE GRACE OF GOD WHICH WAS WITH ME.

ST PAUL

Chapter 2

1. DATE OF THE EPISTLE.   2. LANGUAGE.   3. GENUINE-NESS.   4. QUESTIONS RAISED ABOUT THE CLOSING CHAPTERS, AND,   5. ABOUT THE FINAL DOXOLOGY.

1. The time and place of the writing of the Epistle can both be clearly ascertained. It was written (1) late in the missionary history recorded in the Acts; for St Paul had already done his work in the regions East of the Adriatic (xv. 19). It

---

[1] The impressions of "craft" and "pride" are manifestly intended by the Poet to be false impressions. But things have been sometimes said about St Paul's *tact* which amount to a charge of insincerity; and it seems worth while to observe that a sufficient vindication of his noble straightforwardness is found in his own gentle and affectionate allusions (see 1 Cor. ix. 19—22; 2 Cor. xii. 16;) to his own "craft," "guile," and the like. A man really capable of insincerity, and especially of the insincerity of pious frauds, is not the man to describe himself thus. St Paul's one recorded approach to equivocation (Acts xxiii. 6), if such it was, seems to have disturbed his conscience (Acts xxiv. 20, 21).

was written (2) when he was just about to leave Greece (xv. 25, 26) for Jerusalem, with collected gifts for the poor. These notes exactly agree with allusions in 1 and 2 Corinthians to the collection of such gifts during St Paul's approach to Achaia by Macedonia, at a time when both Achaia and Macedonia were already evangelized. And these allusions, again, fit into the history of Acts xx., xxi., which records his journey from Ephesus, by Macedonia, to Achaia, and his journey and voyage thence (after a brief interval) to Palestine. Our Epistle, then, was written soon after the date of 2 Corinthians, and just before the visit to Palestine of Acts xx., xxi.: that is, it was written early in A.D. 58 (see ante, p. 20), during the fourth year of Nero.

Again, the *place* of writing was Corinth. *Cenchreæ* (xvi. 1), the Saronic port of Corinth, was evidently a neighbour-town ; and in xvi. 23 "*the city*" is a phrase which indicates a capital ; and that capital was, by the obvious meaning of that verse, the place where St Paul was at the time. And this localization is confirmed by comparing xvi. 23, where a *Gaius* is St Paul's actual host, with 1 Cor. i. 14, where a *Gaius* appears as a *Corinthian* specially connected with St Paul.

2. The Epistle, though addressed to Rome, was written in Greek. There is no surprise in this. For (1) Greek was the far more familiar language to St Paul; while there is no proof that the " gift of tongues " was of a kind to neutralize this difference. And (2) Greek was used to a very large extent in Italy at that date. Not only was it universally learnt and spoken by the children of wealthy Romans, but (to point to one fact alone) Southern Italy had been for ages sprinkled with Greek colonies, and between these and the City there must have been abundant intercourse for many generations when St Paul wrote.

Not many years later St Clement, the Roman bishop, wrote to the Corinthians in Greek ; and not long afterwards again St Ignatius of Antioch wrote in Greek to the Romans. Many such examples might be added.

3. The genuineness of the Epistle as a whole is universally admitted : even the extreme school of German criticism, the

"school of Tübingen," did not assail it. The first formal quotations from the Epistle are by St Irenæus, about A.D. 170; but such quotations indicate, of course, an already long established authority. And St Clement of Rome, St Paul's own follower, writes (in his Epistle to the Corinthians, ch. xxxv,) what is plainly a summary of Rom. i. 29, &c. Several other testimonies, also primeval, might be added.

4. The *closing chapters* of the Epistle, however, have been said, by some foreign critics, of the last hundred years, to be either mutilated or misplaced. We here abridge Tholuck's summary of these theories[1], supplemented from Alford's and Meyer's Introductions.

1. *Semler* held that cch. xv., xvi., were not meant for the Romans at all; that the true Epistle was cch. i.—xiv.; that *this* was entrusted to certain Christians moving from Corinth to Rome; that ch. xvi. was a list of disciples resident at different places on the route, who were to be greeted; that Cenchreæ would be the first stage (a very brief one), and that thus Phœbe is first named; that Ephesus would be the next resting-place, where Aquila and Priscilla (whose names thus stand next) would be met with; and so on. Ch. xv., in Semler's view, was merely "a sort of private missive to be communicated to all whom they visited on the way."

2. *Heumann* held that cch. i.—xi., xvi., were the original Epistle; that Phœbe's journey was delayed; and that, in the interval, news from Rome led St Paul to add cch. xii.—xv.

3. *Schulz* held that ch. xvi. has nothing to do with the Epistle, but was written from *Rome* to *Ephesus;*

4. *Schott*, that it is the fragments of an Epistle from St Paul in *Corinth* to some Asiatic Church or other.

(The doubts about ch. xvi. seem to be almost wholly due to the mention there of Aquila and Priscilla, and the supposed difficulty of our having *no account* of a migration of theirs from Ephesus to Rome, and an after migration again (2 Tim. iv. 19) to Ephesus.)

[1] Tholuck *on the Romans, Eng. Trans.; Biblical Cabinet*, Vol. v. pp. 17, &c.

The *internal* evidence for these curiously conflicting guesses is feeble indeed. The best refutation is a consecutive reading of cch. xii.—xvi. by a reader who does not start with a pedantic theory of what St Paul *ought* to have related, or alluded to, or discussed. And what is the *external* evidence? It amounts to this :

(1) The heretical teacher *Marcion* (cent. ii.) "cut off" (so Tertullian tells us) cch. xv., xvi. :—but it was Marcion's principle to reject whatever Scriptures *did not suit his views.*

(2) *Tertullian* (centt. ii., iii.) apparently quotes[1] xiv. 10 as "in the *conclusion*" (of the Epistle):—but this is *in a treatise written against Marcion*, and may be meant to meet Marcion on his own ground.

(3) *Euthalius* (cent. v. ; see p. 258), in his section-headings to St Paul's Epistles, gives no heading for ch. xvi. ;—but probably this was because ch. xvi., as being full of names, was not used as a church-lesson ; and Euthalius elsewhere, in counting the "verses" (of his arrangement) in the Epistle, evidently *reckons in ch. xvi.*

Meanwhile, of the known extant MSS. of St Paul (of which Dr Scrivener reckons about 300[2]), *all the MSS. hitherto collated* (including the very large majority and all the most important), if they preserve the main body of the Epistle consecutively at all, give these chapters in just the received connexion and order.

5. To this statement one reservation must be made, regarding the *closing Doxology*, xvi. 25—27. These verses—

(1) in most of the very oldest MSS. stand where we read them : (2) in a very few MSS. indeed are omitted or (by a later hand) erased : (3) in many MSS., including most of the cursive, or running-hand, MSS., are placed at the close of ch. xiv. : (4) in a very few MSS. are found in *both* places.

The evidence of patristic quotations and ancient versions is

[1] *Against Marcion*, v. 14. The words possibly admit of another rendering.
[2] *Introduction to N. T. Criticism*, 1874, p. 269.

divided. The ancient Greek Lectionaries support the position at the close of ch. xiv.

The evidence for the right of the Doxology to stand *somewhere* in the Epistle is thus most ample. A tendency to place it at the end of ch. xiv. can be fairly explained by early misconception, due (1) to the occurrence of a Benediction (xvi. 24) just before the Doxology, and (2) to the thought that the words "*able to stablish you*" were specially adapted to the plea for the "*weak*" in ch. xiv. And on the other hand it needs only to read the Doxology to see that its main purpose is nothing lower than thanksgiving for the Universal Gospel as a whole, and that its weighty grandeur of tone obviously belongs to the close not of a section (which section, too, the Apostle at once carries on into a new passage, xv. 1, &c.), but of the Epistle.

On the theory of a *pause* in St Paul's dictation after ver. 24 (see note there), the received place of the Doxology entirely harmonizes with its rich contents and sublime expression[1].

Chapter 3

PARALLELS BETWEEN THE EPISTLE TO THE ROMANS AND THE EPISTLE TO THE GALATIANS

Subjoined are the more obvious parallels, arranged under doctrinal heads. A careful study of these, and of the two Epistles generally, will make plain the peculiar connexion of the two, and the remarkable upgrowth, so to speak, of the longer and more deliberate out of the shorter, more personal, and more urgent[2].

1. *The Gospel predestined and prophesied:*
       Gal. iii. 8=Rom. i. 2.
       — iv. 4= — v. 6.

[1] See further Tholuck's Introduction; Alford, *in loc.;* and Meyer's long and careful preliminary note to ch. xvi.
[2] On resemblances between *Romans* and *Corinthians* see Appendix

2. *Sin:*
    Gal. v. 19—21 = Rom. i. 18—32.

3. *Futility of mere Privilege.*
    Gal. v. 6, vi. 15 = Rom. ii. 25—29.

4. *Justification by Faith:*
    Gal. iii. 11 = Rom. i. 17, iii. 26, &c.

5. *Release from the Law:*
    Gal. v. 18 = Rom. vi. 14.
    — ii. 19 = — vii. 4.

6. *Use of the Law:*
    Gal. iii. 19 = Rom. v. 20, vii. 7.

7. *The Holy Spirit:*
    Gal. iii. 14 = Rom. v. 1, 5.
    — v. 17 = — viii. 14.

8. *Sonship of the Justified:*
    Gal. iv. 5, 6 = Rom. viii. 14—16.

9. *Heirship of the Justified:*
    Gal. iv. 7 = Rom. viii. 17.

10. *The Flesh and the Spirit:*
    Gal. iii. 3, v. 16 = Rom. viii. 4, &c.

11. *The inner Conflict:*
    Gal. v. 17 = Rom. vii. 14—24.

12. *Equality (in Guilt and Justification) of Jew and Gentile:*
    Gal. iii. 8, 28 = Rom. iii. 30, x. 12.
    — iii. 22 = — xi. 32.

13. *Abraham, and his Seed:*
    Gal. iii. = Rom. iv.
    — vi. 16 = — ix. 8, 25, 26.

14. *Baptism:*
    Gal. iii. 27 = Rom. vi. 3, 4.

15. *"Crucifixion":*
    Gal. ii. 20, v. 24, vi. 14 = Rom. vi. 6.

16. *"Putting on of Christ":*
    Gal. iii. 27 = Rom. xiii. 14.

17. *Love fulfils the Law:*
    Gal. v. 14 = Rom. xiii. 8.

Chapter 4

NUMBER OF QUOTATIONS FROM THE OLD TESTAMENT

THE reckoning below is approximate only, for in some cases the quotation may be accounted for by more O. T. passages than one. The figures thus tend on the whole to be under rather than over the mark.

Approximately, then, we have in this Epistle—

GENESIS quoted *five times;*	ISAIAH quoted *nineteen times;*	
EXODUS „ *four times;*	EZEKIEL „ *once;*	
LEVITICUS „ *twice;*	HOSEA „ *twice;*	
DEUTERON. „ *five times;*	JOEL „ *once;*	
I. KINGS „ *twice;*	NAHUM „ *once;*	
PSALMS „ *fifteen times;*	HABAKK. „ *once;*	
PROVERBS „ *twice;*	MALACHI „ *once.*	

Thus there are at least sixty-one direct quotations. Cch. v., vi., xvi. alone are without any. The allusions to Old Testament history, type, and doctrine extend, of course, far beyond even these verbal references.

Chapter 5

ARGUMENT OF THE EPISTLE

CH. I. **1—7.** PAUL, a commissioned messenger of the predicted and now exalted Messiah, greets the saints of Rome.

8—17. He hears with joy the report of their faith, and prays to be allowed at length to visit them, both as a friend and as a teacher. Even in the great City he will find courage to teach, for his doctrine is Divine in origin and efficacy, and it is for all. It is the secret of sinful man's acceptance before God—JUSTIFICATION BY FAITH. [And of this, anticipating an oral discourse, he will now treat in writing.]

18—23. First, then, let them consider the *need* of such a Way of Acceptance, in the light of the fact of Divine Wrath against Human

SIN. Such is the sin of man that the sinner, in his rebellion, has resisted and repressed that knowledge of a Supreme Creator which the outward world has always at least suggested to the conscience of the Creature. From this voluntary and most guilty ignorance sprung Idolatry; and, as a judicial penalty upon Idolatry, God gave up the idolatrous world to the worst developments of impurity and unrighteousness.

CH. II. **1—11.** But what, then, of the *Jewish* world, which had now for ages been free from positive idolatry? The exposure of Jewish sin is approached gradually, by an appeal first to the conscience of *self-righteous man in general*, but in terms which more and more mark out Jewish self-righteousness; and closing with a warning that, not only in privilege but in responsibility, the Jew stands first.

12—16. Yes: for sin implies guilt, and guilt implies doom; alike for those who have an explicit Revelation, and for those who have the light and law of Conscience only. [For Conscience, even when addressed by no more than the voice of Natural Religion, is a real, though imperfect, guide; and man's disobedience to it, even in the darkness of heathenism, is sin.] Thus neither the privilege of having a Revelation exempts the Jew, nor the disadvantage of not having it exempts the Gentile, from the judgment of the Great Day.

17—29. These truths are now pressed direct upon the conscience of the Jew. As a well-known fact, self-righteous Jews are not pure. And if not pure, then not safe. For the Covenant of Abraham was never meant to shield impenitent descendants of Abraham from doom. Circumcision is not a substitute for spiritual blessings, but their seal.

CH. III. **1—2.** But if so, how was the Jew better off than the heathen? Why was there a Covenant with Abraham at all? Answer: —chiefly, because of the immense honour and benefit of the possession of Revelation. True, Revelation aggravates responsibility; but none the less is it an inestimable opportunity and privilege.

[This section is an appendage to the section previous.]

3—8. But may not the Jew now urge, on the whole question, a new and subtle objection? May he not take his stand on the fact of the promise to Abraham, and suggest that that promise *may* include the impunity of even impenitent Jewish sinners; because such impunity might "commend," by contrast, the indulgence of God displayed in letting the impenitent alone? Answer:—such reasoning would tend to negative the fear of *any* penalty for *any* sin, whether of Jews or Gentiles. It goes on a principle abhorrent to all righteousness.

9—20. Thus then, as the result of the reasoning, the whole world, mankind in every instance, Jews and heathens alike, is GUILTY before God. Experience attests it, and Revelation (vv. 10—18) plainly declares it. And thus the whole result of the LAW,—in other words, of Revelation as preceptive,—is not the acceptance of man but his conviction. Every explicit demand on obedience, addressed to sinners, does but expose more explicitly the nature of sin as *transgression*.

21—31. [Under these circumstances of fatal guiltiness, is there a means of mercy, a Way of Acceptance? All have sinned, and so sinned that "there is no difference" between man and man—in respect, not of amount of guilt, but of completeness of failure. For all men equally therefore the Law has *no acceptance ;* for its inexorable demand is nothing less than life-long and entire obedience, negative and positive. And meantime God, the Eternal Judge, is fully on the side of the Law ; which is no capricious demand of mere Power, but the expression of His own absolute and necessary Holiness. Thus then if there is a Way of Acceptance for man, it must on the one side stand entirely "*apart from the Law*" (ver. 21), independent (as to its terms,) of man's obedience to the Law—because a *justifying* obedience on man's part is now impossible ; and on the other side it must "*manifest the righteousness*" of Him who accords acceptance ; it must make it plain that the Judge, while accepting the offender, still unchangeably ratifies, maintains, and honours the sanctity of His own Law, His expressed Holiness.]

Such a Way of Acceptance there is ; foretold in the Old Scriptures, and now made actual in the Work of JESUS, the Messiah. He, by the Eternal Judge Himself, is now "*set forth*" in the view of fallen men as their EXPIATORY SACRIFICE. [His Death is that of a vicarious, or substituted, Victim ; a Death endured because Sin (not His own but man's) calls for the retribution of Death. As such, and as the Death of an infinitely sacred and perfectly voluntary *Victim*, it proves beyond doubt that God, who ordained that Death, is indeed not indifferent to His own Law. And again, as the death of a *Substitute*, it is a Redemption, a Ransom :—for those who obtain interest in it, it effects deliverance from legal doom, i.e., Acceptance before God.] And lastly, the way to obtain such interest is FAITH ; sincere and direct *Trust* in the Person and the Work in question, as the revealed Propitiation ;— Faith and no less, Faith and no more.

By this Way of Acceptance, now revealed, God (1) "*declares* (or, *explains*) *His righteousness*," in the pardon of sin, both in the ages before the Gospel (ver. 25), and now. And (2) He "*excludes boasting*," by transferring the element of *merit* in the matter of Acceptance, wholly and for ever, to the Propitiatory Substitute of the sinner; nothing being left to the sinner but the act of trustful acceptance—the act of Faith.

[And even this is left to him only that he, a responsible being, may have a conscious and willing part in the matter; not with any suggestion that *faith carries any merit with it*. For in its proper nature it cannot; and this is specially plain in this case, where Faith is the acceptance of *immense mercy*: and, in any view, the admission of the idea of merit would at once negative the "exclusion of boasting." But this "exclusion" is, says St Paul, the direct and proper result of "the law (or, institute) of Faith."]

These terms of Acceptance are, evidently, as free for Gentiles as for Jews. God, and His procedure in the matter, alike are One (ver. 30).

31. An objection is here, in passing, stated and negatived, and deferred for fuller treatment. That objection is that such terms of Acceptance appear to *dispense in all respects with the Law*. Is the sinner accepted only and absolutely on the merits of the Propitiation; which merits he obtains interest in on the sole condition of his own trustful acceptance of them? What becomes then of his future actions? Will he care to keep rules of righteousness? Has he adequate reasons for so doing? Yes, says St Paul; he has indeed; and they are such as will secure a fulness and reality of obedience unknown before. [But this is to be explained later (ch. vi.)]

CH. IV. 1—5. Another objection is now anticipated and discussed, the discussion forming a strong confirmatory argument. ABRAHAM, it might be urged, the great Paternal Name of the Old Covenant, was surely justified by that covenant and not another. He, at least, won acceptance "*according to the flesh;*" on a standing of his own works. He, at least, might in some sense "*glory*," in the matter of his acceptance.

No: for it is expressly and providentially laid down in Abraham's history that what was "*counted to him for righteousness*" was his entire and self-forgetful *Trust* in the promise of God. [He was regarded as having merit because he had Faith; while yet Faith is not merit, nor can be.] And thus Abraham, instead of being an exception to, is the great example of, the rule of Divine Acceptance; namely, that the sinner's way to that Acceptance is not by merit, whether antecedent, concomitant, or consequent, but by Faith; by "*believing on Him that justifieth,*—that accepteth as righteous,—*the ungodly."* [Yes; even *the ungodly;* the impious and profane. Even in such extreme cases, if the man, with all his guilt unmitigated on his head, yet trustfully accepts the revealed Propitiation, God justifies freely.]

6—8. [A parenthetical illustration follows, perhaps suggested by the word "ungodly."] DAVID, another preeminent Mosaic "patriarch," bears explicit witness to the bliss of non-legal acceptance; [and he does so with the intensity of personal experience of deep transgression.] He testifies to the wonderful and merciful fact that God can, and does, *"reckon* (impute) *righteousness"* to a soul that has nothing of its own but aggravated sin.

9—17. The argument reverts now to Abraham's case; and a new difficulty is anticipated and met. Abraham and David were *Hebrews;* members of the covenant of circumcision. May it not be, then, that this blessing of free Acceptance, albeit so large in itself, is yet *in its application limited to the circumcised alone?* Is it not for them only that Justification by Faith is revealed? No: for again in Abraham's history it is providentially recorded that his acceptance as righteous took place long before his circumcision. The covenant followed his Faith, not his Faith the covenant. And this was thus ordered on purpose to make it quite clear that Gentiles as well as Jews are welcome to the sacred Justification, and to the inheritance of the Promise made to Abraham; [a Promise which pointed to his Great Descendant, Messiah, and to all who should stand vitally connected with Messiah.]

18—22. The *circumstances* under which Abraham "believed God" are now detailed, [to bring out not only Abraham's strength of Faith, but a main characteristic of justifying Faith in general, as the act by which the *man looks wholly away from self and intently regards Another* as the sole ground of trust. And this is taken as an account, in some measure, of the reason why Faith specially is appointed as the condition of Justification. Faith (as directed towards God) is that act of the soul which most entirely *honours* Him. Absolutely devoid of merit, as we have seen, it has however a natural fitness to be the act of acceptance of the blessing.]

23—25. This act of Faith on Abraham's part, and the record of it, have direct reference to believers now. It was recorded not merely as a passage of ancient story, but because God purposed to deal with *us* as He dealt with Abraham; to count us, having Faith in Him, as having righteousness. And we now have a final and special cause for such Faith; for He is known to us as the Father who gave His Holy One to death because we had sinned, and raised Him again because His death had effected our Justification.

CH. V. [Thus far St Paul has established (1) the *need* of Justification; and (2) its *equal terms* for Jews and Gentiles; and (3) that Faith in Christ's blood, (iii. 25,) personal trustful acceptance of the Propitiation, is its one appointed *condition*. And (4) in Abraham's case he has illustrated the *nature and actings* of Faith. Now he is about to deal with the *effects* of Faith in life and character;—but not yet explicitly or exclusively. He has to treat of topics connected with both past and future reasonings. First he must dwell on the Manifestation of *Divine Love* in Justification; then he must further illustrate the *relation between Christ and the justified* by the relation between Adam and the guilty.]

1—11. [Now first he deals with the manifestation of Divine Love in Justification by Faith. The justified are not merely acquitted, in a negative way.] They are in full "*peace*" with God; they "*stand*" in holy nearness to Him; they look with *joy* for His final glory; their very sorrows are used to vivify their hope and perseverance. They have (ver. 5), from the indwelling Divine *Spirit*, a consciousness (not due to their own minds) of the love of God towards them. Meantime this consciousness is conveyed through the amazing objective Fact of the Father's Gift of His Christ to be the Propitiation for souls which, in themselves, were sinful, impious, and hostile to God. This, further, is a sacred pledge that He who so freely loved them before reconciliation will perseveringly love them after reconciliation; and thus their state is one not of safety only but of joy.

12—21. [Now follows a section in which both the vicariousness, and the overflowing efficacy, of the Work of Christ for the justified are illustrated by the doctrine (evidently known and believed in the Church) of the relation of the fallen Race to Adam. This discussion springs, partially, from the immediately previous statement of the abundance of the Divine love in Justification, and of the deep and lasting connexion (ver. 10) of the justified with Christ.] Such, says St Paul, was Adam's position as Head of the Race that by his sin every individual of his sons was subjected to *guilt*. Yes; not to defilement only, but to guilt. Such were the mysterious relations of Law and Sin that Adam's sons, even when [as in the case of infants] no conscious transgression could have been committed by them, yet all without exception have suffered *death*; that is, suffered *penalty for sin*—for such, for man, death is. [Why, we do not fully know; but the fact of infant-death is enough to prove it to be so ; and the Judge of all the earth does right.] Thus, in a sense, Adam's race *penally* dies *because Adam sinned.*

Now this is a counterpart, and strong illustration, of the fact that the Church lives, *meritoriously* accepted, *because Christ obeyed.* As Adam's guilt is reckoned to his sons, so Christ's righteousness is reckoned to His brethren. The parallel only fails (ver. 15) in the *excess* of the wonder of the results in the second case. The Gift of Grace *far exceeds* the Ruin, though each is the result of one Representative's act ; for while the result of Adam's sin was that law merely took its course of condemnation, the result of Christ's work is not a mere return to the *status quo,* but a truly Divine reversal—the Reign of the Justified in eternal glory : and this, meanwhile, in spite of the fact that the Redeemer had to deal not only with the one original Crime but with the countless personal offences of the justified (ver. 16). And the Law, far from doing part of His work, did but *bring out* in its fulness the fatal malady and peril; only, however, that this might be sur- passed by the more than equal fulness of the atoning and redeeming Grace and its results.

CH. VI. **1—15.** [We now come to the question suggested in iii. 31.] What is the *result on conduct* of this proved and illustrated truth that man is justified by faith without works ? Shall we go on in the old life of sin, under the belief that thus the Grace of God will have a wider field for action ? The thought is abhorrent. But it is also clearly unreasonable. For *how* are we set *free from the claim, and doom,* of sin ? By our union with a slain and risen Redeemer. Now as His Death, counted to us, frees us from doom, so His Life, in which He is still our Head and Representative, pledges our continued blessed acceptance before God. But such acceptance before such a God must, inevitably, be a cause of holiness. It is not merely freedom *from doom ;* it is freedom *to God.* And one way in which this effect (holi- ness) is to be realized is by a firm grasp on the truth that the justified, in their Substitute and Head, *have died to sin ;* that is, have borne its penalty and exhausted its claim. Not till that was done could they *truly* love the *true* God ; for they could not have peace with Him, nor He with them. Conversely, now that this is done, *their wills are set free to love Him ;* love to Him, and consequent obedience, are now the true *bias* of their new position "in Christ." Let them realize this and act it out ; still keeping (ver. 14) the fact of JUSTIFICATION full in view as the grand motive and condition for SANCTIFICATION, i. e. attainment of holiness.

16—23. This great subject is further illustrated from the facts of human Slavery. A slave, purchased from one owner, is freed from that owner, but only by the fact of becoming the property of another. Now it is a *purchase*, a *Redemption*, that has freed the justified from doom; but by that very fact therefore they are the *property* of their Redeemer; the *slaves* of holiness, of God. True, the illustration (ver. 19) is in itself low and harsh; but it is used to enforce a strong reality; and meantime that reality is full of dignity, full of the bliss of an immortality of holiness, the Gift of God in Christ.

CH. VII. **1—6.** The same subject is further illustrated from the facts of Matrimony. Matrimony, in its idea, is indissoluble during the lifetime of both partners. But the death of one sets the other free for a new union. Even thus the justified once had for a mystical Husband *the Law* (regarded not as a guiding but as an exacting standard), and the offspring was sin. Now the justified, in Christ, have *died:* the matrimony is dissolved. But also in Christ they are risen, they are in a new life; therefore they are free for a new union. And this union is to the Eternal Bridegroom Himself. Him His Church is both to love and (with a wife's devotedness) to *serve.* And the offspring will be, deeds of holy obedience done for God.

7—13. But the question now has to be answered, *What is the true function of the Law?* St Paul has just said that we, in Christ, are dead to the Law: is the Law then a thing which is evil, and from which it is good to be altogether free? No; the thought is abhorrent. But none the less the fact is plain that the Law, in itself entirely pure and holy, yet *in collision with the fallen soul* does aggravate the developements of sin. Man, antecedent to his knowledge of the Law, was sinful and guilty (ch. v. 12, &c.), but knowledge of the Law gives a new rancour and intensity to his personal sinfulness, because it developes the element of definite resistance to a perfectly Holy Will. It finds this element dormant; it awakens it as from a grave; sin, in this aspect, "revives" at the voice of the Law, and the man [consciously—but not penitently—] is aware of its doom; he "dies." Such then in the present respect is the true function of the Law: as a demand upon the sinful soul, it *does not purify, but only inexorably evokes and exposes the full reality and malignity of Sin.*

14—25. And this, which is true of the unregenerate state, is true also, in measure, of the regenerate state. For in the regenerate man there is still an element, "the flesh," which, though no longer dominant, is present; no longer the practically true Self, yet an almost *alter Ego.*

And this double consciousness (so to speak) is to last as long as the "body of death" lasts—in other words, till the immortal state begins. The conflict is terrible; but the prospect of release is glorious and animating (ver. 24).

The justified man then, (as the result (ver. 25) of the discussion,) is in a certain sense in bondservice both to God and to sin. But it is his true self that serves God; it is his old self that serves sin.

CH. VIII. [St Paul now proceeds to a final application of the whole previous reasonings, to the position, privileges, and hopes of the justified. He has explained and illustrated the absolute freeness of Justification, as effected *wholly* by the merits of Christ conveyed to those who believe in Him. He has explained and illustrated also the relations between the justified and the Law; shewing (1) that their Justification (being a matter of Redemption, and involving a spiritual Marriage-union,) binds them *ipso facto* to a new obedience, that of the reconciled soul to the reconciled God; and (2) that the Law, nevertheless, in no degree is, any more than it was, their Justification; for, alike in the past and the present, its absolute demands— viewed as demands for *satisfying* obedience—serve only to expose the subtle malignity of sin. It is the Guide, but not the Covenant, of the justified.]

1—13. There is therefore now, as the whole result, no condemnation from the Law for those who, by faith, are "in Christ." His Sacrifice has done what the Law could not do; it has, by removing the legal curse, set free the believing soul to choose and love *ex animo* the Law of God: and this not merely by removing a barrier but by admitting a new Energy—even that of the Divine Spirit, who dwells in a mode altogether special in the souls of the justified, and (through their human spirit) rules their nature, which—before this Indwelling—was ruled and characterized by the element of sin, and incapable of true love to the true God. Now, though their body still feels the results of the penalty of sin, (ver. 10,) and though there is still an inherent element of sin to be resisted by the will, (vv. 9, 13,) yet their spirits are already exempt from the spirit's death, (ver. 10,) and their bodies shall hereafter be exempt from the body's death also (ver. 11).

14—17. Further, the justified are (what has not yet been explicitly stated) the SONS of God, [as being "in Christ," the Eternal Son.] They are, in this their filial position, animated by the Divine Spirit with filial feelings—with the will to obey their Father (ver. 14),

and the intimacy of conscious and reciprocal love in His presence (vv.
15, 16). And their Father makes them His *heirs* as well as His sons:
He designs for them His riches of glory in the eternal state.

18—25. So vast is this glory that the manifestation of it is an
object of profound desire not only to the justified themselves, but
(in a different and metaphorical sense) to the sin-affected material
universe, for which is destined a mysterious transfiguration, to be
effected in connexion with the glorification of the justified. They,
meanwhile, recognize this *futurity* of their full blessedness, and patiently wait for it, notwithstanding all sorrows and delays.

26—27. And again, their happy position is further secured by
the Indwelling Spirit's special influences in *prayer;* surely directing
them to effectual petitions for real blessings.

28—30. Finally, all things and events are so ordered by the will
of God as to contribute to the present and final good of those who love
Him; that is to say, of the justified; who are, according to a purpose
of eternal covenant, fore-ordained to their possession of likeness to
Christ, to acceptance in Him, and to glory with Him.

31—39. In view of such sacred facts, as expounded in the whole
previous reasoning of the Chapter and the Epistle, what can be
said in the way of doubt and fear? Who can ruin those thus
secured? He who gave His SON for their deliverance will deny no
subsidiary security. Their Justifier will not be also their Accuser.
Their Substitute and Intercessor will not be their condemning Judge.
And as they have thus the Father and the Son wholly on their side,
no adverse power shall avail for their ruin. Nothing shall pluck them
from the eternal hand; no violence of this world; no powers of the
world unseen; no imaginable obstacle or adversary, present or to come.
Divine Redeeming Love holds them fast.

CH. IX. [St Paul now turns from the abstract explanation of
the ways of Divine Grace, to the discussion of one great and anxious
concrete phenomenon. There is a subtle connexion of thought
in the transition: the freedom of the Christian's justification, the
security of his standing, and the splendour of his hopes, bring up
by way of contrast the dark fact of the UNBELIEF OF ISRAEL. Perhaps
also he is led to deal with it by a consciousness that it was a difficult
question in many Christian minds—how to reconcile the truth of
the Gospel as the final Revelation with the rejection of it by the
Depositaries of the elder Revelation.]

1—5. But St Paul's immediate feeling is the intensest personal pain, and most importunate longing, as he—himself a Jew—contemplates the unbelief, and consequent exclusion from the great Blessing, of the once gloriously privileged Israel; the people honoured above all by the human birth among them of the Divine Messiah.

6—13. The first care in this matter, however, must be to vindicate GOD. Has He failed to keep His promises, by thus suffering the Jewish Nation to fall? Had He not promised Abraham that *his seed* should be blessed, and should be a blessing? Is the present state of Israel, then, a case of *non-performance?*

St Paul meets this, not by making out that the promise was *conditional,* but by proving the *limits* of its intention. By "the seed" was meant, plainly, not all the descendants of Abraham, but some of them. There was a limit in Sarah; another in Isaac; another in Jacob. And the story of Jacob illustrates a fact full of importance in this question; that namely of absolute *Sovereignty of Choice* on the part of the Eternal. He chooses, as the recipients of blessing, "*whom He will,*" antecedently to all idea of merits or character in the persons chosen or not chosen; [—all of whom are, considered *à priori* and in themselves, alike unworthy of choice.]

14—24. Such a fact is unquestionably one of profound mystery, and challenges the most anxious questions. *Is God unrighteous? Is man responsible?* If GOD's Will is the ultimate account of the difference between man and man in respect of religious privileges and the actings of Divine grace, what can we say to these questions?

[St Paul's reply is, to the last degree, uncompromising. He takes his stand on two principles: first, that the Old Testament is a true revelation of the true God; secondly, that whatever the true God, as a fact, does, cannot be unrighteous—whether or no we can fully understand its righteousness.] In this respect he specially insists (ver. 20, &c.) on the ineffable difference of standing-point between the CREATOR and the Creature. St Paul does not *overwhelm* objections by mere power or terror; he *meets* them with the fact that the God who is Sovereign is, not merely an irresistible Potentate, but the Eternal CAUSE of things, and especially the Cause of Man. Before HIM it is indeed reasonable to bow with entire submission when we are once sure of HIS Act or of HIS Word.

Now in this matter of Sovereignty we are sure of *both.* His own Scriptures record His own avowal that—as in the actual case of *Pharaoh*—He applies or withholds gracious influences on human souls as HE will. This is true not only of nations, or churches, but of individuals; for so (ver. 18) St Paul applies the individual case of Pharaoh:—"*He hath mercy on the man on whom He will, &c.*" In His dealings, alike with communities and with persons, His own Glory is the ultimate purpose of the Eternal. [That purpose is sure to be attained through ways of perfect Righteousness, but also through ways of quite unfathomable mystery. For the Glory is the Glory of the Eternal.]

[Meantime, however man may fail to understand the problem, and to reconcile the Decrees and the Benevolence of God, *both are real facts.*] Even with the "*vessels of wrath*" He deals in sincere long-suffering. And on the "*vessels of mercy*" He pours His wealth of blessing, and has destined them for heavenly glory. And these "vessels" are the true Israel; the true "seed of Abraham," blessed and a blessing; some of them Jews, some of them Gentiles, and all sovereignly called to grace.

25—33. And such an Israel, an Israel of election and of spiritual parentage, from which many Jews should be shut out, and to which many Gentiles should be admitted, was *foretold* in Prophecy; by Hosea and by Isaiah. And the actual cause of the ruin of the excluded Jews was foretold also; it was to be their guilty error in taking the Law to be a covenant of self-righteousness, and in stumbling, instead of resting, on the rock of Messiah's Work.

CH. X. **1—13.** St Paul pauses to repeat the assurance of his intense desire for the salvation of the Jews; especially in view of their strong, but misguided, *earnestness.* This gives him occasion to enlarge on the witness of the *Old Testament* to Christ, and to Justification by Faith. For he shews that Israel, in mistaking the purpose of "the Law," mistook it *in spite of its own words.* Christ is the Divine Fulfilment of which the Law was one vast prediction. And, in one remarkable passage, Moses was inspired to specially foreshadow the Incarnation and Resurrection of Messiah, and the offer of salvation to whosoever should confess and accept Him as the Eternal Son thus made Man and sacrificed for sinners. And manifestly such a salvation is as free for Gentile as for Jewish faith; as again Prophecy (ver. 13) has testified.

14—15. And if so, then certainly the salvation thus foretold must now be *proclaimed*, without reserve, to the nations. Apostolic missions, however opposed by misguided Judaism, are the will of God; as again (ver. 15) Prophecy has indicated.

16—21. [But is it objected further that multitudes of the heathen have met those missions with contempt and unbelief, and that this looks as if the Divine Purpose were otherwise?] The reply is that this too was distinctly *foretold*—in words which exactly describe the Gospel and its work (ver. 17); and moreover that the universal spread of the proclamation, and the admission of Gentiles to covenant with God, and the Jews' rejection of the appeals of His patient love, were all foreshewn in Prophecy, and are therefore confirmations, not difficulties, of belief.

CH. XI. **1—10.** [But this is not all that is to be said on the great problem. The Divine Sovereignty of Choice has been asserted, and we have been shewn the clear predictions in the Hebrew Scriptures of the universal Gospel and of Jewish unbelief. Thus far the discussion, as regards the Jews, has been adverse only. Now St Paul will shew proof, in their favour, that their rejection *never has been total.*]

The nation was never so rejected as not to contain within it an elect Church, a true Israel. As in the darkest days of Baal-worship, (ver. 4,) so now in the darkest days of unbelief in Messiah, there is a believing Israel all along. [What no other race can shew, Israel shews; an unbroken continuity of the "holy seed."] This continuity, be it again remembered, is the result of pure sovereign grace (vv. 5, 6), and in it we see the predicted (vv. 8, 9) spectacle of an unbelieving Nation enshrining an elect Remnant—[whose existence proves that Jews *as Jews* have never been excluded from the covenant.]

11—15. But even this is not all. The rejection of Israel has never been total; neither is it, even thus, *final.* Its present phase, in which Faith is the rare exception, is in God's time to close, and a great return to Messiah is to take place. The "*stumbling*" of Israel is not a final "*fall.*" Viewed on a certain side, it was permitted and ordained as a means of mercy to the Gentiles; for (1) it immediately occasioned the Death of the Redeemer, and (2) it compelled the Apostles to turn to the Gentile world. And from this may be anticipated the greatness of the blessing which the Gentile world shall reap from the *Restoration* of Israel. For such a blessing is, in fact, in store. Israel shall in such a sense be "received" into the Covenant of Messiah that the result on the world at large shall be like a spiritual resurrection. (On this prospect St Paul specially dwells because (vv. 13, 14) of his special mission to the *Gentiles;* which gives him an equal concern in the influence of Gentile faith on the Jews and of Jewish restoration on the Gentiles.)

16—24. This predicted restoration, though an act of Divine grace, will yet, in a sense, move in the line of anterior probability. The lineal connexion of the Jews with the Fathers makes it obviously likely that their return to Messiah will be abundantly welcome to the God of the Fathers. To the great Olive Tree of the Church the Jews stand in a specially *congenial* relation; [for, in a certain respect, the Root of that Tree is Abraham and the Hebrew Patriarchs, and its Stem is the faithful Hebrew Church under the Old Testament.] From this Tree the unbelieving Jew is, as it were, a branch *rent off*. Into this Tree the believing Gentile is, as it were, a branch *grafted in* from an alien and uncultured stock. Can it be doubted, then, that when the great Husbandman re-ingrafts the native branches their reception and growth will be, to the full, as *kindly* as that of the alien branches has proved to be?—Let the Gentile Christian beware of the tendency to a proud and exclusive spirit in *his* turn. Let him remember that grace has reached him through Israel, not Israel through him. Let him not be content merely to see that Israel's rejection was the means of mercy to himself; but let him further see in that rejection a caution to himself, a warning that his own personal Faith in the Propitiation is the one—and vital—condition of his own union with the mystic Tree; and let him welcome the prospect of the restoration, on the same condition, of the severed, but native, branches.

25—27. For, be it once more remembered, such restoration is to take place. The present partial unbelief of Israel is to last, not for ever, but till an advanced stage of the in-gathering of the Gentiles. Then the Jews shall be brought back to Messiah in numbers which will be, in at least a general sense, inclusive of the whole race. So Prophecy has foreshadowed: Messiah's coming was foretold as that which, in God's time and way, should bring to *Israel* the blessings of faith and peace.

28—32. To sum up:—In spite of the dark phenomenon of the rejection of Israel, (over-ruled for the spread of the Gospel,) the nation, with a view to the always-existing elect Remnant, is still emphatically within the purposes of Divine Love. And again, there is a *special* purpose of grace in the temporary rejection of Israel: namely, that the salvation of Jews, as well as that of Gentiles, might be conspicuously placed—to God's glory—on a footing of *mere mercy*. Mere mercy had called the Gentiles out of heathenism; mere mercy would *re*-call the Jews out of unbelief. Thus, in both cases, the sovereignty of mercy would stand out unmistakable.

33—36. At the close of this discussion, in which the mystery of the ways of God, and the inscrutable adaptations of judgment to mercy, and of all to the Divine Glory, have been so prominent, St Paul pauses to ascribe adoring praise to HIM whose Will and Wisdom are unfathomable, and absolutely independent of His creatures, and Who is Himself the Final Cause of all His works.

[Here closes the Doctrinal Part of the Epistle, in the stricter sense of the word "doctrinal." The application of doctrine to practice is now to come more definitely forward.]

CH. XII. 1—8. In view of the great Exposition, now completed, of Human Sin and the redeeming, justifying, and electing "Compassions" of God, St Paul beseeches the believers to live as those who are wholly dedicated, with all their energies, to their Lord; finding in the hope of eternal bliss an animating motive; studying the good will of God with the powers of their now renewed intelligence; watching against tendencies to self-assertion, and isolation of spiritual interests, (for each is a part, with all the rest, of one Body); and aiming faithfully to carry out the sacred "division of labour" appointed by the Divine Master.

9—21. They must cultivate love; holiness; courtesy; diligence; hope; patience; prayerfulness; unselfishness; meekness under persecution; sympathy; humility; probity; and that loving requital of good for evil which is the true *revenge* of a Christian.

CH. XIII. 1—7. They must be careful to live as loyal and orderly subjects in the State; for Civil Authority is God's own ordinance. He, the Supreme King, without a moment's abdication of His own royalty (ver. 8, *note*,) yet has constituted human magistrates His delegates. Their work (in spite of all imperfections and abuses) is, on the whole, His work; they bear His credentials; they carry on the work of the State, with its machinery of taxation and the like, in His name— [whether they own it or not.] The Christian therefore must recognize, in "the powers that be," his Lord's order, and must altogether decline, whether by way of craft or of violence, to resist them.

8—10. And as in the public so in the private relations of life, the Christian must sedulously regard the claims of others; avoiding all *indebtedness* save only that of the great debt of brotherly love, which will be ever paying, never paid; and the payment of which is the sure way to an impartial obedience to all the guidings of the Divine Law.

11—14. Meanwhile, to animate these loving efforts, they must live in recollection of the waning of the Night of sorrow and temptation, and of the approach of the eternal Day of purity and joy. [The Lord's Incarnation, like the Star of Morning, has already warned us that] "*the night is far spent:*" the next great crisis is the sunrise of resurrection glory. Let them then, by new efforts of faith and love, cast off the acts and habits of sin and sloth which are, as it were, the nightrobe of the soul; let them dress themselves in the armour that befits the children of the Day —in other words, let them make their Redeeming Lord Himself the safeguard of their souls, and in Him find the true secret of watchful self-denial instead of that *watchful self-indulgence* (ver. 14, *note*,) natural to the sinful will.

CH. XIV. **1—9.** [Yet, with all these exhortations to vigorous decision, St Paul must warn them also to practise, in one direction specially, gentleness and toleration.] There are, he understands, some amongst them whose consciences are not clear on the question whether observance of the Mosaic ritual and calendar is still incumbent on believing Christians;—"brethren" who hold, or at least incline to hold, that the Levitical distinctions in food, and the specially Jewish holy-days, are a part of God's path of duty for the justified. And again there are others amongst them who so strongly take the opposite view as to make their assertion of freedom in these respects a main part of their religion, and well-nigh to excommunicate the Christians who differ from them. Now, in *abstract principle*, the "stronger" consciences are right; St Paul's own convictions are with them. But in *application of principle* they are wrong. For these differences touch not the Foundation. The "weak" and the "strong" alike, their special opinions notwithstanding, may be and are safe in Christ by justifying Faith; accepted, "received," for His sake, by His Father. Both alike, though in different ways, "acknowledge Him" as their rule and principle; and both alike are directly and supremely responsible to Him.—Yes, let them all remember this: His saints, alike in this world and the next, are immediately and inseparably connected with Him as Master and Disposer. The very manner and method of His Redeeming work proves and enforces this.

10—23. But, to revert to the special question:—seeing that each Christian is thus responsible to the LORD, responsible for his *opinions* as for all else, let the "stronger" believer be tenderly respectful towards the conscience of the "weaker." Let him think of the sacredness of Conscience, which—however erring—is never (while it is still conscience) violated without sin. Let him not tempt his brother to trifle with his scruples, and, so far, tend to undo the work of Redeeming Love for that soul. True Christian privilege and liberty has infinitely more to do with justification, peace, and joy before God, than with a self-asserting independence of ceremonial restrictions; and, while a faithful life in the enjoyment of *spiritual* privilege is both acceptable to God and a proof to men of the reality of true religion, [an eager assertion of mere *mundane* privilege is little likely to be either the one or the other.] Faith (ver. 22) is not a matter for personal display. And, once more, the peril of a slighted conscience is great indeed : every *liberty taken against conscience*, and not on the clear ground of acceptance in Christ, is essentially sin, and brings down the displeasure of the holy Judge.

To pursue the same subject :

CH. XV. 1—7. The duty of the " strong" or "able " Christian is to be not the critic but the friend and helper of the " weak ; " to make not the liberty of self but the good of the brotherhood his dearest aim. This is to follow the supreme Example of Him who, for man's salvation, " endured the contradiction of sinners " against His Father and Himself; thus specially fulfilling the prophetic words of Psal. lxix. And (be it said by the way) the whole Old Testament Scriptures are in one respect or another applicable, even as that passage is applicable, to Christian life and duty now ; and specially to the enlivenment of Christian *hope*, which again is one of the surest motives to Christian *unanimity*.

So let Christians *welcome* Christians, into the friendship, sympathy, and forbearance of the Gospel ; remembering each his own merciful welcome to grace: thus glory to God will be the result.

8—13. As one more motive-truth in this direction, let them remember that the Redeemer was "*of* the Jews " and "*for* the Gentiles ; " which latter fact is fully attested by Prophecy. Let this thought draw together the Jewish and the Gentile believer, and conciliate him who still observes the old ceremonial with him who has entirely done with it,

14—21. [Now to draw to an end.] St Paul fully shares the universal high esteem for evangelical maturity in which the Roman Christians are held. Yet he has written as their monitor, (and sometimes in very plain terms); for he stands before them as being, by grace, the Apostle of the Gentiles ; the metaphorical Priest of the great metaphorical Offering ; bringing to the Gospel-altar the "*living sacrifice*" of converted nations. Such is his commission ; and he has been enabled to carry out that commission, in an independent and miraculously-ratified course of apostolic labour, from Jerusalem and the East to the Adriatic province—the next neighbour of Italy.

22—33. The vastness of this field of work, and the knowledge that the Gospel had already struck such root at Rome, has kept him hitherto from visiting the Capital. But now he is planning a journey to Spain, and he will take Rome on the way, and taste there the sweetness of sacred friendship a little while. A visit to Jerusalem, in the matter of alms from the Greek to the Judæan Christians, must first be carried out : then he will come, and blessing from the Lord will attend the visit. Meanwhile, the Romans must now specially remember him in prayer ; for this Judæan visit has many attendant anxieties.—May the God of holy peace be with them !

CH. XVI. **1—16.** He now personally *commends* to their Christian hospitality a pious Visitor from the neighbourhood of Corinth— Phœbe, a female helper in the Cenchrean church. And he *greets* first his honoured and self-devoted friends Prisca and Aquila, and the Christians meeting at their house for worship; and then many other individuals and groups.

17—20. One brief warning more. There are certain teachers of error abroad, specious in tone and exposition, but not pure in intention and practice. Loyal to the Gospel as the Romans are, yet even *they* must be on their guard. And ere long the strife with error, and with its Prince, will be over for ever.

21—24. Timotheus and others desire their salutations to the Roman saints. The amanuensis inscribes his own.

25—27. Lastly, [on review of the Argument in which thus his Inspirer has enabled him to expound the foundation-truths of the Gospel,] St Paul ascribes all praise to the Eternal Father, the Giver and Revealer of this Gospel of Grace and Faith, (in which the Romans will find their secret of stability ;) this Gospel which was the great Secret of the Past, and is the glorious Revelation of the Present ; the embodied Wisdom of the Only Wise. To Him, through His Son, be glory for ever.

COMMENTARY ON ROMANS

Cʜ. I. 1—7 *Greeting*

Pᴀᴜʟ, a servant of Jesus Christ, called *to be* an apostle, 1
separated unto the gospel of God, (which he had pro- 2

Tɪᴛʟᴇ

The oldest form is the briefest, Tᴏ (ᴛʜᴇ) Rᴏᴍᴀɴs. So in the
"Subscription" to the Epistle, q. v.

Cʜ. I. 1—7. Gʀᴇᴇᴛɪɴɢ

1. *Paul*] On the name, see *Introduction*, i. § 2.

a servant] Strictly, **a bondservant.** So Phil. i. 1; Tit. i. 1;
Jas. i. 1; 2 Pet. i. 1; Jude 1. For exposition of the word see vi. 18,
19, with 1 Cor. vi. 19, 20; Tit. ii. 14 (where "a *peculiar* people" means
"a people of possession"). The Christian is his Lord's bondsman
(1) as purchased, (2) as self-surrendered. St Paul thus describes himself before the mention of his special, apostolic, branch of bondservice.
This Epistle is the earliest in which St Paul uses the word in the
exordium.

of Jesus Christ] Cp. xiv. 18; 1 Cor. vii. 22; Eph. vi. 6, &c. To St
Paul the Divine Son, as truly as the Father, is his absolute Master and
Possessor.—The sacred Name and Title (Jesus, Christ,) occur *together* in
the Gospels five times, in the Acts often, in the Epistles perpetually.—
It is most important to remember that *Christ* is merely the Greek
version of the Hebrew *Messiah* (Anointed). As used in Scripture, it
thus constantly refers back to O. T. prophecy, and to the truth (uttered
by Messiah Himself, John iv. 22,) that "salvation is *of the Jews.*"

called] At his conversion. Cp. 1 Cor. i. 1. For the terms of the
call see Acts xxvi. 17, 18. This call is distinct from the *call to be
a Christian*, on which see vv. 6, 7; viii. 28; 1 Cor. i. 24.

an apostle] Lit. **an envoy, missionary**; in Gospels and Acts,
always in the special sense of an immediate Delegate from the Saviour.
In xvi. 7, the sense is, perhaps, more extended[1]; so, too, Phil. ii. 25
(where E. V. "messenger"). St Paul needed often to insist on the
fact and rights of his apostleship. 1 Cor. ix. 1, 2; 2 Cor. xii. 12;
Gal. i. 1.

separated] For the special work of an Apostle. This was (1) in God's
sure purpose (Gal. i. 15, 16; cp. Jerem. i. 5); (2) at his conversion (Acts
ix. 15); (3) at Antioch (Acts xiii. 2; "*separate* me, &c.").

the gospel of God] The Message of Good sent from God and reveal

---

1 But see note there.

3 mised afore by his prophets in the holy scriptures,) concerning his Son Jesus Christ our Lord, which was made of
4 the seed of David according to the flesh; *and* declared *to be*

ing Him. So xv. 16; 2 Cor. xi. 7; 1 Thess. ii. 2, &c. In a special
sense it is the Gospel of *Christ*, in whom alone is the true revelation of
God (Matt. xi. 27; John xvii. 3).

2. *which he had promised afore*] This verse is not properly a parenthesis. See on verse 3. The *Promise* of the great Deliverer, running
through the O. T., is one of the most wonderful of the phenomena of
history. It was such that, beyond all question, it had brought the hope
of Israel to an intense pitch just before, and at, the time of the birth and
life of Jesus of Nazareth. See Bp E. H. Browne's *Messiah Foretold
and Expected*, pp. 1—21.

by his prophets] I.e., probably, by the Scripture-writers generally.
In the O. T., history and prophecy are closely interwoven. In Heb.
i. 1, God's message to "the fathers," though "in divers manners," is *all*
sent "through the prophets." The words here are nearly repeated, xvi.
26, where the O. T. Scriptures are regarded as the great instrument, in
apostolic hands, for spreading the Gospel.

in the holy scriptures] Holy, because divinely planned and guided
throughout. So 2 Tim. iii. 14, 15. The article is wanting in the Gr.
(as it is in xvi. 26, " prophetic writings "), and the translation might
thus be *"in holy writings."* But the article is often omitted where the
thing or class spoken of is unmistakable; and the word rendered
"scripture" is so completely appropriated in N. T. to the contents of the
definite inspired writings, that we must translate " *the* holy Scriptures."

3. *concerning his Son*, &c.] The connexion is with the close of
ver. 2: the "promise through the prophets "was "concerning the Son of
God." In the Gr., the order of words in this verse and the next is
peculiar and emphatic : **concerning His Son, who was made** [lit. **who
came to be, who became] of the seed of David according to the flesh;
who was marked out as the Son of God, in power, according to the
Spirit of holiness, in consequence of the resurrection of the dead,
Jesus Christ our Lord.**

of the seed of David] The N. T. begins with this assertion (Matt.
i. 1), and almost closes with it (Rev. xxii. 16). In 2 Tim. ii. 8, St Paul,
at the close of his ministry, again recites it as a foundation-truth.

according to the flesh] **Flesh**-wards, i. e. "on the side of His manhood." This is said in contrast to the next words, "declared to be the
Son of God." Cp. ix. 5 for an important parallel, where the full significance of the title "Son of God" appears. For another use of the
phrase "according to the flesh," see iv. 1.

4. *declared*] Better, **defined, marked out by sure signs.** Same
word as Heb. iv. 7 ("He *limiteth* a certain day"). His Resurrection
shewed Him to be *none other than* the Son. The same Greek word is
used in e.g. Acts x. 42, xvii. 31; and rendered there "ordained;"
perhaps rightly so. But obviously its meaning will slightly vary as
connected with the *Sonship* or with the *Judgeship* of Christ.

the Son of God with power, according to the Spirit of holiness, by the resurrection from the dead: by whom we have 5

the Son of God] Cp. Acts xiii. 32, 33, for a close parallel; one of the
many between St Paul's Discourses and Epistles. The Sonship of the
Redeemer, the truth proclaimed at His baptism (Matt. iii. 17), is enforced
and illustrated through the N. T. In this Epistle see especially cch.
v. 10, viii. 3, 29, 32.

with power] Lit. **in power.** Cp. 1 Cor. xv. 43. *Power* attended
and characterized His Resurrection, both as cause and as effect. The
practical reference here is to the *fulness of the proof of the fact.* The
true Resurrection was not such as that imagined by e.g. Schleiermacher;
the creeping forth of a *half-slain* Man from his grave. It was miracle
and triumph.

according to the Spirit of holiness] This phrase presents two questions :
(1) what is "*the Spirit of Holiness*"? (2) what is meant by "*according
to*"? We take them in order. A. "The Spirit of Holiness" must
mean either the Holy Paraclete, or the sacred Human Spirit of Christ,
or His Deity regarded as (what it is, John iv. 24,) Spirit. The reference
here seems to be to the Paraclete; for (1) in this Epistle He is very
frequently referred to, in a way which makes an initial reference here
highly probable; (2) the expression "Holy Spirit" is so closely akin to
"Spirit of Holiness" that any reference of the words other than that to
the Paraclete would need special evidence; and such evidence can
hardly be found in St Paul. (See 1 Tim. iii. 16; Heb. ix. 14; for the
nearest approaches to it in N. T.) B. The words "according to"
may refer to the Paraclete, either (1) as the Agent in the Incarnation
(Luke i. 35), or (2) as concerned in the Resurrection (see viii. 11 for
a very partial parallel), or (3) as the Inspirer of the Prophets. Of these
possibilities (1) is most unlikely, for the Sonship of Christ here in question
is plainly the *Eternal* Sonship (see ix. 5), not that of the Incarnation;
(2) accords better with Scripture usage; but (3) far more so, in view of
the frequent mention of the Holy Spirit as the Inspirer. See Acts xx. 23;
1 Tim. iv. 1; Heb. iii. 7, ix. 8, x. 15, (and cp. 1 Pet. i. 11); for places
where "the Spirit" is evidently the Holy Spirit as the Author of Prophecy. The present passage will thus mean: "He was declared to be
the Son of God, with power, (even as the Holy Ghost foretold), in consequence of the resurrection."

by the resurrection] Lit. **out of, from;** i.e. **in consequence, as a
result, of.** The same construction and meaning occur e.g. 2 Cor.
xiii. 4, where lit. "He was crucified *out of* weakness; He liveth *out of*
the power of God; we shall live *out of,* &c." The grand *result* of the
resurrection here stated is that His prophesied character and dignity were,
by the resurrection, made unmistakably clear.

5. *by whom*] Lit. **through whom.** Ultimately from the Father,
but through the Son.

we have received] Better, perhaps, **we received;** (but see below on
ver. 19.)—"*We*" includes, possibly, all the Apostles, as certainly in
1 Cor. xv. 1, 11, &c. (where note the change from plural to singular in

received grace and apostleship, for obedience to the faith
6 among all nations, for his name: among whom are ye also
7 *the* called of Jesus Christ: to all that be in Rome, beloved
of God, called *to be* saints: grace to you and peace from
God our Father, and the Lord Jesus Christ.

vv. 1, 2, 3). Certainly it does not refer to any nominal *associate in the writing of the Epistle*, for none such appears. But most probably the author here uses the plural for the singular, as frequently in the course of the Epistle (see e.g. cch. iii. and iv.).

grace and apostleship] (1) all merciful qualifications for his office; (2) the definite commission.

for obedience to the faith] Better, **to the obedience of faith**; to produce the obedience connected with believing. Justifying faith is itself an act of obedience (see x. 3, "have not *submitted* themselves," and 1 Pet. i. 2), and it results in a life of obedience. The Gr. in xvi. 26, rendered "for the obedience of faith," is identical.

among all nations] Literally so in its intention; and even in St Paul's own experience, a great number of "nations" had now contributed converts. Cp. the strong expressions Col. i. 6, 23; and see xv. 19.

for his name] Practically = **for His sake**. The "*Name*," in general Scripture usage, is *the Person, as revealed and known.* See Exod. xxxiv. 5—7; Matt. xxviii. 19.

6. *the called of Jesus Christ*] **Jesus Christ's called ones**; called, and as such belonging to Him. The "call" here referred to, as almost always in the Epistles, is *the effectual call of Divine grace;* more than the external message. In the Gospels "call" and "choice" are almost contrasted; e.g. Matt. xxii. 14. In the Epp. they are (not indeed identical but) united. See viii. 28, xi. 29; 1 Cor. i. 24; Jude 1; Rev. xvii. 14.

7. *to all that be in Rome, beloved of God*] Better perhaps without comma: **to all God's beloved ones who are in Rome.** The Gr. admits either construction.

called to be saints] Lit. **called saints**; i.e., practically, "converted, so as to be saints." The idea is not of a "call" which may or may not result in sanctification. They were "saints" as being "called." The same phrase occurs 1 Cor. i. 2. See on ver. 6 above.

grace to you and peace] So in the first words of 1 Cor., 2 Cor., Gal., Eph., Phil., Col., 1 Thess., 2 Thess., Philem. In the Pastoral Epp. the remarkable addition "*mercy*" appears. In these salutations, "*Grace*" is all the free and loving favour of God in its efficacy on the saints; "*Peace*" is specially, perhaps, the complacency of reconciliation with which He regards them, but so as to imply also the results of this— their repose in His favour, and consequent serenity of heart, life, and intercourse. See for various illustrations of the word, ii. 10, v. 1; Phil. iv. 7; Col. iii. 15.

from God our Father, and, &c.] To St Paul the Father and the Saviour are equally the Givers of eternal blessing, as they are equally the Possessors of the soul. See on ver. 1.

8—17 *The good report of the Roman Church. Paul desires
to visit them, and to preach the gospel of faith to them*

First, I thank my God through Jesus Christ for you all, 8
that your faith is spoken of throughout the whole world.
For God is my witness, whom I serve with my spirit in the 9

8—17 THE GOOD REPORT OF THE ROMAN CHURCH. PAUL DESIRES
TO VISIT THEM, AND TO PREACH THE GOSPEL OF FAITH TO
THEM

8. *First, I thank my God*] First, before any other message. Such
messages of *thanksgiving* are characteristic of St Paul. See 1 Cor. i. 4 ;
Eph. i. 16; Phil. i. 3; Col. i. 3; 1 Thess. i. 2, ii. 13; 2 Thess. i. 3,
ii. 13; Philem. 4.—"*My* God :" again characteristic.   1 Cor. i. 4 ;
2 Cor. xii. 21; Phil. i. 3, iv. 19; Philem. 4. Cp. Acts xxvii. 23, and
Gal. ii. 20, for the *spirit* of the words.

through Jesus Christ] As the Mediator. See viii. 34. The idea
includes both His merit as opening the path of prayer, and His present
agency in commending the suppliants.

your faith] The strength and simplicity of your reliance on your
Lord, and allegiance to Him. See, for full illustration, 1 Thess. i. 8—10.

is spoken of] Lit. **is being proclaimed**, as a thing of public interest and notoriety. The reference doubtless is only to the intercourse
between Christian Churches ; for, as yet, the conduct of the Roman
disciples would hardly attract the notice of the heathen public. A few
years later, St Paul's Roman residence, and then the Neronian persecution, altered the case in this respect.—See 1 Thess. i., just quoted,
for a beautiful illustration both of the fact of such Christian communication and its power.

throughout the whole world] See Col. i. 6 for same words. The
phrase would be perfectly intelligible as meaning "through the Roman
empire." In Acts xi. 28, xvii. 6, xix. 27, xxiv. 5, the same phrase and
sense appear, but with a different word in the Gr.

9. *For God is my witness*] A characteristic appeal. Cp. 2 Cor.
i. 23, xi. 31, xii. 19; Gal. i. 20; Phil. i. 8; 1 Thess. ii. 5, 10. This
is traceable in part, perhaps, to the incessant calumnies against his
sincerity and veracity which grieved St Paul's heart.

whom I serve] The word here rendered "serve" has special reference
to religious *worship*, whether paid by priests or by people. But
it naturally implies also active obedience to the God so worshipped,
and its *classical* usage points entirely this way.

with my spirit] Lit. **in my spirit.** Much has been said on the
risk of confounding "*in*" and the instrumental "*with*," in such cases ;
and this risk must never be slighted. But in Heb. both ideas have the
same sign, and the Hebraistic tinge of N. T. Greek makes it highly
likely that in many instances there will be no practical distinction of
"in" and "with." We may well explain the present phrase, "I serve
Him *with* my spirit as the instrument." The spirit was *used* in every
various way in the Master's work.

gospel of his Son, that without ceasing I make mention
10 of you, always in my prayers, making request, if by any
means now at length I might have a prosperous journey by
11 the will of God to come unto you. For I long to see you,
that I may impart unto you some spiritual gift, to the end

in the gospel of his Son] Here obviously, on the other hand, *"in"* bears
its proper meaning. The Gospel was the field of energy and effort; *in
it*, in expounding and spreading its message, St Paul spent his spiritual
powers.—"*Of His Son* :"—see for the same idea in fuller terms, 2 Cor.
iv. 4, where lit. "The Gospel of the glory of Christ, who is the image
of God." The Eternal SON is Himself "the Gospel." The Gospel
is His, because He is not only the great Teacher but the essential
Doctrine.

without ceasing] As a continual and diligent habit. The same word
occurs 1 Thess. v. 17, in the same sense.

always in my prayers] Lit. **always, upon my prayers**; i.e., "on
every occasion of prayer."—"*My* prayers;"—no doubt specially "my
private prayers." The Apostle did indeed "labour fervently in prayer"
for his beloved converts and brethren, in his hours of direct intercourse
with God. From ch. xvi. we gather how individual and detailed his
remembrance at such times would be.

10. *making request*] Connect this with the previous verse, and read
**without ceasing I make mention of you, always in my prayers
making request, if by any means,** &c. The special "request made
known to God" was that the Apostle might, after long delays, be
allowed to visit the Roman Christians. Cp. Acts xix. 21, where the
phrase "I *must* see Rome" probably indicates a Divine purpose revealed.

might have a prosperous journey] Perhaps more briefly, **might be
prospered, might have the way smoothed.** Little did he foresee
how this was at last to be. See xv. 23, 24, 32; and cp. Acts
xxvii. 24.

by the will of God] Lit. **in the will of God.** See on ver. 9. If
the construction is to be pressed, the implied thought is that the visit
to Rome would be *within the limits of God's will;* guided by its lines.
The Gr. of Heb. x. 10 presents the only close parallel in N. T.

11. *that I may impart unto you some spiritual gift*] Some "*charisma.*"
The exact reference is not quite certain. It has been explained of miraculous gifts, which (on this view) St Paul desired to impart, by imposition
of hands, to the Roman saints. And certainly it appears that these
"gifts" were *as a rule* conveyed only by immediate apostolic ministry
(and therefore only to Christians of the first age). See Acts viii. 14—17,
xix. 6. But the word *charisma* ("gift of grace,") is used with the widest
reference. See e.g. vi. 23, where it is Salvation itself. And from
xii. 6 it appears that at least the Apostle might, "gift" of prophecy, or inspired
preaching, was then possessed by Roman saints; (though to be sure no
other miraculous gift is there named, and even this may have been
received from Apostles *elsewhere* as it was e.g. by Aquila, xvi. 3).

you may be established; that is, that *I* may be comforted 12
together with you by the mutual faith both of you and me.
Now I would not have you ignorant, brethren, that often- 13
times I purposed to come unto you, (but was let hitherto,)
that I might have some fruit among you also, even as
among other Gentiles. I am debtor both to the Greeks, 14

The sequel of this passage (esp. vv. 12, 16,) points rather to the "gift"
of holy intercourse, and above all to that of instruction. St Paul
desires to "preach the Gospel" to the Roman believers; i. e. to do
what in fact he does in this Epistle, "expound to them the way of Christ
more perfectly," "to the end they might be *established*," by maturer
and ampler knowledge of the eternal Truth.

12. *that is, that I may be comforted together*, &c.] We have here
St Paul's fine *tact*, to use a word "soiled by ignoble use," because
sometimes associated with insincerity. The tact of the Apostle is
only an exquisite combination of sympathy and judgment; he speaks
the true word, in the right place, and from the heart. It would be
shallow criticism indeed which would see here only an ingenious
religious *compliment*. To the sincere Christian teacher nothing is more
real than the reflex aid he receives among Christian learners[1].

with you] Better, **in you**; **among you**; "that I may share consolation among you."

by the mutual faith] Lit. **the faith which is in one another**; a
pregnant phrase; q. d., "the faith which dwells in each, and which
each manifests to the other."

13. *Now I would not have you ignorant*] A characteristic phrase.
See xi. 25; 1 Cor. x. 1, xii. 1; 2 Cor. i. 8; 1 Thess. iv. 13.

I purposed to come unto you] *Within limits*, evidently, St Paul's plans
were no more inspired than those of modern missionaries; his most
deliberate intentions were liable to correction by his Master. The
correction came often in the form, not of silent providence, but of
miraculous intimation. See Acts xvi. 6, 7, and cp. 2 Cor. i. 15—17.

but was let hitherto] Lit. and **was let (hindered)**. Practically,
though not in grammatical form, this clause is a parenthesis. For
the nature of the hindrance, see xv. 22, 23.

that I might have some fruit] Some results of my ministry. The
"results" here contemplated would be not so much conversions as the
deeper instruction of the converted.

other Gentiles] Properly, **the other Gentiles**. This clause proves
that the large majority of the Roman Christians were converts from
paganism. The drift of the whole Epistle says the same.

14. *I am debtor*] I.e. "I owe it to them to impart to them the
Gospel." See 1 Cor. ix. 16, 17; where St Paul speaks as a "dis-
penser" or "steward" of the Gospel, who is absolutely bound ("it is
laid on me") to give the "portion of food in due season" to those
whom he can reach.

1 See *Introduction*, i. § 33, note.

and to the barbarians; both to the wise, and to the unwise.
15 So, as much as in me is, I am ready to preach the gospel
16 to you that are at Rome also. For I am not ashamed
of the gospel of Christ: for it is the power of God unto

the Greeks, and to the Barbarians] A familiar division of mankind.
Barbarus originally meant "a speaker of an unintelligible tongue;"
then, in Greek, the speaker of a language *not Greek*. Thus the Romans
were as much *barbari* as the Scythians; and indeed in the older Latin
writers we find the word used by themselves, with reference to their
own language, as a sort of synonym for "non-Greek." But when
Rome more and more added culture to power the word was practically
restricted to nations *other than Greek and Latin*, and so probably here.
The word "Greeks" (*Hellenes*), in such contrasts as this, had come, by
St Paul's time, to include Romans. Every educated Roman was trained
in Greek speech and literature. Some of the "Roman" Christians
were no doubt true Hellenes, and, as a body, evidently, they understood Greek. See *Introd.* ii. § 2.

the wise, and to the unwise] Practically, **the cultured and the un-
educated.** He contemplates *literary* hearers on one side, and on the
other rude tribes, and peasantry and workmen, and women and children.
The word rendered "*unwise*" is a strong one; elsewhere (e. g. Luke
xxiv. 25; Gal. iii. 1; Tit. iii. 3;) rendered "fools," "foolish," or the
like. Here the Apostle probably uses it as from the point of view of the
"wise:"—"those whom the philosopher would think to be mind-less."

15. *as much as in me is*, &c.] Lit. **that which relates to me is
ready,** &c.; "*my side* is ready." Perhaps the point of this periphrasis
for "I" is the hope of an equal willingness on the side of the Romans
to *hear* the message.

to you that are at Rome also] This was the *climax* of his apostolic
courage. It was no light matter to St Paul, keenly sensitive as he was,
to face the metropolitan world of life and power. See Acts xxviii. 15,
where we can trace previous anxiety in the words "*he took courage.*"

16. *For I am not ashamed*] The "*for*" links this verse to the last
thought. At Rome, if anywhere, he might be "ashamed" (Mark viii.
38) of the message of a *crucified* Saviour; a message, too, which pronounced "the whole world *guilty* before God." But he was *not* ashamed
of his message, and so was ready to "see Rome."

the gospel of Christ] Omit the words "of Christ," on evidence of
MSS., &c.

the power of God] So 1 Cor. i. 18, where "the message of *the cross*"
is spoken of. See too ibid. 23, 24: "we preach *Christ crucified...Christ
the power of God*, and the wisdom of God." Cp. 1 Cor. ii. 5. The
doctrine of the true Messiah brought to bear God's energy, to the result
of "salvation."

salvation] This word is here probably used in its largest meaning,
including the whole process of mercy from the time of belief onwards;
deliverance from doom, sin, and death. Its very frequent reference in

salvation to every one that believeth; to the Jew first, and *also* to the Greek. For therein is the righteousness of God 17

N. T. is to the resurrection-glory (see xiii. 11; 1 Thess. v. 8, 9; 2 Tim. ii. 10; Heb. i. 14, ix. 28; 1 Pet. i. 5), but it is also used of the present results of grace (2 Cor. vi. 2) as (much more often) its cognate verb, *to save*. See Matt. i. 21; Rom. viii. 24; Eph. ii. 5, 8; 2 Tim. i. 9; Tit. iii. 5. The Greek verb and noun include the ideas of *rescue from peril*, and (more rarely) *healing*, according to their connexion. But their prevailing reference (in religion) is to *rescue* rather than to *amelioration*.

to every one that believeth] Here is given out the "theme" of the Epistle, or more properly of the first chapters; viz., FAITH, a trustful acceptance of the Divine Saviour; Faith as the only way of rescue for the human soul from doom and sin; absolute and alone, because of the supreme and absolute glory of the Person, and so of the Work, accepted by "the believer."—See Appendix C.

to the Jew first] More strictly, **both Jew, first, and Greek.** So it was historically. But the reference is also to the special relationship of the Jew to the *Messianic* hope. The Deliverer was of the seed not of Adam only but of David; and the Deliverance therefore had a peculiar and endearing claim on the acceptance of the Jew. The reasoning of the Epistle quite excludes the thought that a Gentile, once believing, was in the least less welcome or less secure than a believing Jew; but this fact leaves room for such a "priority" as that indicated.

17. *the righteousness of God*] A phrase occurring elsewhere seven times in this Epistle (iii. 5, 21, 22, 25, 26, x. 3 twice), once in the Gospels (Matt. vi. 33), once in 2 Cor. (v. 21), once in St James (i. 20), and once in 2 Pet. (i. 1). As regards Pauline usage, it is plain that Rom. iii. is the *locus criticus* for its leading meaning, which meaning we may expect to find here. iii. 26 appears to supply the key to this meaning: the "righteousness of God" is something which is reached, or received, "through faith in Jesus Christ;" and it is "declared" in such a way as to shew Him "just, *yet justifying*." On the whole it is most consistent with most passages to explain it of the "righteousness imputed by God" to the believer. (See esp. cch. iii. and iv. for explanations of *imputation*.) It is "*God's* righteousness," as being provided by Him and availing with Him. (" Die Gerechtigkeit *die vor Gott gilt*," "the righteousness *which avails with God*," is Luther's paraphrase.)

It is objected that the word rendered "righteousness" denotes a *real moral state.* But this is only partially true. It quite as much tends to denote what makes a man clear *in the eye of the law, satisfactory to justice;* and just such is the effect, according to this Epistle, of the Work of Christ accepted by faith. With proper caution we may thus say that "righteousness," in this and similar phrases, is often a *practical* equivalent for "Justification."—In Matt. vi. 33 the reference at least *may* be as above; in 2 Cor. v. 21 we have another but cognate reference, viz. to the *aspect of the justified* before God; in 2 Pet. i. 1 and Jas. i. 20, the meaning seems to be quite different, though equally proper to

revealed from faith to faith: as it is written, The just
shall live by faith.

18—23 *The necessity for the Gospel: Divine wrath; human (especially heathen) sin*

16 For the wrath of God is revealed from heaven against all

the Greek words, viz. "the will of the righteous God." For variations
in this Epistle see notes on successive passages.

revealed from faith to faith]   Q.d. "is unfolded, and displays faith,
and only faith, as its secret, at each disclosure."   (1)   The initial step,
the *entrance* to justification, is faith: (2) The *life* of the justified is
maintained by faith: faith is the starting-point and the course.—"*Is
revealed*:"—a present tense in the Gr.:—**is revealing.**   The idea is
of a perpetually recurring process: "to each fresh discoverer it is revealed."   So of the *opposite* "revelation," i. 18.

as it is written]   The formula of quotation, sanctioned by the Saviour
Himself in His own all-significant use of Scripture at the Temptation.
"It is written; it is written again."   (Matt. iv. 4, 7, 10.)

This is the first direct quotation in this Epistle.   In the 16 chapters
the O. T. is *directly* quoted about 60 distinct times.   See *Introd.* iv.

The original is in Hab. ii. 4, and is lit. rendered, "And [the] just
man, by his faith shall he live."   The context there defines the meaning
of faith to be *trust, confidence in another*, as opposed to self-confidence.
Such humility of trust marks the "just" man, the man *right in God's
sight;* and thereby he stands possessed of "life," i.e., peace and security
before God.   This brief but profound sentence is here taken by the
Apostle as the text of his great statement of JUSTIFICATION.   So again
in Gal. iii. 11.—"*By faith:*"—lit. **out of faith**; i. e. in consequence of
it, after it, as the *condition* on which "life" is given.

18—23   THE NECESSITY FOR THE GOSPEL: DIVINE WRATH; HUMAN (ESPECIALLY HEATHEN) SIN

18.   *For the wrath of God*, &c.]   The "for" marks the connexion
as follows: "The Gospel is the secret of *salvation*, of justification
before the eternal Judge; and as such it is a thing of supreme importance; *for* the Judge has proclaimed the doom of human sin.   The
question is not of mere theory, but of life or death."

the wrath of God]   A phrase frequent in the N. T.   All attempts to
explain it away involve violence to the sense of Scripture : it would be
as legitimate, in point of language, to explain away the Divine Love.
Strong and even vehement accessory language is sometimes used with
the word *wrath*: see ii. 8; Rev. xvi. 19, xix. 15.   On the subject generally, see especially Joh. iii. 36; Eph. ii. 3; Rev. vi. 16.

It must, of course, always be remembered that the "wrath of God" is
the wrath of a Judge.   In its inmost secret it is the very opposite of an
arbitrary outburst, being the eternal repulsion of evil by good.

ungodliness and unrighteousness of men, who hold the truth
in unrighteousness ; because that which may be known of 19
God is manifest in them ; for God hath shewed *it* unto

is revealed] A present tense in the Gr. See on ver. 17. This
"revelation" is a *standing* one, for all places and all times, and ever
repeated to individual consciences.

from heaven] A pregnant phrase. The wrath is "revealed" as
about to be inflicted from heaven ; by Him "who sitteth in heaven,"
and who "shall descend from heaven" in "the day of wrath and
righteous judgment."

against] Or, **upon**; i.e. "to descend upon."

ungodliness and unrighteousness] Sin, in its aspect as offence (1) a-
gainst God, (2) against man; the awful opposite to the Two Great
Commandments. "*Unrighteousness*," however, is obviously a wider
word than "*ungodliness*," including the idea of injustice to God as well
as to man; spiritual rebellion.

of men] I.e. mankind; not a class, but the race. This is plain
from the sequel, though the Gr. leaves it possible (grammatically) to
render "of those men who hold, &c."

who hold] Lit. **who hold down.** The verb has several shades of
meaning, and frequently = "to hold fast." So e.g. 1 Cor. xi. 2 ; (E. V.,
"keep;") 1 Thess. v. 21. But the context here decides for the meaning
"hold down, hold back, suppress." The verb occurs once again in this
Epistle, vii. 6: "wherein we were *held*," i.e. "held down as captives."
Here the phrase is pregnant:—"who suppress the truth, living in unrighteousness the while." "The Truth" (of the awful Majesty of God)
is, as it were, *buried* under sinful acts, though still *alive*, still needing
to be "held down," if sin is to rule.

19. *that which may be known of God*] Lit. **that which is known**;
i.e. ideally known; that which, under any circumstances, man has
known. The E. V. is thus practically right.

The word "knowable" has of late years become fashionable in philosophic language; and some writers have boldly taught that God is
"The Unknown and Unknowable." This direct contradiction of the
Lord and the Apostles seems to be largely due to a confusion of real
knowledge with perfect knowledge. Meanwhile Scripture itself teaches
that *in an inner sense* God *is* "unknowable," until revealed. (Matt.
xi. 25—27.)

The "*because*" points to the "holding down" just before: q. d.,
"they hold down the truth; and it *needs* holding down, as a living
thing, if it is to be kept out of the way; because it is, as a fact, known
to them."

in them] Or, **amongst them.** The Gr. bears either meaning; and
on the whole the context favours the latter.

for God hath shewed it] Lit. **for God did manifest it.** The verb
is in the aorist, and thus seems to point to a *complete* past; perhaps
to the ideal time of creation, when the "eternal power and Godhead"
were manifested. It must be observed in general, however, that in the

20 them. For the invisible *things* of him from the creation of the world are clearly seen, being understood by the things that are made, *even* his eternal power and Godhead; so that 21 they are without excuse : because that, when they knew God, they glorified *him* not as God, neither were thankful ;

Greek of the N. T. the aorist *sometimes* practically covers the ground of the perfect.—The point of this verse thus may be that "God *hath* [in abiding effect] manifested, &c."

20. *from the creation of the world*] I. e. "since the world was created." The Gr. scarcely allows the interpretation "from the frame-work, or constitution, of the world."—He means that ever since there was a universe to observe, and man to observe it, the being and will of a Divine Artificer have been discernible.

are clearly seen] The Gr. verb hardly gives the emphatic "*clearly*," though it distinctly states that they "are under observation," "in view."

eternal] The Gr. word here (*aïdios*) is only found besides in N. T. in Jude 6. By derivation and usage it is connected with the Greek equivalent for "*ever*" or "*always*." The point of the word here is that creation condemns the guilty vagaries of Idolatry by witnessing to a God *everlastingly* One and the Same.

Godhead] Lit. **Divinity**; character or capacity worthy of God.

so that they are without excuse] Better perhaps, (comparing similar constructions in this Epistle) **so that they may**, or **might, be without excuse** ; to remove all cause of inevitable ignorance, and to throw the whole blame of declension from primeval truth on the perverted Will.

21. *because that, when they knew God*] I. e. as primevally revealed, and then constantly witnessed to by the visible Creation as Eternal and Omnipotent. "*To know God*" is a phrase capable of many degrees of meaning, from the rational certainty of a Supreme Personal Maker and Lord up to that holy intimacy of divinely-given communion with the Father and the Son, to which the words of John xvii. 3 refer. In this passage all that is necessary to understand is the certainty (however learnt) of the existence of a Personal Omnipotent Creator.

they glorified him not as God, neither were thankful] The verbs throughout this passage are aorists. The *process* of declension from the truth is not dwelt upon, so much as the *fact* that it did take place, at whatever rate. There was a time when man, although knowledge of God had been given him, ceased to praise Him and to thank Him for His "great glory" and His rich gifts ; turning the praise and thanks towards idol-objects instead. We must note that these first marks of decline (failure to praise and to thank Him), indicate a subtle and lasting secret of idolatry. Man, conscious of guilt before the Eternal, shrinks from *direct* worship. In mistaken reverence, it may be, he turns away to "the Creature," to address his praises there. But the result is inevitable; the God unworshipped rapidly becomes unknown.

but became vain in their imaginations, and their foolish heart
was darkened.   Professing *themselves* to be wise, they be- 22
came fools, and changed the glory of the uncorruptible God 23
into an image made like to corruptible man, and to birds,
and fourfooted beasts, and creeping things.

24—32   *The same subject: heathen sin judicially aggravated*

Wherefore God also gave them up to uncleanness through 24

but became vain in their imaginations]   "*Vain*," here, as often in
Scripture, is "*wrong*," morally as well as mentally.   "*Imaginations*"
is rather **thinkings** : the Gr. is a word often rendered "thoughts,"
(as e.g. Matt. xv. 19.)   In Phil. ii. 14 it is rendered "disputings;" in
1 Tim. ii. 8, "doubting."   The verb is used in e.g. Luke xii. 17, for
the balancing of thing against thing in the mind.   Both verb and noun,
when the context gives them an unfavourable reference, indicate a habit
of captious and hesitating thought such as would ignore plain testimony
and attend to abstract difficulties by preference.   Thus here, man,
growing unused to adoration of his God, fell to independent thinking,
(in however rude a form,) and "*in*" this, occupied in this, "*became
vain*," went astray altogether.

their foolish heart]   "*Foolish*," more strictly **unintelligent**; failing to
see connexions and consequences.   Same word as Matt. xv. 16.   The
"*heart*" may here mean merely the intellect, as perhaps in Mark ii.
6, 8.   It is almost always difficult, however, to trace in Scripture (as
indeed so often in constant experience) the *border* between reason and
conscience.   "Heart" certainly includes both in the majority of N. T.
passages.

22.   *Professing themselves to be wise*, &c.]   A severe but just description of speculation, primitive or modern, which ignores Revelation
where Revelation has spoken.   St Paul does not mean that in such
speculations no intellectual power was exerted; surpassing power often
was, and is, displayed in them.   But the premises of the reasoners, and
their moral attitude, in view of the real state of the case, were fatally
wrong.   In the very act of "professing to be" *competently* "wise"
they proved themselves "fools," and further proved it by palpable acts,
as follows.

23.   *into an image made like to*]   Lit. **in the resemblance of the
likeness of**; i. e. "*so as to appear in* a form like man, bird, beast,
snake, and insect."   Deity, and its prerogatives, were so degraded as
to be (in the idolater's act) transferred to idols.   The illustrations of
the Apostle's words from ancient and modern heathenism are too
abundant to need special mention.

24—32   THE SAME SUBJECT : HEATHEN SIN JUDICIALLY
AGGRAVATED

24.   *Wherefore God also gave them up*]   The inevitable connexion
of idolatry with debased morality is stated here.   Nothing but the

the lusts of their own hearts, to dishonour their own
25 bodies between themselves: who changed the truth of
God into a lie, and worshipped and served the creature
more than the Creator, who is blessed for ever. Amen.
26 For this cause God gave them up unto vile affections:

knowledge of the Holy One, Eternal and Almighty, can ever really
teach and enforce human purity; even though conscience (up to its light)
always takes the part of purity. Manifold experience shews that mere
social civilization and mental culture can never really banish even the
grossest lusts. Nothing but the knowledge of God as He is can reveal
to man both his fall and his greatness, his sin and his sacred duty.

God also gave them up] So Psal. lxxxi. 11, 12; Acts vii. 42. On the
other hand man "gives himself over;" Eph. iv. 19. Experience as
well as Revelation says that the most terrible, and just, penalty of sin
is the hardening of the sinning heart. It is a "law;" though in using
that word we must here specially remember that, as with physical
so with moral laws, "their ultimate reason is God." The "law" of
judicial hardening is His *personal* will, and takes place along with His
personal displeasure.

through the lusts] Lit. **in the lusts**: a pregnant phrase; q.d. " He
gave them up *to live in* vile desires."

to dishonour] The dignity and sanctity of the body is a main and
peculiar truth of Revelation.

between themselves] Another reading gives "*among them;*" but the
evidence is not decisive, and general reasons support the E. V.

25. *who changed*] The Greek relative pronoun implies that this
was the *cause* of the special turn taken by the judicial hardening:
seeing they had changed, &c.

the truth of God] I.e. that which is true of Him alone, and revealed
by Him; Omnipotence and Deity. Cp. ver. 18.

into a lie] Lit. **in falsehood**; they degraded it so that it was *lost
in* falsehood; falsehood took its place. This "falsehood" is, of course,
the grand error—Idolatry.

more than the Creator] Lit. **Him that created [it]**. The idolater
reverenced and did ritual service to his idol "*more*," or "*rather*," than
to the Creator, whether he wholly ignored the Eternal, or recognized
Him as a shadow or mystery in the background only.

who is blessed] *Benedictus* here, not *Beatus*. The glorious epithet
indicates the Creature's right attitude toward the Creator; that of
adoring praise and love. (The same phrase occurs ix. 5; an important
doctrinal parallel.)

26. *For this cause*] Resuming ver. 24.

vile affections] Lit. **passions of disgrace**; stamped with essential
degradation. (Far different is the Greek, where (in E. V.) the same
word "vile" appears, in Phil. iii. 21: "the body *of humiliation.*")
On this and the next verse we must not comment in detail. The
hideous vices here plainly named, one of them in particular, frightfully

for even their women did change the natural use into that
which is against nature: and likewise also the men, leaving ²⁷
the natural use of the woman, burned in their lust one
towards another; men with men working that which is un-
seemly, and receiving in themselves *that* recompence of
their error which was meet.   And even as they did not like ²⁸
to retain God in *their* knowledge, God gave them over to
a reprobate mind, to do those *things* which are not convenient; being filled with all unrighteousness, fornication, ²⁹
wickedness, covetousness, maliciousness; full of envy, murder, debate, deceit, malignity; whisperers, backbiters, haters ³⁰

deface some of the very fairest pages of ancient literature.   The tremendous condemnations of Scripture have made the like display almost
impossible in modern writings; but the human heart is the same.   (Jer.
xvii. 9.)

It is noteworthy (as an act of tenderness, perhaps,) that the sin of ver.
26 is touched more rapidly than that of ver. 27.   It is also remarkable
that in the Greek we have not "*women*" and "*men*," but "*females*"
and "*males*."—Bengel's remark on this passage is excellent: "Often, in
exposing sin, we must call a spade a spade (*scapha debet scapha dici*).
They often insist on an excessive delicacy who themselves are void of
modesty."   These words apply to many passages of Scripture besides
this.

28.   *And even as*, &c.]   In this and the following verses the developements of sin are followed into less monstrous but more pervading and
not less guilty forms.

as they did not like]   **did not approve.**   The Gr. is akin to the
Gr. of "reprobate" just below.   Knowledge of God met with no
approbation, and He gave them over to *reprobation*.

to retain God in their knowledge]   Lit. **to have God in real (or
full) knowledge.**   There was an antecedent knowledge of God; partly
by the universe, partly by the constitution of their nature, partly by
primeval revelation.

a reprobate mind]   Lit. **a mind, or state of thought, rejected after
test.**   The Gr. word, from this literal meaning, comes habitually to
mean "refuse, outcast, **abandoned.**"

convenient]   I. e. **becoming.**   So Philem. 8, where the Greek word
is nearly the same.   The euphemism here is most forcible.

29.   *fornication*]   This word is to be omitted.

maliciousness]   Same word as 1 Pet. ii. 1, (where E. V. "malice,") 16.
The Gr. is a wider word than these English words; **evil** in its largest
sense, but specially, moral evil.

full of envy]   Lit. **brimful;** a word as strong as possible.

malignity]   Our "*ill-nature*" exactly.

30.   *backbiters*]   Rather, **evil speakers,** without the special notion
of speaking in the *absence* of the person attacked.

of God, despiteful, proud, boasters, inventors of evil *things*,
31 disobedient to parents, without understanding, covenant-
breakers, without natural affection, implacable, unmerciful:
32 who knowing the judgment of God, that they which commit
such *things* are worthy of death, not only do the same, but
have pleasure in them that do *them.*

haters of God] The Gr., by formation and classical usage, should
rather mean **hateful to God**; men whose character is peculiarly abhorrent to Him. Similar words or phrases were familiar at Athens to
denote *defiant* evil; and this would well suit the two words here following.

disobedient to parents] A symptom of deep moral and social disorder.
Parental authority stands in the Decalogue among the great foundations
of virtue and duty; and our Lord Himself is significantly said (Luke ii.
51) to have been "subject" to Joseph and Mary.

31. *without understanding, covenant-breakers*] The Gr. words are
almost identical in form and sound. On "*without understanding*" see
note on ver. 21, where "foolish" represents the same Greek word ; an
epithet full of deep meaning.

implacable] Lit. **truce-less** ; an adjective used in the classics for
inevitable *death* and internecine *war.* The word is perhaps to be omitted
here ; but evidence is far from decisive.

32. *who knowing*] The Gr. relative is same word as ver. 25, where
see note. Thus what is here stated of the world of sinners is, as it
were, the *condition* for the special vices just enumerated : men are such
because they resist conscience.

knowing] The Gr. is strong, **well knowing**. The witness of conscience is here intended, enforced by traditions of primeval truth and
by the majesty of creation.

the judgment of God] Rather, His **ordinance**, His statute of retribution. It is not necessary to understand that they explicitly know that
the statute is "ordained of God." God, as a definite Object of thought,
may be to them as if He were not; but a voice not their own bears
witness to the eternal difference of right and wrong, however broken
that witness may be. They are aware, however imperfectly, of a
"statute" whereby impurity and cruelty are evil and condemnable.

death] The extreme penalty of the Divine "judgment." It is in fact
"the death that cannot die ;" whether the transgressor estimates it so
or not.

have pleasure in] Rather, **feel with them and abet them.** This
is certainly a greater depth of transgression even than personal, and
thus perhaps solitary, wrong-doing. It indicates *complete* victory
over conscience, and *complete* callousness to the moral ruin of others.
On the whole of this terrible passage, see as a Scripture parallel Tit.
iii. 3. On that verse Adolphe Monod (*Adieux* I) remarks: "For a long
while I found it impossible to admit this declaration; even now " (on
his death-bed) "I cannot understand it in its fulness. But I have

CH. II.   1—16   *Human sin, continued: Jews and Gentiles
equal in guilt and peril: gradual approach to the Jewish
question*

Therefore thou art inexcusable, O man, whosoever thou **2**
art that judgest: for wherein thou judgest another, thou
condemnest thyself; for thou that judgest doest the same
things.   But we are sure that the judgment of God is ac- ₂
cording to truth against them which commit such *things.*

come, by God's grace—very slowly indeed—to see this doctrine more
clearly, and sure I am that, when this veil of flesh shall fall, I shall find
in it the perfectly faithful likeness of my natural heart."

CH. II. **1—16**   HUMAN SIN, CONTINUED: JEWS AND GENTILES
EQUAL IN GUILT AND PERIL: GRADUAL APPROACH TO THE
JEWISH QUESTION

1.   *Therefore*]   It is difficult to state the precise bearing of this word ;
the exact premiss to which it refers.   It is, perhaps, best explained by a
brief statement of the apparent general connexion here.

St Paul has described the great fact of Human Sin.   He has done so
in terms which point specially to heathendom, but not exclusively.   Two
points, the universality of sin, and the universality of conscience (vv. 18,
32), are plainly meant to be true of all men, idolaters or not.   But now,
in our present verse, he has it in view to expose specially the state of
Jewish sinners; but to do this by leading *gradually* up to the convincing
point, which is not reached till ver. 16.   Really, but not explicitly, therefore, he here addresses the Jew, as included in the previous condemnation, but as thinking himself all the while the " judge " of heathen sinners.   In words, he addresses *any* self-constituted "judge ;" while in
fact he specially, though still not exclusively, addresses the Jew.   And
he addresses him as "inexcusable," *because* of his sin, and *because* of his
conscience, a conscience in his case peculiarly enlightened.

The " *therefore*" thus points mainly to the words just previous; to
the fact of a knowledge of God's penal statute against sin, while yet sin
is committed and abetted.

doest the same things]   The reference is doubtless to the passage from
about i. 26.   External *idolatry* had vanished among the Jews since the
captivity; but other forms of the subtle "worship of the creature" had
taken its place; a gross immorality was far from rare ; and sins of
"strife, craft, and malignity," were conspicuous.

2.   *we are sure*]   This is spoken as by the Apostle, not as by the
Jew.   He solemnly repeats the thought that man knows that judgment
is to come.

judgment]   The original word is almost always in N. T. used of *adverse* decision, and in most cases of the *execution* of the sentence, as in
the next verse.

according to truth]   Rather, **according to reality ;** in awful earnest
and fact.

₃ And thinkest thou this, O man, that judgest them which do such *things*, and doest the same, that thou shalt escape the ₄ judgment of God? Or despisest thou the riches of his goodness and forbearance and longsuffering; not knowing ₅ that the goodness of God leadeth thee to repentance? But ·after thy hardness and impenitent heart treasurest up unto thyself wrath against the day of wrath and revelation of the

3. *that thou shalt escape*] *"Thou"* is, of course, emphatic. We must remember how often the Jews of that age clung to national privilege as if it were personal immunity. It was a saying, that to live in Palestine was "equal to the observance of all the commandments." "He that hath his permanent abode in Palestine," so taught the Talmud, "is sure of the life to come." (Edersheim's *Sketches of Jewish Life*, p. 5.) The tendency betrayed in such thoughts is deep as the fall of man, but it has its times and ways of special manifestation.

4. *the riches*] A frequent word with St Paul, in reference to Divine goodness and glory. See ix. 23, x. 12, xi. 33; Eph. i. 7, 8, ii. 7, iii. 8, 16; Phil. iv. 19; Col. i. 27, ii. 2.

goodness] Specially the goodness of **kindness.** So the same original is rendered 2 Cor. vi. 6; Eph. ii. 7; Tit. iii. 4.

to repentance] See, as an illustrative parallel, 2 Pet. iii. 9; where perhaps render "willing to *receive all* to repentance." The Gr. of *"repentance,"* here as elsewhere in N. T., means far more than alarm or grief; rather, a change of thought and will. See especially 2 Cor. vii. 9, 10; 2 Tim. ii. 25.

The point of this verse is specially for the (still unnamed) Jew. He thought his spiritual privilege and light, so long and lovingly continued, a mere honour, instead of a peculiar call to conscience.

5. *after*] **according to,** in a way traceable to.

hardness] **insensibility,** whether to love or reason.

treasurest up] Possibly this word alludes to the "riches" of ver. 4; q. d., "the Divine store of loving-kindness is exchanged by the sinner for the Divine store of holy wrath."

unto thyself] Emphatic; more than merely "for thee." The wrath is pure retribution, the result of sin. The sinner is the cause of his own doom.

against the day of wrath] Lit. **in the day of wrath;** a pregnant phrase; "which *will take effect in* the day." On *"wrath,"* see note on i. 18: *"The day:"*—i.e. the definite time of the Lord's Appearing, to raise the dead (Joh. vi. 39, 40, 44, 54, xi. 24); to judge the world (Joh. xii. 48; Acts xvii. 31); and to receive the saints to final glory (2 Tim. iv. 8). In one remarkable passage (1 Cor. iv. 3) the Greek of the word "judgment" (in E. V.) is lit. *"day;"* and a probable account of this use of the word is the inseparable connexion of thought, in the early church, between the *day* and the *judgment* of the Lord.

revelation of the righteous judgment of God] The "wrath" is as pure, just, and Divine as the mercy. Its *"revelation"* will be only

righteous judgment of God; who will render to every *man* 6
according to his deeds: to them who by patient continu- 7
ance in well doing seek for glory and honour and immortality, eternal life: but unto them that are contentious, and 8

the revelation of the absolute equity of "the JUDGE of all the earth."
This deep righteousness of the Divine anger is its most awful element.

6. *who will render to every man*, &c.] According to the promise,
Matt. xvi. 27; Rev. xxii. 12. (Note that the very phrase used here of
the Father, is used there of Himself by the Son).

7. *to them who by patient continuance*, &c.] More lit., **to those
who according to patience of** (i.e. **in**) **a good work seek**, &c.;
i.e., who, in that method, by that path, seek for eternal bliss. *"Patience"* here, as often in N. T., practically means active patience, perseverance. (Cp. Luke viii. 15; Heb. x. 36, xii. 1). *"Work"* is here,
as often, used in the singular as a summary of the Christian's whole
course of obedience.

It is very remarkable to find here, in the first pages of this great
Treatise on Gratuitous Salvation, the distinct mention of the blessed
result of *"good work."* (See specially, by way of contrast, iv. 2, 6,
xi. 6; and also Eph. ii. 9, 10.)—It must be remembered that St Paul
expressly teaches that man's knowledge and love of God in this life,
and by consequence its practical results, are as much His gift, a gift
perfectly free and special, as is the bliss of the life to come;
and that the two are inseparably connected. Divine mercy gives the
"patient continuance in well-doing" as well as the "glory, honour,
and immortality." It is most true that the just freedom of Scripture
language frequently leaves this connexion out of *explicit* statement; but
this whole Epistle tends to remind us that it is among the very foundations of truth.

seek] As a traveller on his homeward road seeks for (aims at,
moves toward) his home. Cp. Heb. xiii. 14.

glory] The heavenly state, on its side of exaltation; the *dignity* of
the vision and the likeness of God. See ch. **v. 2** for its deep connexion
with His presence: it is "the glory *of God."*

honour] Often associated with "glory." See 1 Pet. i. 7 for an
instructive parallel. St Paul here speaks of "perseverance in good
works;" St Peter there of the "fiery trial" of faith; both as preliminary to the Master's welcome.

immortality] Lit. **incorruptibility.** Same word as 1 Cor. xv. 42,
50; 2 Tim. i. 10. (E. V., "immortality.") It indicates perpetuity
not merely of existence but of purity and power, the immortality of
heaven. See further, next note.

eternal life] On these two most weighty words we can only summarize
thus. (1) *"Life,"* beyond question, may, and very often does, mean more
than bare existence. A "lifeless" tree, or body, yet exists, though in
another state than before. In regard of *spiritual* life, it is clear that
existence may be strong and conscious where there is no such "life."
See Joh. vi. 53; Eph. ii. 1. Existence. to be in this sense "life," must

do not obey the truth, but obey unrighteousness, indigna-
9 tion and wrath, tribulation and anguish, upon every soul of
man that doeth evil, of the Jew first, and *also* of the Gen-

contain happiness and holiness, whether in the germ (as here), or in
maturity (as hereafter). (2) "*Eternal*." Much has been written on
the Greek of this word; *aionios*. But its connexion with *duration*,
in derivation and usage, is certain. For N. T. usage in this respect,
see e.g. 2 Cor. iv. 17, 18. And it is equally clear that its ruling idea
is *duration unending in respect of the period referred to.* If used e.g.
with regard to the present world, or a human lifetime, it naturally
means unending while that world, or lifetime, lasts. When applied
to the unseen and ultimate world, it appears equally naturally to mean
unending while that world lasts. "*Everlasting*" is thus no arbitrary
equivalent for it, for both words have much the same consistent elasticity
of meaning.

8. *contentious*] Lit. **out of partizanship**, or **factiousness**; (the
same construction as "of the truth;" Joh. xviii. 37). The phrase
implies connexion and attachment; as here, "those who belong to, can
be classed under the character of, the factious."

The "faction" in question is that of the sinful soul against the
humbling terms of the Divine peace and love. Cp. x. 3 for a special
example of this in the case of the Jews. A pointed, though not explicit,
reference to Jewish opponents of the Gospel lies in the word here.

do not obey] The Gr. is sometimes rendered, "disbelieve." In all cases,
however, the resistance of the *will* is implied in it; the element of
disobedience in *unbelief* towards God. See, for a suggestive example,
Heb. iv. 6, compared with the history there referred to.

the truth] The revelation of the eternal reality of the glory of God.
(See on i. 18, 25.) It is Truth, not in mere generality, but in that
speciality which attaches to the Truth of truths. See, for an important
parallel, 2 Thess. ii. 10, 12; where "the truth" and "unrighteousness" are contrasted, as here. See also Joh. viii. 32.

obey unrighteousness] Yielding the will to the impulse of sin;
"having pleasure in unrighteousness" (2 Thess. ii. 12). Cp. vi. 6, 16, &c.;
Tit. iii. 3. "*Unrighteousness*" here, as often, means sin in its largest
sense. All wrong, civil, social, moral, personal, overt, secret, violates
the *eternal rights,* even when it least seems to touch temporal and human
interests.

indignation and wrath] See on i. 18 and ii. 5.

9. *tribulation and anguish*] Both words, in Greek as well as in
English, indicate the crushing and bewildering power of great grief or
pain. "*Anguish*" is the stronger of the two; for see 2 Cor. iv. 8,
where the original of "distressed" is cognate to that of "anguish" here.

It is remarkable that the antithesis here to "eternal life" is the
conscious experience of the effects of Divine anger.

doeth] The Gr. is somewhat emphatic; **practiseth, worketh, worketh out.** A *habit* of sin is intended. Same word as "worketh" in next
verse.

tile; but glory, honour, and peace, to every *man* that work- 10
eth good, to the Jew first, and *also* to the Gentile: for 11
there is no respect of persons with God.   For as many as 12
have sinned without law shall also perish without law: and

of the Jew, &c.]   Lit. **both of the Jew, first, and of the Greek.**
The phrase is as if St Paul had been writing simply "of the Jew and
of the Greek," "of Jew and Greek alike;" and then, as by a verbal
parenthesis, inserted the word *"first"* to emphasize what was all along
most in his view in the simple phrase; viz., the special accountability
of the Jew.   On *Jew* and *Greek*, see on i. 16.

10.   *glory, honour, and peace*]   A beautiful return to the thought of
ver. 7, as if out of an abundance of inspired love and hope.   *"Peace"*
may here bear a special reference to the *peace of acceptance*, of which
the Epistle is to say so much.   Not that this would exclude the larger
meaning of all safety and happiness.

to the Jew first]   See on i. 16.

11.   *for there is no respect of persons*]   *"For"* points to the last
words of ver. 10, and shews that though St Paul has just emphasized
the special privilege of the Jew, ("to the Jew *first*,") as balanced with
his special accountability, yet his main emphasis of thought is on the
position of the Gentiles as side by side with the Jews.   See Acts x. 34,
35, where St Peter at length admits the equal acceptability of pious
Jews and pious Gentiles before God.

with God]   The Greek construction is one often used in judicial
connexions;=**before God;** "in His court, at His bar."   It may,
however. mean no more than "with," "in the case of;" French *chez*,
German *bei*.

12.   *For as many as have sinned*]   The equality of Jew and Gentile
is here pursued, not (as might have been expected from ver. 11) in the
direction of privilege, but in that of responsibility and judgment.   The
reason for this direction is, no doubt, that the main subject of the
Epistle here is SIN and its results.—*"Have sinned"* is literally in the
Greek **sinned**; an aorist, not a perfect.   It is not safe to press *far*
the distinction of these tenses in N. T. Greek.   (See on i. 19.)   But the
aorist, if taken strictly, would here point to the time when earthly life
is closed, and judgment is come; to the sinner's actions as looked back
upon from that point.

sinned without law]   Lit. **lawlessly.**   The context here shews that
the word means "in the absence of a law;" and that this means
"in the absence of an explicit, revealed law;" other law than the
law of conscience.   Similarly, the context proves that to *"perish* without law" means to perish not *"arbitrarily,"* but *"without an explicit
code* as the standard of guilt."   This verse no doubt implies the truth,
elsewhere so clear, that no man shall be condemned for ignorance
of what was in no wise revealed to him; but its main purpose is to
teach the awful truth that *even without the revealed law* there is yet
real sin and real doom.

perish]   "Be doomed to death;" lose the soul.   The Gr. word,

as many as have sinned in the law shall be judged by the
13 law; (for not the hearers of the law *are* just before God,
14 but the doers of the law shall be justified. For when *the*

which some have held to imply *annihilation of being*, by no means
does so. Its true import is rather ruin and loss in regard of condition.
The Latin *perditio* exactly renders the idea.

in the law] Where it is revealed; within range of its explicit precepts.

judged by the law] To "judge" here means practically, as so often
when the context is clear, to "*condemn:*" so e.g. Heb. xiii. 4.--"*By* the
law," as the *instrument* of the doom; as used in determination of the
doom.

The whole argument of this passage sufficiently decides what is
meant by the Law. It is the Moral Law, the revealed Divine Will concerning right and wrong in respect both of God and man. That it is
not specially the Ceremonial Law (which was a divinely-given but
temporary and special code) is plain from ver. 14 of this chapter, where
the witness of conscience must, of course, concern not the legal cere-
monies but the principles of duty.

13. *for not the hearers*] A parenthesis is usually begun here, and
continued to the close of ver. 15. We prefer to dispense with it, for
reasons to be given there. The present verse is naturally connected
with the close of ver. 12.—"The *hearers* of the law:"— as we too speak
of "*hearers* of the Gospel," even now when *reading* is so vastly prevalent.

before God] See last note ver. 11. The Gr. is the same here.

the doers of the law shall be justified] See Gal. iii. 12. . For the express citation cp. Lev. xviii. 5: "Ye shall keep my statutes...which if a
man do, he shall live in them; I am the LORD." How deep the tendency of the Jew was to build safety upon privilege and knowledge,
appears from Matt. iii. 9; Joh. vii. 49. See on ii. 3, and Appendix A.

shall be justified] The future tense, perhaps, refers to Lev. xviii. 5
just quoted; "shall live." Supposing the law kept, this stands in
God's word as the *promised result.*

The meaning of the verb "to justify" will be fully illustrated as we
proceed. Here it is enough to remark that it signifies not *amendment*,
but *acquittal;* or, rather, a judicial *declaration of righteousness.* See
for an excellent illustration from the O. T., Deut. xxv. 1. (The LXX.
there employ the same Gr. word as St Paul's here). The present
verse does not, of course, assert (what would be so clearly contradicted
by e.g. iii. 20) that the law ever is, or can be, so kept as to justify the
keeper. It merely states *the conditions of legal justification*, whether
fulfilled in fact or not.

14. *For when the Gentiles*, &c.] The connexion marked by "*for*"
is not easy to state. We take it to refer (*over* ver. 13, which is an explanation of the previous words) to ver. 12, and to be connected with
the words "shall perish without law." *How* this shall be St Paul
now suggestively states, by explaining that Conscience is to the heathen

Gentiles, which have not the law, do by nature the *things* contained in the law, these, having not the law, are a law unto themselves: which shew the work of the law written 15

a substitute for Revelation, in regard of responsibility. Q.d., "Heathen sinners shall be justly condemned; *for* though without the law, they have a substitute for it."

by nature] This phrase here has to do with a contrast not of *nature and grace*, but of *nature and law*. "*Nature*" here means impulses which, however produced, are not due to known Revelation, or indeed to any precept *ab extra*. Cp. 1 Cor. xi. 14.

the things contained in the law] Lit. **the things of the law.** It is just possible to explain this as "things both commanded and *forbidden* by the law." But far more naturally it means the "principles of the law," i.e. the grand Difference of right and wrong; and thus the whole phrase = "to act on the principles of the law." Nothing is here stated as to perception, or love, of holiness by heathen; but it is certainly stated that they had conscience, and could, up to a certain point, act upon it. It is scarcely needful to say that this is fully illustrated by ancient literature, while the same literature illustrates fully the mysterious limits of conscience and tremendous force of evil. See Appendix E.

having not the law] I.e. "*though* not having it." Their lack of the law gives special importance to the fact of conscience.

a law unto themselves] This may mean "each to himself," or "each and all to the community." As to facts, both explanations would hold. Without individual conscience, there could be no public moral code. But we believe the *main* reference here to be to the public code; to the *general* consciousness and opinion of heathens that right and wrong are eternally different, and that judgment is to be accordingly hereafter. This consciousness and opinion St Paul regards as influencing heathen minds *mutually*; as "*shewn*" in intercourse of thought and speech; as "*witnessed to*" by individual consciences; as coming out in "*reasonings*," philosophic or popular, concerning right and wrong; and as all pointing to a great manifestation of the truth of the *principle* at the Last Day.

15. *which shew*] The relative pronoun is the same as in i. 25, where see note. It marks a condition: "they are a law to themselves, **inasmuch as, &c.**"

shew the work of the law written in their hearts] "*The work* of the law" has been explained as if collective for "*works;*" but this is ill-supported by real parallels. It is better to explain it as "what the law does," than as "what is done for the law's sake;" and thus it means the teaching of the Difference of right and wrong (see iii. 20). This "work," done in an intense degree by the law, is done in a lower degree by conscience alone; but the work is the same in kind. The sense of wrong and right, which it is the law's work to produce fully, is somehow and in some measure, without the law, "*written*" in heathen "*hearts.*" (On the word *heart* see note to i. 21.)—" They *shew:*"—this word may of course refer to *subjective* discovery; each man shewing it

in their hearts, their conscience also bearing witness, and
their thoughts the mean while accusing or else excusing one
16 another;) in the day when God shall judge the secrets of
men by Jesus Christ according to my gospel.

to himself, finding it in his experience. But it better suits the word to
take it of *mutual* manifestations: language and conduct, in heathen
communities, shewing the objective reality of the convictions which
individuals are aware of.—" *Written:*"—for this metaphor, no doubt
suggested by the tablets of Sinai, cp. 2 Cor. iii. 2, 3.

their conscience also bearing witness] Lit. **bearing witness with,
bearing concurrent witness.** What is the *concurrence?* It may be
"of conscience with itself," in its different verdicts. But, on our view
of the passage, it is "*with the common conviction.*" Individual consciences affirm the common conviction of moral distinctions which they
find around them.

In ix. 1 the witness of conscience is again appealed to, with the same
verb: lit. "bearing witness *with me.*" See note there.

and their thoughts, &c.] Better, **and between one another their
reckonings** (or **reasonings**) **accusing, or, it may be, defending.** The
Gr. of "thought" specially means *reasoning* thought, not intuition. It
can hardly be a mere synonym of conscience, which (at least in practice)
is intuitive. The meaning is either "their consciences are ratified in their
verdicts by their private reasonings on particular cases;" or, as seems
better on our view, "the fact of their moral sense is evinced by their
reasonings on right and wrong;" e.g. by Treatises and Dialogues in
which ethical questions are discussed. "*Between one another*" thus
refers not to one mind's balance of thought with thought, but to arguments of man with man. St Paul says nothing of the rightness of these
reasonings in particular cases, but of the *moral significance of the fact
of them.*

16. *in the day*, &c.] This sentence is often connected with the close
of ver. 12. But the parenthesis is thus, even in the style of St Paul,
highly difficult and peculiar; and ver. 13 stands in close natural connexion with ver. 12. Meanwhile the sequence of ver. 16 on ver. 15 is not
hard to trace; the allusion to the Great Day is *anticipatory;* q.d., "These
moral convictions and verdicts have their good and final confirmation in
the day, &c.;" "all that was true in them will be recognized and carried out in Divine action then."

the secrets of men] I.e. of men in general, heathens as well as Jews.
The "*secret* things" are here named, as implying also of course the
judgment of all that is "*open* beforehand." Perhaps the word alludes
too to the "cloke" of Jewish formality, and faith in privileges.

by Jesus Christ according to my gospel] The word "Gospel" is
here used (a deeply significant use) of the entire contents of the
Apostle's teaching; of holy principles and threats of condemnation
as well as holy promises of life.—"*My* Gospel:"—same word as
xvi. 25. The original of the phrase is not strongly emphatic, but
certainly not without point. It indicates on one hand St Paul's deep

17—29 *Explicit exposure of Jewish responsibility, guilt, and peril*

Behold, thou art called a Jew, and restest in the law, 17 and makest thy boast of God, and knowest *his* will, and 18 approvest the *things* that are more excellent, being instructed out of the law ; and art confident that thou thyself art a 19

certainty of his direct Divine commission and its precise import, and on the other his consciousness (much more strongly expressed in the Galatian Epistle) of *opposition* to his position and doctrine. Cf. e.g. Gal. i. 6—12.—" By *Jesus Christ:*"—the words emphatically close the sentence; perhaps with implicit reference to the rejection, by the unbelieving Jews whom the Apostle now more distinctly addresses, of Him who is to judge the world.

17—29 Explicit exposure of Jewish responsibility, guilt, and peril

17. *Behold*] Better, **But if.** A single additional letter in the Gr. makes this difference; and it should certainly be so read. The framework of the sentence is thus somewhat altered : "But if thou art a Jew, and dost glory in the name and privilege,—say, dost thou act up to thy light?"

thou] Emphatic, "thou, my supposed hearer or reader."

art called] Lit. **art surnamed.** Perhaps in the word "named" lies a slight reference to the contrast between external and internal "Judaism." See ver. 28.

restest in] Lit. **restest upon.** The *possession* of the Law was the foundation-rock of the man's peace and hope. On this he reposed himself, thanking God that he was "not as other men were." The Divine exposure of his sin he perverted into a reason for self-righteousness !

makest thy boast of God] Lit. **boastest, or gloriest, in God.** A "boast" either most holy or most sinful according to the man's view of God and of himself. See Isai. xlv. 25, for the sacred promise perverted by Pharisaic pride.

18. *his will*] Lit. **the will.** Cp. 3 Joh. 7, where the original is "for the sake of *the* Name." Possibly the phrase here was a " stereotyped" formula, which St Paul quotes. But in any case its form (as that of the parallel above) is one of peculiar solemnity and dignity.

approvest the things that are more excellent] Better, **assayest, puttest to the test, things which differ.** Exactly the same words occur Phil. i. 10. The Jew had the touchstone of Divine Revelation to apply to questions of wrong and right ; he claimed to be a perfect *casuist.*

19. *thou thyself*] Strongly emphatic. The person supposed is not only sure of the privileges of Jews in general, but of *his own* spiritual competency, by virtue simply of his position and light.

Surely the Apostle is recalling, in part, his own ideas as a Jewish Rabbi of "the straitest sect;" and we may be certain that in the mass of Rabbis and their followers of that time all the features of pride and

guide of the blind, a light of them which are in darkness,
20 an instructor of the foolish, a teacher of babes, which hast
21 the form of knowledge and of the truth in the law. Thou
therefore which teachest another, teachest thou not thyself?
thou that preachest *a man* should not steal, dost thou steal?
22 Thou that sayest *a man* should not commit adultery, dost
thou commit adultery? thou that abhorrest idols, dost thou
23 commit sacrilege? thou that makest thy boast of the law,

blindness he here draws were at least as strongly marked as in his
own past.—See Appendix A.

a guide of the blind] A very frequent and expressive metaphor. See
Matt. xv. 14, xxiii. 16, &c.

20. *the foolish*] **the thoughtless.** Same word as Luke xi. 40;
1 Cor. xv. 36; Eph. v. 17, &c.

hast the form, &c.] Read, **having in the law the form of knowledge and of truth.**—"The *form:*"—same word as 2 Tim. iii. 5, where
certainly it means *outward form* as separate from inward life. Here
the same meaning is present, but not as the only or chief one. The
Greek word (not found in the classics) strictly means "shaping,"
"moulding;" but this must not be pressed: it may well mean, practically, the result of shaping—i.e. *form*. And certainly in the derivation of the word there is no necessary idea of *unreality;* rather the
opposite. The natural reference here is to the divinely-drawn outline
and scheme, the delineation, of spiritual "knowledge and truth" in the
Old Testament. But beneath the word, *in this context*, inevitably lies
the thought that this delineation is (in the self-righteous Jew's use of it)
taken apart from life and love.

21. *Thou therefore*, &c.] In this and the following verses St Paul
does not charge every individual Rabbinist with immorality. He
exposes the spirit and principles of Rabbinism, as evinced and proved
only too abundantly in multitudes of lives. Not every unconverted
Rabbinist was a thief or adulterer; but in one aspect or another he
did not "teach himself;" allowing in his own heart principles of self-
righteousness and formalism which *really* cut at the root of his moral
teaching of others. Meantime, the Jewish malpractices of that age
were terribly real, frequent, and notorious.

preachest] Lit. **proclaimest**: e.g. in synagogue-discourses.

22. *commit sacrilege*] Lit. **plunder sacred things,** or **plunder from
sacred places.** The Gr. word is the same as that translated "robbers
of churches," Acts xix. 37. The idea of plunder is not *necessary*
in the word, however; other forms of sacrilege may be included.
Thus the reference may be to such profanations as that of the
traders in the Temple (Joh. ii. 14, &c.), and the appeal will be,
"Thou, who art so jealous for God against idolaters, dost thou worship
self and mammon in His presence?" But if the special thought of
robbery is kept (as is certainly more natural, with the derivation and
usage of the Greek word in view), the reference probably is to Jewish

through breaking the law dishonourest thou God? For the 24 name of God is blasphemed among the Gentiles through you, as it is written. For circumcision verily 25 profiteth, if thou keep the law: but if thou be a breaker of the law, thy circumcision is made uncircumcision. There- 26 fore if the uncircumcision keep the righteousness of the law,

thefts from pagan temples, where meanwhile the strict Jew professed not to dare to set his foot for fear of pollution. Scruple broke down before thievish avarice.

23. *dishonourest*] **disgracest.** The crimes of Jews made their Lord's "name to be blasphemed among the Gentiles;" as, alas, the name of Christ is, for exactly similar reasons, often blasphemed among the heathen now.

24. *as it is written*] In Ezek. xxxvi. 20—23. In that passage the special reference is to the evil example of the dispersed Jews of the captivity.

25. *For circumcision verily profiteth*] With this verse a minor section or paragraph begins. The thought is not in strict sequence with what has just been said, though in full connexion with the same general subject.—"*Profiteth:*"—for comment on this word, see iii. 1. Circumcision was the gate to ample privileges; above all to the familiar knowledge of the written oracles. But these privileges would finally benefit only the personally pious Jew.

if thou keep the law] Lit. **if thou do the law.** The reference, probably, is not to *absolute* righteousness (q.d., "if thou act with sinless obedience"), but to practical sincere piety, as contrasted with neglectful or wilful disobedience. The emphasis here is on the destructive effect of this latter. In Gal. v. 2, 3, where a widely different error is combated (not native Jewish pride, but Judaical ritualism creeping back amongst Christians), the Apostle emphasizes as he does not here the vast demands of the covenant of circumcision viewed as terms of justification.

is made uncircumcision] The benefits of thy circumcision are as if they had not been.

26. *Therefore*, &c.] St Paul reasons from his last statement, as from what is self-evident to conscience.

the uncircumcision] I.e., probably, "the uncircumcised man;" for see below, "*his* uncircumcision." The form of speech is most unusual; such a word as "uncircumcision," when used personally, almost always referring to a class, not an individual. *Perhaps* even here it is so used, but then immediately (in the words "his circumcision") an individual specimen is considered.

keep the righteousness, &c.] See above on ver. 25. Here again, practical piety, the will to do God's revealed will, is in view; not sinless obedience. Cornelius (Acts x. 35) is a case exactly in point. He was not sinless; he needed "*saving*" (a significant word there); but he "feared God, and worked righteousness," and the Divine welcome was his.

shall not his uncircumcision be counted for circumcision?
27 And shall not uncircumcision which is by nature, if it fulfil
the law, judge thee, who by the letter and circumcision dost
28 transgress the law? For he is not a Jew, which is one outwardly; neither *is that* circumcision, which is outward in the
29 flesh: but he *is* a Jew, which is one inwardly; and circumcision *is that* of the heart, in the spirit, *and* not *in* the letter; whose praise *is* not of men, but of God.

the righteousness] Better, **the ordinances**; the special precepts, of
whatever kind.

27. *uncircumcision which is by nature*] Better, **the uncircumcision**, &c.; a phrase not easy to explain exactly. Perhaps (though
the Gr. of the two passages is not quite parallel) we may illustrate by
Gal. ii. 15: "Jews by nature," Jews born and bred. Here thus the
sense would be "Gentiles born and bred, with no *physical* succession to
Jewish privilege."

if it fulfil] Lit. **fulfilling**; as e.g. Cornelius did in the sense
pointed out above.

judge] **criticize and condemn.** Perhaps the phrase arises from
the solemn words of the Saviour Himself, Matt. xii. 41, 42. A stronger
Gr. verb is used in that passage, however.

by the letter and circumcision] The phrase is a verbal paradox.
The "letter and circumcision" are properly the *means* to a knowledge
of the law, to obligation to it, and obedience under it; here they are,
by paradox, the *means* to the wilful breaking of it, and not mere
obstacles overcome by the transgressor.—"*The letter*" is the "letter of
the law" of circumcision: q. d., "thou usest thy literal circumcision as
a means to transgression," a salve to thy conscience.

28. *he is not a Jew*] Obviously, in the sense of exclusive privilege.
Q. d., "If a Jew means (as the word would mean from Pharisaic lips)
a member of a body which is specially entitled to salvation, then a Jew
is not made by physical circumcision, for a title to salvation must be
sought in things spiritual not physical." See for similar forcible statements, Gal. iii. 7, &c., vi. 15, 16; Phil. iii. 2, 3; Rev. iii. 9.

29. *inwardly*] Lit. **in that which is hidden, in secret**; same word
as Matt. vi. 4, &c. Just above, "outwardly" is lit. **in that which is
open.** The contrast is between an external seal on the body and an
internal change in the soul. See 1 Pet. iii. 4 for an illustrative phrase,
"the hidden man of the heart."

in the spirit, and not in the letter] The same contrast appears vii. 6,
and 2 Cor. iii. 6—8. Here practically the contrasted things are,
(1) circumcision, a literal act done on the body; (2) that state of the
soul, the result of a change spiritual and unseen, of which circumcision
was a symbol. "*In*" this latter, in respect of it, in relation to it,
the pious Gentile was "circumcised." See further below on vii. 6.

whose praise] "*Whose*" refers to the man. The "praise" of such

CH. III.   1—2   *The advantage of the Jew: Revelation*

What advantage then hath the Jew? or what profit *is* 3
there of circumcision?   Much every way : chiefly, because 2
that unto them were committed the oracles of God.

a "Jew in the hidden man," his commendation as a true son of
Abraham, may be refused by the Pharisees, but will be given by God
when He gathers His Israel in.   The whole two verses (28, 29) are
more exactly rendered thus: **For not the outwardly-sealed Jew is
a Jew, and not the circumcision outwardly wrought in the flesh
is circumcision ; but the inwardly-sealed Jew, and the circumcision
of the heart in spirit, not in letter ; of whom the praise is not from
men, but from God.**

CH. III.   **1—2**   THE ADVANTAGE OF THE JEW: REVELATION

1.   *What advantage*]   Lit. **what excess**, i. e. of privilege.
St Paul here corrects, though only in passing, the possible inference
from the previous passage that circumcision was valueless in all respects,
and that the Jew as such had nothing special to thank God for.   It is
remarkable that his chief reply to such a thought lies in the fact that the
Old Covenant secured the immense practical benefit of *Revelation.*
(Cp. Ps. ciii. 7.)   This correction is aside from the main argument of
this part of the Epistle, in which St Paul aims to prove the equality of
Jew and Gentile not in respect of privilege but in respect of *reality of
guilt, and of need of a Divine justification.*   Yet even here the main
argument is not forgotten: the gift of Scripture brings the *responsibility*
of the Jew into the fullest light.   His "advantage" is his accusation.
2.   *every way*]   For a comment see ix. 4, 5; part of an argument of
which this verse may be regarded as the germ or first suggestion.
chiefly]   Lit. **first.**   Perhaps this is the first step in an enumeration
which is not carried on.   Cp. i. 8.   But the rendering *"chiefly"* is
quite possible and natural.
unto them were committed]   Lit. **they were trusted with** ; for their
own benefit in the first place, and then as the "keepers of Holy Writ"
for the world—for enquirers and proselytes under the Old Covenant,
and for the universal Church under the New.
the oracles]   **the utterances.**   Same word as Acts vii. 38; Heb. v.
12 ; 1 Pet. iv. 11.   The Gr. word is occasionally used in the LXX. for
ordinary human utterances; e. g. Ps. xix. (LXX. xviii.) 14: "the *words*
of my mouth."   The context of the passages of N. T. just quoted leaves
no doubt that it refers here to the utterances of God through the prophets of the Old Covenant; in short, to the O. T. Scriptures.   The
Apostle's testimony to the unique dignity of the Scripture Revelation
could not be stronger.   And so when he elsewhere contrasts "letter"
and "spirit," his meaning, whatever it is, is not to diminish the Divine
authority of the written "oracles."

3—8   *The Divine Judge will not connive at sin*

3   For what if some did not believe? shall their unbelief make
4   the faith of God without effect? God forbid : yea, let God be

3—8   THE DIVINE JUDGE WILL NOT CONNIVE AT SIN

3—8. *for what if some*, &c.] Verses 3—8 form a passage of much
difficulty in detail, though clear as a whole. The difficulty results
partly from a doubt as to where the Opponent speaks, and partly from
the Apostle's own thought modifying the words put into the Opponent's
mouth. It will be best to waive a minute discussion of interpretations,
and at once to give our own in the shape of a paraphrase.

Ver. 3. (*The Jewish Opponent*). "You say the Jew has advantage.
He has indeed : God's veracity (truth, faithfulness) is pledged to give
him eternal life.   For can we think that the unfaithfulness of some
Jews to God annuls His faithfulness to the race? Will He fail in His
purpose?"

Ver. 4. (*The Apostle.*) "God forbid! Rather should we admit
any charge of untruth against man, than the least against God.   So
David saw, and wrote, in his confession of his own sin; his main
thought was (Ps. li. 4) that he would even own the very worst against
himself, that God might be seen to punish him justly."

Ver. 5. (*The Opponent.*) "But hear me further. The sinful unbelief of some Jews, as you own, cannot change HIS purpose. May I not
say more? does it not, by bringing His faithfulness into contrast, glorify
Him? and if so, will He punish it? What say you of His justice or injustice in visiting even wicked Jews with wrath?"

Vv. 6, 7, 8. (*The Apostle.*) "I say, God forbid the thought that He
will *not* punish them. For, on such a principle, how shall God be the
universal Judge at all? I too, be I Jew or Gentile, might say as well as
you, 'I choose to tell a lie; somehow or other this will illustrate God's
truth, e. g. by *contrast;* therefore I ought to be acquitted; I ought to be
allowed to act on the principle of evil for the sake of good;'—a principle
with which we Christians are charged, but which we utterly condemn."

We now remark on details.

3. *For what*] Here a formula of argument, introducing an objection.

if some] A euphemism, most natural in the words of a supposed
Jewish Opponent. As a fact, it was the "some" who believed, the
many who did not; as of old at Kadesh-barnea. (Numb. xiii. and xiv.)

the faith of God] i.e. His **good faith**, faithfulness to His promise.
The same Gr. word appears with the meaning "faithfulness" in e.g.
Gal. v. 22 (where E. V. has "faith"), Tit. ii. 10, and perhaps 1 Tim.
iv. 12.—See Appendix C.

4. *God forbid*] Lit. **may it not be ; be it not**; and so always
where the words "God forbid" occur in the Eng. N. T.—The Apostle
more than accepts the opponent's position, but not in his sense. God's
promise should indeed stand; the mere thought of a failure there is
shocking. But that promise had never said that *impenitent individuals*
of the chosen race should be safe from doom.

true, but every man a liar; as it is written, That thou
mightest be justified in thy sayings, and mightest
overcome when thou art judged. But if our un- 5
righteousness commend the righteousness of God, what
shall we say? *Is* God unrighteous who taketh vengeance?
(I speak as a man) God forbid: for then how shall God 6

let God be true, &c.] Q. d., "If there is failure, it is safer and truer
to believe the truest man false, than 'God who cannot lie.'"—It is a
profound characteristic of all Scripture to be always *on the side of God*.
In this lies one pregnant evidence, to those who will think it out, of the
"Supernatural Origin of the Bible."

that thou mightest, &c.] The Gr. words are verbatim the LXX.
of Ps. li. (LXX. l.) 4. The lit. Hebrew is exactly as E. V. there,
"clear when thou *judgest;*" and probably the Gr. of LXX. and
of St Paul here is really the same, or nearly so, in effect: "clear when
thou impleadest; when thou *procurest judgment.*" Same word as "go
to law," 1 Cor. vi. 1. On the special force of this thought *in Psalm li.*
see paraphrase above.

5. *unrighteousness...righteousness*] General terms, but implying the
special forms of *unbelief* and *fidelity*. Man's mistrust is awfully *unjust
to God ;* God's fidelity to His promise is *just to Himself* and His holiness.
—See below on ver. 21 for the *exceptional* meaning here of "*the
Righteousness of God*[1]."

Is God unrighteous, &c. ?] This question (the Opponent's) is a
serious grammatical difficulty in the Gr. The interrogative particle is
that which regularly expects the answer "*No.*" But the turn of this
argument suggests a question (*from the Opponent*) expecting "*Yes.*"
(The above use of the particle in question is not *quite* invariable in Gr.,
but it holds in all other cases *in St Paul*.) To us it seems that the
solution is as follows: The Apostle gives the Opponent's question, but
jealousy for God's honour compels him to modify it by his own intense
sense of the Divine righteousness. The Opponent demands the answer
"*Yes;*" St Paul is forced to make him, grammatically, demand the
answer "*No.*" Instead of his would-be "*Is not* God unrighteous, &c. ?"
it thus stands, "*Is* God unrighteous, &c. ?"—in which at most the
question is left, verbally, open.

taketh vengeance] Lit. **inflicteth the wrath ;** i.e. the wrath merited
by the special sin; the wrath which had fallen on Israel.

I speak as a man] I.e. "on merely human principles, from mere man's
point of view." This serious questioning about right and wrong in the
Eternal and His acts is, in St Paul's view, "speaking as man." In the
light of the Holy Spirit's teaching it is impossible, unless (as here) by
way of a mere argumentative formula.

6. *how shall God judge the world?*] The emphasis is on "judge,"

[1] It is *possible*, however, that the meaning assigned to the phrase in note on i. 17,
may be the meaning even here: q.d., "What if our sin should illustrate (by contrast
or otherwise) God's Way of Acceptance?"

7 judge the world? For if the truth of God hath *more* abounded through my lie unto his glory; why yet am I also
8 judged as a sinner? And not *rather*, (as we be slanderously reported, and as some affirm that we say,) Let us do evil, that good may come? whose damnation is just.

not on "world." It is needless to suppose the word "world" here to stand in opposition to *the Jewish people.* The point of the question is, that if God could not righteously punish sin when sin illustrated His glory, not only would He not punish those particular sins, but He would (as to principle) *entirely* abdicate His office as "Judge of all the earth." *All* sin, in one respect or another, illustrates His glory, if only as a black contrast: therefore, in *no* case would punishment be just!—On the truth that the Lord *is* the "Judge of all" the Apostle falls back as on a "first ground."

7. *For if,* &c.] Here St Paul takes up the Opponent on his own ground ; speaking as a human being whose sin (e.g. a falsehood) serves to make God's truth "abound to His glory;" i.e. be more largely manifest in a way to win Him fresh praise:—in such a case is not Paul, is not A, B, or C, equally entitled with the Jewish opponent to be excused penalty?—In the Gr. of the clause "why am I yet, &c.," the word "I" is strongly emphatic; **I also**; i.e. "I, as well as my opponent."—"Why am I *yet*, &c.:"—i.e. "after the recognition of the effect of my sin on the advancement of God's glory."—"*By my lie;*" lit. **in my lie;** i.e. "on occasion of it, in connexion with it."

8. *And not rather,* &c.] The grammatical difficulty of this verse is great. The words, up to the brief last clause, are a question. This question is introduced (like that in ver. 5) by the particle which *expects a negative reply.* But again the drift of the reasoning seems to demand, though not so clearly as in ver. 5, an *affirmative,* thus: "*Is it not* (as we are slanderously reported, and as some affirm that we say) a case for the maxim ' Let us do evil that good may come'?" Here, in our view, the wording presents a compound between the simple statement of the argumentative question, and St Paul's abhorrence of the moral wrong involved in an affirmative answer. He cannot bear to state the case without conveying, *while he does so,* his deep protest, both in the words " as we be *slanderously* reported " (lit. "as we are *blasphemed*"), and in the choice of the interrogative particle which demands a *negative.*

The "slanderous report" in question is illustrated by iii. 31, and vi. 1, 15. It was a distortion of the doctrine of free grace. St Paul was charged, by his inveterate adversaries in the Church, with teaching that complete and immediate pardon for Christ's sake makes sin safe to the pardoned, and that, consequently, the more "evil" is "done" by such, the more "good" will "come," in the way of glory to God's mercy.

whose damnation is just] I.e. the condemnation, moral and judicial, of *all* who can hold such a principle. This is a more natural reference of the words than that to the slanderers, or to the Apostle and his followers as holding (by the false hypothesis) immoral principles. It is

9—20   *Man universally and fatally guilty: no hope in human merit.   This with special reference to Jewish prejudice*

What then? are we better *than they*?   No, in no wise: 9
for we have before proved both Jews and Gentiles, that
they are all under sin; as it is written, There is none 10
righteous, no, not one: there is none that under- 11

the brief elliptic statement of his abhorrence *in toto* of all and any who
could maintain the lawfulness of wrong.   What a comment upon
Jesuitical maxims, and "pious frauds" in general!   See *Introduction*,
i. § 33, note.

damnation]   In the Gr. strictly **judgment**. So 1 Cor. xi. 29 margin.   The Gr. word is inclusive.   In Rom. xi. 33, in plural, it signifies
the Divine counsels or decisions; in 1 Cor. vi. 7, acts of going to law;
in 1 Cor. xi. 29, 34, inflicted penalty; in Rev. xx. 4, judicial power.
In almost every other N. T. passage it means "condemnation," whether
that of opinion (Matt. vii. 2) or of a judicial (usually capital) sentence,
either human (Luke xxiv. 20) or Divine (Rom. ii. 2, 3; Heb. vi. 2).
Here undoubtedly it is the latter.

**9—20.   MAN UNIVERSALLY AND FATALLY GUILTY: NO HOPE IN
HUMAN MERIT.   THIS WITH SPECIAL REFERENCE TO JEWISH
PREJUDICE**

9.   *What then? are we better?*]   I.e., probably, "we Jews."   The
effect of the last passage has been specially to convince *the Jew* of his
sin and danger; and here the Apostle speaks, as he was so ready to do,
as a Jew with Jews.   The delicacy of his so doing here is remarkable,
where it is a question of humiliation.

proved]   Or **charged**, as in margin.—"*We* have before proved:" a
use of plural for singular frequent with St Paul.

under sin]   The grammar of the Gr. suggests *motion* under; q. d.,
"*fallen* under sin," i.e. from an ideal (not actual) state of original
righteousness, such as is implied when we speak of individuals as
"fallen human creatures."—"*In Adam* all" *fell*, as from a standing.—
"*Under sin*:"—i.e. so as to be subject to its weight, its power and
doom.   This is the first occurrence of the word SIN in the Epistle.   It
is repeated nearly fifty times in the first eight chapters.

10.   *There is none*, &c.]   In vv. 10—18 we have a chain of
Scripture quotations.   The originals are found, verbally or in substance,
in Psal. v. 9, x. 7, xiv. 1—3, xxxvi. 1, cxl. 3; Prov. i. 16; Is. lix. 7.
In the Alexandrine MS. of the LXX. of Ps. xiv. (LXX. xiii.) 3, appears
a singular phenomenon: the Gr. is much ampler than the original
Hebrew (for which see E. V.), and is verbatim the same as the Gr. of
vv. 12—18 of this chapter.   There can be little doubt that this was
the work of a copyist acquainted with this passage of St Paul.—Ver. 10
would better read: **as it is written that there is none righteous, no,
not one.**   The precise quotations would then begin at ver. 11.   The

standeth, there is none that seeketh after God.
12 They are all gone out of the way, they are together become unprofitable; there is none that
13 doeth good, no, not one. Their throat *is* an open
sepulchre; with their tongues they have used de-
14 ceit; the poison of asps *is* under their lips: whose
15 mouth is full of cursing and bitterness: their
16 feet *are* swift to shed blood: destruction and mi-
17 sery *are* in their ways: and the way of peace
18 have they not known: there is no fear of God
19 before their eyes. Now we know that what *things* soever
the law saith, it saith to them who are under the law: that
every mouth may be stopped, and all the world may be-
20 come guilty before God. Therefore by the deeds of the law

words of ver. 10 are not found in the O. T., and read rather as a
summary of what is to follow.

The awful charges of vv. 10—18 are specially pointed at the Jews:
see ver. 19. The passages quoted are descriptive of Israelites, some
of them of Israelites of the best days of Israel. What *at least* they
establish is that the root of sin was vigorous in Jewish hearts, and that
its fruits in Jewish lives were abominable in the sight of God. Meantime we must not narrow the reference too closely. The Apostle's
doctrine of human sinfulness (see e.g. Tit. iii. 3) is that the worst
developments of individual sin only indicate the *possibilities of the sinful
heart in general.* Passages like those cited here thus prove, not only
what certain men were, but what man is. See Jer. xvii. 9.

13. *an open sepulchre*] Perhaps as "*uttering abomination.*" " Emit-
ting the noisome exhalations of a putrid heart " (Bp Horne on Ps. v. 9).

19. *the law*] Here not the Pentateuch, but the O. T. as a whole.
So Joh. x. 34, xv. 25. The O. T. does indeed predict and reveal much
of redeeming mercy; but its main characteristic work (apart from prophecy) is to reveal the *preceptive will* of God and the sin of man.

under the law] Lit. **in the law**; within its precincts, its dominion.
These persons are here the Jews, the primary objects of the O. T.
message. The Gentiles are *otherwise* convicted; and the Jews being
now also thus convicted (from the very title-deeds of their privileges)
both of sin and of exposure to its doom, "the *whole world* is found
guilty." We must remember that the Apostle has had in view the
Pharisaic prejudice that the only really endangered sinners were the
"sinners of the Gentiles." See Appendix A.

guilty] The original word occurs here only in N. T. A common
classical meaning is "liable to legal process, actionable." Every
human soul owes to God the awful forfeit for sin. Strong, indeed, is
the language of this verse, but no conscience that ever really awoke to
the holiness of God thought it at last too strong.

20. *Therefore*] This verse sums up the great argument begun at

there shall no flesh be justified in his sight: for by the law *is* the knowledge of sin.

21—31 *The Divine method of holy pardon, alike for all*

But now the righteousness of God without the law is 21 manifested, being witnessed by the law and the prophets ;

i. 18, and more especially that begun at ii. 1. The Apostle has laid deep the foundation of the fact of universal and intense sinfulness and guilt. Now he will, in the true order, speak of the Divine Remedy.

deeds of the law] I. e. "prescribed by the Law," specially by the O. T. as the preceptive revelation; but practically also by its counterpart in every human being—Conscience (see i. 14). That the ceremonial law alone is not meant is particularly plain from the recent quotation of purely moral passages as "the Law" (ver. 18). The subsequent argument of the Epistle entirely accords with this, and practically explains that "works of the law" are acts of human obedience viewed as satisfactory, or meritorious, in regard of salvation.

no flesh] "No human being." So 1 Cor. i. 29; Gal. ii. 16. See too Joh. xvii. 2.

justified] See note on ii. 13.

by the law is the knowledge of sin] The Gr. for "knowledge" is a special word, meaning **full** or **particular knowledge**. The idea of sin does indeed always exist in conscience. But the express revelation of the holy will of God calls out and intensifies that idea, and also makes plain the results and doom of sin, without stating any terms of pardon, which it is not the business of the PRECEPT to offer. See the Apostle's own comment, vii. 7, 8. It is the revealed Precept which, above all things, makes sin known as *evil done against the Holy One*.

21—31 THE DIVINE METHOD OF HOLY PARDON, ALIKE FOR ALL

21. *But now*] i. e. "But as things are, as the fact is."

Here the great argument of Pardon and Salvation begins, to close with the triumphant words of viii. 37—39.

the righteousness of God] See note on i. 17. In iii. 5 this phrase had a reference different from that of most other passages in this Epistle[1]. Its meaning in that verse is modified and determined by the words "our unrighteousness," which, by contrast, fix it to mean there the *Divine veracity and fidelity*. Here, and through the rest of this argument, it means the divinely-granted, and righteous, acceptance of believers.

without the law] "Apart from the code of precepts." The best comment on this most important phrase is the rest of this chapter and iv. 4—8. The very essence of the argument here demands that the words should mean "to the *total exclusion* of any work of obedience of man's *from the matter of his justification.*"

is manifested] Lit. **has been manifested**; i. e. historically, "by the appearing of our Saviour Jesus Christ." 2 Tim. i. 10.

---

[1] See however the footnote there.

22 even the righteousness of God *which is* by faith of Jesus
Christ unto all and upon all them that believe : for there is
23 no difference : for all have sinned, and come short of the

witnessed by the law and the prophets] Its reality and virtue is by
them attested, confirmed, to those who accept the O. T. as the Word of
God.—" *The Law*" is here, by the context, the Pentateuch, with its
prophecies of redemption, and its Levitical ritual, priesthood, and
tabernacle, all which was (see the Epistle to the Hebrews) a "prophecy
in act " of the " better things to come."—" *The Prophets,*" including
the Psalter, are full not only of direct predictions of the Redeemer and
His Work, but of language of love and pardon from the Holy One which
only that Work can reconcile with the awful sanctions of the moral
law.

22. *even*] Perhaps translate **but**, i. e. with a sort of contrast to
the words just before. The "righteousness" was witnessed indeed by
the O. T., *but* it resided in Christ and His work.

faith of Jesus Christ] **Faith in Jesus Christ** is certainly the meaning. The same Gr. construction occurs in Mark xi. 22; Acts iii. 16;
Gal. ii. 16, 20; Eph. iii. 12; Phil. iii. 9; with the same sense.

In this verse the Saviour's NAME is first brought into the argument.

unto all and upon all] The Gr. phrases respectively indicate *desti-
nation* and *bestowal*. The sacred pardon was prepared *for* all believers,
and is actually laid *upon* them as a " robe of righteousness." (Is. lxi.
10.)

no difference] I.e., in respect of the need of the revealed justification.
Between Jew and Gentile, and soul and soul, there were and are countless other differences; but *in this respect, none*. A mountain-top differs
in level from a mine-floor; but it is as impossible to touch the stars from
the mountain as from the mine. The least sinful human soul is *as hopelessly* remote from the Divine standard of holiness as the most sinful,
and that standard is inexorable.

23. *all have sinned*] Lit. **all sinned** : the Gr. aorist. Probably
the time-reference of the tense is to the original Fall of Man, regarded
as involving the individual experience of sinfulness in the case of each
person. See however on i. 19.

come short] A present tense. The result of the Fall is that they *are
now* "short of the glory of God." The word translated "come short"
is translated "to be in want " (Luke xv. 14); "to suffer need " (Phil.
iv. 12); "to be destitute " (Heb. xi. 37). Here the context suggests
that modification of its root-meaning given in E. V.: "to suffer from
defect," "to fail to attain."—" *The glory of God*" must here be His
moral glory, His holiness and its requirements. In many passages the
word "glory " is used with evident reference to the Divine moral attri-
butes—mercy, faithfulness, love—as well as to Divine power. See vi. 4;
2 Cor. iv. 4 ("the gospel of the glory of Christ "); Eph. i. 12, 14;
1 Tim. i. 11 ("the gospel of the glory of the blessed God "). Fallen
man lies hopelessly below the standard of the spiritual law which is the
expression of the essential holiness of God.

glory of God; being justified freely by his grace through 24
the redemption that is in Christ Jesus: whom God hath 25
set forth *to be* a propitiation through faith in his blood,

24. *being justified*] A present tense; indicating a constant procedure, in the case of successive individuals.

freely] Lit. **gratis, gift-wise.** Same word as Joh. xv. 25 ("without a
cause," E.V.); 2 Cor. xi. 7; Gal. ii. 21 ("in vain," E. V.; i.e., "without
equivalent result"); 2 Thess. iii. 8 ("for nought"); Rev. xxi. 6, xxii. 17.

The word here expresses with all the force possible the entire absence
of human merit in the matter of justification.

grace] The loving favour of God, uncaused by anything external to
Himself. For explanatory phrases specially to the point here, see
v. 15, 17, vi. 14, 15; Eph. ii. 8, 9.

through the redemption] The Divine Grace, because Divine and therefore holy, acts only in the *channel* of the Work of Christ.—"*Redemption:*"—this word, and the corresponding Gr., specially denote "deliverance as the result of *ransom.*" There are cases where its reference
is less special, e.g. Heb. xi. 35. But the context here makes its strict
meaning exactly appropriate; the sacrifice, the blood, of the Saviour is
the ransom of the soul. See for a similar context the following passages, where the same Gr. word, or one closely cognate, occurs: Matt.
xx. 28; Eph. i. 7; Col. i. 14; Tit. ii. 14; Heb. ix. 15; 1 Pet. i. 18.
See below on viii. 23 for another reference of the word.

in Christ Jesus] It resides in Him, as the immediate procuring
cause; for He "became unto us Redemption," 1 Cor. i. 30. To Him
man must look for it; in Him he must find it.

25. *hath set forth*] Lit. **did set forth**; the aorist (see on ver. 23).
The Gr. verb bears also the derived meaning "to purpose, design," (so
Eph. i. 9), which would not be unsuitable here. But the E. V. is made
more probable by the context, which dwells on the fact of the *manifestation* of redemption.

a propitiation] The Gr. word is only found elsewhere in N. T.,
Heb. ix. 5, where it means the golden lid of the Ark, the "Mercy-seat."
(In 1 Joh. ii. 2, iv. 10, where E. V. has "propitiation," the Gr. has
another but cognate word.) The translation "Mercy-seat" is insisted on here by many commentators, and it is a fact on their side that
in the LXX. the Gr. word is always used *locally,* of the Mercy-seat, or
the like. But on the other side are the facts (1) that the word, as to its
form, can quite well mean **a price of expiation**; (2) that it is found,
though very rarely, in that sense in secular Greek; and above all (3)
that the context here is strongly in favour of the sense "an expiatory
offering." He *becomes* "a propitiation" to the soul "*through faith in
His blood;*" an expression which naturally points to the Victim, not the
Mercy-seat, as the type in view.

through faith] This, as always in the Scripture doctrine of salvation,
is the necessary *medium of application.* In *Himself* the Saviour is what
He is, always and absolutely; to *the soul* He is what He is, as Saviour,
only when approached by faith; i.e. accepted, in humble trust in the

to declare his righteousness for the remission of sins that
26 are past, through the forbearance of God; to declare, *I say*, at this time his righteousness: that he might be just,

Divine word, as the sole way of mercy. The progress of the Epistle will be abundant commentary.

in his blood] The same construction as in Gr. of Mark i. 15: "believe *in* the Gospel." The idea is of faith as a hand, or anchor, finding a *hold in* the object. Here first in the Epistle the holy Blood is mentioned; once again at ch. v. 9, in precisely the same connexion. For similar mentions see Matt. xxvi. 28; Joh. vi. 53—56; Acts xx. 28; Eph. i. 7; Col. i. 20; Heb. ix. 12, 14, 22, x. 19, xii. 24, xiii. 12, 20; 1 Pet. i. 2, 19; 1 Joh. i. 7; Rev. i. 5, v. 9, vii. 14, xii. 11.

to declare his righteousness] Lit. **to be a demonstration, or display, of his righteousness.** The Redeemer's expiatory death, and the gift of pardon solely "through faith in" it, *explained* beyond all doubt that the Divine mercy *did not mean indifference to the Divine Law.* Many questions regarding the atonement may be beyond our knowledge; but this at least is "declared," as the sinful soul contemplates it.—Here, probably, the phrase "Righteousness of God" bears a sense (suggested in the note) exceptional to the rule given in note on i. 17. But the meaning as in i. 17 is not wholly out of place.

for the remission, &c.] Lit. **on account of the letting-pass of the fore-gone sins in the forbearance of God.** Almost every word here needs special notice. "*Letting-pass:*"—a word weaker than full and free pardon, and thus specially appropriate to God's dealings with sin *before the Gospel*, when there was just this *reserve* about the forgiveness, that the Reason of it was not fully revealed.—"*Fore-gone*, or *fore-done, sins:*"—i.e., those before the Gospel. These are specially mentioned here, not because sin was more, or less, sinful then than now, but because the matter in hand here is the *display of the righteousness of the Divine pardon of any sin.* Cp. Heb. ix. 16.—"*In the forbearance*, &c.:*"—perhaps=**in the time when God forebore,** i.e. did not punish sin, though without a *fully-revealed* propitiation. But the words may mean, practically, as E.V., **through, &c.;** i.e. "His forbearance was the *cause* of that letting-pass; of that 'obscure' pardon."—Lastly, "*On account of the letting-pass:*"—the point of this phrase will now be clear. The pardon of sinners under the O. T., being (in a certain sense) unexplained, *demanded* such a *display* at last of the Righteousness of Pardon as was made in the Cross.

26. *at this time*] The word translated "time" means usually **occasion,** "special time," "due time." Same word as ch. v. 6. Such a sense is natural here. The "declaration" of God's righteousness in pardon was made not only "at this time," as distinct from a previous age (that of the O.T.), but "at this *due* time," the crisis fixed by the Divine purpose.

that he might be] I.e., practically, "might be seen to be," "that He might be *in His creatures' view.*"

just] With the justice of a judge; giving full honour to the Law.

and the justifier of him which believeth in Jesus. Where *is* 27
boasting then? It is excluded. By what law? of works?
Nay: but by the law of faith. Therefore we conclude that 28
a man is justified by faith without the deeds of the law. *Is* 29
he the God of the Jews only? *is he* not also of the Gentiles? Yes, of the Gentiles also: seeing *it is* one God, 30

and the justifier] "And" here plainly = **even whilst.** The Cross
reconciled two seeming incompatibles—jealousy for the Law, and
judicial acquittal of the guilty.

him which believeth] Lit. **him who is out of, or from, faith.** This
Gr. idiom may mean "one who belongs to the *class of faith*," i.e. of the
faithful, the believing. Nearly the same Gr. occurs Heb. x. 39.

in Jesus] Some critics omit these words, but without sufficient
reason.

27. *boasting*] Lit. **the boasting;** i.e. probably "the boasting of
the Jew in his pride of privilege." This reference is supported by the
next three verses, especially if "for" is read in ver. 28 (q.v.).

It is excluded] Lit. **It was excluded,** by the "declaration" made
in the Redeemer's death.

the law of faith] The word "law," in Greek as in English, is
elastic in its reference. In English it is freely used for two almost
opposite conceptions, a moral law and a law of nature; of which the
first is a precept of duty *à priori*, the second a statement of observed
facts *à posteriori*. Here the word, connected with *faith*, evidently
means not a moral code but a rule of procedure; the Divine *institute*
that justification is reached only by faith.

28. *Therefore*] Another reading of the Gr. gives **For.** Evidence
of MSS., &c. is strong on both sides: but the internal evidence, in the
coherence of the argument, is decidedly for "*For.*" Ver. 28 is then a
resumé of what has gone before; a brief restatement of the "law of
faith:" q.d. "for this *is* what our facts go to prove, that a man is justified, &c."

If "*therefore*" is retained, this verse begins, or rather forms, a new
minor paragraph, summing up indeed what has preceded, but with no
bearing on what follows. If "*for*" is adopted, vv. 27 and 29 are in
close connexion: the Jew's boasting is "excluded," because the "law
of faith" is as much for the Gentile as for the Jew. "*We conclude*"
should rather be **we reason, we maintain.**

29. *Is he the God,* &c.] More lit. **Does God belong to the Jews
alone?** i.e. as the Giver of peace and life by covenant.

30. *seeing it is one God*] This ver. may be lit. rendered thus:
**if indeed God is one, who will (= and He will) justify the circumcision
in consequence of faith, and the uncircumcision by means of its faith.**
"*If indeed*" is an argumentative formula, assuming its hypothesis to be
true. Q.d., "God is one; hence it is but likely that His action on this
great principle will be one also."—"*Will justify:*" this future, like many
others in this argument, refers to what *is and will be the Divine method*

which shall justify the circumcision by faith, and uncircum-
31 cision through faith. Do we then make void the law
through faith? God forbid: yea, we establish the law.

CH. IV. 1—25 *Abraham, an apparent exception to the rule
of gratuitous acceptance, really the great example of it*

4 What shall we say then that Abraham our father, as per-

through the Gospel age.—"*The circumcision in consequence of faith, and
the uncircumcision by means of*, &c." It is hardly possible that a distinction is to be insisted on here, as the point of the passage is *similarity,
equality, oneness,* in regard of justification. The fulness of thought and
language delights, as it were, to dwell on justifying faith in one case as
God's reason why pardon is applied to the believer, in the other as *the
believer's way* of accepting the pardon. The whole passage proves that
Jewish and Gentile faith is one and the same in kind and effect.

31. *Do we then*] This verse stands very much by itself, a sort of
brief paragraph. A serious objection (on the part of the Jew) is anticipated and strongly negatived; but the discussion of it is postponed. It
springs out of what has gone before, but is not connected closely with
the next passage.

make void] **annul, cancel.** Same word as iii. 3.

the law] It has been much doubted what exact reference the word
bears here. But the previous context seems to fix it to the moral law,
and primarily as embodied in the O. T. (See on ver. 20.) For we have
been just occupied with the contrast between "faith" and "works of
the law;" and what St Paul *intended* by the latter (viz. moral, not
ceremonial, obedience) is fully shewn by e.g. iv. 4—8. Here in fact is
suggested and dismissed the objection which is discussed at length in
ch. vi.; that Justification by Faith not only annuls Jewish privileges,
but seems to repeal the moral law. Alford takes this verse in close
connexion with ch. iv.; but ch. iv. is not at all occupied with the
"*establishment* of the law," in any usual sense of the word "law."

CH. IV. 1—25 ABRAHAM, AN APPARENT EXCEPTION TO THE RULE
OF GRATUITOUS ACCEPTANCE, REALLY THE GREAT EXAMPLE OF IT

1. *What shall we say then?* &c.] Here a new and independent
objection is anticipated. ABRAHAM, the great Head of the Old Covenant, would be appealed to by the Jew, as on the assumption that *he*
at least was justified by its terms; and on him now the argument turns.
—See Appendix B.

The reading of the Gr. varies in MSS.; but the most probable reading will be rendered thus, **What therefore shall we say that Abraham
our father hath found, according to the flesh?**—" *Therefore:*"—this,
in our view, refers to the general previous argument from iii. 21, not
specially to iii. 31.— "*Our father:*"—i.e. of the Jews.—" *Hath found:*"
—i.e., in the way of acceptance and privilege. The perfect tense suggests
the *permanence* of Abraham's position in men's thoughts.—"*According to*

taining to the flesh, hath found? For if Abraham were 2
justified by works, he hath whereof to glory; but not before
God. For what saith the scripture? Abraham believed 3
God, and it was counted unto him for righteous-

the flesh:"—these words do not, as in E. V., belong to "our father,"
but to "hath found." To interpret them here we must remember (what
will come out in the course of the Epistle) St Paul's doctrine of "the
flesh." It is, briefly, that "the flesh" is *human nature, in the Fall, as
unrenewed and unassisted by Divine special grace.* "According to the
flesh" will thus mean here "in respect of his own independent works
and merits." Did Abraham win acceptance as meritoriously keeping
the covenant of works, which demands obedience and provides no
grace? In brief, was he justified by works?

2. *For*] Q.d., "the question is asked, because if the answer is *yes*,
Abraham stands in a position of independence before God."

by works] Lit. **out of works**; in consequence of them.

he hath] "As he stands before us in Scripture;" a frequent and
natural use of the present tense.

whereof to glory] Lit. **a boast**; a ground of self-congratulation.
The word is nearly the same as that in iii. 27. Both Gr. words are good
or bad according to their connexion; meaning sometimes rightful and
even holy exultation (e.g. ch. v. 2; Heb. iii. 6, "rejoicing"), sometimes
vanity and self-assertion.

but not before God] Lit. **but not towards God;** i.e. "not as
looking Him in the face." **Before** is thus a fair rendering. The
phrase seems to be pregnant: instead of a mere negative to the
question proposed, St Paul suggests the ultimate reason of the negative
—the impossibility that man can boast rightly before God. We may
paraphrase: "But as a fact he had no ground of boasting; for, in view
of the holiness of God, that could not be, even for him. And (ver. 3)
Scripture bears this out in direct terms; for it records that he was
accepted as believing."

3. *what saith the scripture?*] See on i. 17.

Abraham believed, &c.] Lit. **But Abraham believed,** &c. The
particle is, perhaps, significant; emphasizing the verb. The Gr. is
verbatim from LXX. of Gen. xv. 6, save that *"but"* is *"and"* in LXX.
See by all means Gen. xv. 5, 6, as a leading illustration of what faith
is in St Paul's sense; personal trust in God; acceptance of His word
absolutely, because it is His. (See further on ver. 22 below.)

it was counted] The same Gr. verb is rendered in this chapter
"reckoned," vv. 4, 9, 10; "counted," ver. 5; "imputed," vv. 11, 22,
23, 24: see too vv. 6, 8. (In 2 Tim. iv. 16 it is "laid to charge.")
Its plain meaning is (like that of the Lat. *imputare*) to *put down on an
account* (whether as debt or credit the context decides). *The reason
why* of the "imputation" does not lie in the word itself, which may
equally be used where merit and grace, wages and gift, are in question.

for righteousness] I.e. "as if it were righteousness" (in respect of
results) Same construction as ii. 26, a passage which illustrates this.

₄ ness. Now to him that worketh is the reward not reck-
₅ oned of grace, but of debt. But to him that worketh not,
but believeth on him that justifieth the ungodly, his faith is

There the (supposed) Gentile who keeps the law, is treated as if he
were circumcised, *though he is not.* Here Abraham, because he believes,
is treated as having personal (justifying) righteousness, *though he has it
not.* In other words, he is justified on a ground which is *not his own
works.* It is specially needful to notice (what this particular passage
brings out) that faith is in no sense regarded as, *in itself, righteousness.*
(See below, on ver. 26.) The statement is that, "by grace," the same
result, viz. acceptance before God, follows faith that would follow the
possession of merit. Faith is the condition, but not the ground, of
this acceptance. The ground is the Propitiation.

[In Ps. cvi. 31 we have the very words used of Phinehas which are
here used of Abraham. But comparing the Psalm with Numb. xxv.
11—13 we see the difference of application. In Phinehas, an act of
holy zeal was honoured by a special temporal favour, the permanence
of the priesthood in his family. It was no question of *acceptance in
respect of salvation;* a matter which lies on a totally different level
from that of temporal rewards. On that lower level, the act of Phinehas
was one of merit, and was "reckoned" as such to him and his house.
In Abraham's case we have two notes of difference from that of Phinehas: (1) faith in God, not an act of zeal, is the occasion; (2) the
"imputation" is mentioned absolutely and with peculiar solemnity,
unconnected with any temporal results. And thus it is taken by
St Paul here, as his whole reasoning shews, as a Divine intimation of
the true conditions of the acceptance of man by God "without works."]

On Jas. ii. 14, &c., see Appendix C.

4. *to him that worketh,* &c.] A general principle and fact, instanced
here with special reference to human obedience to the Law of God.
The terms of the Law are tacitly compared to a human contract, with
definite pay for definite work.

of grace] Lit. **according to grace;** "on the principle of undeserved
kindness." So just below, **according to debt;** "on the principle of
obligation."

5. *to him that worketh not*] The Gr. implies a general statement;
Abraham's case in universal application.—"*Worketh not:*"—i.e., of
course, in respect of justification. It is another form of the truth
expressed iii. 28 and iv. 6 by "*without works;*" and the phrases singly
and together go as far as language can in defining faith to be the *sole*
condition of Justification.

on him that justifieth the ungodly] These words, with numberless
others, remind us that justifying faith is not trust in "*anything,*" but
trust in God and His Word. See below on vv. 20—22.—"*The ungodly:*"—a very strong word—**the impious man.** Same word as ch. v.
6; 2 Pet. ii. 5; Jude 4, &c. Here St Paul leaves the special features
of Abraham's case, to enforce the principle of Justification by an
extreme case. He contemplates a man so emphatically "without works"

counted for righteousness. Even as David also describeth 6
the blessedness of the man, unto whom God imputeth
righteousness without works, *saying*, Blessed *are they* 7
whose iniquities are forgiven, and whose sins are
covered. Blessed *is* the man to whom the Lord 8
will not impute sin. *Cometh* this blessedness then upon 9

as to be an open sinner: now, *this* man is justified, is declared to be accepted as righteous, on the sole condition of faith in the Justifier. And God is, as it were, *characterized* here as He who (habitually) so acts; doubtless to encourage the most unreserved trust. The word "ungodly" is not descriptive of every man: "all have sinned" fatally (iii. 19, 23); but not all are openly *impious*. And as men look on these latter as extreme cases, just these are selected for special mention as proper objects of Justification.

6. *Even as David also*] In Ps. xxxii. This quotation is specially to the point, being not only an inspired statement of truth, but made by one who had been guilty of deep "ungodliness," and had himself experienced justification under that condition.—"*Also:*"—i.e. as well as Moses in Genesis.—Vv. 6—8 are quite subordinate to the main argument, which is throughout based on *Abraham's* justification.

describeth the blessedness] More lit. **expresses the congratulation.** The word rendered "blessedness" here and in ver. 9 is properly "the pronouncing happy." It is just this which is done in Ps. xxxii. 1, 2.

imputeth righteousness] As it is implied that He does when we read that He "will *not* impute *sin*" to him (ver. 8). Not that the two phrases are exactly coincident: to "impute *righteousness*" implies a largeness of acceptance not *necessary* in the other phrase. But, taken with the word "*blessed*," the non-imputation ·of sin is practically equivalent to the imputation of righteousness; for such "blessedness" imports a full and solemn acceptance.—The latter phrase well illustrates the former: in the latter, man has sin, but is treated as having it not; in the former he has not righteousness, but is treated as having it:— "righteousness is *reckoned* to him *without works.*"

7. *Blessed*, &c.] The Gr. is verbatim from LXX. It is worth remarking that the words (in the Psalm) following this quotation ("and in whose spirit is no guile ") are in full accord with its application here. The "guile" there is evidently "*insincerity* in coming as a penitent to God." The "blessed" are they who are really forgiven— who have *really sought* forgiveness.

are forgiven] Gr. aorist; **were forgiven.** The probable reference is to the definite act, past and complete, of remission. So just below, **were covered.**

covered] The literal translation of the Hebrew word very often translated "atoned for."

8. *will not impute*] I. e. at any time of enquiry and judgment that may arise. They "shall not come into condemnation." (Joh. v. 24.)

9. *Cometh this blessedness*, &c.] Here the reference to David's words merges again into the main argument from Abraham's case.

the circumcision *only*, or upon the uncircumcision also? for
we say that faith was reckoned to Abraham for righteous-
10 ness.   How was it then reckoned? when he was in circumcision, or in uncircumcision?   Not in circumcision, but in
11 uncircumcision.   And he received the sign of circumcision,
a seal of the righteousness of the faith which he had *yet*
being uncircumcised: that he might be the father of all
them that believe, though they be not circumcised; that
12 righteousness might be imputed unto them also: and the

This is indicated by the word "then." The literal rendering of this
verse is, **This assertion of blessedness therefore – does it concern the
circumcision, or the uncircumcision as well?   For we say that to
Abraham his faith was reckoned for righteousness.** This may be
paraphrased: "Can it then be applied only to the circumcised? (for it
may be urged that David was a circumcised Hebrew); or can we
extend it to the uncircumcised?   We ask this; for *Abraham's* is the
case now in hand; and we may look to that case for an answer."

10. *Not in circumcision*] Gen. xv. precedes Gen. xvii. by at least
fourteen years.

11. *the sign of circumcision*] I.e. circumcision as a physical mark
to denote the accomplished fact of justification.

a seal of the righteousness]   A formal, legal attestation that He who
prescribed the rite held to His grant already made.

the righteousness of the faith, &c.] Lit. **the righteousness of that
faith which was in his uncircumcision: i.e.** "the righteousness (i. 17)
connected with the faith which he exercised in the days of his uncircumcision."   For a passage illustrative of the words "the righteousness of
the faith" see Phil. iii. 9; "the righteousness which is through faith of
(in) Christ, the righteousness granted from God on condition of faith."

that he might be, &c.]   This refers to the whole previous immediate context.   Q. d., "It was divinely ordained that Abraham's
justification should precede his circumcision, and so that his circumcision should not *convey* but *attest* his justification,--in order that his
relationship to *all* the believing, Gentiles and Jews, might stand clear
of the circumcision-covenant."

the father]   The progenitor; in a sense figurative but quite natural.
It implies here not only priority in time and example, but that Abraham
received a blessing which was *the title-deed of inheritance* to all who
should "walk in the steps of his faith."   On the doctrine of this great
spiritual Fatherhood cp. Gal. iii. 7, 9; and see Matt. iii. 9; Joh. viii.
39; Gal. vi. 16.

them that believe, though, &c.] Lit. **them that believe through uncircumcision.** The Gr. idiom indicates merely the state in and under
which the belief is exercised.

righteousness] Lit. **the righteousness**; i.e. perhaps "the righteousness
in question, that which is by faith."

father of circumcision to them who are not of the circumcision only, but who also walk in the steps of *that* faith of our father Abraham, which he had being *yet* uncircumcised. For the promise, that he should be the heir of the world, 13 *was* not to Abraham, or to his seed, through the law, but through the righteousness of faith. For if they which are 14

12. *of circumcision*] Practically = **of the circumcision;** (see last note on i. 4). Abraham is here said to be the (spiritual) Father of the circumcision; i.e. of the circumcised; and then at once this is limited to the *believing* circumcised.

to them who] I.e. "to the benefit of those who, &c." They *inherit* the eternal promise made to their great Father.

but who also walk] There is a grammatical difficulty in the Gr.; but it leaves the sense exactly as in E.V.

in the steps] Better, **by the steps,** as rule and model. Cp. Phil. iii. 16. In the Gr. the verse closes with the words *"of our father Abraham;"* thus with an emphasis on the fact and nature of the fatherhood.

13. *For the promise,* &c.] Here again the Gr. order is emphatic: **For not through the law came the promise, &c.**

that he should be the heir] Perhaps better, **namely, his being heir,** in apposition with "the promise." The promise made him *heir at once,* and foretold actual possession. The Gr. word rendered "heir" sometimes means one with a prospect of possession, more rarely an actual possessor.

the world] Perhaps here in its widest meaning; "heaven and earth," "the universe." · In Christ, the Son of Abraham, to whom "all power is given in heaven and earth," the inheritance is seen to be universal. And even a Rabbinic phrase is quoted in which "heaven and earth" are named as promised to Abraham. (See too p. 260.) But looking at Gen. xii. 3, xxii. 18, and at the frequent use of "the world" for "the world of *man*" (e. g. ch. i. 8, iii. 19; Col.i.6; 1 Tim. iii. 16;) and at the special doctrine of this passage (that of a righteousness for believers of *every nation*), it seems best to understand it here as = "every land." Abraham was to possess, in "his seed," every land; "all kindreds, peoples, and tongues." Comparing Gal. iii. 16 and its connexion, it seems clear that the reference here is to the dominion of Christ, "the Prince of the kings of the earth," to whom "the utmost parts of the earth" are given "for His possession," —a possession real now, and indeed manifested as real in the important respect that the redeeming power of Messiah is felt in every region, and in an ever-growing degree.

14. *of the law*] Lit. **out of the law.** On the Gr. construction see on iii. 26 (*ad finem*).—"*Law*" here is without article, and *possibly* its reference is general; q.d. "If those who in any sense claim on grounds of *a law*, &c." But it is far better to read (in *English*) "*the* law." The lack of the article is quite natural where the thing is conspicuous and well known.

of the law *be* heirs, faith is made void, and the promise
15 made of none effect: because the law worketh wrath: for
16 where no law is, *there is* no transgression. Therefore *it is*
of faith, that *it might be* by grace; to the end the promise
might be sure to all the seed; not to that only which is of

heirs] I.e. of the world, as promised to Abraham.

faith] Gr. **the faith**; i.e., probably, "the faith in question;" justifying faith, and Abraham's in particular.

made void...of none effect] Both verbs in Gr. are in the *perfect;* and the probable point is q.d., "If the Law becomes the condition of heirship, *ipso facto* the faith and the promise are void;" they *have been cancelled* by the mere fact of a *legal* condition.

the promise] I.e. "that he" (Abraham, in his seed) "should be heir of the world." In other words, that Messiah, the Son of Abraham, (and thereby His "Israel"), should enjoy a sacred victory and dominion.

15. *the law worketh wrath: for*] "For" indicates that this statement confirms that just made, namely, that inheritance by law must bar the fulfilment of the promise.—"The faith" in question was said to be "reckoned for righteousness" to the believer; "the promise" in question was that that believer, as such, should "inherit the world." But if once the Law, with its only possible terms, interposes between the sinner and justification, he is hopelessly cut off (1) from a valid "righteousness," and (2) therefore from the "heirship" attached to it. Justification and inheritance are equally out of his reach; because inevitably, *as applied to fallen man*, the Law (just because holy and absolute) "works wrath;" produces what in the nature of things calls down the Judge's pure but inexorable wrath; for it produces "transgression" by the fact of its application to *man as he is.*—Note that *"transgression,"* not *"sin,"* is St Paul's word here. "Sin" is wherever the Fall is; "transgression" is a narrower word; the "overstepping" of a definite condition.

16. *Therefore,* &c.] Lit. **Therefore out of faith, that according to grace**; a singularly terse sentence even in Gr. " *Therefore:*"—q.d., "such being the case under Law, the Divine mercy *acted accordingly* on our behalf." The clause may be expanded: "Therefore God took faith as the one condition of justification, so that justification might stand clear of the conditions laid down necessarily in His Law; i.e. those of perfect obedience, outward and inward. That is to say, the justification was 'according to grace,' for it treated man as *having what he had not*—meritorious righteousness." We might of course supply "the promise," or "the inheritance," instead of "justification," as the subject in these clauses. But the latter idea is so much the more prominent, that it is the safer suggestion.

sure] I.e. not imperilled by the conditions of the Law for the Jewish believer, and by the lack of its privileges for the Gentile believer.

not to that only] The Gr. has grammatical difficulties, but the sense is practically as in E.V. The "seed" is regarded as in its two great divisions; and here first, that which is "of the law," i.e. Jewish

the law, but to that also which is of the faith of Abraham; who is the father of us all, (as it is written, I have made 17 thee a father of many nations,) before *him* whom he believed, *even* God, who quickeneth the dead, and calleth those *things* which be not as though they were. Who against 18

believers, not as really having a claim from the law, but *taken as having one*, to bring out the validity of the claim of faith on the Gentiles' part.

the faith of Abraham] Abraham is here the example of *manifestly extra-legal* faith, and therefore the case in point for the Gentile. Not that the Jewish believer (ver. 12) did not equally need "Abraham's faith," but the *stress* here is on the case of the Gentile.

us all] I. e. all believers; the "nations of the saved" (cp. Gal. iii. 7). Here first St Paul seems distinctly to turn from his Jewish opponents to his co-believers, Jewish or Gentile. Henceforth there is little if any anti-Jewish reasoning.—Wonderful was the triumph of the Gospel, which made it not only possible but profoundly *natural* for former Pharisees and former idolaters to unite as "we" and "us" in Christ.

17. *as it is written*] Gen. xvii. 5, when the name Abraham was given.—Cp. the remarkable phrase of Gal. iii. 8, where Scripture is, as it were, identified with its Inspirer, and the words of Genesis are distinctly claimed as a prophecy of the Gospel.—It is a shallow criticism that objects that *Moses* probably had no such design. Whether so or not, the Apostle, like his brethren (1 Pet. i. 11) and his Lord (Matt. xxii. 43), claims that behind the knowledge, thought, and words of the prophets, lies everywhere the thought and purpose of Him "who spake by them." And if indeed Jesus is the Eternal SON, is such a preparation for Him *out of proportion?*—The quotation here is lit. from LXX.

before him, &c.] More lit. **in the presence** (i.e. in the judgment) **of the God whom he believed.** The clause is connected with "who is the father of us all." Q. d., "little as *man* may see in Abraham the forefather of believing Greeks and Scythians, *God* both ordained and acts upon such fatherhood."

quickeneth] I.e. (as always in Bible-English) **maketh alive.** This noble description of Omnipotence has immediate reference to the miracle of the birth of Isaac in the childless old age of Abraham and Sarah (see ver. 19, and cp. Heb. xi. 11, 12).

calleth] I.e., practically, **treats as being.** Cp. the quotation at ix. 25 for a similar use of the verb. The Almighty addresses (i.e. deals with) non-existent things, and even things which from man's point of view *cannot* exist (e.g. a son of one who was "as good as dead"), as if existing, because soon to exist according to His purpose.

18. *against hope...in hope*] Lit. **beyond hope...upon hope.** Here perhaps the first is subjective hope, the second objective. Abraham was asked to believe in a way which went *beyond* all mere impressions of probability; but he rested *upon* the "hope set before him" by the Divine promise, and believed.

hope believed in hope, that he might become the father of
many nations; according to that which was spoken, So
19 shall thy seed be. And being not weak in faith, he
considered not his own body now dead, when he was about
an hundred year old, neither *yet* the deadness of Sara's
20 womb: he staggered not at the promise of God through
21 unbelief; but was strong in faith, giving glory to God; and

that he might become] **with a view to becoming.** Not that this was
the radical motive of his trust; knowledge of God was that motive. But
this great "joy set before him" was strongly present in his believing
soul.

So shall thy seed be] Gen. xv. 5. This is interesting, as an example
of *allusive* quotation. St Paul takes it for granted that the reader
knows the context, and thus understands the force of the "so." Cp.
Heb. vi. 13, 14, where the very point of the quotation lies in the unquoted
context. But that passage, addressed to Jewish disciples, is less remarkable than this, addressed to a mixed, and chiefly Gentile, Church.
We have here a significant note of the Apostle's encouragement of
minute study of the O. T. among his *Gentile* converts.—No doubt
allusive quotation was much used by the Rabbis; but St Paul would
not have used it with Gentiles had he not felt it to be in place.—Notice
that the words here quoted immediately precede (in Gen. xv.) the words
"Abraham believed God, &c."

19. *being not weak*] I. e., at that crisis; so the Gr. implies. *Under
that strain* he did not succumb; in faith he rose to the effort.

he considered not] So as to distract his view of the fact of the
Promise. He was conscious of the physical impossibility (at least in
Gen. xvii. 17), but he looked away from it, and rose above it. See
below, vv. 20, 21.

now dead] Same word as that translated "as good as dead," Heb.
xi. 12.

about an hundred year old] Ninety-nine (Gen. xvii. 1). Bengel remarks that between Shem and Abraham none of the patriarchs had
begotten a first son (so far as recorded) when 100 years old. Indeed,
none did so at above 34, except Terah.

20—21. *he staggered not*, &c.] The Gr. suggests the paraphrase;
"he looked away from his own physical state, only at the Promise, and
did not doubt its terms—just because they were the Promise. So he
rose in a great effort and exercise of faith, which consisted in giving
glory to God (the 'glory' of absolute and adoring trust in Him as God);
in being perfectly sure of His ability to keep whatever promise He
should in fact make."

We have here a fuller account than anywhere else of the nature of
Faith as essentially Trust; not mere historic belief, nor mental assent,
but personal Trust; reposed, with application to self of the consequences,
on the Divine Promiser as such. We have also a precious suggestion of
some reasons (if we may say so) *why* God prescribes Faith as the con-

being fully persuaded that, what he had promised, he was able also to perform. And therefore it was imputed to him 22 for righteousness. Now it was not written for his sake 23 alone, that it was imputed to him; but for us also, to whom 24 it shall be imputed, if we believe on him that raised up Jesus our Lord from the dead ; who was delivered for our 25 offences, and was raised *again* for our justification.

dition of the justification of a sinner. Faith, we see, is an act of the soul which looks wholly away from "self" (as regards both merit and demerit), and *honours the Almighty and All-gracious* in a way not indeed *in the least meritorious* (because merely reasonable, after all), but yet such as to "touch the hem of His garment." It brings His creature to Him in the one right attitude—complete submission and confidence. We thus see, in part, *why* faith, and only faith, is the way to reach and touch the Merit of the Propitiation. This is suggested in the next verse.

22. *And therefore*, &c.] This quality of faith *accounts* for its imputation in justification.

23. *Now*, &c.] In this ver. and 24, 25, St Paul sums up this part of his argument;—the proof from Abraham's ·case. He shews its full applicability to those who now likewise "give glory" to the same God·by like absolute trust in respect of His explicit Promise of Justification, a Promise finally sealed by the Resurrection of His Son.

for his sake] Lit. **because of him**; i.e. "because Abraham was justified by faith; merely to tell us that."

24. *for us also*] Lit. **also because of us**; "because we were to be likewise dealt with, and therefore needed to know it."

shall be] Lit., fully, **is about to be**. The reference of the *futurity* is to the abiding *intention* of the Justifier. Justification is, individually, *present* on condition of belief; but with regard to all who "shall believe," it is in intention, a *future* thing.

if we believe] More lit. **even us who believe**. The faith is assumed.

on him that raised up, &c.] The Father. (Cp. Psal. xvi. 10; Acts ii. 24, xiii. 30, xvii. 31; Eph. i. 20, &c.; Heb. xiii. 20.) His "bringing Jesus again" stands here as a Divine pledge of His infinite *trustworthiness*. "He hath given assurance unto all men," not only of judgment (Acts xvii. 31), but of a present and complete justification, "in that He raised Jesus from the dead." Abraham believed Him specially as the God of the primeval Promise, and of particular providence and love to himself: we believe Him now *also* as the Father who raised His Son to life after propitiatory death.

our Lord] The title of Majesty enhances the significance of the Resurrection.

25. *delivered*] As the Victim. Cp. viii. 32. Here the Father delivers up His Son. In Gal. ii. 20; Eph. v. 2, &c.; we have the self-surrender of the Son. See Psal. xl. 8, 9, for the union of the two truths. "Lo, I come;...*I delight* to do *Thy will*."

Ch. V. 1—11 *The security and happiness of the state of Justification; its basis being the Divine Love*

5 Therefore being justified by faith, we have peace with

for our offences] Lit. **because of our offences;** "because we had offended." Such is the natural meaning of the Gr. The fact of our sins demanded, for their just remission, nothing less than the Lord's Death.

for our justification] Lit. **because of our justification.** The construction is identical. This, and the balance of the clauses, seem to demand the exposition: "He was raised, *because our justification was effected;*" not, "*in order to give us* justification," as many interpret it. The parallel is complete: "We sinned, therefore He suffered: we were justified, therefore He rose."—To this it is objected that the thought is not doctrinally true; justification being, for each believer, *dated* not from the Lord's death, but from the time of faith (see ch. v. 1). But the answer is obvious: the Apostle here states the Ideal of the matter; he means not individual justifications, but the Work which for ever secured Justification for the believing Church. A close parallel is the "It is finished" (John xix. 30). (See too the *ideal* language in viii. 30; and instructive parallels in Heb. i. 3 and x. 14.) In the Divine Idea every future believer was declared to be justified, through an accomplished Propitiation, when Jesus rose. His resurrection proved His acceptance as our Substitute, and therefore our acceptance in Him. No doubt the other interpretation is true as to *fact:* He was raised that, through the Gospel, (which but for His resurrection would never have been preached,) we might receive justification. But the Gr. construction, and the balance of clauses, are certainly in favour of that now given.

Ch. V. 1—11   The security and happiness of the state of Justification; its basis being the Divine Love.

1. *Therefore being justified*] Here opens a leading section. The preliminaries are now over:—The need of Justification is established; and its equal terms for Jew and Greek; and the fact that Faith is its one appointed condition; and the nature and actings of faith, specially as in Abraham's example. We now come to a fuller statement of some important details, which will lead up to a view of the *effects* of faith in the character and life of the justified.

being justified] An aorist. The time-reference is probably to the definite crisis of acceptance in each individual case; not to the ideal justification just expounded (iv. 25). Because the words "by *faith*" point here to *our acceptance* of the Lord's work.

we have peace] The Gr. has an important and strongly supported *various reading:* "*Let us have peace.*" Without attempting to discuss the documentary evidence here, we merely state the case thus:—There is, on the whole, a greater weight of MSS. and ancient Versions in favour of "*let us have.*" But on the other hand there is a greater weight of internal evidence for "*we have.*" In other words,

God through our Lord Jesus Christ: by whom also we have 2

"*we have*" exactly *fits into the context; "let us have*" is *foreign to it.* The whole context is one not of exhortation, but of dogmatic assertion:—"we have access;" "we rejoice;" "the love of God has been poured out into our hearts;" "we shall be saved;" "we are reconciled;" "we have received the reconciliation."—How then can we account for the "Let us have"? Probably, by early failures to grasp the complex but consistent argument of the whole long context, and the inevitable tendency due to such misapprehension to substitute aspiration or exhortation for (what the text speaks of) a present possession.— It is an obviously right principle, though calling for most cautious application, that no amount of MS. evidence ought ever to force on us a reading which mars the context.—A *single stroke* in the Gr. MSS. makes the only visible difference between the readings.

peace with God] Lit. **towards God.** That is, "in view of Him, as regards Him, we possess the security and calm of acceptance." Practically the phrase thus = "He has admitted us to peace;" "He is at peace with us." The whole previous argument shews that His reconciliation to us, not ours to Him, is the main point; in other words, the *justice of forgiveness* on God's part, not the *yielding of the will* on man's part, which latter, though an all-important thing, is not directly in view *now.* —Much has been said against the phrase "God's reconciliation to us," as if it made Him out to be a hostile Power. But the justice of the words is seen when we (like St Paul here) look on Him as on the JUDGE. As Creator and Father, He loves the sinner; as Judge, He must condemn him—if it were not for His own gift of a Propitiation. And the judge who sentences a criminal is, however personally kind, *judicially hostile.* And again, the judge who for a good cause removes the sentence is then *judicially reconciled* to the accused, though he may personally need no reconciliation of *feeling.*—Scripture plainly reveals that the God of Love proclaims "no peace" to the impenitent. Therefore when He "speaks peace" there is a change, not in His benevolence but in His judicial attitude: in other words, reconciliation.—For instructive parallels where the word "peace" occurs see Isai. liii. 5; Luke ii. 14, xix. 38; Heb. xiii. 20; 2 Pet. iii. 14.

through our Lord Jesus Christ] The sacred Propitiation, provided and accepted by the loving and righteous Father; once offered, and continuously ("we *have*") availing.

2. *by whom*] Lit. **through whom;** the same construction as that just before.

also] I.e. "we owe to Him our entrance to grace, *as well as* our standing in it."

we have access] Lit. **we have had;** "we have found." The time-reference is to a past reception resulting in present possession.—"*Access:*"— lit. **the introduction;** "our introduction." Same word as Eph. ii. 18, iii. 12 (though the reference there is not precisely that here), and 1 Pet. iii. 18 (where E. V. has "bring us to God"). The idea is of the acceptance of the acquitted. Both ideas, acquittal by a Judge and acceptance by a reconciled Father, reside in Justification.

access by faith into this grace wherein we stand, and rejoice
3 in hope of the glory of God. And not only *so*, but we glory
in tribulations also: knowing that tribulation worketh pa-
4 tience; and patience, experience; and experience, hope:

by faith] Our side of the matter. The Lord's "introduction" of us
to His Father's acceptance takes effect individually when we individually
believe.

this grace] I.e. "acceptance" (Eph. i. 6) and resulting "peace."
The word recalls the fact that acceptance, as previously proved (see ch.
iv.), is "according to grace," not debt.

wherein we stand] The word "stand" is in contrast to the "fall" of
the rejected and condemned. See xi. 20; also Psal. i. 5, cxxx. 3; Rev.
vi. 17; and I Cor. xv. 1, where the context gives the idea of *acceptance*
and safety, as here. That of *perseverance* (as in Acts xxvi. 22, E. V.
"continue") may *also* be present; but the context shews that acceptance is at least the main point.

rejoice] A word elsewhere rendered "glory" (as just below, ver. 3),
or "boast." See on iv. 2. The reasoning here rises, from the foundation-truth of *lawful justification*, to the holy elevations of consequent
joy and energy in the justified.

in hope] Lit. **on hope.** Perhaps here (as in iv. 18, q. v.) the
"hope" is objective; "the hope *set before us*" (Heb. vi. 18), i.e. the
promise and pledges of glory. On this our joy is *based*.

the glory of God] For commentary, see viii. 18, 21, 30.—The eternal
bliss of the justified is called "the glory *of God*" because it is a state of
joy, love, majesty, and holiness, bestowed by God; in the presence of
God; and being in its essence the Vision of God, and likeness to
Him. Cp. Joh. xvii. 24; 2 Cor. iv. 17; Phil. iii. 21; Col. i. 27; 2 Tim.
ii. 10; I Pet. iv. 13; Rev. xxi. 11, 23.—This ver. is a brief anticipation
of ch. viii.

3. *but we glory*] For the present, St Paul puts the eternal future
out of view again, in order that present grace may be better explained.
—"*We glory*."—same word as "rejoice" in ver. 2. Wonderful is the
force of this repetition, in connexion with *tribulation!*

tribulations] Lit. **the tribulations;** "our troubles." See viii.
35—39 for a noble example of such rejoicing. See too Matt. v. 11;
Acts v. 41; Heb. x. 34; I Pet. i. 6—9; and esp. Jas i. 2—4.

patience] The patience of *perseverance*. See on ii. 7. "Tribulation"
teaches the believer the possibility, and blessedness, of "patient *continuance in well-doing*."

4. *experience*] The Gr. properly means "*a proof, a test*." So
usually in N. T.: e.g. 2 Cor. viii. 2 (where E.V. "trial"), xiii. 3 (where
E. V. "proof"); Phil. ii. 22 ("proof"). The word here cannot refer to
the *testing of the believer by his Master*, for the next clause shews it is
something in his own consciousness, producing *hope* there. It is rather
his own testing of himself; his discovery of what he can bear and do,
through grace; promoting courage for future efforts, and steady hopes of
final victory.

and hope maketh not ashamed; because the love of God is 5
shed abroad in our hearts by the Holy Ghost which is given
unto us. For when we were yet without strength, in due 6
time Christ died for the ungodly. For scarcely for a righte- 7

hope] Of future grace and (perhaps mainly here) of the glory to follow. Each "test" of the power given enhances the *confidence* that
He who gives it will continue it till the course of "patience" ends in
the eternal welcome.

5. *hope*] Lit. **the hope**; not any hope, but the hope thus produced.

maketh not ashamed] Same word as ix. 33; 2 Cor. vii. 14, ix. 4;
nearly the same as Phil. i. 20; 2 Tim. i. 12. In all these passages the
idea of *disappointment* is in the verb. So here: "the shame of disappointment never follows this hope."

because] The connexion of thought is illustrated by e.g. Eph. i. 13,
14. See too viii. 11, 16, 17. Our certainty that the hope will end in
fruition is deepened, if not begun, by the fact that the Holy Spirit is
already given to us, and so given as to assure us of the love of God.

the love of God] I.e. His love to us. So ver. 8; viii. 35, 39. The
following context decides against the meaning "our love to Him."

is shed abroad] Lit. **has been poured out**, as rain from a cloud.
The tense indicates the lasting result of that past act by which the Holy
Spirit first revealed the Divine Love to the soul.

by the Holy Ghost which is given] Better, **which was given**; a past
bestowal, whether viewed ideally as to the Church, or actually as to
each justified person. The Divine personal Spirit is here seen working
as in viii. 15, 16; and in such work He is recognized as the "earnest" of
heaven, where the Love of God will be fully realized for ever.

6. *For when*, &c.] From this ver. to ver. 11 St Paul expands the
words "the love of God." He explains this love, as "poured out"
by the Spirit, to be specially *redeeming and justifying love.*

without strength] **Impotent** to deliver ourselves from sin and judgment. The words are in contrast to the might of the Deliverer.

in due time] That of the Eternal Purpose; "the fulness of the time;"
Gal. iv. 4. See Mark i. 15.

Christ] In the Gr. this word has a slight emphasis, pointing to the
wonder of *such* a Deliverer's appearance.

died] Also emphatic by position. His death is both the supreme
proof of Divine love and the supreme requirement of the Divine Law.

the ungodly] Better, **us the ungodly**. Same word as iv. 5, q. v.
Here probably this intense word is used of *all* sinners as such; in
view of the contrasted holiness of the Substitute, and also to suggest
that the "impotence" of ver. 6 is not merely negative, but is the re-
fusal (due to moral evil) truly to love the true God. See on viii. 7.

"*For*" = **for the sake of.** The special bearing of the Gr. preposition
here used depends on the context. In *itself* it does not necessarily indicate "substitution in the place of," "vicariousness." But the illustration
in ver. 7 at once suggests that idea; and the preposition neither compels
nor excludes it.

ous *man* will one die : yet peradventure for a good *man*
8 some would even dare to die. But God commendeth his
love toward us, in that, while we were yet sinners, Christ
9 died for us. Much more then, being now justified by his
10 blood, we shall be saved from wrath through him. For if,

7. *For*, &c.] The connexion is somewhat thus: "He died for the
godless: a proof of unequalled love; for hardly will you find any one
die for a just, a good, man; you may find such a case, but it will be
rare."—No marked distinction is meant between "*just*" and "*good*."
Justice and goodness are equally contrasted with godlessness and sinfulness here. As regards the wording of the verse, it is lit. **For hardly for
a just man will one die; for for the good man, perhaps, one actually
dares to die.** The first "*for*" in the second clause may be explained
by a paraphrase: "Death for even a just person is hardly known. I
say, *hardly* known; not quite *unknown;* for cases of death for one who
is good do occur." The whole point of the verse is that such acts of
even such love among men are very rare and very limited indeed. (The
translation "for a just *cause*," "for *that* which is good," is precluded,
as Meyer points out, by the *personal* words in contrast; "the godless,"
"sinners.")

8. *commendeth*] Same word as (for instance) xvi. 1. Infinite con-
descension lies in this simple word.

his love] Fully, **His own love**; the love peculiar to Himself who is
Love: perhaps too with a hint that it is uncaused by any previous love of
ours for Him.

yet sinners] " *Yet* " implies the gracious *after-change* which Christ's
death was to produce in the justified.—For a full parallel to this verse
see Tit. iii. 3—5, where the dark picture of ver. 3 brings out in contrast
the "love toward man" of ver. 4.

Christ] The Beloved of the Father, viii. 32.

9. *Much more*] I.e. as to our apprehension. After this amazing
first step of unmerited love we can, with less *surprise*, rely on its
gracious continuance.

now] "As the case stands."

by his blood] Lit. **in His blood**. If " *in* " is to be pressed, the idea
may be that of washing, (Rev. i. 5,) though this would not be strictly
germane. It is most difficult to pronounce on such uses of "in" in
N.T. Greek, in which "in" certainly often="by." See on ch. i. 9.

saved] I.e. "*kept safe*," till the final preservation at the last day.
See 1 Thess. i. 10, where lit. "Jesus, who rescues us (or, is our
rescuer) from the wrath to come." Not only did He once die as our
Propitiation, but, as the sure sequel, He lives, now and ever, to be,
every moment, our accepted Representative and Intercessor; a Saviour
in permanence. See viii. 34.

wrath] Lit. **the wrath**; the wrath of final doom. The justified shall
be preserved by their Lord unto, and through, even that crisis. Cp.
John v. 24; 1 John ii. 28.

10. *if*] I.e. **as**. The hypothesis is also a fact.

when we were enemies, we were reconciled to God by the death of his Son, much more, being reconciled, we shall be saved by his life. And not only *so*, but we also joy in God 11 through our Lord Jesus Christ, by whom we have now received the atonement.

enemies] *Personal* enemies; the proper force of the Gr. word. Cp. Col. i. 21. See below on viii. 7.

reconciled to God] On "reconciliation," see on ver. 1. Here certainly the idea of the *conciliation of man's will to God* (as a result of the Propitiation revealed) is suggested. But even here it is scarcely the main idea. The language, carefully weighed, points more to God's acceptance of the sinner than to the sinner's acceptance of God. For the case is put thus:—"When we were enemies, God was *gracious to us:* much more (as to our apprehension) will He be gracious to us still." How was He gracious to us then? Surely by the gift of justification (see ver. 9). As our Judge, He acquitted us; in other words, He was reconciled to us, and adopted us. Therefore, as our reconciled Father, He will surely be equally gracious to us still.—Through this context St Paul has not yet come to the *result of pardon on the will*. When he here uses the phrase "reconciled to God" it is evidently with main reference to the removal of a judicial bar.—Absalom, for instance, was reconciled to David—restored to his filial position—only when David put aside his just wrath : *till this was done,* no change of will in Absalom would be reconciliation.

by the death] As propitiation, with a view to justification ; iii. 24, 25.

being reconciled] He does not say "being *friends;*" which, as just stated, is not yet the idea in point. The *barrier of condemnation* is taken away; therefore *à fortiori* the Judge, who is also the Father, will continue to us His love.

we shall be saved] See on ver. 9.

by his life] Lit. **in His life.** The *"in"* here is probably strictly appropriate: "in His life"="in Him who lives." The justified are "in Christ Jesus" (viii. 1).—Cp. Col. iii. 4, where the reference to the final appearing of the Saviour, (the appearing to judgment and salvation,) serves to explain this passage. Q. d., "We shall be *saved in the day of the Lord* because He, who died for us, *ever lives* as our Life."

11. *not only so*] We shall not only be welcomed *then*, but we are permitted to feel *now* the bliss of our position.

we...joy] Lit. **joying**; the participle. The meaning is practically the same as in E. V. Grammatically the word perhaps connects with "being reconciled;" q. d., "We shall surely be 'saved' then, because we are now admitted not to acquittal only, but to rejoicing confidence of Divine Love," "we are not reconciled only, but rejoicing."

now] See on ver. 9.

received] Ideally, when He died and rose ; actually, when we believed (ver. 1). The Gr. is an aorist.

the atonement] **the reconciliation**; the cognate noun to the verb in ver. 10. According to the explanation there, it here means the grant of

12—21   *The same subject, illustrated by the connexion of fallen man with Adam, and justified man with Christ*

12   Wherefore, as by one man sin entered into the world, and death by sin; and so death passed upon all men, for that

"peace with God through our Lord Jesus Christ," in virtue of His propitiation. The Gr. noun occurs elsewhere in N. T. only xi. 15, and 2 Cor. v. 18, 19.

12—21   THE SAME SUBJECT, ILLUSTRATED BY THE CONNEXION OF FALLEN MAN WITH ADAM, AND JUSTIFIED MAN WITH CHRIST

12. *Wherefore*, &c.]   Here begins an important section, closing with the ch.   In point of language, and of links of thought, it is occasionally difficult, and moreover deals with the deep mystery of the effects of the Fall.   We preface detailed comments with a few general remarks.

1.   The section closes one main part of the argument—that on the *Way* of Justification; and it leads to another—that on its *Results*.   It is connected more with the former than with the latter.

2.   Its main purpose is unmistakable.   It brings out the grandeur and completeness of Christ's work by contrast with the work (so to speak) of Adam.   It regards the two as, in some real sense, paralleled and balanced.

3.   Without explaining (what cannot be explained, perhaps, in this life,) the *reason* of the thing, it states as a *fact* concerning the Fall that its result is not only inherited sinfulness, but inherited guilt; i.e. liability to punishment, (that of *death*,) on account of the primeval Sin. *Death* (in human beings) *is penalty:* but e.g. infants, void of actual moral wrong, die: therefore they die for inherited (we may say for vicarious) guilt.

4.   From this admitted mystery and fact (as plainly it was with the Romans) St Paul argues to the corresponding "life" of believers in virtue of the vicarious righteousness of Messiah, whom here (and in 1 Cor. xv. 22, 45, 47,) he regards as the Second Adam.

5.   Unquestionably the mystery of the Effects of the Fall is extremely great and painful.   But it is the mystery of *facts;* and it is but one of the offshoots of the greatest and deepest of all distressing mysteries, the Existence of Sin.—See further, Appendix D.

Wherefore, as, &c.]   There is no expressed close to this sentence. But a close may be taken as implied in this first clause: q.d., "Wherefore [the case of Justification is] just parallel to the entrance of sin by one man, &c."   Ver. 12 will then be a complete statement.

by one man]   Cp. 1 Cor. xv. 21, 22, 45—49.

sin...death]   See vv. 17, 18 for the implied antithesis: *Christ, righteousness, life.*

death by sin]   In the case of Man.   Scripture nowhere says that death in *animals* is due to human sin.   Death was the specially threatened penalty to the sole race which was on the one hand created with an animal organism, which could die, and on the other, "made in

all have sinned: for until the law sin was in the world: but $_{13}$
sin is not imputed when there is no law. Nevertheless $_{14}$
death reigned from Adam to Moses, even over them that
had not sinned after the similitude of Adam's transgression,
who is the figure of *him* that was to come. But not as the $_{15}$

the image of God." The *penal* character of death is essential to St
Paul's argument.

passed] Lit. **went through,** traversed, penetrated.

upon] Better, **unto**; so as to *reach* all men. *"Men"* is expressed
here in the Gr., marking the special reference to *human* beings.

for that all have sinned] Better, **for that all sinned**; the aorist. St
Paul refers to the First Sin, to the guilt of the *Representative* of the
race. A close parallel, in contrast, is 2 Cor. v. 15, where lit. "since
One died for all, therefore they all died;" i.e. ideally, in their Divine
Representative. See too 1 Cor. xv. 21, where our *death* in Adam is
spoken of just as our *sin* in Adam here.

13. *for until the law*] This and the following verses are not a
parenthesis: see on ver. 12.—"*Until*" here practically = "*before.*" The
period "from Adam to Moses" is in view, the Law of Moses being
taken as the first *elaborate* statute-giving of God for man. "Laws" existed long before Moses; e.g. those of Marriage, of the sanctity of Life,
and of the Sabbath. But the Mosaic Law *covered the field of
duty* in a way unknown before; so as to suggest the question whether
human beings, in *the previous ages,* in *some instances,* had not satisfied
the claims of *then-known* duty, and so *escaped death.* But no: in those
ages, as in the Mosaic, "death reigned;" therefore there was sin; therefore there was broken law; and that law, in numberless cases, (viz.
infantine,) must have been broken *only* "in Adam;" for it was unknown
to the persons in question.

law...law] Both these words in the Gr. are without the article. In
spite of some difficulty, we must interpret the first of the Mosaic Law,
and the second of Law in some other sense; here probably in the sense
of the declared Will of God in general, against which, in a particular
case, Adam sinned, and we "in him."

is not imputed] So as to bring penalty. Therefore, had there been
in no sense a (broken) law in the primeval age, there would have been
no death. But death was universal.

14. *reigned*] See below, on ver. 21. The idea is of unquestioned
dominion.

after the similitude, &c.] I.e. *by conscious transgression of express
precepts.* The phrase thus exactly meets the case of infant-death, and also
includes all other cases, supposed possible, in which no distinct violation
of then-known law was traceable.

the figure] Lit. **a figure.** The word "type," (derived from the Gr.
word used here,) expresses the meaning exactly. Adam so sinned that
his sons, even irrespective of personal sins, *died*—a penal death. Christ,
the last Adam, so lived and suffered that his "brethren," irrespective of
personal merit, *live,* with the life of the justified.

offence, so also *is* the free gift. For if through the offence of one many be dead, much more the grace of God, and the gift by grace, which is by one man, Jesus Christ, hath 16 abounded unto many. And not as *it was* by one that sin-

him that was to come] Christ; mysteriously foretold from the first as "to come." A sentence is quoted from the Rabbis: "*The last Adam is Messiah*."—Observe that the doctrine of the imputed guilt of the First Sin is distinctly found in Judaic literature. As Meyer says on ver. 12, (Germ. ed., p. 241,) it probably was a part of the Apostle's belief before his conversion, but one "which he found, in his Christian enlightenment, no reason to reject;" on the contrary, he incorporated it as an integral part of his Gospel-teaching.—(And this he did, let us add, as the *commissioned* messenger of the Truth.)

15. *But not*] Here, after the parallel of Adam and Christ, is stated the glorious *difference* of the work of Christ. This occupies vv. 15—17. —The difference is, the vastly greater *wonder* of His Work and its Result.

offence] Lit. **stumbling**. Our word "offence" comes from the Latin for the same, and is so used here by E. V.

if] Here (as in ver. 10,) the "if" nearly = "as."

of one] Lit. **of the one**; the one personal Offender in view.

many be dead] Lit. **the many died.** See on "all have sinned," (an exact parallel,) ver. 12. "*The many :*"—"*many*," in contrast to their one forefather; "*the* many," as those in question here. They are, in this case, *all mankind*.

much more, &c.] Here notice the *respect in which* Redemption is so far "in excess of" Ruin. Not in respect of *numbers* affected; because, on any theory, the redeemed are *no more numerous* than the ruined, who are the whole race. It is in respect of the *quality* of the cause and the effect. Redemption is a positive exercise of surpassing grace and love, resulting in a glorious and eternal reversal, in the subjects of it, of the previous ruin; indeed, more than a reversal, because it brings with it the *exaltation* given to the brethren of the Second Adam.—The "much more" here, and in ver. 17, is thus q. d., "The fall of the First Adam caused vast results of evil; the work of the far greater Second Adam shall much more cause vast results of good."

the grace of God] His *positive* favour; whereas He merely *let the law take its course* at the Fall.

the gift, &c.] Lit. **the gift in the grace of one Man, Jesus Christ.** The "*grace of Christ*" is the loving favour to man shewn by Him in His work. The "*gift*" which was given "*in*" (i. e. practically "through," or "by,") that grace is the eternal life of the justified.—"*The one Man :*"—"*Man*" is emphatic, indicating the Lord's position as the Second Adam, and, (as this Man is JESUS CHRIST,) the supreme greatness of the Second Adam.

hath abounded] Lit. **did abound unto the many.** The reference is to the historic fact of His Work. "*The many :*"—here again, "*many*" in contrast to the One-ness of their Head; "*the* many," as the persons here in question. These here, (as e.g. vv. 13—19 explain,) are the

ned, *so is* the gift: for the judgment *was* by one to condemnation, but the free gift *is* of many offences unto justification.   For if by one man's offence death reigned by one; 17

justified.   See below on ver. 18.—"*Abounded:*"—the idea is of Divine
liberality in mercy, as opposed to the *no more than legal justice* of the
condemnation.

16.   *And not,* &c.]   The line of thought here is less difficult if we
take ver. 17 in close connexion, and read the words from "*for the judgment*" to "*unto justification*" as a parenthetic statement of the two facts
before us.   We may then paraphrase vv. 16, 17 thus: "The Gift, in
wonder and greatness of quality, far exceeds the Ruin, though each is the
result of one Person's act: (for, as we know, the sentence and execution
was the result of one man's one sin, while the atonement and justification
is the result, in a sense, of many men's many sins :)—I say the Gift exceeds the Ruin; for while the result of Adam's sin was just the lawful
reign of death over *men* as sinners, the result of Christ's work shall be
not a mere reversal of this, but the reign of *justified men* over death in
glory."

And not, &c.]   The Gr. here is more exactly, **And not as by
means of the sinning of one, [is] the gift: for the sentence [resulted]
from one [person] unto condemnation; but the boon [resulted] from
many offences unto acquittal.**   Here the "*one*" is plainly Adam; and
the contrast is between his *one-ness,* and that of his sin, and the *many*
offences of his many sons.   St Paul estimates the greatness of the
pardon of all the sins of all the justified from the tremendous legal
results of the one sin of Adam.   Such is sin, that Adam's *sin* brought
death on all men; such is grace, that innumerable *sins* are, through the
Propitiation, "abundantly pardoned."—The phrase above, "resulted
from," has of course a different bearing in the two clauses.   The first
sin was the *strict* cause of the sentence; while the "many offences"
"caused" the boon, only as *calling forth* the mercy.—"*The sentence...unto
condemnation;*" "*the boon...unto acquittal:*"—in each of these phrases the
last word explains the first: the sentence *amounted to* sentence of death;
the gift was *nothing less than* acquittal.—The hereditary guilt and doom
of the Fall is very distinctly taught in this verse.   The sentence of death
on man as man came "by means of the sinning of *one,*" in a sense expressly distinguished from the guilt of the "many offences" of the
many.

17.   *For,* &c.]   "For" refers mainly to the last clause of ver. 16.   The
contrast of "one" and "many" is now dropped, but we find another
contrast; that between the legal results of evil and the overflowing
results of Divine goodness, the goodness which grants acquittal to the
"ungodly."   Q. d., "The free gift is a gift indeed, liberal and glorious:
for if the result of Adam's one sin was the reign of death, far more amply
shall the result of God's grace be the reign of the justified in life!"—In
this verse the "glory to be revealed," as a *necessary sequel* of justification, first distinctly appears.

by one man's offence]   A better reading gives **in one offence.**   The

much more they which receive abundance of grace and of
the gift of righteousness shall reign in life by one, Jesus
18 Christ. Therefore as by the offence of one *judgment came* upon

First Sin was the occasion *"in"* (or *on*) *which* death acquired its
tyranny over man.

by one] Lit. **through**, or **by, the one.** So just below. See on
ver. 15.

they which receive] From time to time; a continuous process, as regards successive generations.

abundance] The word implies the *necessary* fulness of a gift of
Divine love. Justification, with its sequel, is *always* "abundant," both
in itself and as to its recipients.

grace] Lit. **the grace**; i.e. that in question; acceptance for Christ's
sake.

the gift of righteousness] I.e. here, practically, Justification. What
is "given" is a *standing of acceptance in the eye of the Law.* And the
Law, as such, accepts *only* on the ground of "righteousness," freedom
from guilt. How such freedom from guilt is attained is another question: in the present case, it is attained as "a gift," given by "the
Justifier of him that believeth in Jesus."

shall reign in life] Amply reversing the "reign" of death over them.
Probably the chief idea is of a *triumph,* full and lasting, *over death.*
Cp. 1 Cor. xv. 55—57, an instructive parallel. But no doubt the
words refer beyond this to all the *majesty* of the coming "glory" of the
justified, figured elsewhere by the "crown" of life, righteousness, or
glory; and by the "throne." See the marvellous union of *service and
royalty*, Rev. xxii. 3, 5.—"*Life*" is here the future, heavenly life;
life in its full sense. Cp. Matt. xviii. 8, 9, xix. 17.

by one, &c.] Lit. **through the One, Jesus Christ**. Here is the
secret of the "much more." The surpassing glory of Him who is the
Cause accounts for the Divine quality of the Result.

18. *Therefore*] In vv. 18, 19 the argument, from ver. 12, is summed
up as to its main substance; namely, the parallel of Adam and Christ;
the illustration of the work of Christ by Adam's position in respect of
his descendants and the effect on them of his sin.

as by the offence of one] Better, **as by one offence,** as in marg.
E.V.—The Gr. is elliptical here. We may supply "the result was,"
in each part of the verse; **as through one offence the result was,
unto all men, to condemnation; so through one righteous act the
result was, unto all men, to justification of life.**—The word rendered here **righteous act** is the same as that rendered "acquittal" in
the note on ver. 16, q.v. Its strict original meaning is a *thing righteously
done.* Its usual actual meaning is *an ordinance of justice.* But in one
N.T. passage at least it appears to mean *a righteous act* or course of
acts. (Rev. xix. 8, "the *righteousnesses* of the saints.") It thus is possible to interpret it in one place here as an *ordinance of acquittal,* in the
other as the great *act of righteousness* (which becomes also, as it were,
a *statute* of righteousness,) done by the Redeemer for His brethren.

all men to condemnation; even so by the righteousness of one *the free gift came* upon all men unto justification of life. For as by one man's disobedience many were made sinners, 19

Such a change of reference is not alien to St Paul's style.—If, however, the interpretation *righteous ordinance* should seem more necessary than it seems to us, it would fairly suit the context. Christ's obedience is (as suggested just above) viewed thus as the embodied ordinance, or institute, of Justification. This last, on the whole, is Meyer's explanation.

all men...all men] What is the reference of these words in the two cases respectively? In the first, certainly, *all mankind* is meant. Every man, not in theory only but fact, incurred sentence of death in Adam. In the second case also, many commentators, (e.g. Meyer,) hold that all mankind is intended: not that all actually receive justification, but that all are within the scope of Christ's work. Without entering on the profound question of the Divine Intentions, and merely seeking for St Paul's *special thought here*, we prefer to take the second "all men" *with a limit*, as meaning "all who are connected with the Second Adam;" all "His brethren." For through this whole context St Paul is dealing with results and facts, not with abstract theory. From the dreadful fact of the result of death from the Fall he reasons to the results of Christ's work; and the parallel would be most imperfect (and such as precisely to *contradict* the "*much more*" of vv. 15, 17,) if while in the one case condemnation was a fact and act, Justification should be only a possibility in the other. If Adam brings death *in fact* on all concerned, Christ must bring life *in fact* on all concerned also. Again, a limitation is suggested by the whole reasoning of the Epistle, and specially by viii. 30, where the justified are identical with the "foreknown" and "glorified," in the plain sense of the passage.—The use of "all men" with this change of reference is fairly illustrated by 1 Cor. xv. 22, 23. For through that whole ch. the Resurrection *of the Church* is the sole subject; and ver. 23 explicitly refers to "them that are Christ's:" and yet, when the parallel of Adam and Christ is in view, the word "all" is equally used there in both cases.—See for other illustrations, though less exact, John xii. 32; Tit. ii. 11.

The view of Christ as the Head of *all Mankind* is, to say the least, far less distinct in Scripture than that of Christ as the Head of *justified Mankind*, the true Church. Bearing this in mind, a difference of reference here will surely seem more natural than a sameness which can only be explained by admitting profound differences along with it.

justification of life] I.e. which confers, and results in, life; both by reversal of the sentence of death, and (as in ver. 17) by the gift of the life of glory in consequence.

19. *For*, &c.] This verse is in close connexion with ver. 18. St Paul recurs to the central truth in view, now from this side now from that, so as to leave the one deep and distinct impression of the *vicariousness* of the unique Work of the Second Adam; the truth that the justification of all the justified *wholly* results therefrom.

so by the obedience of one shall many be made righteous.
20 Moreover the law entered, that the offence might abound.
But where sin abounded, grace did much more abound:
21 that as sin hath reigned unto death, even so might grace

made sinners...made righteous] Better, **constituted**, "put into a position" of guilt and righteousness respectively. Here the whole context points to not a moral change but a legal standing. In Adam "the many" became, in the eye of the Law, guilty; in Christ "the many" shall become, in the eye of the same Law, righteous. In other words, they shall be justified.—"*Shall be made:*"—the future refers to the succession of believers. The justification of all was, ideally, complete already; but, actually, it would await the times of individual *believing.*—"*Many:*"—lit., in both cases, "the many." See on ver. 15.
—"*Obedience:*"—here probably the special reference is to the Redeemer's "delight to do the will" of His Father, "even unto the death of the cross." (Psal. xl. 8; Phil. ii. 8.)

20. *Moreover*] More simply, **But**, or (better) **Now**. In this verse and 21 a new consideration comes in, almost independent of the chain of reasoning, but meant to illustrate the surpassing "abundance" of grace (vv. 15—17).

the law] Lit. **Law**; but probably the reference is definite, as implied by the mention of *Moses* in ver. 14. See note on ver. 13, on the peculiar position of the Mosaic law.

entered] Lit. **entered by the side**; as if an afterthought in the great plan.—Cp. Gal. iii. 19.

that the offence might abound] Q.d., "that the disease might be brought to the surface." This bringing out of latent sinfulness was a real mercy. Cp. vii. 13. Obviously St Paul does not mean that this was the only, or chief, aim of the holy Law; but that *in view of the question in hand* (justification of sinners for Another's sake,) such was its function. It was to bring out the fact that men were not only *guilty* "*in Adam,*" but *personally sinful.*

the offence] Man's offences, regarded as a single whole. Just below we have "the *sin;*" the *principle* of which "the *offence*" was the *expression.*

sin] Lit. **the sin**. So just below, **the grace**. The reference is to sin and grace in their special aspects here.

much more abound] These words represent one compound verb in the Gr., and that verb is strengthened by the compounded preposition, and is itself a stronger word than that just used for "the abundance" of sin: **where the sin multiplied, there the grace superabounded.** On the thought here, see notes on ver. 16.

21. *that as sin,* &c.] More lit. **that as the sin reigned in death, so also may the grace reign through righteousness,** &c.— "*The sin reigned in death:*"—i.e., death was the expression of its power. Cp. vv. 12—14 and notes.—"*May grace reign:*"—such is the exact rendering, which should be kept, though Gr. idiom makes E.V.

reign through righteousness unto eternal life by Jesus Christ our Lord.

CH. VI. 1—14   *Justification organically connected with sanc-*
   tification: grace the supreme motive to obedience

What shall we say then?   Shall we continue in sin, that **6**

("*might*") grammatically possible.   St Paul is still thinking of the succession of future believers.

through righteousness]   I. e.   "through the gift of righteousness," (ver. 17,) Justification.   Grace provides the Method of the justification of the ungodly; it gives them a position of acceptance in the eye of the sacred Law; constitutes them, for the purposes of that Law, righteous persons.—We do not for a moment here forget that a *moral change* is intended, and effected, in the subjects of grace; but the argument, up to this point, has in view *not this yet*, but the judicial acceptance which is the prior condition of it;—Justification, not yet Sanctification.

unto eternal life]   The final issue of the "reign of grace."   See vi. 22, viii. 32, and note on ii. 7.

by Jesus Christ our Lord]   Well do these holy words close that great section of the argument which specially explains the WAY of Pardon.   Jesus Christ is the one Cause and Means of Pardon, and therefore indeed also the "LORD" of those who through Him are accepted and glorified.

CH. VI. **1—14** JUSTIFICATION ORGANICALLY CONNECTED WITH SANC-
      TIFICATION: GRACE THE SUPREME MOTIVE TO OBEDIENCE

1.   *What shall we say then?*]   Here begins the direct treatment of a great topic already suggested, (iii. 5—8,) the relation of gratuitous Pardon to Sanctity.   This discussion occupies ch. vi. and vii. 1—6; and is closely connected with the rest of ch. vii.

Let us distinctly note that up to this point *it has not been explicitly in the argument at all*.   The strongest *statements* of the evil and the doom of sin were made e. g. in cch. i. and ii.; but the *argument* thus far has been wholly occupied with acceptance; with JUSTIFICATION.   No part of the passage from iii. 9 to this point, has *purification of heart* for its *proper* subject.

continue, &c.]   Lit. **remain upon sin**.   The phrase is frequent in other connexions, and tends to mean not mere continuance, but *perse-verance in will and act*.   See e.g. 1 Tim. iv. 16.—The objection anticipated in this verse is abundantly illustrated in Church history.   It may be prompted either by the craving for sinful licence, or by a prejudice against the doctrine of purely gratuitous pardon under the belief that it does logically favour security in sin.   It is all the more noteworthy that St Paul meets it *not* by modifying in the least the gratuitous aspect of pardon ; *not* by presenting any merit of the pardoned person as even the minutest element in the *cause* of pardon.   He takes sanctity as entirely the *effect* of Justification, not at all its cause.

₂ grace may abound? God forbid. How shall we, that are
₃ dead to sin, live any longer therein? Know ye not, that
so many of us as were baptized into Jesus Christ were bap-
₄ tized into his death? Therefore we are buried with him by

2. *we, that are dead*, &c.] More lit. and fully, **we, as those who
died to sin.** The reference is again to a single past act; the death of
the Second Adam, *at which* His brethren too, regarded as "in Him,"
"died to sin." See last note on ch. v. 12.

dead to sin] See below, ver. 10: "He died to sin, once and for
ever." It appears then that *our* "death to sin" (in Christ) must be
explained by what *His* death to it was. And His was a death such as
to free Him not from its *impulses* (for He was essentially free from
them) but from its *claim*, its *penalty*, endured for us by Him. His death
once over, the claim of sin was cancelled[1]. Therefore, for those who
"died in Him," it was cancelled likewise. The phrase thus has, in the
strict sense of it, not a moral but a legal reference. But the transition
to a moral reference is inevitable when the REDEEMER'S DEATH is
seen to be the act which exhausted the claim: in that death we see
not only the strength of the claim, but the *malignity of the claimant*.

live any longer therein] "*Live*" is emphatic, in contrast to "*dead*."
St Paul puts it as inconceivable that the soul which is *so freed from such
claim* can endure, after its death in Christ to sin, (or, in other words,
after His death to sin for it,) to yield its faculties as before to sin's influence.—Strictly, *death* and *life* are used here in different respects;
death in a legal respect, life in a moral; but see last note for the
reconcilement of the seeming inconsistency.—"*Therein*:"—surrounded
by it, as the body by the air it breathes; in vital connexion.

3. *so many of us*, &c.] Not implying that some were, and some
were not. This is plain from the Gr. *All* Christian believers are
contemplated; for each his baptism was all this, if a true baptism.—
This and ver. 4 contain the only mentions of Baptism in the Epistle.
He refers the converts to their baptism as to the great crisis of their
lives, when, having already, by Divine grace, "turned from idols to
serve the living God," they made (so to speak) their formal self-surrender to their Redeemer, and received His formal acceptance of them as
His own.

into Jesus Christ] I.e. so as to belong to Him, to obey Him, and
to learn of Him. Cp. the parallel phrase "baptized into Moses,"
1 Cor. x. 2.

into his death] I.e. so as to come into special relations with it.
We may paraphrase, "into Him *as the Slain One*." His atoning
death was the primary point of apostolic teaching. See 1 Cor. xv. 3.

4. *we are buried with him*] Better, **we were buried**, &c.; the reference being to the past fact of baptism. *Burial* is the final token of

[1] Sin here, obviously, is used as a practical synonym for the broken Law;
but so that its proper meaning is ready at once to reappear. Properly, sin's only
"claim" is *to be itself put down*; but by a natural modification it appears as
that which *exacts the punishment of the sinner.*

baptism into death: that like as Christ was raised up from
the dead by the glory of the Father, *even* so we also should
walk in newness of life. For if we have been planted to- 5
gether in the likeness of his death, we shall be also *in the*

death, and so the strongest expression of death as a fact. Perhaps
there is an allusion to the immersion of baptism, as a quasi-burial. (The
only parallel passage is Col. ii. 12.) But the significance of the rite
would not depend on such a form of it: the essential is that every true
baptism is the ratification of covenant connexion with Christ and *His
Death*. It thus lays the baptized Christian, as it were, *with the Lord in
that grave* where He lay as the slain Propitiation; i.e. it ratifies our
share in the Justification of the Cross.

by baptism] **by means of baptism,** i.e., of course, not by the mere
act, but by all that is involved in a true baptism. Baptism is not an
isolated thing, but a summary and seal.

into death] Better, **into the death,** the Lord's Death. Connect
these words with "we were buried." The whole idea is a union with
Christ *as the Slain One*, so real that it is expressed by the figure of a
share in His grave.

that, &c.] The sequence indicated is as follows:—Our new position
and conduct as Christians was both to be, and to seem, radically new;
as new as resurrection-life after death. Therefore our admission to the
covenant was by a rite essentially connected with the Lord's DEATH,
and thus intended both to remind us of the price of justification, and
of the totally new position, principles, and conduct, of the justified.

by the glory of the Father] By the majestic harmony of His Power,
Holiness, and Love; all consenting in the great miracle. Perhaps the
thought is suggested here that the same "glory" shall be exercised in
the "new life" of the justified.

walk in newness of life] I.e. move and act with the new principles
and powers of those who, as the justified, are "*born again* to a *living*
hope."—"*Newness:*"—the Gr. word expresses not so much *youth* as
novelty; a condition *without precedent* in our experience.—"*Life:*"—in
the sense not of a *course of life*, but of the *principle of life*. Through
the Death of Christ, the justified "live;" in the "newness" of that
condition they are to "walk."—Here again (as in ver. 2) note the *transition* of ideas; from a "death to sin" (with Christ) in respect of
penalty, to a "life" (with Christ) in respect *not merely of remission* but
of new principles and acts; i.e. from Justification simply to Justification
as resulting in Sanctification. The "life" is not merely the extension
of existence to a pardoned man, but the condition and use of that existence where the pardoned are also, as such, accepted among the
"brethren" of Christ.

5. *if*] I.e. "*as;*" an assumed fact.

planted together] Better (with regard to the form of the Gr. word),
vitally connected. Not *implanting* but *coalescence* is the idea. (The
word occurs nowhere else in N. T.)

6 *likeness* of *his* resurrection: knowing this, that our old man
is crucified with *him*, that the body of sin might be de-
7 stroyed, that henceforth we should not serve sin. For he

in the likeness] Not His Death, but its Likeness; i.e. *our* "death
unto sin" in Him. (See on ver. 2.) As believers, we have become
vitally, inseparably, connected with that "death;" in other words,
freedom from the claim of doom is an *essential* of our condition "in
Him." (viii. 1.)

we shall be] I.e., practically, "we are and shall be." This *is to be*
the sequel of justification, now and ever.

his resurrection] Which was not merely the reversal of His Death,
but His entrance on the *"power* of an endless life." So the justified
live, not merely "not unto sin," but "unto God."

6. *knowing this*] Not precisely = "for we know this;" but more
fully, *"as those who know this."* This *knowledge* is to be a working
motive in the new life.

our old man] Cp., for illustrative passages, vii. 22; 2 Cor. iv. 16;
Eph. iii. 16, iv. 22, 24; Col. iii. 9; 1 Pet. iii. 4. In view of these, the
word *"self"* in its popular use ("a man's true self," &c.) appears to be
a fair equivalent for *"man"* here. Meyer here gives *"unser altes Ich,"*
("our old Ego"). Here the Apostle views the Christian before his
union to Christ as (figuratively, of course,) *another person;* so profoundly different was his position before God, as a person unconnected
with Christ.

is crucified with him] Better, **was crucified.** Here again the idea
is the Representative Death of the Substitute, appropriated and made
efficacious for justification, by faith. Not merely Death, but the CROSS,
is here named; the ideas of shame and pain being specially fit here, to
emphasize both the requirements of the law and the claims of grace.

the body of sin] I.e. the body regarded as the special seat and stronghold of sin. Cp. 1 Cor. ix. 27; and below, vv. 12, 13. The body is
"the external basis of human nature;" "the medium for the reception
...of life;" and thus "the sinfulness of human nature is...manifested
by means of it." (Cremer.) In connexions like the present it nearly =
"the flesh."

destroyed] Better, **cancelled,** as to its fatal power on the spirit. Same
word as iii. 3, 31; where see notes. Cp. especially 2 Tim. i. 10; where
E. V. "abolished." For a comment on the meaning here see viii. 3,
and 1 Cor. ix. 27.

serve] Lit., **be slaves to;** and so in the whole context. This clause
explains the last: "The body of sin" is so "cancelled" as to its power
that the "inner man" no longer is the slave, or obedient victim, of sin,
but combats it, with final victory. Before our "death with Christ," the
will, although it was swayed by conscience away from single acts or
courses of sin, had never decisively revolted from sin as such, under
the one effective motive—supreme love to the Holy God as the God of
Peace. Hence, little as he might know it, the man's will was, in the
main respect of all, in harmony with sin, and the tool of sin; for sin in

that is dead is freed from sin. Now if we be dead with 8
Christ, we believe that we shall also live with him: knowing 9
that Christ being raised from the dead dieth no more;

its essence is the not-loving the true God. And the *impending doom* of
sin, (in other words, *sin as unforgiven sin*,) was the strength and secret
of this bondage; for till the removal of the doom the man could not
love God; God could not be to him the God of Peace. Hence St Paul
speaks now immediately of deliverance from the *doom* of sin as *implying
deliverance from its bondage.*

7. *For he that is dead,* &c.] Better, with a slight paraphrase, **for he
who has once died to sin now stands free from its claim.** The *legal
claim* of sin is meant here, not its *moral dominion,* for the Gr. word
rendered "freed" in E. V., is lit. (see margin of E. V.) **justified.** The
argument is that, since death is the penalty of sin, then if death has been
suffered and *passed,* the penalty is exhausted and the claim cancelled:
now such is the position of the justified in Christ; His death *was
endured, and is now past, for them and as theirs;* therefore they live
as those who have exhausted penalty and are free from its claim—in
fact, "justified from sin."

8. *Now,* &c.] This ver. and vv. 9, 10, 11 carry on, in a brief paragraph, the truth just stated, with special reference to the permanence
and power of the Lord's resurrection-life, which is the pledge of the
Christian's "new life." Here too the view of His resurrection-life as
a life "*unto God*" is distinctly stated; (see below on ver. 12;) the
point which specially affects the argument then following.

if we be dead with Christ] Better, **as we died with Christ**; (see on
ver. 2).—Here observe that it is in different senses respectively that
man "*dies in Adam*" (1 Cor. xv. 22), and "*dies with Christ.*" "In
Adam," he incurs death *in his own person,* as penalty for inherited
guilt (see on ch. v. 12). "With Christ" he, *not in his own person,
but in that of Christ, his Representative,* suffers death as expiation; is
viewed as having thereby exhausted the claim of the law against him;
and thus arrives in the happy state of justification, with its attendant
results of sanctifying change in affections and will.

we believe] On the firm ground of our "death with Him."

we shall also live] The future points not so much to bodily resurrection
and life in glory, as to the immediate prospect, on justification, of "newness of life." Q. d., "We live, and shall continue to do so, in our
near and distant future." The future "glory" is not yet the direct
subject, as it is in parts of ch. viii.: the future of the life of *grace* is
in view here.

with him] I.e., by connexion with Him as the Second Adam.

9. *knowing*] As an admitted foundation-truth. Christian *faith* is
always viewed as grounded upon *knowledge,* upon *fact.*

dieth no more] His life is continuous and endless; such then also is
that of those to whom He is the Second Adam; who therefore "shall
live with Him." Through this whole context the parallel of Adam and
Christ needs to be borne in mind.

₁₀ death hath no more dominion over him. For in that he
died, he died unto sin once : but in that he liveth, he liveth
₁₁ unto God. Likewise reckon ye also yourselves to be dead
indeed unto sin, but alive unto God through Jesus Christ
₁₂ our Lord. Let not sin therefore reign in your mortal body,

---

death hath no more dominion over him] "*Him*" is emphatic.—The
Second Adam, as Representative and Substitute, submitted to the "dominion," or mastery, of death as the appointed penalty of sin. But by
that very act He exhausted death's claim on Himself and His brethren;
He "cancelled death." (2 Tim. i. 10.)

10. *in that he died*] Lit. **that which He died**; His dying, in all
that it involved. So below, **that which He liveth**.

unto sin] I.e., as the previous argument shewed, "with reference to
the *claim* of sin;" to meet and cancel it; and therefore so as now to be
out of reach of its doom.

once] **once for all,** "once and for ever." The word here is not
necessary to the argument, but it enforces, by contrast, *the continuousness
of His life.* It also, though less pointedly, suggests the completeness of
the atonement, and so the greatness of its results. (On the latter reference see Heb. vii. 27, ix. 12, x. 10; where "once," "once for all,"
is the same word as that here, in the Gr.).

unto God] I.e. **with respect to God**; as having obtained (representatively for us) God's acceptance, and having thus entered on an immortal
permanence (representatively for us) of joy and power before Him.
(The same phrase, but with different special reference, occurs Luke
xx. 38.)

11. *Likewise*] Here is the *strict result* of the truth just stated, when
the position of Christ as the Second Adam is remembered. What He
did and does, as such, was done and is done by those who are "in Him"
as their Head.

reckon] This word, just as in iii. 28, (E. V., "conclude,") marks a
solid inference from facts. It *implies* also here an *application* of that
inference to conscience, affections, and will; such as is now developed
by the argument.

through Jesus Christ] Lit., and far better, **in Jesus Christ**. The
word "in" is quite strictly used here, of the relation of the Second Adam
to His brethren.—"*Our Lord*" should be omitted, on evidence of MSS.,
&c.

12. *Let not sin therefore reign*] Here begins the direct moral appeal
to the will. This till now has been either withheld, (while the *Divine motive* was being explained,) or made only indirectly, as in vv. 2, 6, and
iii. 31.—Notice how perfectly free and natural is the appeal to the will.

reign] This word implies sin's presence still in the "mortal body" of
the justified; a presence dwelt upon so fully in ch. vii., at the close. But
they are to resist and subdue it, just because they are (1) judicially free
from its claim, or doom; and (2) freed by a means, exactly such as to
bring them into the "newness" of a "life unto God;" i.e. a totally new

that *ye* should obey it in the lusts thereof.   Neither yield ye 13
your members *as* instruments of unrighteousness unto sin :
but yield yourselves unto God, as *those that are* alive from
the dead, and your members *as* instruments of righteousness

condition of connexion and intercourse with Him as the Father of their
Head.   Such a condition, in the nature of things, cannot be *merely
objective*.   It *is objective* as regards the acceptance of believers in the
Risen Lord, and His intercessory life for them; but it must *also* inevitably be *subjective* on its other side, because the final cause of the objective
position is the realization of a subjective spiritual *state;* namely, that of
holiness and love before God.   The *facts* are expressly given in order to
work upon the conscience and will.   See further, *Postscript*, p. 268.

in your mortal body]   See on "the body of sin," ver. 6.   Here the
"mortality" is emphasized, because it marks the fact (see further on
viii. 23) that the deliverance of the body is still incomplete, so that it is
still a special field for the action of sin.   See below on vii. 24.

that ye should obey it, &c.]   Better read, **so as to obey the lusts
thereof**; i.e. of the body.   This clause explains the word "reign."   Sin
"reigns" when the will *goes with* solicitations to evil—as it does on
the whole go, since the Fall, till Redemption gives it the motive power
to resist and prevail.—"*Lusts:*" desires after evil, and away from God,
of every kind; whether "sensual" or not.   The most refined æstheticism
may be as truly a "lust of the mortal body" as the grossest vice, if
it perverts the will from holiness.

13. *your members*]   **your limbs**; the bodily organs and their constitution.   The words thus = "your body," (see xii. 1,) only with the
suggestion of its *varied* powers for good or evil.   See on ver. 6 (on
"the body."   Cp. Col. iii. 5).

instruments]   Lit., **weapons**.   The word in classical Gr. has very
various references, but N. T. usage makes it best here to keep the
military reference.   The will is regarded as *at war*, whether for or
against holiness.

unto sin]   Connect these words with "*yield;*" q. d., "Do not put
them as weapons into the hand of sin to use for unrighteousness."   So
below, "Put them into the hand of God as weapons to use for righteousness."

yourselves]   This word was not used in the previous clause, and here
emphasizes the *cordial* allegiance resulting from justification.

as those that are alive, &c.]   Rather better, **who were dead and are
alive**.   The facts both of death and life are emphatic in the Gr.—The
reference is to *acceptance* in Him who "was delivered because of our
offences and raised again because of our justification" (iv. 25).   *In Him*
the believer has, as it were, suffered expiatory death and passed into
"newness of life."   This seems to be the reference *proper to this context*,
rather than a reference to the *spiritual death-state* of unrenewed man.
(Eph. ii. 1.)

righteousness]   Here, of course, in the sense of *active good;* not, as so
often before, in that of "righteousness in the eye of the law."

14 unto God. For sin shall not have dominion over you: for
ye are not under the law, but under grace.

15—23   *The same subject.   Illustration from slavery*

15   What then? shall we sin, because we are not under the
16 law, but under grace? God forbid. Know ye not, that to
whom ye yield yourselves servants to obey, *his* servants ye

14. *For sin*, &c.] It is not quite clear whether this verse closes or
opens a paragraph. Meyer takes it as opening the new section of
argument. But it is quite in place as closing the previous one, while
yet pointing forward also. On this view, St Paul makes the statement
on purpose to animate the disciple to that exercise of will which yields
his whole being to God. He is reminded of the *reality of Justification*,
with its results of strength-giving peace and joy.

shall not have dominion] I.e. in the way of claim and doom. Same
word as ver. 9, where see note. The future means that this freedom
from condemnation shall be mercifully continued to them *in their
conflict;* they "shall not come into condemnation." This truth was to
be their invigoration.

for] This clause fixes the reference of the last to *justification*, when
read with the commentary on "law" and "grace" supplied by ch. iv.

under the law] Lit. **under law**; and so best here. Law in its
widest reference is meant; a code of precepts, to be fulfilled as the preliminary to acceptance.—The Gr. suggests the paraphrase, "Ye are
now *placed* not under the law but under grace;" with the idea not of
the mere position, but of the *transferring process.*

15—23   THE SAME SUBJECT.   ILLUSTRATION FROM SLAVERY

15. *What then?*] This takes up the question of ver. 1, and introduces the explicit answer, for which the passages between have fully
prepared us. The form of the question here, as there, helps further
to fix the reference of ver. 14 to *justification*. Sin was there said to
have "no dominion" over the believer, in such a sense as to give
(momentary) *colour* to such a question; therefore we now are shewn
that the "dominion" there referred to was one of *claim*, not of *influence.*

16. *Know ye not*] As a self-evident truth, that bond-service, once
accepted, becomes binding. This general principle is at once applied
to the special cases of Sin and Obedience regarded as personified Masters.
The clauses to the end of ver. 18 may be thus summarized:—"All
bond-service, once accepted, is binding, and forbids divided servitude;—
this is as true of the obligations of Pardon as of those of Condemnation;
of Justification as of Death. And you, thank God, have now passed
from the latter to the former. Remember then, that in the very act of
leaving the bond-service of sin you entered that of Pardon as taught in
the Gospel, and are thus bound to *obey* as much as ever, though in the
opposite direction."

are to whom ye obey; whether of sin unto death, or of obedience unto righteousness? But God be thanked, that 17 ye were the servants of sin, but ye have obeyed from the heart *that* form of doctrine which was delivered you. Being 18

unto death—unto righteousness] The *results* ("death," "righteousness") of the respective "servitudes" are not *necessary* to the immediate statement, but are brought in as inseparable from the whole subject.

obedience] This is here the personified Master, the antithesis of Sin. The context, (ver. 17,) and x. 3, (see also 1 Pet. i. 2,) shew its meaning here to be *the act of submission to the Divine terms of pardon*. It is thus the practical equivalent of those terms, which are to be the *ruling principle* of the new life.

righteousness] The Gr. may here be *paraphrased* (not *translated*) by Justification. In such a paraphrase we are far from shutting a moral meaning out of the word; but a careful collation of passages *in this Epistle* makes it reasonably clear that its ruling reference in this argument is to the *legal side* of righteousness; i.e. to what *the Law will view as righteous*, and so to the persons whom it will view as possessing righteousness. Such a possession, in the case of "the ungodly" (iv. 5), is explained by St Paul as wholly due to the righteousness of their Representative. In other words they are justified for His sake.—Thus "righteousness" is used as a summary for the process of justification, though strictly applicable only to one part of the subject. Here we may paraphrase: "Ye became the bond-servants of God's Terms of Pardon, to which you submitted with a submission that resulted in your being reckoned righteous in the eye of His Law." '

17. *that ye were*] I.e. obviously, "that whereas you were, &c."

servants of sin] Such, without exception, was the former state and position of the justified. They were ruled by the principles, and under the claim, of sin; the will alienated from God, the person liable to doom.

ye have obeyed] Better, **ye obeyed**; at the time of faith. See note on *obedience*, ver. 16.

from the heart] The words are added as indicating the grand requisite of *reality*, and as implying the *heartiness* of the consequent life of holy "bond-service" (see x. 9, 10); perhaps too in allusion and contrast to any idea of a *forcible* subjection which might be suggested by the phrase "ye were *delivered over*" just below. See next note.

that form of doctrine which was delivered you] This rendering of the Gr. cannot stand. The margin E. V. is correct: **the form of doctrine into which you were delivered.** Here we have to ask, (1) what is the "*form of doctrine*"? The word rendered "form," (same word as ch. v. 14, but there certainly with different reference), usually means, in St Paul, something *guiding* or *formative*—whether fact, principle, or person; (e.g. Phil. iii. 17; and 1 Cor. x. 6, where literally "figures, types, of us"). The phrase here would thus mean, "the *principle*, the *rule* of doctrine;" i.e. that rule of life which the "doctrine" in question, viz. the apostolic teaching, furnishes. Such a reference of the word "form" is

then made free from sin, ye became the servants of righte-
19 ousness. I speak after the manner of men because of the
infirmity of your flesh: for as ye have yielded your members
servants to uncleanness and to iniquity unto iniquity ; *even*

specially apt here, since the moral results of faith are now in view. The
reference of the phrase to *shades and varieties of Christian teaching* is
certainly wrong; for such a reference would be out of place here, where
the subject is the antithesis of the *main truths* of sin and salvation.—
The phrase thus = " The guiding principles learnt from the preaching of
the Gospel."—(2) What is the meaning of "*into*, or *unto*, *which ye
were delivered*, or *handed over*"? The allusion is to that metaphor of
slavery which runs through the context. The Christian has been taken,
by Divine mercy, from the hands of one Master to be *put into the hands*
of another. The transference is, in one aspect, voluntary, ("yield
yourselves," "from the heart,") but in another aspect it is the sovereign
act of grace. (See Col. i. 13 for similar imagery). The new Master
is here the Ruling-Principle of the Gospel, just as, in ver. 16, it was
Obedience to that Gospel.

18. *Being then*, &c.] This verse is a brief summary, in more direct
terms, of the previous two verses. The emphasis is the reality, and
immediateness, of the new servitude.—" *Then* :"—better, **But.** A
slight contrast of thought is indicated, between the *willingness* of the
obedience (ver. 17), and the consequent *obligation*.

righteousness] See last note on ver. 16. The same reference of the
word will hold good both here and there. The practical meaning thus
is that pardon, as conveyed in the Divine justification, is now the (as
it were) Master, the possessor of the obedience of the will; in other
words, the ruling principle and motive.

19. *after the manner of men*] More lit., **humanly.** He apologizes,
so to speak, for using the peculiarly earthly image of the slave-market
to enforce a truth of the most exalted spiritual dignity ; namely, the
necessary conformity of the wills of the justified to the will of God.

because of the infirmity of your flesh] I.e., because you are "weak " to
apprehend spiritual truth, as being still "in the flesh;" affected by that
element of your nature which (besides being the stronghold of sin) is
always the antithesis of "the spirit." This is his reason for going so
low for his metaphor ; for boldly depicting their state of justification as
one also of slavery. No illustration less *harsh* would convey the full
reality of obligation to their minds.

to uncleanness and to iniquity] Two main aspects of sin. "Iniquity "
is lit., and better, **lawlessness.** The first of the two words means,
the craving for evil as such ; the second, the hatred of holy restraint as
such.

unto iniquity] Lit., again, **unto lawlessness;** i.e. "with the result
of lawless acts on the lawless principle." See 1 John iii. 4, where the
Gr. precisely means, "sin and lawlessness are convertible terms."

servants] The word is, of course, emphatic in both parts of the verse.

so now yield your members servants to righteousness unto
holiness. For when ye were the servants of sin, ye were 20
free from righteousness. What fruit had ye then *in those* 21
things whereof ye are now ashamed? for the end of those
things is death. But now being made free from sin, and 22
become servants to God, ye have your fruit unto holiness,

righteousness] See notes above on vv. 16, 17, 18, in favour of still
referring this word to justification, the "gift of righteousness" (see
on ch. v. 17) regarded as the new *motive* in the life of the justified ;
the new power which was to use their "members" as its "weapons"
against sin. (See on ver. 13.)

unto holiness] Lit., and better, **unto sanctification.** The Gr. noun
indicates rather a process than a principle or a condition. (So too Heb.
xii. 14.) The result of the new "bondage" was to be a steady *course
of purification;* a *process* of self-denial, watchfulness, and diligent observance of the holy will of the God of Peace.

20. *For when*, &c.] This verse enforces the exhortation just given,
by reminding the Christian that once he was emphatically *not* the
"bond-servant of righteousness."

free from righteousness] Lit. **free unto righteousness;** i.e. with respect to it, both as to its mercy and as to its consequent claim. There is
here a deep and solemn irony, (if we may venture the word), which has
some parallel in 1 Pet. iv. 3; q. d., "You had nothing to do with
the righteousness of God ; you were not justified before Him : therefore
His righteousness had, as it were, nothing to do with you ; it laid no
bond of grateful love upon you."

21. *What fruit had ye then*] "Then," or "therefore," points to the
resulting practice due to their just-described *position.*

fruit] The word is very often used as a figure for "result," and
almost always in a good sense. The probable meaning here will
thus be, "*Did you find any happiness or profit resulting?*" For
a comment on these clauses see the passage 1 Pet. iv. 1—4, which is
pregnant with illustration of this whole context. (Cp. e.g. Rom. vi. 3,
7, with 1 Pet. iv. 1; Rom. vi. 12, 13, with 1 Pet. iv. 2.) See too, for
the deep and gracious contrast between the past and the present of
other Christian converts, 1 Cor. vi. 9—11.

death] See on i. 32. From. ver. 23 here it is plain that this "death"
is the correlative of "eternal life." It is the "second death" of the
Revelation ; the "destruction," or "ruin," of Matt. vii. 13.

22. *now*] I.e. **as things are,** by Divine mercy.

to God] The real Master of the justified. The figures, "Obedience,"
"Righteousness," "Rule of Doctrine," &c., are now laid aside, that
HE to whom they refer may at last appear in the Divine simplicity of
His ownership over the soul.

ye have your fruit] The verb, by position, is emphatic. "You
now *have*, what you then lacked, namely *fruit;* 'your' fruit, a real and
happy profit and result from your new principle."

₂₃ and the end everlasting life.   For the wages of sin *is* death;
but the gift of God *is* eternal life through Jesus Christ our
Lord.

CH. VII. 1—6   *The same subject.   Illustration from
matrimony*

7   Know ye not, brethren, (for I speak to them that know

unto holiness]   **unto sanctification**; see on ver. 19.   The "fruit"
amounted to, consisted in, a steady *course* of self-denial and conflict
against sin.

everlasting life]   I.e. in this context, the bliss of the life to come; the
"sight of the Lord" which is attained only by the path of "sanctification"
(Heb. xii. 14); being, as it is, the issue and crown of the process.—Here,
as in many other cases, note the varying reference of a single phrase.
"Eternal life" is sometimes viewed as present (John iii. 36, v. 24;)
sometimes, and more often, as future (e.g. John iv. 36).   In the first
case it is the grace of regeneration, in the second, the developement of
this in the glory to come.

23. *For*]   The "for" refers to the last statement.   The verse may
be paraphrased, "For whereas the wages of sin is death, the gift of God
is, as we have now said, *eternal life.*"

wages]   The Gr. is same word as Luke iii. 14; 1 Cor. ix. 7; 2 Cor. xi. 8.
It strictly denotes pay for military service; and the metaphor here therefore points not to *slavery* so much as to the *warfare* of ver. 13 (where
see note on *weapons*).   The word is full of pregnant truth.   Death, in
its most awful sense, is no more than the reward and result of sin ; and
sin is nothing less than a conflict against God.

gift]   The Gr. is same word as **free gift**, ch. v. 15.—This word here is,
so to speak, a paradox.   We should have expected one which would
have represented life eternal as the *issue of holiness*, to balance the
truth that death is the *issue of sin*.   And in respect of holiness
being the *necessary preliminary* to the future bliss, this would have
been entirely true.   But St Paul here all the more forcibly presses the
thought that salvation is a *gift* wholly apart from human *merit*.   The
eternal Design, the meritorious Sacrifice, the life-giving and love-im-
parting Spirit, all alike are a Gift absolutely free.   The works of sin *are*
the *procuring* cause of Death ; the course of sanctification *is not* the
procuring cause of Life Eternal, but only the training for the enjoyment
of what is essentially a Divine gift "in Jesus Christ our Lord."

through]   Lit., and better, **in.**   The "life eternal" is to be found
only "in Him," by those who "come to Him."   His work is the one
meritorious cause ; and in His hands also is the actual gift.   (Joh. xvii.
2, 3).

CH. VII. 1—6   THE SAME SUBJECT.   ILLUSTRATION FROM
MATRIMONY

1. *Know ye not*, &c.]   The passage from hence to end of ver. 7 is
closely connected with the last chapter.   By a perfectly new simile

the law,) how that the law hath dominion over a man, as long as he liveth? For the woman which hath a husband 2 is bound by the law to *her* husband so long as he liveth; but if the husband be dead, she is loosed from the law of the husband. So then if, while *her* husband liveth, she 3 be married to another man, she shall be called an adulteress: but if *her* husband be dead, she is free from *that* law; so that she is no adulteress, though she be married to 4 another man. Wherefore, my brethren, ye also are become

(marriage), it illustrates further what has been just illustrated by the metaphor of slavery, and (in the first part of ch. vi.) by the union of the justified with Christ;—namely the Christian's entire disconnexion from the claims, and so from the ruling influence, of sin, in virtue of the new and sacred union.

to them that know the law] Lit. **law**; without article. But the immediate context shews that the Mosaic Law, (and probably especially its sanctions regarding marriage), is meant. The whole Roman Church, whether Jewish or Gentile, would be familiar with it; many of them having been disciples of the synagogue, and all being directed constantly to the use of the Old Testament by apostolic precept and example. See on iv. 18.—This brief parenthesis is quite in keeping with the courtesy of St Paul's writings.

hath dominion] I.e. **has a claim on him**; same word as vi. 9, where see note.

a man] Lit. **the man**; the individual, as the second party in any given case—the Law being the first party.

as long as he liveth] Not "*only* as long as he liveth," as this is sometimes explained. The emphasis is on the abiding claim of the Law up to death, which alone can cancel it. This general and certain principle is now at once applied to the special case at which St Paul aims in illustration—the case of marriage.

2. *to her husband so long*, &c]. Lit. **to the living husband.** So it should be rendered; q. d., "to the present, not to a past or future, husband."

she is loosed] Lit. **she has been cancelled from,** &c. The perfect tense indicates the *ipso facto* character of the release. The obvious equivalent of the phrase is, "the law of her husband has been cancelled *ipso facto* in respect of her."

the law of the husband] I.e. "that special part of the law which affects her husband and his claim;" viz. the sanctions of marriage.

3. *she shall be called*] The Gr. verb indicates a *deliberate* "calling;" the *winning of a title*. Same word as Acts xi. 26.

that law] Lit. **the law**; i. e. of her husband.

married] Lit., in this ver. and 4, the verb is merely **be,** or **become: if she be** [joined] **to another husband**—lawfully or not.

4. *Wherefore*] The word marks transition from the facts to the spiritual inference.

dead to the law by the body of Christ; that ye should be
married to another, *even* to him who is raised from the dead,
5 that we should bring forth fruit unto God. For when we
were in the flesh, the motions of sins, which were by the

are become dead] Lit., and better, **were made dead**; a passive verb,
suggesting the external, objective work which caused their "death;"
viz., the Death of their Representative and Head, the Second Adam.

to the law] To its claim on you as a covenant of salvation.

by the body of Christ] Which was slain for you. No reference to
the mystical Body, the Church, (xii. 5; 1 Cor. x.; Eph.; Col.;) is to be
sought here. The word "*body*" is used, instead of "*death*," probably
to remind the readers that the Lord "took our nature upon Him"
expressly in view of His death. (See Heb. ii. 14.) Meanwhile the
truth of the connexion between believers and their Head, their Second
Adam, is still full in view. By virtue of it the death of the Lord counts
as the death of His brethren, in respect of the claim of the Law upon
them—here figured as the claim of one marriage-partner over the other,
to be broken only by the death of one of the two.

to another] I. e., another than the Law, now regarded as defunct in
respect of its claim on them. Observe that the metaphorical language
here is not strictly consistent. In vv. 2, 3, the death of the husband is
contemplated; in ver. 4 the death of the wife. The change may be explained partly by St Paul's desire to avoid an expression so easily misunder-
stood as the *death of the Law* (see on ver. 6); and partly by the unique
character of the spiritual fact illustrated here by a new marriage; viz.
the *death and resurrection* (in her Representative, who now becomes
her Husband also,) of the mystical Bride.—The change in the metaphor,
whatever its cause, leaves it unchanged as an illustration.—The figure
of Marriage, passingly employed here, (and still more so, Gal. iv.
21—31,) is worked out more fully in Eph. v. 23, &c., and in the
Revelation. It is largely foreshadowed in O.T.; e.g. in Ps. xlv.;
Canticles; Isai. liv.; Jer. iii.; and in the many passages where idolatry
is pictured by sin against wedlock.

to him who is raised] The Lord's resurrection is here brought in,
because the "death" (in Him) of His people has just been mentioned.
The thought suggests both that they are "risen in Him" to the life of
peace with God, and that they partake with Him, as their Risen Head,
"the power of an endless life."

fruit] **offspring**. The metaphor is carried into detail. (See for a
parallel of more elaboration, Jas. i. 15.) The "offspring" here is,
obviously, the "fruit of the Spirit" (Gal. v. 22), Christian virtues; just
as the "offspring" of the former marriage had been acts of sin (ver. 4).

unto God] The Father, not Christ. The phrase does not suggest
the bearing children to a Husband, but the bearing children to be then
dedicated to God. So Hannah bore Samuel "unto God."

5. *when we were in the flesh*] For illustration of this important
phrase see especially viii. 8, 9. St Paul here assumes of Christians
(1) that they were once "in the flesh;" (2) that they are so no longer.

law, did work in our members to bring forth fruit unto
death. But now we are delivered from the law, *that* being 6
dead wherein we were held ; that we should serve in newness of spirit, and not *in* the oldness of the letter.

To be "in the flesh" thus describes the man's condition previous to the
special gift of the Holy Spirit connected with justification; (see ch. v. 5,
and Gal. iv. 6;) the condition in which the dominant element was the
very antithesis of the Spirit—the "carnal mind." (See on viii. 6, 7.)
Such passages as Gal. ii. 20 shew that "in the flesh" may, with a proper
context, mean no more than "in the body," "in the surroundings of
material, earthly, life." But when, as here, the context points to a
contrast between "the flesh" and *better* things, it is plain that the
essential idea of "the flesh" is that it is the special vehicle of sin.

It is most needful to observe that, according to St Paul, the dominance
of this element is the *invariable* condition of man before special grace.

motions] Lit. **passions**, as marg. E.V. ; *instincts* of evil.

by the law] I.e., to which the law, as calling out the rebellion of
the carnal will, gave special direction and energy. See below on
vv. 7, 8.

did work] **were active.** The Gr. verb is the original of "energize."

in our members] I.e. in our body, viewed in the variety of its parts
and powers. See on vi. 13.

unto death] The doleful parallel to "unto God" in ver. 4. Death
was, as it were, the Power to which the results of the unregenerate life
were dedicated. He "who had the power of death" (Heb. ii. 14) was
the usurping god.

6. *now*] **as the fact stands.**

are delivered] Lit., and better, **were delivered** ; by our Representative's death ideally, and actually through faith in Him.

delivered.] Lit. **cancelled, abolished.** This peculiar expression confirms the remark above on ver. 4, that St Paul designedly avoids the
idea of the Law's death, though the metaphor in strictness suggests it.
Here, similarly, the Law "was cancelled from us;" but
we are said to be "cancelled from the Law."—"*From the Law:*"—
a pregnant phrase=**so as to be free from it.**

that being dead] I.e. the Law. But a better-supported reading
(with a change of one letter only in the Gr.) gives, **we being dead to
that wherein,** &c. This precisely accords with the evident avoidance
hitherto of the idea of *the Law's death ;* for our death (in Christ) to the
claim of the Law is thus put where we should expect to read of the
death of its claim to us.

we were held] Lit. **held down ;** i.e. from freedom; both as to the
claim of the law and as to the consequent influence of sin.

that we should serve] Here the metaphor of marriage gives way to
that of bondservice once more. The *obedience* of the wife is the
connecting idea of the two.

newness of spirit] Better, **of the Spirit** ; though the word is without
article. The contrast of *Spirit and letter* has occurred ii. 29, (see too

7—25 *The true function of the Divine Law : to detect and condemn sin, both before and after Justification*

7 What shall we say then? *Is* the law sin? God forbid.

ii. 27,) and occurs also 2 Cor. iii. 6, twice. Comparing those passages, we find that the practical meaning here of "the letter" is the *Law* (as a covenant), and that of "the Spirit," the *Gospel*. The common ground on which they are compared and contrasted is that of Obedience; at which both Law and Gospel ultimately aim. The Law does so "by the letter," by prescribing its own inexorable terms. The Gospel does so "by the Spirit;" by the Divine plan of Redemption, which brings direct on the soul the influence of "the Spirit of the Son of God," who "pours out the love of God in the heart" (ch .v. 5). The Gospel thus both intends, and effects, the *submission of the will* to the will of God; a submission absolute and real; a bondservice. But the bond is now the power of adoring and grateful love.—It will be seen that we take "Spirit" here to mean the Holy Paraclete. The Gr. word rarely, if ever, bears our modern sense of "the *spirit* of a law, of an institution, &c." It must here be, then, either the human spirit or the Divine Spirit. And as the idea of "the letter" is that of an objective ruling power, so it is best to explain "the Spirit" as objective also to the man, and therefore here the Divine Spirit.—We may now paraphrase the last words, "so that we might live as bondmen still, but in the sacred novelty of the bondservice which the Holy Ghost constrains, not in the now-obsolete way of the bondservice prescribed by the covenant of merit."

7—25 THE TRUE FUNCTION OF THE DIVINE LAW : TO DETECT AND CONDEMN SIN, BOTH BEFORE AND AFTER JUSTIFICATION

7. *What shall we say then?*] Same words as vi. 1.—Here opens a new and important section, including the remainder of ch. vii., and passing on in close connexion into ch. viii. The dogmatic statement and illustration of the Union of the justified with Jesus Christ as (1) the Second Adam, (2) the new Master, (3) the mystic Husband, is now closed. All these aspects of redemption, but especially the last, have suggested the question now to be definitely treated; namely, *What is the true Nature and Work of the Law?* The expressions just used regarding the Law;—the "death" of the justified to it; "the holding down" which it inflicted on them; the "oldness of the letter;"—all point the new enquiry "*Is the Law sin?*" We have just read (ver. 5) that "the instincts of our sins were *by the Law*." Does this mean that the Law is a sinful principle and motive? Is it the origin of sin? Is it sin itself?—"*The Law*" here, and through most of the context, (exceptions, of course, are vv. 21, 23,) is the Moral Law, with a special, but not exclusive, understanding of the Mosaic Code. See above on ch. v. 13.

God forbid] See on iii. 4.—The vehement negative is, of course, only in keeping with the many incidental assertions hitherto (e.g. vi. 19) of the reality of the *obedience* of the justified.

Nay, I had not known sin, but by the law: for I had not known lust, except the law had said, Thou shalt not covet. But sin, taking occasion by the commandment, 8 wrought in me all *manner of* concupiscence. For without the law sin *was* dead. For I was alive without the law 9

Nay] Lit., and far better, **But.** St Paul entirely rejects the suggestion that the Law *is* sin, but all the more insists on the fact that it does both detect sin and (in a certain sense) *evoke* it.

I had not known] See on iii. 20.—The reference of the words there "by the law, &c.," and that of this clause, are not precisely the same. There, the law is regarded more as *detecting the evil* of sin; here, more as *evoking its power*. But the two ideas are nearly akin.—Here St Paul means that without the Precept he would not have seen, in evil thoughts, &c., that element of *resistance to a holy Will* which carries with it a mysterious attraction for the fallen soul. He would not have known sin *as sin in this respect.*

Through the whole context, to viii. 3 inclusive, he speaks in the first person. This change is most forcible and natural. The main topic before this passage, and very much so after it also, is *objective* truth;— the Propitiation, and the legal results, and logical effects, of belief in it. Here comes in *subjective* truth; the inner experience of the conflict of the soul. How could this be better stated than through the writer's *own* experience, as the experience of a typical (but real) man?

lust] **desire** after forbidden things. The desire might, of course, be felt "without the law;" but the law gives it a new character and intensity.

covet] Lit. **desire.** This verb, and the noun rendered "lust," are cognates. "I had not known lust as lust, but for the Law's word, 'Thou shalt not lust.'"—The reference is to Exod. xx. 17; where the terms of the commandment illustrate the meaning of the word "desire" here.

8. *But*] This word refers to the statement "I had not known lust;" and this verse explains the action of the law in causing (indirectly) the knowledge of sin.

sin] As a principle, "working" evil desires as its result.

occasion] The Gr. word = the French *point d'appui.* The positive inexorable precept, *presented to the fallen will*, became the *fulcrum* for the energy of the evil principle.

concupiscence] The same word as that just rendered "lust."—The verb is aorist; **wrought**; but the reference is not necessarily to any single crisis of the past. St Paul probably views the whole past action of the Commandment and of Sin respectively as, in idea, one thing. Not, however, that there *may* not have been a crisis of "fierce temptation" in his recollection.—These remarks apply to vv. 9—11 also.

sin was dead] The context explains this phrase. Sin, as sin, as resistance to God, (see fourth note on ver. 7,) was *torpid* till the Law

once: but when the commandment came, sin revived, and
10 I died. And the commandment, which was *ordained* to life,
11 I found *to be* unto death. For sin, taking occasion by the
12 commandment, deceived me, and by it slew *me*. Wherefore

called it out. It was present; for certainly he does not mean that he
was once *sinless;* but it was present as a blind negative bias rather
than otherwise.

9. *For I*] The "**I**" is emphatic. Through this section, as often
elsewhere, Sin is quasi-personified, and distinguished from the Self which
nevertheless it fatally infects. It is an alien thing, an invasion, which
(at the Fall) broke in on Man's nature created upright. In this repre-
sentation of Sin, no extenuation of personal guilt is meant : with St Paul
"every soul that doeth evil" incurs for itself the Divine wrath. But the
separability in thought of Sin and the Self is not only true in fact, but
suggests the gracious coming deliverance of the Self from Sin.—We
are not to view the Self as a *good principle opposed to the evil principle;*
it is the *subject* on and in which the èvil principle works; but it is not
therefore identical with it, and is capable of being worked on and in by
the Divine Principle.

was alive] Here the context explains again. *Subjectively* he was
"alive;" unconscious of resistance to God, and alienation from Him,
and condemnation. See note on vi. 13, ("as those that are alive, &c.,")
where the *true* "life" (of acceptance) is remarked on. The state here
referred to was, as it were, the phantom of that. In this, he took for
granted his acceptance before God, or at least did not realize the
opposite.

the commandment came] Came home to conscience and will, in the
midst of this fancied "life" to God.

revived] Sin is viewed as (1) invading the soul (ideally, in the
Fall); then as (2) dormant till the Law crosses it; and now as (3)
roused to direct energy.

I died] I.e., "my previous state of consciousness was reversed." I
became *subjectively* dead; I "found myself" alienated and doomed.
Evidently the ideas of "death" and "life" here vary, as applied to Sin
and Self. The "death" of sin before its "revival" was *torpidity.*
The "death" of self on that revival of sin was *sense of doom.*

10. *ordained to life*] In the Gr. simply **to life.** Such was its natural
tendency. "This do and *thou shalt live*" is the statement of a deep
and holy sequence. The failure lies not in the commandment but in
the fallen will. And meantime no *modification* in the commandment
is conceivable ; for that would be to bend an eternal principle, the basis
of all peace and hope, namely, Holiness.

11. *For sin*, &c.] A reiteration of ver. 8, with more detail. The
"deception" here is fully illustrated by the history of the Fall. (Cp.
carefully Gen. iii. 4, 5.) The Tempter "took occasion by" the prohi-
bition to "deceive" the woman as to the character of God for truth
and love; alienated her will from Him; and so brought in death. Since
then, alas, he finds the human will ready-alienated to his hand.

the law *is* holy, and the commandment holy, and just, and
good. Was then that which is good made death unto me? 13
God forbid. But sin, that it might appear sin, working
death in me by that which is good; that sin by the commandment might become exceeding sinful.

For we know that the law is spiritual: but I am car 14

12. *Wherefore*, &c.] This is not a direct inference from the preceding passage. The holiness of the Law is rather assumed as an axiom
than proved. But the *fault of Sin* has been so brought out as to leave
the *faultlessness of the Law* vividly in view.

the law—the commandment] The general and the particular. Here
" Thou shalt not lust " is the specimen-commandment. Observe the
emphasis on the goodness of the *commandment;* it is not merely "holy"
but " holy, and just, and good:" q. d., "not only is the Law in the
abstract a sacred thing, but its most *definite and restraining precepts*
are so also, in the fullest sense." See Matt. v. 19; (also ch. xii. 2.)

This verse is sometimes arranged as the close of a sub-paragraph.
It seems better to take it as equally connected with the past and *coming*
contexts ; introducing now the fuller and deeper statement of the case.

13. *that which is good*] These words are emphatic in the Gr.—He
has said (ver. 10) that the commandment was found to be, in respect of
him, "*unto* death." Here he rejects the thought that it *was death ;* a
principle, or true cause, of death.

made] The Gr. verb is simply **did it become?**

But sin] Supply, **became death to me.**

that it might] Q. d., "it was permitted to do its work, that it might
expose its true nature."

appear] I.e. **come out to light**, "shew in its real character."

death] I.e. practically, "condemnation."

by that which is good] Namely, the Law. The sacredness of the
instrument enhances the evil of the agent which so uses it.

might become] Not merely "might *appear*." Sin, as it were, *sur-
passes itself* when it takes occasion from the pure Law to awake the soul's
resistance to the Blessed Lawgiver. Thus it "*becomes exceeding sinful*
through the commandment;" and thus its developement is overruled to
its effectual detection, which is the leading thought here.

14. *For we know*] The "*for*" points to the fact just cleared up
that sin, not the law, is the true cause of the soul's misery; which
results from the *collision of sin* with the law.—"*We know;*"— as an
admitted foundation-truth among Christians ; a truth not only implied
by the whole drift and often by the words (e.g. Psal. xix. 7, 8, and cxix.
passim,) of the Old Testament, but explicitly taught in the Sermon on
the Mount.

spiritual] Coming from Him who is a Spirit, and addressed to
man's spirit. The practical force of the word here, is to shew the law
as claiming internal as well as external obedience ; that of thoughts as
well as acts.

I am carnal] The pronoun is emphatic, and the form (in the best reading) of the Gr. word rendered "carnal" is emphatic too, as meaning that the very *material* (as it were) of the Ego was "flesh." It is remarkable how on the other hand, in e.g. ver. 25, he distinguishes the Ego from the flesh. But the contradiction is in form only. In the present verse he contrasts *Paul* with *the Law*. In ver. 25 he contrasts the "mind" of Paul with his "flesh;" and views the "mind" as influenced by Divine grace. *Paul*, as in contrast with the absolutely spiritual *Law*, is in his own view emphatically *carnal;* falling as he does (because of the element of the "flesh" still clinging to him) far indeed below its holy ideal. But *Paul's will*, in the regenerate state, (and the will is the essence of the person,) is, in contrast with *the same element of the "flesh"* still encumbering it, *not carnal*. In view of the Law, he speaks of the whole state of self as, by contrast, fleshly. In view of the "flesh" he speaks of his self, his rectified will, as not fleshly.

We here remark on the general question whether he means the veritable Paul, and Paul in the regenerate state, in this passage. (See on ver. 7 for some previous remarks to the point.)

It is held (*a*) by some expositors, that the "I" is purely general; a human soul relating a conceivable experience. But such a reference is so extremely artificial as to be not only unlike St Paul's manner, but *à priori* unlikely in *any* informal composition.

It has been held again (*b*) that he speaks as Paul, but as Paul quite unregenerate: or again (*c*) as Paul in the first stage of spiritual change, struggling through a crisis to spiritual peace; having seen the holiness of the Law, but not yet the bliss of redemption. As regards (*b*), this surely contradicts St Paul's doctrine of grace; for he views the soul, before special grace, as (not without the witness of *conscience*, which is another matter, but) "alienated and hostile as to the mind" towards the true God. (See Col. i. 21; Rom. v. 10, viii. 7, 8, &c.) But the "I" of this passage "hates" sin, (ver. 15,) and "delights in the Law of God" (ver. 22; see note below). As regards (*c*), the same remarks in great measure apply. In St Paul's view elsewhere *hostility* and *reconcilement* are the only alternatives in the relations of the soul and God. But the "I" of this passage is not hostile to God.

The *primâ facie* view of the passage, certainly, is that by the first person and the present tense St Paul points to (one aspect of) *his own then present experience*. And is not this view confirmed by what we know of his experience elsewhere? See 1 Cor. ix. 27: "I buffet my body and drive it as a slave;" words which, on reflection, imply a conflict of self with self, just such as depicted here. See too Gal. v. 17; where the conflict of *regenerate* souls is evidently treated of. The language of 1 Cor. xv. 10, *ad fin.*, must also be compared.

The records of Christian experience, and particularly of the experience of those saints who, like St Augustine, have been specially schooled in spiritual conflict, surely confirm this natural view of the passage. It is recorded of one aged and holy disciple that he quoted Rom. vii. as the passage which had rescued him from repeated personal despondency. It would be a very shallow criticism here to object that the Paul of ch. viii. could not be, in the same part of his history, the Paul of ch. vii.

nal, sold under sin. For *that* which I do I allow not: 15 for what I would, that do I not; but what I hate, that do I. If then I do that which I would not, I consent 16 unto the law that *it is* good. Now then it is no more 17

The language of the present passage is indeed strong; but it is the strength of profound spiritual insight. The man who here " does what he hates " is one who has so felt the absolute sanctity of God and of His law as to see sin in the *slightest* deviations of will and affection from its standard. Such penitence, for such sin, is not only possible in a life of Christian rectitude, but may be said to be a natural element in it[1].

sold under sin] I.e. **so as to be under** its influence. The metaphor is from the slave-market; a recurrence to the topics of ch. vi. But the difference here is that the redeemed and regenerate man is now in question, and the slavery is therefore a far more *limited* metaphor. He is now only so far under the mastership of sin as that he is still in the body, which is, *by reason of sin*, still mortal and still a stronghold of temptation. As regards *a claim on the soul to condemnation*, he is free from sin; as regards *its influence, its temptations*, he is liable. And such is now his view of holiness that the presence of these, and the *least* yielding to them, is to him a heavy servitude.—To the question, When was he thus sold? we answer, At the Fall and in Adam.

15. *I do*] The Gr. word is strong; **carry out;** perhaps with allusion to servile task-work.

allow] In the old English sense of the word; "to allaud," "to praise, or approve:" so "the Lord *alloweth* the righteous," Psal. xi. 6, Prayer-Book. But the common meaning of the Gr. is **I know**, in the sense of recognition; and this has a fit application here: q. d., " I know not, in a proper sense, what I do; it is done only under the (partial) *obscuration* due to the presence of the flesh." This is further explained in the next clauses.

what I would, &c.] Lit., and better, **not what I will, do I; but what I hate, that do I.** Here the " willing " and the " hating," if carefully weighed, are good evidence for the reference of this whole section to the *regenerate* soul in its conflicts. It is certainly out of harmony with St Paul's doctrine of grace to represent the soul, before special grace, as "*hating*" sin as sin, and "*willing*" pure holiness as holiness.—On the whole passage we must again remember that a soul *fully* alive to the profound sanctity of the Law is in view. *Not gross but minute deviations* (minute on the human standard) occasion these complaints.

16. *If then*, &c.] The emphasis is obviously on "that which I would not:" q. d., " If my faulty course of action is contradicted by my will, I thereby consent to the goodness of the Law, which also contradicts it."

17. *Now*] I.e. **in this state of the case.**

it is no more I] The Gr. is lit. **but now no longer I do it**, &c. The "*no longer*" is noteworthy, as implying (in the natural and common meaning of the words) a *different previous* state. It is possible

[1] See further remarks on this whole passage in Appendix E.

18 I that do it, but sin that dwelleth in me.   For I know
that in me (that is, in my flesh,) dwelleth no good *thing:*
for to will is present with me; but *how* to perform that
19 which is good I find not.   For the good that I would I do

indeed for the Gr. phrase to mean "no longer" with a *logical* reference
only: q. d., "you can no longer maintain, *after this statement,* that I, &c."
But the large majority of New Testament parallels are for the *time*-
reference: q. d., "it was once my true self, it is now no longer my true
self, which works the will of sin."   Divine grace has now so altered the
inner balance that the *conscious will* hates sin as sin and loves holiness
as holiness.—See meanwhile note on ver. 9; where it is pointed out
that even before grace *self* and *sin* are not, in strictness, to be identified.
But the present verse goes further; indicating a real antagonism now
between sin and the (regenerated) self.

18.   *For I know,* &c.] This verse intensifies the statement just made.
"Sin dwells in him" to such a degree that "no good thing dwells in
him:" the intruder has occupied the whole dwelling, and *every part* of
it is *infected:* by vitiating the affections and will, sin has spoilt *all.*—
Notice that the emphasis is on "good;" "no *good* thing:" q. d.,
"nothing that dwells 'in me' is unspoiled, however good originally and
in itself. For instance, affections, right and wholesome in themselves,
are spoiled by the absence of right affections *towards God.*"

It is possible to explain the Gr. words somewhat differently, though
in a way which alters the sense hardly, if at all: "For I know that it is
not a *good* thing that dwells in me, [but that *sin* does.]"   There is a
languor however about the form of such an assertion, quite unlike the
context, which insists upon a terrible reality of evil.

in me (*that is, in my flesh*)] See below on viii. 7, 8. "The flesh,"
practically, is the man as unregenerate, and then (after grace) the *Alter
Ego* of the still-abiding impulses and tendencies of evil.   Here St Paul is
careful not to say that in his whole condition then present there was no
good thing dwelling; for the Divine Spirit (viii. 9) and His influences
"dwelt in him."   And yet he calls "the flesh" still his *Ego;* because he
is contrasting his condition as a whole with the absolute and holy Law.
See note on ver. 14, ("I am carnal,") where is explained the apparent
inconsistency of the Ego being sometimes distinguished from, sometimes identified with, what is evil.

is present with me] **Is within my reach.** Meyer takes this to refer
to the unregenerate man; and such is his view of this passage throughout.   But see Gal. v. 17, and Phil. ii. 13.   In this context, the will
is represented as *uniformly* biassed against sin and for holiness; this,
surely, cannot be the unregenerate will.—Logically, no doubt, the will
of the *believing* soul ought always to conquer evil, because faith calls
in Divine power.   But then just here comes in the mystery stated in
Gal. v. 17, and which is a permanent *fact* of Christian experience.

I find not] The will is, on the whole, really sanctified; but its
exercise is impeded. The counter-influences of "the flesh" *bewilder* it
in the struggle. Its weapons, so to speak, are not always *drawn.*

not: but the evil which I would not, that I do. Now if I [20] do that I would not, it is no more I that do it, but sin that dwelleth in me. I find then a law, that, when I would do [21] good, evil is present with me. For I delight in the law of [22] God after the inward man: but I see another law in my [23]

Another reading, but not so well attested, is, "To will is present with me, but to perform that which is good, *is not so.*"

19, 20.] These verses almost repeat vv. 15, 17; not however as a tautology, but as emphasizing by repetition the two main facts in view, the reality of the renewal of the will, and the reality of the struggle of the flesh.

21. *I find then,* &c.] The Gr. construction of this verse is difficult. But the explanation is helped by remembering that **the law**, not "*a* law," is the right version; and all analogy of passages leads us to refer this to the Divine Law. There can thus be little doubt of the practical meaning of the verse:—"such is the relation between me and the Law, that my will is with it, my action is against it." The Gr. is (as nearly literally as possible), **So then I find the Law, with me willing to do what is good, [I find, I say,] that with me what is evil is present.** The construction is rapid and broken, but characteristic of St Paul. It is as if he had written, "I find the Law *thus* in its attitude; I find that what is evil is present with me, while yet my will is for the good."

He thus states, (what it is one main object, if not the chief of all, to state in this whole remarkable passage of the Epistle,) that the *subjugation of sin is not the function of the Law.* The awful holiness of the Law both evokes the resistance of sin, and, (in the regenerate) ever more and more detects its presence in the minutest shades. Another Influence (viii. 3) is needed, *side by side with this detection,* if sin is to be subdued.

Meyer suggests a rendering of the above clauses which is perfectly possible as regards construction, but in our view less natural, and less proper to the context: "I find then that with me, choosing [willing, lit.] the law, so as to do right, evil is present."

22. *I delight in*] Lit. **I delight with.** The Law, as the will of God, is quasi-personified, and the regenerate soul "rejoices *with it*" in its delight in holiness and truth. The Law's loves and hatreds are those also of the soul. Cp. 1 Cor. xiii. 6, where render, "rejoiceth *with* the Truth."

the inward man] The regenerate Self. Not that the phrase *necessarily* means the regenerate self, as does the phrase "the *new* man" (Eph. ii. 10, iv. 24). In itself it may mean (as Meyer holds) no more than "the rational and moral element in human nature." But surely this does not, according to St Paul, "delight"—with the delight of the *will*—"with the Law," until grace has rectified its fall. See Col. i. 21, where "the *mind*" is the *seat of* "*enmity.*" The phrase in this context therefore points to the regenerate state; the self as it is by grace, distinguished from "the flesh."—A fit illustration of this verse is Psal. cxix., where

members, warring against the law of my mind, and bringing
me into captivity to the law of sin which is in my members.
24 O wretched man that I am ! who shall deliver me from the
25 body of this death ?   I thank God through Jesus Christ our

the inspired Saint indeed "delights with," and in, the Law, and yet
continually makes confession and entreaty as a sinner.

23. *I see*] The true Self contemplates, as it were, the perverting
element, the *Alter Ego*, the flesh.   Such conscious contemplation surely
befits the idea of the regenerate state rather than that of the state of
nature.

another law] See on iii. 27.   The word "law" is used here with
the elasticity of reference pointed out there.   It means here a force
making itself felt consistently, and so resulting in a *rule of* (*evil*)
procedure so far as it acts.—It is called more explicitly "the law of sin,"
just below.

in my members] See on vi. 13.

warring against] The Gr. word implies not only a battle but a
campaign.   The conflict is a *lasting* one in this life.   See it described
from the other side, 1 Cor. ix. 27.

the law of my mind] I.e., practically, *the law of God*, "with which
my mind delights," (ver. 22,) and which in that respect it makes *its
own*.   The "*mind*" is here the "inner man" of ver. 22: so too in
ver. 25.—The word "*mind*" sometimes denotes specially the reason, as
distinguished e.g. from spiritual intuition (1 Cor. xiv. 14, 15).   Sometimes (Col. ii. 18), apparently, it denotes the rational powers in general
as in the unregenerate state; and again, those powers as regenerate
(xii. 2).   In Eph. iv. 23 it seems to denote the *whole* inner man, and
thus includes the "spirit."   So here.

bringing me into captivity] The word indicates captivity *in war*.—
The Gr. is a present participle, and thus need not imply a successful
effort; it cannot imply a completed one.   The *aim* of the "campaign"
is described.   And no doubt St Paul means to admit a *partial* success;
he feels, *in the slightest sin*, however it may be (in the world's estimate)
involuntary or inadvertent, a victory of sin and a "capture" of the
better self.   See note on ver. 14 ("sold under sin").—See 2 Cor. x. 5
for the same metaphor on the other side of the contest.

24. *O wretched man*, &c.] Lit. **Miserable man [am] I.**   The adjective indicates a state of *suffering;* the *pain* of the inner conflict as
felt by the regenerate "mind[1]."

from the body of this death] Better, perhaps, **out of this body of
death.**   The Gr. admits either translation.   The best commentary on
this ver. is viii. 23, where the saints are said to "groan, waiting for the
redemption of their *body*."   Under different imagery the idea here is the
same.   The body, *as it now is*, is the stronghold of *sin* in various ways,

[1] In Lord Selborne's *Book of Praise* will be found a most remarkable Hymn,
(No. CCCLXX), beginning "O send me down a draught of love."   The whole Hymn
forms a profound and suggestive commentary here.

Lord. So then with the mind I myself serve the law of God ; but with the flesh the law of sin.

CH. VIII. 1—13   Security of the justified. The mind of the Spirit, not the mind of the flesh, is their characteristic

There is therefore now no condemnation to them *which* **8**

(see on vi. 6,) and is that part of the regenerate man which yet has to *die*. The Apostle longs to be free from it *as such*—as sinful and mortal; in other words, he "groans for its redemption." Cp. Phil. iii. 21; 2 Cor. v. 4, 8.

Such an explanation is surely preferable to that which makes "body" mean "mass" or "load." Some commentators, again, trace a metaphorical reference to the cruelty of tyrants, (e.g. Virgil's Mezentius,) who chained the living and the dead together. But this is quite out of character with the severely simple imagery here.

25. *I thank God*]   Here first *light* is let in; the light of hope. The "redemption of the body" shall come. "He who raised up Christ" shall make the "mortal body" immortally sinless, and so complete the rescue and the bliss of the whole man. See viii. 11.

through Jesus Christ our Lord]   "In whom shall all be made alive" (1 Cor. xv. 22). He is the meritorious Cause, and the sacred Pledge.

So then, &c.] The Gr. order is **So then I myself with the mind indeed do bondservice to the law of God, but with the flesh the law of sin.** On "*the mind*" here, see note just above, last but one on ver. 23.   On "*the law of sin*" see second note *ibidem*.—"To do bondservice to the law of God," and that with "the mind," can only describe the state of things when "the mind" is "*renewed*" (xii. 2).—What is the reference of "*I myself*"? (for so we must render, and not, as with some translators, "*The same I*"). In strict grammar it belongs to *both* clauses; to the service with the mind and to that with the flesh. But remembering how St. Paul has recently dwelt on the Ego as "willing" to obey the will of God, it seems best to throw the emphasis, (as we certainly may do in practice,) on the *first* clause. Q. d., "In a certain sense, I am in bondage both to God and to sin ; but my *true* self, my now regenerate 'mind,' is *God's* bondservant; it is my '*old*' man,' my flesh, that serves sin." The statement is thus nearly the same as that in vv. 17, 20.

The Apostle thus sums up and closes this profound description of the state of self, even when regenerate, *in view of the full demand of the sacred Law*. He speaks, let us note again, as one whose very light and progress in Divine life has given him an intense perception of sin as sin, and who therefore sees in the faintest deviation an extent of pain, failure, and bondage, which the soul before grace could not see in sin at all. He looks (ver. 25, *init*.) for complete future deliverance from this pain; but it is a real pain now. And he has described it mainly with the view of emphasizing both the holiness of the Law, and the fact that its function is, not to subdue sin, but to detect and condemn it. In the golden passages now to follow, he soon comes to the Agency which is to subdue it indeed. See further, *Postscript*, p. 268.

are in Christ Jesus who walk not after the flesh, but after

CH. VIII. 1—13 SECURITY OF THE JUSTIFIED. THE MIND OF THE
SPIRIT, NOT THE MIND OF THE FLESH, IS THEIR CHARACTERISTIC

1. *therefore*] To what does *"therefore"* refer? To the discussion
of the inner conflict just previous? Or to something remoter in the
argument? The text is sometimes so printed as to carry on the connexion unbroken from ch. vii. some distance into this ch., and thus to
make the discussion in vii. 7—25 the premiss of this "therefore." But
against this we think that, (*a*), both in contents and in tone, ch. viii. is a
whole in itself, with one grand topic, the Security of the Saints, traceable
throughout; and that (*b*) there is nothing in the last paragraphs of ch. vii.
to *suggest directly* the present statement, though much to illustrate and
enforce it. Had ch. vii. *ended* with "I thank God, through Jesus
Christ our Lord," it might have *seemed* otherwise, (though see note
on those words;) but ch. vii. actually ends with the strongest assertion
of the sin-awaking and sin-detecting power of the Law and the consequent strife of the soul. It is thus far better to refer this exordium of
ch. viii. to the *whole* previous argument, but specially to such parts of it
as detail the way of Justification. More specially still it is connected
with chh. v. and vi., and the first section of ch. vii., which state (under
various imagery) the union of the justified with their Head, Master, and
Bridegroom.

Hitherto the Epistle has discussed and explained, from many sides,
the great matter of JUSTIFICATION, and its immediate results, (union
with Christ, bondservice to God, the liberation of the will, &c.). The
last topic thus considered is the *attitude of the Law* towards the soul—
an attitude such that the Law cannot (in the regenerate or unregenerate)
subdue sin, but can only expose and condemn it. This has been shewn
partly to vindicate the holiness of the Law, partly to expose the
malignity of sin, partly to re-inforce the truth, already proved, that
Justification is to be attained by another way.

Now, to the close of ch. viii., the argument (without wholly leaving
former topics and reasonings) rises to a fuller view of present results,
and to the first full statement of the eternal Sequel. It is needless to
point out the majesty and splendour which mark the whole passage.

no condemnation] The word *"no"* is strongly emphatic in the Greek.
The Gr. for *"condemnation"* here occurs elsewhere in N. T. only
ch. v. 16, 18. The cognate verb is frequent, and occurs e. g. Mark xvi. 16;
1 Cor. xi. 32 (last clause). As regards the soul, the verb means *to
pass sentence of death.* Such sentence *"is not,"* for those who are in
Christ; they "shall not come into condemnation, but are passed from
death unto life." (John v. 24.) "Who is he that condemneth?" (ver. 34.)
Observe that the word *"is"* is not in the Gr. There is no specifica-
tion of time. Q. d., "such a condemnation is inconceivable."

in Christ Jesus] See for parallels to this important phrase, vi. 11,
(E. V. *"through,* &c.,") xii. 5, xvi. 7; 1 Cor. i. 2, xv. 18; 2 Cor.
v. 17, &c. And cp. Eph. v. 30, where the key to its special meaning
appears. The brethren of the Second Adam are regarded as *solidaire*

the Spirit. For the law of the Spirit of life in Christ Jesus [2]
hath made me free from the law of sin and death. For [3]

with Him in the sense both of holy dearness and inseparable interest; specially the latter. The former idea is conveyed rather under the figure of the Spouse; the latter under that of the Body and the Head.—The whole previous argument of the Epistle makes it plain that those who are "in Christ" are those who have been "justified through faith." (Ch. v. 1.) No merely external position of opportunity or privilege can satisfy the phrase, in view of such a verse as this, or as 2 Cor. v. 17. On the other hand, the phrase (strictly speaking) indicates not the *inner experience* of the justified—which rather appears in the phrase of "*Christ in them*" (Col. i. 27, &c.,)—but their *standing and interest.*

who walk, &c.] Better, **walking, as they do, not according to the flesh, but according to the Spirit.** If these words are retained, they must be taken as a *description* rather than a *definition*. The *condition* of freedom from doom is, to "be in Christ Jesus;" but that happy position does, as a fact, result in, and so is characterized by, a "walk after the Spirit." The words will thus serve as a caution against the abuse of the doctrine of gratuitous justification ; *but not as a modification of it*. The point is admirably elucidated by Calvin's remark, that "it is faith alone which justifies, but the faith which justifies can never be alone."

But it is probable that the words from "who walk" to "after the Spirit" are to be *omitted* here. Almost for certain the *last* clause, "but after the Spirit," must so be omitted. Very possibly they were inserted here by copyists, who conceived the previous statement *too absolute to be trusted alone to the reader*, and so borrowed a quasi-note from ver. 4.

2. *For the law*, &c.] What is this law? We take it to be a *phrase by way of paradox*, meaning the institute, or procedure, of the Gospel of Grace. Cp. "the law of faith," iii. 27. It is the Divine Rule of *Justification*, (which alone, as the whole previous reasoning shews, removes "all condemnation,") and is thus "a law" in the sense of "fixed process." But also it is here "the law *of the Spirit*," because its necessary sequel (indeed we may say its final cause as regards man) is the impartation of the Holy Spirit, (see John vii. 39,) of whose influences so much is now to be said. And He is here specially "*the Spirit of Life*," because He is the Agent who first leads the soul to believe in the Propitiation (see 1 Pet. i. 2), and so to escape sentence of "*death ;*" and who then animates it with the energies of the *new life*. Lastly, this whole process is "*in Christ Jesus*," who is the meritorious Cause of Justification, the Head of the Justified, and the Giver of the Spirit.— The sum of the meaning thus is that the deliverance from doom is by faith in the Justifying Merit of Christ, which faith is attended, as well as produced, by the influences of the Holy Spirit, given through and by Christ.

hath made me free] An aorist in the Gr.; probably referring to the

what the law could not do, in that it was weak through the
flesh, God sending his own Son in the likeness of sinful

definite past fact of the delivering Work. The phrase thus refers to
Justification rather than Sanctification, which is a present process, not
a past event.—"*Me:*"—there is another reading "thee;" but "me" is
certainly right. The word is an echo from ch. vii. Cp. Gal. ii. 17—21,
where the Apostle similarly turns from the plural of general truth to
the singular of his own appropriation of it.—"*Free:*"—i.e. in respect of
condemnation—not in respect of influence; which indeed (see next note)
would be an alien idea here. He is here summing up the whole previous
argument of the Epistle.

the law of sin and death] I.e. the Law, which, as regards man apart
from Christ, is invariably linked with *sin*, as evoking it, and with
death, as thus, in the nature of things, calling it down on the sinner.
In other words it is the Divine Law, (instanced in that of Moses,)
which, as a Covenant, is by its very holiness the sinner's doom. The
word "law" is (though not at first sight) used in the sense of a fixed
process in both parts of the verse: the "new covenant" is linked, *by
the chain of cause and effect*, with the Spirit of Life; the "old
covenant," with sin and death.

3. *what the law could not do*] Lit. **the Impossible of the Law.**
What was this? The answer lies in ver. 4. The Law could not procure
the "fulfilment" of its own "legal claim;" could not make its subjects
"live after the Spirit." This was beyond its power, as it was never
within its scope: it had to prescribe duty, not to supply motive.—
Here, obviously, the Law is the Moral Code; just alluded to as inseparably connected with sin and death in its effects (apart from Redemption) on fallen man.

in that it was weak] Better, **in which it was weak**. It was "weak"
(i.e. "powerless," in fact,) *"in"* its impossibility" (see last note); in
the direction, in the matter, of producing holiness of soul.

through the flesh] The construction is *instrumental;* the flesh was, as it
were, the instrument by which sin *made the Law powerless* to sanctify.
—Observe how St Paul here again (as in vii. 7, &c.) guards the honour
of the Law; laying the whole blame of the failure on the *subject* with
which it deals.—On "*the flesh*" see below, on ver. 4.

God] Not in antithesis to "the Law," which, equally with grace, is
from Him. The antithesis to the Law here is the whole idea of the
Gift and Work of His Son.

his own Son] So ver. 32; though the Gr. is not precisely identical.
In both places the emphasis is on the Divine nearness and dearness
between the Giver and the Given One. The best commentary is such
passages as John i. 1, 18; Col. i. 13—20; Heb. i. 1—4.

in the likeness of sinful flesh] Lit. **in the likeness of the flesh of sin;**
i.e. of the flesh which is, in us, inseparably connected with sin. The
Apostle is careful not to say "in sinful flesh;" for "in Him was no sin"
as to His whole sacred being. But neither does he say "the likeness of
flesh," which might seem to mean that the flesh was unreal. The

flesh, and for sin, condemned sin in the flesh: that the 4
righteousness of the law might be fulfilled in us, who walk

Eternal Son took real "flesh," (John i. 14; Rom. ix. 5; Col. i. 22; &c.,
&c.;) and it was "like" to our "flesh of sin" in that it was liable to all
such needs and infirmities as, not sinful in themselves, are to us
occasions of sinning. He felt the strain of those conditions which, in
us, lead to sin. See Heb. iv. 15.—This is kept in view here (by the
phrase "flesh *of sin*") because the *victory over sin in its own stronghold*
is in question.

and for sin] The Gr. preposition is one specially used in sacrificial
connexions in LXX. Sin-offerings are frequently there called "*for-
sins*," (to translate literally). So in the quotation Heb. x. 8.—We are
prepared for a sacrificial phrase here, not only by the idea of Substitution so often before us in the previous chapters, but by the explicit
passage iii. 25.

condemned sin] I.e. *in act:* He *did* judgment upon it. Perhaps the
ideas of disgrace and deposition are both in the phrase: the sacrifice of
the Incarnate Son both exposed the malignity of sin and procured the
breaking of its power. But the idea of *executed penalty* is at least the
leading one: Christ as the Sin-offering bore "the curse;" (see Gal.
iii. 13;) sin, in His blessed humanity, (representing our "flesh of sin,")
was punished; and this, (as is immediately shewn,) with a view to our
deliverance from the *power* of sin, both by bringing to new light the
love and loveliness of God, and by meriting the gift of the Holy Ghost
to make the sight effectual. (See ch. v. 1, 5.)

in the flesh] I.e. in our flesh as represented by the flesh of Christ;
our sinful by His sinless flesh.—Meyer and others take the words as =
"in humanity in its material aspect." But through this passage the
idea of the flesh is an idea *connected with evil:* even the Lord's flesh is
"in the *likeness* of the *flesh of sin;*" and St Paul goes on at once to the
hopeless antagonism of the flesh and the Spirit. It seems consistent then
to refer the word here, in some sense, to the unregenerate state and
element in man; to man, in fact, as unregenerate. On man as such
the doom of sin behoved to fall: but in his place it was borne by his
Representative, who, to do so, behoved to come "in the flesh;" "in
the likeness of *sinful flesh;*" with *that* about Him, as part of His being,
which in us is unregenerate and calls for doom. Thus the idea is of
substitutionary penalty; fallen man's sinfulness was punished, but in
the incarnate Manhood of the Son.

4. *that the righteousness of the law*, &c.] Here is the (for us) Final
Cause of the Atonement. Both as a satisfaction of the Law as regards
God, and as the manifestation and pledge of Divine Love as regards
man, it was to give man peace with God (see on ch. v. 1, &c.), and so
to bring his will into real working harmony with the will of God. Atonement was to result in love and holiness.

righteousness] Better, **legal claim**; that which the Law laid down as
the requisite for man, as his only possible right state. (The form of the
Gr. word is different from that usually rendered "righteousness.") What

₅ not after the flesh, but after the Spirit.   For they that are

this "claim" is we find in the Lord's definition of the Great Commandments ; supreme love to God, and unselfish love to man.

fulfilled]   The context, as now interpreted, will explain this word.
The saints "fulfil" the law's "claim" not in the sense of sinless perfection, (for see last chapter, and cp. 1 John i. 8—10,) but in that of a
true, living, and working consent to its principles; the consent of full
conviction, and of a heart whose affections are won to God.   The Law
could not compel them to "delight with" itself; but the gift and work of
the Son of the Father do draw them "with the cords of love" to find
the Law (as the expression of His now all-beloved will) "good,
perfect, and *acceptable*."   This state of things is further described in
the next clause.

in us]   The justified.

who walk, &c.]   "Who live and act;" a very frequent Scripture
metaphor, from Gen. v. 22 onwards.—"*After the flesh :*"—on its
principles, by its rule.   So "*after the Spirit :*"—as the Spirit animates
and guides.

THE FLESH—THE SPIRIT

This seems to be a proper place for a few general remarks on these
two important words.

A.   *The Flesh.*   In N.T. usage, on the whole, this word bears in
each place (where its meaning is not merely literal) one of two meanings.
It denotes either (*a*) human nature as conditioned by the body; (e.g.
ix. 3, 5, 8; 2 Cor. vii. 5, &c. &c.;) or (*b*) human nature as conditioned by the Fall, or in other words by the dominion of sin, which
then began, and which works so largely through the conditions of *bodily*
life that those conditions are almost, in language, identified with
sinfulness.   (See e.g. the present passage, and vii. 5, 18, 25, xiii. 14;
Gal. v. 17—24, &c., &c.)   In the *first* connexion "the flesh" may bear
a neutral, or a holy, meaning; (John i. 14;) in the *second*, it means a
state which is essentially evil, and which may be described with practical
correctness as (1) the state of man unregenerate, and (2), in the regenerate, the state of that element of the being which still resists grace.
For manifestly (see Gal. v. 17) "the flesh" *is* an element still in the
regenerate, not only in the sense of *corporeal* conditions, but in that of
sinful conditions.   But, in the latter sense, they are no longer *characterized* by it; they are not "fleshly," because the *dominant* element is now
not "the flesh," but the renewed will, energized by the Divine Spirit.

B.   *The Spirit.*   In the present context this word, in our view,
denotes the Holy Ghost, except in vv. 10, 16, where the *human* spirit is
spoken of.   That it means here the Holy Ghost seems plain, because it
is regarded as a *regulating* principle, and immediately below (vv. 13, 14)
the Divine Spirit is described as the *regulator* of the will of the saints.
We do not of course deny the reality of the *human* spirit, even in the
unregenerate (1 Cor. ii. 11; Eccl. xii. 7).   But here, as in a large
majority of N.T. passages, the personal Divine Spirit is depicted as in
such a sense inhabiting and informing the regenerate human spirit that

after the flesh do mind the *things* of the flesh ; but they *that are* after the Spirit the *things* of the Spirit.   For to be car- 6

He, rather than it, is regarded as the dominant rule and influence in the being.   Thus, ver. 9, the regenerate are said to be "in the Spirit," not "in the flesh," not because their *human spirits* are in command of their being, but because *the Divine Spirit dwells in them*.   He does not dispossess their spirit, but so possesses it that He in and through it is the ruler of the man.

As regards the *human spirit*, (vv. 10, 16;) the word, in both O. T. and N. T., has now a wider, now a narrower meaning.   Now it is the whole incorporeal element of the being—the whole antithesis of *"the body;"* now it is the "nobler powers" of that element—the antithesis of *"the soul,"* in that narrower sense of "soul" which concerns instincts rather than conscience, reflection, and deliberate affections.   Man is thus sometimes "body and soul;" (e.g. Matt. x. 28, and cf. Rev. vi. 9;) and sometimes "body, soul, and spirit;" (e.g. 1 Thess. v. 23).   And in 1 Cor. xv. 44, in the Gr., a remarkable contrast is drawn between the present body, *"characterized by soul,"* and the future body, *"characterized by spirit."*—It must be remembered, however, that, unless in passages of exceptional antithesis, the distinction of soul and spirit may easily be pressed too far, and that in no case are they to be thought of as distinct in the sense in which they both are distinct from the body.   We have no hint that they are two separable elements; they are rather different aspects and exercises of the same incorporeal element.

5.   *they that are*]   This *"being* after the flesh" is the state of which *"walking* after the flesh" is the exhibition and proof.—St Paul here, and in a measure to the close of ver. 11, expands and illustrates the difference between the past and present state of the Christian.

after the flesh]   I.e. obeying it, (as the organ of sin;) making it their rule, in spite of their knowledge of right and wrong.

do mind]   Same word as Col. iii. 2, where E.V. has "set your affection on."   It means far more than to "like," or "care for;" it indicates the full preoccupation of thought and will with a chosen and engrossing object.—Such, according to St Paul, is the natural state of men, as regards any real bias of will and love to the *true* claims of the *true* God.

the things of the flesh]   All things that the unregenerate nature prefers to the "things above," whether in themselves guilty or innocent.

they that are after the Spirit]   Ruled and determined by His awakening, regenerating, illuminating presence; characterized by the fact that He dwells in them.—It is plain (*a*) that St Paul regards the two classes as mutually exclusive, and together exhaustive of mankind; (*b*) that he makes the "being in the Spirit" to be a strictly *super*natural state, the result of a Divine Indwelling once unknown to the soul, but now real and living; and (*c*) that this state is, in his teaching, an absolutely necessary condition of the true "sonship" of men towards God.   Further, he does not mean by it a state of *un*natural exaltation, (for nothing can be more practical than his view of daily life and duty; see ch. xii. &c., &c.,)

nally minded *is* death ; but to be spiritually minded *is* life
7 and peace. Because the carnal mind *is·* enmity against
God : for it is not subject to the law of God, neither indeed

nor of freedom from trial, (ver. 17,) nor of absence of inner conflict with
sin (ver. 13). He means a state in which the will is decisively roused to
that conflict, by the knowledge and love of God.

6. *For*] The reference of this "for" is not clear at first sight.
Probably the sequence of thought is that the difference of carnal and
spiritual preferences is profoundly real; *for* the former involves death,
the latter, life and peace. And it is implied that the respective persons
cannot possibly therefore interchange their preferences.

to be carnally minded] Lit. **the mind of the flesh.** The noun
rendered "mind" is cognate to the verb rendered "do mind" in ver. 5.
See note there. The idea includes choice, engrossment, affection towards
a congenial object. See Art. IX. of the Church of England, where "the
wisdom of the flesh" is the only phrase *not* admissible in a strict explanation. The E. V. here gives the sense as well as is possible, perhaps, in
a brief form.

death] Is this legal or moral death? On the whole, we explain it of
legal death, i.e. of *doom*. This idea implies the other, for the soul
which is incurring the Divine Sentence cannot be *morally* "alive to God"
in the sense of peace, love, and purity. But the connexion makes the
idea of *doom* more prominent : see ver. 7, where antagonism to the *Law*
is specified as the inevitable state of the "carnal mind." Thus the words
here mean that to have the choices and affections of unregenerate
humanity is to lie under God's sentence, and to be on the way to its in-
fliction.

to be spiritually minded] Lit. **the mind of the Spirit.** See last note
but one.

life and peace] This (by analogy with the view of "death" just above)
means a state of *acceptance*, in its aspect (*a*) of pardon and consequent
glory; (see last note on ch. v. 18;) and (*b*) of secure and loving intercourse with God, with all its attendant blessings. See on ch. v. 1.—Here
of course, in view of the argument of cch. iii. and iv. especially, we must
note *how* the being spiritually minded "is" life and peace; viz. not as the
procuring cause of these blessings, which cause is the Propitiation (accepted by faith) alone; but as the state of mind in which only they can
be realized and enjoyed.

7. *Because*] The *reason* of the radical difference of the two "minds"
is now further shewn by a description of the essential condition of the
"mind of the flesh."

the carnal mind] Lit. **the mind of the flesh** ; the same phrase in Gr.
as that rendered "to be carnally minded," ver. 6.

enmity] Cp. ch. v. 10. The expression here is as forcible as possible.
As truly as "God *is* Love," so truly, essentially, and unalterably *is* the
"mind of the flesh," the liking and disliking of unregenerate man,
"enmity," "personal hostility," towards the true God and His real
claims.

can be. So then they that are in the flesh cannot please 8
God. But ye are not in the flesh, but in the Spirit, if so be 9

Nothing short of this is St Paul's meaning. It is not to be toned
down, as by the theory that other impulses in the unregenerate may
counterbalance, or at least modify, this enmity. We must keep clearly
in view the reality of the claim of the Holy Creator to the *love of the
whole being.* To decline this, when it is the *creature* that declines it, is
not mere reserve; it is hostility.

the law] In its two great Precepts. Matt. xxii. 37—39.

can be] Again a perfectly uncompromising statement. The will of
the unregenerate, *as such*, is incapable of cordial submission to the claim
of the true God. Its essence is alienation from HIM; self, not God, is
its central point. When the man in reality "yields himself to God,"
ipso facto he is proved to be no longer "in the flesh," (see next verse,)
but "in the Spirit."

8. *So then*] Lit. **But;** and perhaps better thus. The *opposition* is to
the *idea implied* by the *previous clauses* of a condition which *can* love and
submit.

in the flesh] Of course in the *moral* sense of "the flesh," and as being
not merely beset by it, but characterized and determined by it.
Practically the phrase=*"after* the flesh" (ver. 4). The difference in
idea is that between a condition and the resulting action.—It is clear
that "they that are in the flesh" means "all men before special grace."
For the only other condition of the soul contemplated by St Paul is the
being "in the Spirit," i.e. actuated and ruled by "the Holy Ghost given
unto us."

cannot please God] See Col. i. 10 for the bright contrast of the
state of grace.—This ver. proves that "the mind of the flesh" is viewed
by St Paul as the true, ruling, determining, "mind" of the unregenerate
man. It is not only a dangerous element, but that which gives its quality
to his whole attitude towards God. He "cannot" (a *moral* impossibility of course is meant) "please God;" he cannot make God his
supreme choice, object, and rule; in short he cannot "love Him with
all his mind;" and no other condition of the soul than this can, in the
true sense of the word, *"please* God." Particular acts, in themselves,
He may approve; but not the real attitude of the doer's soul.

9. *But*, &c.] After this dark foil, in the picture of the fleshly state,
St Paul now gives (what is his main aim all the while) the opposite
picture; that of the spiritual, regenerate, state.

ye] Who are "in Christ Jesus;" "Jesus Christ's called ones." (i. 6.)

in the Spirit] See long note on ver. 4; and note on "in the flesh,"
ver. 8. To be *"in the Spirit"* is to be in that state of soul which
results in a "walk after the Spirit;" a state therefore in which the Holy
Ghost is the ruling influence.—The meaning is illustrated by the use of
the same phrase for ecstatic inspiration, (another result of the same
Agency,) Rev. i. 10.

if so be] The Gr. particle is more than merely "if," (which often =
"since," or "as,") and suggests just such *doubt and enquiry* as would
amount to self-examination. See 2 Cor. xiii. 5.

that the Spirit of God dwell in you. Now if any *man* have
10 not the Spirit of Christ, he is none of his. And if Christ
be in you, the body *is* dead because of sin; but the Spirit

dwell] See Joh. xiv. 17, and cp. Eph. iii. 16. The word indicates
the intimacy and permanence of the Holy Spirit's action and influence
in the regenerate man.

in you] I.e. of course, as individuals. For see the next words "If
any man have not, &c."

the Spirit of Christ] Evidently not in the *essentially modern* sense
of His (Christ's) *principles and temper*, but in that of the Personal Holy
Spirit as profoundly connected with Christ. Same word as Phil. i. 19;
1 Pet. i. 11; and see Gal. iv. 6.—The phrase is indeed remarkable, just
after the words "the Spirit of God:" it at least indicates St Paul's view
of the Divine majesty of Messiah. On the other hand, it is scarcely a
text in point on the great mystery of the "Procession" of the Holy
Ghost; the emphasis of the words here being rather on the *work* of the
Holy Ghost as the *Revealer of Christ* to the soul. See again Eph. iii. 16.

none of his] See again 2 Cor. xiii. 5, as the best comment on this
brief warning. Evidently St Paul reminds the reader that a vital
requisite to union with Christ is the present veritable indwelling
of His Spirit; such an indwelling as he is treating of here, which deter-
mines the man to be "not in the flesh."—The question thus solemnly
suggested was to be answered (we may be sure) by no visionary tests, but
by a self-searching enquiry for "the fruit of the Spirit." See the whole
passage, Gal. v. 16—26; and cp. 1 Joh. iii. 24.

10. *If Christ be in you*] Observe the immediate transition from
"the Spirit of Christ" to "Christ." See again Eph. iii. 16, for a deeply
suggestive parallel. See too each of the Seven Epistles (Rev. ii. and
iii.) for the identification (in a certain sense) of the Voice of Christ and
the Voice of the Spirit. The supreme work of the Spirit is to acquaint
the soul with Christ; hence the indwelling of the Spirit as the Divine
Teacher results by holy necessity in the indwelling of Christ as the
Divine Guest. Again cp. 2 Cor. xiii. 5.

the body, &c.] Lit. **the body indeed is dead**, &c. The sentence may
be paraphrased; "though the body is dead, &c., yet the spirit is life."
—"*The body*" is here the literal body (see next ver.), doomed to death,
and so already "as good as dead;" not yet "redeemed" (ver. 23).
It cannot here mean "the flesh" (in the sense of that word in this context)
because just below it is promised that the body shall be "*made alive*"
hereafter by the Holy Ghost; whereas "*crucifixion*" is the doom of
"the flesh." In short, the Christian is here reminded that the penal
results of sin still affect the *body* so that it must *die;* but that the regenerate spirit is rescued from the spirit's death.—Many bodies, indeed,
(those of the living at the Last Day) will not, in the common sense,
die; but they will cease to be "flesh and blood." (1 Cor. xv. 50—52.)

the spirit] Here the context seems to give the sense of the *human*
spirit; that which now "liveth unto God" in the regenerate man; the
soul, in the highest sense of that word. See long note on ver. 4.

is life because of righteousness. But if the Spirit of him 11
that raised up Jesus from the dead dwell in you, he that
raised up Christ from the dead shall also quicken your
mortal bodies by his Spirit that dwelleth in you. There- 12
fore, brethren, we are debtors, not to the flesh, to live
after the flesh. For if ye live after the flesh, ye shall 13

is life] A powerful phrase. Cp. "ye are light," Eph. v. 8. The spirit
is not only "alive:" life is its *inmost characteristic*. The "life"
here is that of acceptance and peace with God; the antithesis of the
doom of death. Of course the idea of the "life" of *love and energy* is
inseparably *connected* with this; but it is not identical with it.

Observe here that "Christ in us" is presented as the proof that the
"spirit is life." Here again (as on ver. 6; see last note there,) we
must remember that "Christ *for* us" is the procuring cause of life;
"Christ *in* us" is the evidence that that cause has, for us, taken effect.
See next note.

righteousness] Here, surely, the Righteousness of Christ, the meriting
cause of justification, and so of the gift of the Spirit, and so of the
indwelling of Christ. See on i. 17; v. 17, 21; where it is explained
in what way "righteousness" may be taken as a practical synonym (in
proper contexts) for Justification.

11. *But*] Here the fact of the death-state of the body is *met* and
qualified by the prospect of life for it also.

the Spirit of him that raised, &c.] I.e. of the Father; so described
here because of the following statement. See vi. 4, and cp. Heb. xiii.
20.—Here again the indwelling of the Spirit is practically identical with
the indwelling of Christ in ver. 10.—"*Jesus*" and "*Christ*" are not
mere synonyms here: Jesus is the Risen One as to Himself; Christ the
Risen One as the Head of His people. So Bengel.

quicken] **make alive.** Though the word "*raise*" is not used, the
reference is to the resurrection-day. Cp. 1 Cor. xv. 22. The word is
no doubt chosen to include the case of those who shall "remain to the
coming."

your mortal bodies] The Religion of Scripture alone of religions
(excepting Mahometanism, whose element of truth is all borrowed from
it) promises immortal bliss to the body.

by his Spirit] Lit., and far better, **on account of His Spirit.** The
body is the Spirit's "temple" now, (1 Cor. vi. 19,) and as such
it is for ever "precious in the sight of the Lord." Our Lord indicates
this same deep connexion between the soul's intercourse with God now
and the body's glory hereafter, Matt. xxii. 31, 32.

12. *debtors*] An emphatic word in the verse. Q. d., "We *are
debtors* to the Giver of the Spirit; to the flesh we indeed *owe nothing*,
for its result is death." The first part of this statement is unexpressed,
but obviously in point.

13. *ye shall die*] Lit. **ye are about to die;** on the way to die. The
phrase indicates a sure effect from the given cause.

die: but if ye through the Spirit do mortify the deeds of the body, ye shall live.

14—39 *Security of the Justified : the Holy Spirit's aid given to them : Eternal Glory prepared for them : the Divine purpose leads them thither*

14 For as many as are led by the Spirit of God, they are 15 the sons of God. For ye have not received the spirit

through the Spirit] The Holy Spirit; see next verse, and note above on ver. 4.

mortify] **put to death;** an antithesis to the "death" just mentioned as the result of sin. The verb is in the present tense, and indicates a continued process of resistance and self-denial. For the metaphor, so strong and stern, cp. Gal. v. 24; Col. iii. 5.

the deeds of the body] **the doings,** almost **the dealings.** ("*Praktiken, Machinationen;*" Meyer.) On "the body," as used here, see note on vi. 6. Cp. also the instructive parallel, Col. iii. 5, where "your limbs that are on the earth"="the body of sin."—This passage, and the parallels, shew how fully St Paul recognized the element of sinfulness as present still in the regenerate—so present as to call for intense resistance.

14—39. SECURITY OF THE JUSTIFIED : THE HOLY SPIRIT'S AID GIVEN TO THEM : ETERNAL GLORY PREPARED FOR THEM : THE DIVINE PURPOSE LEADS THEM THITHER

14. *For*] This word points back to "*through the Spirit*" in ver. 13. That brief reference to the Divine Helper of the soul suggests and brings in the marvellous passage now following, down to ver. 27, in which the Holy Spirit's work is the primary subject throughout.

as many as are led, &c.] The emphasis in this ver. is about equal on each clause; on the *condition*, (spirituality of will,) and the *privilege*, (son-ship). *Only* the spiritual are children of God; and the spiritual are *nothing less than* children of God.

led] As by their ruling principle. For illustration of the truth here referred to, see Joh. xvi. 13, and Gal. v. 18, 22, 23. The phrase is exactly parallel to "walk after the Spirit." The Galatian passage is enough to shew that St Paul intends not enthusiastic exaltation, but heart-subjection to the pure rule of God's will, in thought, word, and work; a subjection on the one hand perfectly voluntary in man, on the other hand perfectly due to the Divine Agent and Teacher.

sons] On this sacred word, as used here, cp. Joh. i. 12, 13; 2 Cor. vi. 16—18; Gal. iii. 26; Phil. ii. 15; 1 Joh. iii. 1, 2, v. 1, 4, 5; and below.

15. *have not received*] Better, **did not receive;** a reference to definite past bestowal. See on ch. v. 5, last note.

the spirit of bondage] **of slavery.**—The verse practically means

of bondage again to fear; but ye have received the Spirit
of adoption, whereby we cry, Abba, Father. The Spirit ₁₆
itself beareth witness with our spirit, that we are the chil-

"Ye received the Holy Spirit not as a Spirit of (connected with)
slavery, but as a Spirit of (connected with) adoption."—See vi. 19,
where we have a seeming discord, but real and profound harmony, with
this verse. The Holy Spirit's influence leads the regenerate to "yield
their members as slaves to righteousness;" but his *method of compulsion*
(see ch. v. 5) is such as to make their real subjection "perfect freedom,"
because divinely *filial*.

again] As in the old days of their "ignorance," when they knew
God only as a justly offended King and Judge. Cp. Heb. ii. 14, 15;
1 John iv. 18. It is scarcely needful to point out the difference between
the "fear" of the unwilling slave, or criminal, and the reverent and
sensitive "fear" of the child of God; (1 Pet. i. 17).

adoption] Same word as Gal. iv. 5; Eph. i. 5. The relationship of
God's children to their Father is sometimes viewed as *generative*, for the
change in their wills amounts to a change, as it were, of life and person
—a new *birth* (see 1 Pet. i. 3; &c.): sometimes as *adoptive*, in respect
of the divinely *legal* redemption which procures to them this inner
change, and also in distinction from the essential and eternal Sonship of
Christ, the "Own Son" of the Father.

whereby] Lit. **in which**; surrounded and animated by His influence.

we cry] Whether in supplication, or in praise. Observe the change
again to the first person, suggesting St Paul's sense of the holy community of the family of God.

Abba, Father] Same words as Mark xiv. 36; Gal. iv. 6.—The first word
is the Chaldee for "Father." St Paul places the Gr. equivalent after it,
not for explanation, (which was surely needless, in view of the well-
known use of the word by the Lord,) but probably because in prayer
and praise the Gentile Christians themselves did so. To them the
Chaldee word would sound as a quasi-Name, and would be as it were
supplemented by their own word; q.d., "Our Father Abba." So
Meyer; who suggests that the word "Abba" was already familiar in
Jewish prayers, but now specially sanctified for Christians by the Lord's
Gethsemane-prayer.—The present verse does not, of course, mean that
the view of God as the Father of His People was unknown in O.T. (see
e.g. Ps. ciii. 13; Isai. lxiii. 16), but that the Gospel had both extended
this view to others than Jews, and had intensified and glorified it by
fully revealing the Eternal Son as the Firstborn among Brethren (ver.
29). The knowledge of the Father as our Father because the Father
of the Son is among the greatest of the treasures of grace.

16. *The Spirit itself*, &c.] The "Spirit of Adoption" is here
seen, as it were, at His mysterious work, teaching us to "cry Abba,
Father." He "witnesses" with a witness which *concurs* with a witness
borne by our own "spirit,"—our own consciousness of will and affection.
On this "secret of the Lord" (Psal. xxv. 14) some light is thrown by
ch. v. 5. There the Holy Spirit is said to "shed abroad the love of God

17 dren of God: and if children, then heirs; heirs of God, and joint-heirs with Christ; if so be that we suffer with 18 *him*, that we may be also glorified together.   For I reckon

in our hearts;" i.e., in ways of His own, to assure the believer of the *love of the Father for him*. Meantime, the human heart thus visited is humbly but clearly conscious that it *loves the Father*. Thus the family affection of Divine Grace is owned *on both sides*. The Divine Spirit evermore *meets* the Christian's filial love with fresh assurances of the Paternal Love which is the origin of the whole blessed relationship. —The witness of "our spirit" is *so met as to be verified* by the witness of the Paraclete.

are]   The word is slightly emphatic by position in the Gr.

17.   *and if children*, &c.]   Here St Paul reasons onward from the primary fact, witnessed to by the Spirit, of the Christian's sonship.   He has in view now, more than ever yet in the Epistle, the hope of eternal Glory, when in the fullest sense the saints shall possess the Kingdom of God.   This possession he views as an Inheritance by virtue of Birth into the Family of God.—For the figure, cp. Matt. xxv. 34; Acts xx. 32; 1 Cor. xv. 50; Gal. iv. 7; Eph. i. 14; Jas. ii. 5; 1 Pet. i. 4; &c., &c.

joint-heirs with Christ]   The Divine and Human Eldest Brother (ver. 29.)

if so be]   Same word as ver. 9.   St Paul reminds his readers of the great fact and principle that the path of obedience and self-denial is the one path to Heaven.   And he chooses phraseology (see note on *"if so be,"* ver. 9,) which suggests to the reader's soul the self-enquiry whether the will is really brought into "the fellowship of the sufferings of Christ." (Phil. iii. 10.)—To *"suffer with the Lord"* is not only generally to follow Him in patience and meekness; but specially to bear, in loving fidelity, the pains of that conflict (outward, or inward, or both,) *against sin*, to which we are inevitably called by the fact of our union to Him as His brethren.   Such "sufferings," in one form or another, are never out of date.

that we may be, &c.]   "Suffering with Christ" is the necessary antecedent to "glorification with Him;" by way, not of merit, but of preparation.   The eternal bliss is a *gift* in the most absolute sense; (vi. 23, &c., &c.,) but the capacity to enjoy it is, certainly in a great measure, imparted only in the school of trial.   See, for an illustration of this passage, 1 Pet. i. 5—7.

together]   I. e. "together *with Him*;" in His eternal presence, and as sharers in the joy and dignity of His eternal kingdom.   Before the throne of the Lamb, His servants "shall reign for ever and ever." (Rev. xxii. 5.)   See too Col. iii. 4; 1 Pet. iv. 13; 1 John iii. 1—2; Rev. iii. 21.

18.   *For*, &c.]   St Paul here follows out the last previous thought, and especially the last word; the prospect of *glorification* with Christ after suffering with Him.   He dilates on its immensity and bliss, and never quite leaves the subject through the rest of the chapter.

I reckon]   A favourite word with St Paul.   There is the finest justness

that the sufferings of *this* present time *are* not worthy
to be compared with the glory which shall be revealed
in us. For the earnest expectation of the creature waiteth ₁₉

in the use of this word of *calculation* here, where the subject—so
full of rapture—stands in profound contrast to all *mere* calculation.
And this force is intensified to the utmost when we think *who* it is that
speaks thus; what was meant in PAUL's case by "the sufferings of this
present time."

time] The Gr. word is same as iii. 26, where see note. The choice of
word is most significant: the longest life of trial is but a soon-passing
occasion, compared with the eternal Future. See 2 Cor. iv. 17; 1 Pet. i. 6.

revealed] "When His glory shall be revealed;" "at the revealing of
Jesus Christ;" (1 Pet. i. 7, iv. 13, v. 1. See too Col. iii. 3.)

in us] Lit., and better, **unto us, upon us**; q. d., "to be revealed as
ours and laid as a crown, or robe, upon us."—With this verse on his
lips Calvin died, in extreme suffering, and unable to finish the quotation.

19. *For the earnest expectation*, &c.] The connexion of thought is:
"A glory is to be revealed for us, the children of God; and so real and
momentous is that glory, and its revelation, that it is intently expected
by 'the creature.'"—"*The manifestation of the sons of God:*"—more
lit., and better, (as referring back to the word "revealed," ver. 18,) **the
revelation,** &c.

THE EXPECTATION OF THE CREATURE

The remarkable passage, vv. 19—23, demands a few preliminary
general remarks. Among the many explanations of its meaning, two
are the most representative and important. Of these (A) takes the
passage to refer to the vague but deep longings of mankind for a better
future; (B) to the longings, in a certain sense, of "creation" as
distinguished from man, for a coming glory. According to (A) the
doctrine is that humanity, outside the pale of the believing Church,
shews in many ways its sense of weariness and aspiration; that this is
an unconscious testimony to the fact of a glorious futurity; and that
this futurity will be realized at the Consummation, when (not indeed all
mankind, but) all from all mankind who shall have believed, will inherit
the glory prepared for God's children. According to (B) the doctrine is
that the non-intelligent universe has before it a glorious transformation;
that this is to take place when the saints "appear with Christ in glory;"
and that in some sense there is a longing for this in "mute and material
things."

The decision lies in the true meaning here of the word rendered
"Creature" and "Creation"—the same word in the Greek.

Now certainly in one remarkable text (Mark xvi. 15,) that word
means *mankind*; so too Col. i. 23, (where render, "in *all the creation*
under heaven.") And the peculiar intensity of the language of thought
and feeling here ("earnest expectation," "hope," "groaning and tra-
vailing,") makes it certainly *difficult* to apply it, in so dogmatic a

20 for the manifestation of the sons of God.   For the creature

passage, to "rocks and stones and trees." The longings, however vague, of human hearts are certainly suggested at the first thought.

But, on the other hand, there are many well-known places (e.g. Psal. xcviii. 7, 8; Isai. xxxv. 1; Hos. ii. 21;) where rejoicing, or even prayer, is represented as uttered by inanimate things.   The whole tone of Scripture makes it certain that this is purely figurative; a reflection, as it were, of the feelings of conscious beings; for Revelation recognizes no "soul of the world."   But the language of such passages is a fact, and throws some light on this passage;—though this differs from those in respect of its *dogmatic* character.

And again, the "Creation" here is said to have been "*unwillingly*" (ver. 20) "subjected to vanity," i.e. to evil.   Now the doctrine of sin, so fully expounded in the previous chapters, forbids us to refer this to the unrenewed human heart, in which the perverted *will* is the secret of all transgressions.

On the whole, notwithstanding serious difficulties, it seems necessary to take the word "Creation" here to mean what we popularly call "Nature."   Thus the passage reveals that, in *some sense*, a future of glory, a transfiguration, awaits "Creation;" and the shocks and apparent failures in the present universe are, in a figure, taken to be this (absolutely impersonal) "Creation's" longing and expectancy.   We learn also that this transfiguration will not come till the final glorification of the saints; i.e. till the eternal state.   Our best comment will be, then, 2 Pet. iii.; where we find (1) that the "Day of the Lord" (i.e. of resurrection and judgment) will be attended with the fiery dissolution of the present frame of things; and (2) that then, in modes absolutely unknown to us, there will be, as it were, a resurrection of the "heavens and earth;" or, to keep close to Scripture, "new heavens and a new earth."

There is ample Scripture evidence (Psal. cii. 26; Isai. li. 6; Matt. xxiv. 35; &c.) that "*all these things must be dissolved.*"   The resurrection of Creation will be indeed as from a tomb.   And who shall *describe* "the body that shall be" of that New Universe?   Or who shall reconcile with *eternity* the idea of *materiality*, even when that idea is refined to the utmost?   But we believe, in our own case, that "*body*" as well as "spirit" will live for ever, in a state at present inconceivable.   A Universe *in some sense material* may therefore also be to last for ever, by the Divine will.

Note meanwhile that St Paul nowise dilates on this prospect.   It is mentioned by the way, to vivify the idea of the greatness of the glory of the saints in their final bliss.

earnest expectation]   Lit. **waiting with outstretched head**; a single and forcible word in the Gr.   See previous note for remarks on this and like words as in this passage.

creature]   Better, in modern English, **creation**; and so through the passage.

waiteth for]   The Gr. word again is intense; almost q. d., "is absorbed in awaiting."

the manifestation, &c.]   I.e. the "glorification together with Christ;"

was made subject to vanity, not willingly, but by reason
of him who hath subjected *the same*, in hope, because the 21
creature itself also shall be delivered from the bondage of
corruption into the glorious liberty of the children of God.
For we know that the whole creation groaneth and travail- 22

"the revelation of glory upon them," (vv. 17, 18.) They shall at
length be "manifested" to one another, and to the universe, in their
true character as the children of the King Eternal.

20. *was made subject*] Apparently, at the Fall. Not that there
was no animal suffering and death previously. God pronounced His
creation "good;" but this "goodness" may mean only *goodness in
respect to its then work and purpose;* and this may have included
death and suffering, as in fact it seems to have done. (1 Cor. xv. 21
refers to human death, as that alone is in question there.) From Gen.
iii. 17—19 we find that *some* change for the worse passed over man's
abode when he fell; a change impossible now to define. But it may
be that all distress and failure in creation are, in the sight of the Eternal,
connected with the entrance of sin, whether or no they have followed
the Fall in order of time.

vanity] Same word as Eph. iv. 17; 2 Pet. ii. 18. The word means
evil, whether physical or moral, regarded as (what all evil ultimately
proves to be) delusion and failure.

not willingly] See note just above on "The Creature." The word
here implies merely the absence of personal wrong and demerit in the
subject of the change.

by reason of him, &c.] Who was this? It is very difficult to decide
whether it is (*a*) the Tempter, who procured the Fall; (*b*) Man, who
fell; or (*c*) the Judge who punished the Fall. But we incline to the
latter, because the next words point to *Hope* in a way that suggests the
connexion of a Promise with the subjugation.—The sin-caused "vanity"
was thus inflicted "by reason of" the righteous doom of God.

in hope] These words form a brief clause by themselves.

21. *because*] Better than "*that*," as in some translations. St Paul
justifies the "hope," by stating the fact in which it will be realized.

itself also] As well as the children of God; though in other modes
from theirs.

the bondage of corruption] "Corruption" here (as in 1 Cor. xv. 42,
50,) is probably **decay**; physical, not moral, detriment. This, to
creation, is "bondage," in that it represses and foils its fulness of peace
and splendour.

the glorious liberty] Lit., and better, **the liberty of the glory**; i.e.
connected with the glory; attendant on it, involved in it. The period
of that glory is to be (not only for the saints, but, in another mode,
for the new heavens and earth,) a period of "liberty;" of developement
in undecaying power and bliss.

22. *we know*] By observation of the pain and disturbance everywhere in the material world.

23 eth in pain together until now. And not only *they*, but ourselves also, which have the firstfruits of the Spirit, even we
ourselves groan within ourselves, waiting for the adoption,
24 *to wit*, the redemption of our body. For we are saved by

travaileth in pain] A powerful and expressive word, indicating both
great present distress and the *definite result* which is to close it.

together] This word is to be taken with both "groaneth" and "travaileth." It refers to the complex whole of "creation;" all its kinds
and regions *share* the distress and anticipation.

until now] I.e. ever since the primeval "subjugation." The
"*now*" perhaps refers specially to the Gospel Age, as that which
heralds the final and eternal Age of Glory.

23. *not only they*] The word "*they*" (inserted by our Translators)
perhaps indicates that they understood the passage of conscious individual beings; the world of *man*. (See long note on ver. 19.)

the firstfruits] Same word as xi. 16, xvi. 5; 1 Cor. xv. 20. The idea
is not that "we" have the Spirit *before others have it*; but that we have
that measure of the Spirit which is the specimen and pledge of the
fulness hereafter. St Paul now contrasts the impersonal and unconscious creation, utterly incapable of the Divine Gift, with the human
subjects of grace.   The word "*firstfruits*" is used to suggest the
thought of incompleteness and anticipation.—Cp. the similar word
"earnest;" 2 Cor. i. 22, v. 5; Eph. i. 14.

groan within ourselves] As our Lord once did (Joh. xi. 33, 38). In
vii. 14—24, we see one great instance of this "groaning" of the
saint for entire freedom, in his whole being, from the power of sin.
There too we see that the longing for freedom is linked with the thought
of the *body* as the citadel of temptation, in its present state. Cp. 1 Cor.
ix. 27 for another vivid picture of a "groaning" conflict, and there too
in view of the *body*.—"*Within ourselves:*"—because the cause of the
groan is emphatically *within*. Not outward afflictions so much as inner
conflict are our burthen.

waiting for] Same word as "waiteth for," ver. 19; where see note.

the adoption] I.e., obviously, the final realization of our adoption;
for already the believer *is* "the child of God;" vv. 14, 16. So great
and blissful a crisis will the "manifestation" of the son-ship be that it
is here viewed as the beginning of the son-ship.

the redemption, &c.] The realized adoption will bring this with it, will
imply and involve this. The Brethren of the INCARNATE Son of God
will not realize the fulness of their Brotherhood till their *bodies* shall be
"like the body of His glory," (Phil. iii. 21.)—The Adoption, and the
Redemption of the Body, are not identical terms; but the former includes the latter, as necessary to it.—"*Redemption*" here (as Luke xxi.
28; Eph. i. 14, iv. 30; but *not* Eph. i. 7,) obviously means the actual
and realized deliverance. The redemption-price is paid already; the
redemption-liberation is to come.—See note on vii. 24.

Again remark this unique feature of Revealed Religion; an immortal
prospect for the *body*.

hope: but hope that is seen is not hope: for what a man seeth, why doth he yet hope for? But if we hope for that 25 we see not, *then* do we with patience wait for *it*. Likewise the 26 Spirit also helpeth our infirmities: for we know not what we

Some expositors take the body here to be the "mystical body;" the Church. But the context is clearly against it, giving us as the main idea the struggles and longings for a better future in respect of *material* things.

24. *For we are saved*] Lit., and better, **we were saved;** at the time of our deliverance from darkness into light.

by hope] "*Hope*" has the article in the Gr.—If our English Version is retained, the meaning will be that our conversion was effected, in one sense, by the discovery of "the hope laid up in heaven" for the justified. But the connexion of salvation with *faith* is so marked and careful in N. T. doctrine that it seems far more likely that the true version (equally proper in grammar) is, **we were saved in hope;** i.e. when we believed we accepted a salvation whose realization was future, and could therefore be enjoyed only *in the hope we felt in view of it*.— "*Salvation*" here is used (as e.g. 1 Pet. i. 5,) for the crown of the saving process; final glory.

hope that is seen] I.e. "the hoped-for object, once seen, (as present,) ceases *ipso facto* to be hoped for."

25. *But if we hope*, &c.] The emphasis here is double; (*a*) on the fact that we do *hope* for a given thing; i.e. look for it with a reason for so doing; (*b*) on the fact that it is (by its nature as an object of hope) *out of sight*. Of this general statement, the particular case is the Hope of Glory; and the inference is that we must be at once *patient* and *intent* (see next note) in waiting for it. But this particular application is left to be understood.

wait] Same word as ver. 19, where see note.

26. *Likewise also*] Probably the reference of these words is to the thought just previous; the *help* given to the anxious and weary Christian by a clear view of the ground and object of his Hope. Q. d., "as this view of hope calms and cheers you, *so too* calm and strength come from a yet higher source—from the direct influences of the Holy Ghost."— It is possible to refer "*likewise*" back to ver. 16, q. d., "*as* the Spirit witnesses to our son-ship, *so too* He cheers our weakness." But the reference is too remote to suit the character of this passage, where one reason for confidence is heaped at once upon another.

helpeth] Not *removeth*. The causes for "groaning" (ver. 24) remain, mysteriously permitted still, until the final rest.

infirmities] Or **infirmity**, as a better reading has it. The word includes all that encumbers and obstructs the "patient expectation;" and, as a special example, weakness and indecision in prayer. It may well indicate (as ch. v. 6) not mere imperfection of strength, but absence of strength; a condition of *helplessness* without Him.

for we know not, &c.] An illustrative case of the general truth.—The "*know not*" cannot mean total ignorance, but ignorance in details. St

should pray for as we ought: but the Spirit itself maketh
intercession for us with groanings which cannot be uttered.
27 And he that searcheth the hearts knoweth what *is* the mind
of the Spirit, because he maketh intercession for the saints
28 according to *the will of* God.   And we know that all *things*

Chrysostom (quoted by Meyer) gives as an example St Paul's own
mistaken prayer, (2 Cor. xii. 8,) which was not granted by the wise love
of his Lord.   We may instance also St Augustine's remark on the
prayer of Monnica that he (Augustine) might not leave her for Italy.
He went to Italy, but to be converted there; and thus the Lord
"denied her special request to grant her life-long request." (*Confessions,*
v. 8.)

maketh intercession, &c.]   The practical meaning of these profound
words seems to be that the Divine Spirit, by His immediate influence
in the saint's soul, which becomes as it were the organ of His own
address to the Father, secures the rightness of the *essence* of the saint's
prayer. .E.g. in Monnica's case (see last note) He so worked that her
desire to keep Augustine by her was not a mere craving of natural love,
but the expression, though imperfect, of a spiritual and intense longing
(infused by the Spirit of Adoption) that her child might become a child
of God.—It is true that in strict language, and no doubt in mysterious
reality, the Holy Spirit is said here *Himself* to intercede and groan;
but we mean that *to our understandings* such intercessions take the
form of desires of ours, inspired and secured by Him.

which cannot be uttered]   I.e. in all the depth of HIS meaning;
which must indeed pass human words, even when He inspires them.   In
any special case of prayer the saint may or may not *use words;* but, anywise, the root-desires that underlie the prayer, being the Holy Spirit's
promptings, are "unutterable" to the full.

27. *He that searcheth the hearts*]   Certainly here, the Father.   But it
is the more noteworthy that the same words are used of the Son, Rev.
ii. 23.—"*The hearts*" here are human hearts.   In them the Father sees,
below the surface of "ignorance what to pray for as they ought," the
sacred longings which are the expression of the Spirit's influence.

knoweth]   And meeteth with a corresponding answer; crossing perhaps the saint's *explicit* prayer, but granting the *implicit.*

the mind]   The whole Aim and Choice of the great Intercessor.

because]   If this rendering is kept, the connexion is ; "The Father
knows (and welcomes) the 'mind of the Spirit,' *because* in its requests
it is in Divine harmony with His own."—But it is better to render **that.**
"The Father knows the mind of the Spirit; He knows *that* He inter-
cedes in harmony with His Own will and purpose, and for His Own
children."

the saints]   Lit. **saints** (without article).   Such is the *character* of
those for whom He pleads.

according to the will of God]   Lit. **according to God**; in unerring
coincidence with the Father's will.   The words are used in emphatic

work together for good to them that love God, to them who
are *the* called according to *his* purpose. For whom he did ₂₉

contrast to the possible errors in detail of the saint's unaided desires
and prayers.

28. *And we know*, &c.] Here appears a fresh assurance of safety.
We have seen (1) the certainty of the son-ship of the believer; (2) the
fact that his sorrows are only the prelude of glory; (3) the Divine assist-
ance afforded him by the Holy Spirit, especially in prayer. Now, before
the final appeal, we have an express statement of the truth that the
children of God are the objects on His part of an Eternal Purpose,
which must issue in their final blessedness, and must thus turn "all
things" at last to good for them. This is stated as a confessed certainty,
well known in the Church.

all things] In the amplest sense. See vv. 38, 39 for illustration.
No doubt St Paul has specially in view the *sufferings* of the saints,
which would often tempt them to say "these things are against me."
But peace and rest, on earth, are perils also; and even such trials there-
fore need a similar assurance.—St Chrysostom's dying words were,
"Glory be to God for all things."

work together] As means in the great Worker's hand. It is instructive to note this expression in a passage where also the Divine Decrees
are in view. The eternal Will takes place not arbitrarily, but through
means; and those means are immensely various, and mutually adjusted
by supreme Wisdom only.

for good] Chiefly, no doubt, the *final* Good is meant, the fruition of
God in eternal Glory. But all true good by the way is included, as
part of the path thither.

that love God] As His children; in whose hearts His love has been
"outpoured by the Holy Ghost" (ch. v. 5). Observe that this note of
saintship stands *first* in this memorable passage; not eternal election,
but that conscious love to God in Christ which is its sure fruit, and
without which no speculation of mysteries brings the soul near to Him.
—It is the True God alone who makes this His unalterable demand;
"THOU SHALT LOVE ME."

to them who are the called] Identical with "them that love Him."
See on i. 6, for the profound meaning of "the call." 1 Cor. i. 24, 26,
27 is a clear illustration, in contrast with Matt. xx. 16, xxii. 14. In
the Gospels the word "call" refers to outward hearing; in the Epistles
to inward reception, due to a special and sovereign influence from
above.—See too Rev. xvii. 14.

according to his purpose] Same word as ix. 11; Eph. i. 11, iii. 11;
2 Tim. i. 9. See especially the last passage and Eph. i. 11, for the
sense in which St Paul uses the word here. It is the intention of
"Him who worketh all things after the counsel of His will;" and it is
absolute and sovereign, in the sense not of arbitrary caprice, (God
forbid,) but in that of its being *uncaused by anything external to
Himself*. The gift of life is "*not* according to our works, but according
to His own purpose." His "good pleasure" was, "before the world

foreknow, he also did predestinate *to be* conformed to the image of his Son, that he might be the firstborn amongst
30 many brethren.   Moreover whom he did predestinate, them he also called : and whom he called, them he also justified:

began," "*purposed in Himself*." (2 Tim. i. 9; Eph. i. 9, 11.) In the next verses, St Paul explains his meaning further.—(The word "*His*" is not in the Gr., but is certainly right in translation.)

29.   *For*] The word introduces a fuller account of the "Call according to Purpose."

he did foreknow] Same word as xi. 2; 1 Pet. i. 20 (E.V. "foreordained"). The noun occurs Acts ii. 23; 1 Pet. i. 2.—Comparing this passage with 2 Tim. quoted above, it is clear that the foreknowing is of persons, not of merit in those persons. It thus nearly approaches in meaning here to sovereign Choice of souls. See too xi. 2, and cp. with it e. g. Deut. vii. 7, 8.—Fully to understand and estimate such Foreknowledge, we should need to be the Eternal Being Himself. But our recognition of the extreme *mystery* should dispose us more, not less, to bow to the revelation of the *fact*. It is surely dangerous, if only in view of the context and tone of this great passage, (where all is made to bear on the safety of the children of God,) to attempt explanations which lower the idea of a sovereign choice to life and glory.—Cp. on the general subject, (on which it is obviously best to keep as close to Scripture as possible,) John vi. 37, 39, 44, 64—66, xvii. 2; Eph. i. 4; and below, ix. 11, &c., xi. 5, 7, 28.—See further, Appendix G.

did predestinate] Lit. **defined beforehand**; "marked out, set apart, ordained beforehand." Same word as Acts iv. 28; (E. V. "determined;") 1 Cor. ii. 7; (E.V. "ordained;") Eph. i. 5, 11.   All idea of *blind destiny* must be excluded; the "pre-ordination" is the act of the Living and Holy God.   But while we can thus repose on its justice, it is none the less real, effectual, and sovereign.

to be conformed, &c.] Here is the special regard of the pre-ordination; not merely escape from doom, but *sanctity*, the likeness of Christ. See Eph. i. 4. All the great Doctrines of Grace are, in Scripture, connected with holiness as their supreme aim.—The "*conformity*" here is illustrated by 2 Cor. iii. 18; 1 John iii. 3. It is incipient here, entire hereafter.   It is a spiritual likeness; for while the son-ship is in one respect adoptive, in another it is generative. See on "adoption," ver. 15.—The Gr. implies a *real and permanent* likeness.

firstborn] Same word as Col. i. 15, 18; Heb. i. 6; Rev. i. 5.   He is prior (1) as to time, "begotten before the worlds," *eternally* the Son; (2) as to dignity; "in all things pre-eminent."

many brethren] Cp. Heb. ii. 10—17; a passage remarkably parallel in some respects. See also Matt. xii. 48—50.

30.   *them he also called*] See above, on ver. 28, last note but one. In this chain of past tenses, the whole process is viewed as in its eternal completeness. We *look back*, as it were, from the view-point of glory.

justified] See on ii. 13. The links in this golden chain are strictly

and whom he justified, them he also glorified.   What shall 31
we then say to these *things?*   If God *be* for us, who *can be*

consecutive.   The "*call*" was to obedient *faith; therefore justification,*
by the Divine order, followed.   See cch. iii., iv., v.

glorified]   A past tense used, with wonderful power, of a thing future.
(See ch. v. 2, where we have the "*hope* of the glory of God.")   So indissoluble is the chain that the last link is here viewed as an accomplished
fact because the first links are so.   See, for a remarkable illustration,
Eph. ii. 4—6.   There the saints are already "seated in the heavenly
places *in Christ Jesus:*"—such is their union with Him that, just as
they are viewed as having gone through penal death, because He died, so
they are viewed as having entered heaven, (as regards *right* of entrance),
because He ascended.

It seems difficult, without violence to both the letter and spirit of this
passage, to deny that it represents the salvation of "the children of God"
as a line drawn from eternity to eternity: first, a sovereign Choice of
souls; then the Call of the chosen, resulting in their Faith and their
Acceptance; then the final entrance on heavenly Bliss of these same
called ones; and also their Note and characteristic now,—Love to God.
The "scheme" thus indicated, called by whatever name, has always met
with earnest criticism and opposition; but it is the only one which
naturally fits St Paul's language here and in ch. ix.   It is *really* alien
from Scripture only when it is stated as if it were a plan *of which we
saw the whole:* assuredly in these things "we know *in part.*"   But this
does not mean that we are not to accept what is revealed, just so far as
it is revealed, with sincere submission, and with that encouragement and
joyful assurance which certainly this passage, on any view of it, was
meant to excite.—See, on the whole subject, the equally careful and
decided language of the 17th English Church Article; especially noting
that the doctrine here stated is there viewed (in the spirit of this passage)
as "full of *unspeakable comfort*[1]."—It must also be remembered that in
the scheme in question the *sanctification* of the saved is viewed as quite
as much fore-ordained, and quite as necessary a part of the process, as
any other; and that the *only evidence to the conscience* that the person
is "foreknown" lies, not in any intuition of a Divine decree, but in the
presence of faith and love, and their fruits, in heart and life.   These
will be always attributed, and justly, to *Divine grace alone:* but the
presence of that grace will be traced *in them alone.*

31.   *What shall we then say*, &c.]   St Paul now applies the whole
previous facts and reasons to the final proof of the Safety of the children
of God.   He seems to refer not only to the former part of this chapter,
but to the whole previous argument of the Epistle; for there, rather than
in ch. viii., we find the doctrines which are here applied—the *sacrifice* of
Christ, a1 ⸤ consequent *justification.*   No eloquence could be nobler than
that of the ⸤ closing verses, taking them merely in point of language.   It
is the eloquence of profound fact and truth, expressed with the sublime
force and beauty of a lofty mind filled with the love of God.

[1] See further, Appendix **F.**

32 against us? He that spared not his own Son, but delivered him up for us all, how shall he not with him also
33 freely give us all *things?* Who shall lay any thing to the
34 charge of God's elect? *It is* God that justifieth: who *is* he

> *against us*] So as to prevail.—"*Who*" points the reference to
> personal adversaries; persecutors and tempters, seen or unseen.
>
> **32.** *He that spared not*] From all the humiliation and anguish in-
> volved in His incarnation and passion. For comment, see Ps. xxii. 1;
> Isai. liii. 6, 10; Matt. xxvi. 38, 39.
>
> *his own Son*] The word "*own*" is of course emphatic, marking the
> infinite difference, as to the Divine Generation, between the son-ship of
> Christ and that of Christians. Note that the Lord, in Joh. xx. 17, says
> not "our Father and our God," but "my Father and your Father, my
> God and your God."—For comment on the doctrine of the Divine Son-
> ship of Christ, as revealing the supreme love of both the Giver and the
> Given One, see e.g. Joh. i. 18, iii. 16, 35, 36; Rom. v. 3, 10; Eph. i. 6;
> Col. i. 13, 14; Heb. i. 2, 3.—"He spared not His Son: 'Tis this that
> silences the rising fear; 'Tis this that makes the hard thought disappear:
> He spared not His Son." (Bonar.)
>
> *all things*] Lit. **the all things**; all those things needful to the safety
> and bliss of the children of God.—See for comment, 1 Cor. iii. 21—23;
> and ver. 28.
>
> **33.** *Who shall lay any thing to the charge*] The Gr. word is technical
> and legal. The legal ideas of accusation, condemnation, acquittal, which
> have been so prominent through the Epistle, here reappear, in a final
> statement of the certainty of the Divine Acquittal of those who are in
> Christ.—No doubt the great "Accuser of the Brethren" (Rev. xii. 10) is
> in view in this phrase, though not exclusively.
>
> *God's elect*] The persons chosen by Him and belonging, as such, to
> Him; identical, manifestly, with the "foreknown, foreordained, called,
> justified, and glorified." The phrase occurs Matt. xxiv. 31; Mark xiii.
> 27· Luke xviii. 7; Col. iii. 12; Tit. i. 1. The word "elect," (chosen,)
> is always used in N.T. in connexions that indicate the highest dignity
> and worth in the sight of God. The present passage throws as much
> light on the greatness of its meaning as any other. Cp. with it specially
> Eph. i. 4, 5.—In the O.T. Israel is "My people, My chosen," (Isai.
> xliii. 20.) In the N.T. the chosen are "the Israel of God," (Gal. vi.
> 16: cp. Gal. iii. 29; Rom. iv. 11.) As with the old so with the new
> Israel, the choice is emphatically sovereign. On the other hand, the
> choice of the "justified and glorified" *takes effect through means;*
> through the Gospel. See 2 Tim. ii. 10; (a passage sometimes, but not
> justly, quoted against a sovereign election to salvation;) and *ante,* note
> on "work together," ver. 28.
>
> *It is God,* &c.] The Gr. equally allows the rendering **Is it God,** &c.?
> And this on the whole is more likely to be right, if only because we are
> here in a series of questions, (from vv. 31—35 inclusive,) the force of
> which is surely greatest when unbroken.—The doctrine of the passage is
> unchanged by the difference of rendering. The only *finally effective*

that condemneth? *It is* Christ that died, yea rather, that
is risen *again,* who is even at the right hand of God, who
also maketh intercession for us.   Who shall separate us 35
from the love of Christ? *shall* tribulation, or distress, or

Accuser must be God Himself; but He is pledged to be the very
opposite.

that justifieth]—"him that believeth in Jesus." (iii. 26.) The use
of this word here, so amply illustrated already, shews how entirely the
acquittal and acceptance now in question are "not of works."

34. *condemneth*] Or perhaps (by a change of Gr. accent) **shall condemn** (at the Great Day).

It is Christ] Here again, **Is it Christ,** &c.? should be read.—Observe
the level on which "God" and "Christ" are set in the language of
this great passage. The One is as truly the Supreme Judge as the
Other.

that died]—"FOR US" (ch. v. 8).

yea rather, that is risen again]—"by reason of our JUSTIFICATION,"
(iv. 25.) The Resurrection is "*rather*" emphasized because it not only
involves the Death, but is the proof of its Divine efficacy.

who is even at the right hand] As the Incarnate, Slain, and Risen
One; as wielding, in that character, "all power in heaven and earth;"
not merely accepted as our Representative, but *so* accepted as to be on
the eternal Throne.—Cp. Heb. i. 3; Rev. v. 6—9; &c., &c.—This is
the only direct reference to the Ascension in the Epistle; but what a
pregnant reference!

who also maketh intercession] Another item in this solemn enumeration. The enthroned Son of God is actually pleading for the justified,
in such a sense as to secure "*that their faith fail not.*" (Luke xxii. 31,
32.)—The fullest comment is Heb. iv. 14—16, vii. 25, ix. 11, 12, 24;
1 John ii. 1; and such O.T. passages as Exod. xxviii. 29.

35. *Who shall separate us*] He speaks in view of these amazing
proofs of the grace and truth of the Father and the Son.—"*Who,*"
not "*what;*" although the following words are of things, not persons.
This is in harmony with the intense and vivid tone of the whole passage.
Cp. John x. 28, 29; "*no one* shall pluck them out of my hand; *no one*
can pluck them out of my Father's hand."—"*Us*" is slightly emphatic
by position: q. d., "us, thus cared for and pleaded for."

the love of Christ] Same word as 2 Cor. v. 14; Eph. iii. 19. It is the
love of Christ for us, not ours for Him. The whole context here relates
to our security through the goodness of God.—In what sense are the
things now to be named viewed as "*not separating*" us from this love?
Probably they are to be taken as so many veils or clouds between us and
the (outward) manifestation of the love; things which might tempt the
believer to think that his Lord had forsaken him. St Paul assures him
that this cannot be really so; the separation is but seeming; the love is
indissoluble.

tribulation, &c.] St Paul had indeed a right to use such language as

persecution, or famine, or nakedness, or peril, or sword?
36 As it is written, For thy sake we are killed all the
day long; we are accounted as sheep for the
37 slaughter. Nay, in all these *things* we are more than
38 conquerors through him that loved us. For I am persuaded,
that neither death, nor life, nor angels, nor principalities,

the language of experience. See e.g. 2 Cor. xi. 23—27; 2 Tim. iii.
10—12. Cp. Heb. xi. 35—38, (of the O.T. saints.)

It will not be out of place to quote from the letter of a sufferer for
his faith, in the French galleys, 1739: "Having, by the grace of God,
made a Christian profession, we are bound to be faithful soldiers and
submit to the Lord's will. Our chains are where He has placed them.
Our persecutors think to disgrace us by putting us with malefactors;
but in this we are honoured of God, who gives us cause for rejoicing
that He counts us worthy to bear shame for the name of Jesus....God
has predestinated us to be conformed to the image of His Son, that
suffering with Him we may also be glorified together. Our life is hid
with Christ in God; but when Christ who is our life shall appear, then
shall we also appear with him in glory." (Letter of M. Villevaire, in
Bonnefon's *Life of B. du Plan*, p. 241, Eng. Trans.)

36. *As it is written*] In Psal. xliv. (LXX. xliii.) 22. The Gr. is
verbatim from the LXX. The quotation refers specially to the last
previous word, "*sword*."—By thus quoting the Psalm of the O.T.
confessors and martyrs as divinely meant also for N.T. saints, St Paul
indicates (as so often) the continuity of the believing Church of all time.

37. *Nay*] Lit., and perhaps better, **But:** q. d., "Such are indeed
our sufferings; *but* in all these things &c."

we are more than conquerors] "Wir überwinden weit;" Luther.—If
this glorious utterance (a single word in the Gr.) must be analyzed, we
may explain it as saying that through these sufferings the saints come out
not only unhurt, but with the precious *advantage* of a firmer faith, and
more burning love, and so a deeper capacity for eternal bliss. See
2 Cor. iv. 17.

through Him that loved us] Even in the thought of personal victory
St Paul does not forget that the *source* of strength is wholly above.—
For this Title of the Saviour see Rev. i. 5; (where however read
"loveth us.") See too Gal. ii. 20.

38. *I am persuaded*] Same word as xiv. 14, xv. 14; 2 Tim. i. 5, 12;
Heb. vi. 9. The word implies firm assurance on good grounds. Here,
of course, this amounts (unless the passage is to end with an anti-
climax) to the utmost certainty of expectation.

death] Through which we "depart, and are with Christ." Phil. i.
23. Cp. also, throughout this passage, 1 Cor. iii. 22, 23.

life] With its allurements or its sufferings.

angels, principalities, powers] The last word is to be transferred,
perhaps, to stand after "things to come." In that case it may include
the widest meanings of the word "power." As placed in E.V., it

nor powers, nor *things* present, nor *things* to come, nor 39
height, nor depth, nor any other creature, shall be able to
separate us from the love of God, which is in Christ Jesus
our Lord.

CH. IX. 1—6 *The problem of Jewish unbelief: Paul's
distress in view of it*

I say the truth in Christ, I lie not, my conscience also 9

must specially refer to (evil) *angelic* powers,—"*Principalities :*"—cp.
Eph. iii. 10, vi. 12; Col. i. 16, ii. 15; which assure us that the word
here, standing close to "angels," means not earthly but *supernatural*
(and here evil) dominions.—For suggestions *how* such powers might seem
to tend to "separate" the saint from the love of God, see Eph. vi. 12.

things present—things to come] Phrases in themselves quite exhaustive, whether or no they refer (as they may) to the present world
and the future world respectively. He who holds His saints in His
hand "is, and is to come."

39. *height—depth*] Vastness of intervening space. The Lord who
loved us is "above all Heavens" as to His bodily presence: but His
love reaches thence to our "depth" below, and holds us fast.

any other creature] A phrase meant to be absolutely inclusive—of
everything except the Uncreated One. And it is the Uncreated who
loved us!—The previous phrases had *logically* included "all creatures;"
but St Paul would fain preclude even the least definable causes of
apprehension.

shall be able] At any possible future time.

the love of God, which is in, &c.] A deeply instructive equivalent for
"the love of Christ," ver. 35. The "love of Christ" is the Divine
Love felt for us by the Eternal Son. And this, because He is the
Eternal SON, is also the Divine expression of the love felt for us by the
Eternal FATHER, who "sent His Son to be the Propitiation for our sins,"
and, in giving His Son, gave His Son's love to be our bliss and light.

This closing passage of ch. viii., taken as the climax of the whole
previous part of the Epistle, is a remarkable illustration of the vital
connexion between revealed Truth and sacred Love. It is out of the
dogmatic statements and discussions of the previous passages that this
utterance of adoring love and confidence comes forth.

Here closes the more strictly dogmatic part of the Epistle. But the
next three chapters, though less purely dogmatic, are, incidentally, full
of definitions of truth. Not till ch. xii. comes in the "practical" part
of the Epistle, in the ordinary sense of that word.

CH. IX. **1—6** THE PROBLEM OF JEWISH UNBELIEF: PAUL'S
DISTRESS IN VIEW OF IT

1. *I say the truth in Christ,* &c.] The discussion of the case of
Israel occupies this chapter and the next two. On the general subject

2 bearing me witness in the Holy Ghost, that I have great
3 heaviness and continual sorrow in my heart. For I could

thus introduced, we offer a few remarks. (See also *Introduction*, I.
§ 26.)

(1) The dedication of this large section to this special case is not
out of proportion. Israel not only was immensely important as the
Depositary of Revelation for ages past and the possessor as such of
inestimable privileges, (vv. 4, 5,) but at the time of St Paul it formed the
vast majority of all professed believers in the God of Revelation. The
unbelief of the great majority of Israel was therefore not only a distress
to the Christian's heart, but a perplexity to his mind, and so needed
very special treatment and explanation.

(2) He distinctly foretells a future of grace and mercy for Israel, on
a grand scale of conversion. A time is to come when "blindness in
part" is no longer to characterize Israel as a people; that is to say, a
time when unbelief, if existing still at all, shall be the exception, not
the rule.

(3) He does not touch on any other than the spiritual aspects of that
future. As to the question of a political, or local, restoration of Israel,
or both, he is entirely silent whether to affirm or deny; and so in all
his Epistles. So it is also in all the N.T. Epistles. St Paul's great
object here is (1) to explain the spiritual alienation of the mass of
Israelites, and (2) to open the prospect of its blessed reversal.

in Christ] As a "member of Christ," and so bound to inviolable
truthfulness; and as speaking to other "members." (Eph. iv. 25.)

I lie not] On this and similar appeals see on i. 9.—The special
reason for such words here is, perhaps, the thought that both Gentile
Christians and unbelieving Jews (for different reasons) might think him
now regardless of his earthly kindred, because so resolute in teaching
the entire spiritual equality of all believers, Jew or Gentile. The
Epistle might possibly be heard or read by unconverted Jews; and such
words as these might reach their hearts.

my conscience also bearing me witness] Paul, as a man speaking to
men, was corroborated (in his own consciousness) by Paul speaking to
himself. *Word* and *conscience* coincided in statement.

in the Holy Ghost] Who, as the Sanctifier, pervades the conscience
with new and intense light and sensibility. The reference is not to
inspiration but to *spirituality*, of which he has said so much in ch. viii.

2. *that I have*, &c.] More lit. **that I have great grief, and my
heart has incessant pain.**—Very wonderful, and profoundly true, is
this expression of intense grief just after the "joy unspeakable" of
ch. viii. The heart is capable of a vast complexity of emotions, and
none the less so when it is "spiritual." Cp. 1 Pet. i. 6.—No doubt the
expressions here are the more intense *because* of the contrasted recent
view of the coming glory of believers, and their security in the love
and covenant of God.

3. *I could wish*] Lit., **I was wishing**; the imperfect. A similar
imperfect occurs Gal. iv. 20; where lit., "I was desiring." Without

wish that myself were accursed from Christ for my brethren, my kinsmen according to the flesh: who are Israel- ⁴
ites; to whom pertaineth the adoption, and the glory, and

discussing the grammatical theory of the construction we may *paraphrase*, **I was on the way to wish**, or, **I was in course of wishing**.
Two things are implied; the *tendency* to the wish; and the *obstruction*
of it.—The Gr. for "to wish" here means specially to *express* a wish;
almost, "to pray." Paul's love for Israel is such that, but for certain
preventing reasons, he would form a wish to be cut off from Christ for
their sakes.

myself] Strongly emphatic in the Gr. His intense love for his
brethren constrains him to contemplate *himself* as their victim, if such
a victim there could be.

accursed] Lit. **an anathema**; a thing devoted to ruin by a solemn
curse. Such is the meaning of the word wherever else used by St Paul;
1 Cor. xii. 3, xvi. 22; Gal. i. 8, 9. (See Bp Lightfoot's note on Gal.
i. 8.) No milder meaning will suit the intensity of this passage. St Paul
could even have asked for the extremest imaginable suffering possible
for man—but for certain reasons in the nature of things which forbade
him. These reasons may be given thus:—To desire the curse of God
would be to desire not only suffering, but moral alienation from Him,
the withdrawal of the soul's capacity to love Him. Thus the wish
would be in effect an act of "greater love for our neighbour than for
God[1]." Again, the redeemed soul is "not its own:" to wish the self
to be accursed from Christ would thus be to wish the loss of that which
He has "bought and made *His own*."—But, the logical reason of the
matter apart, we have only to read the close of ch. viii. to see how
entire a moral impossibility it was for St Paul to *complete* such a wish.—
The words here were perhaps written with a tacit reference to the
memorable passage, Exod. xxxii. 32, 33. The answer there given to
the request of Moses would alone suffice to forbid the *completion* of any
similar request thereafter.

4. *Israelites*] "The absolute name, that which expressed the whole
dignity and glory of a member of the theocratic nation, of the people
in peculiar covenant with God, was *Israelite*." (Abp Trench, *New Testament Synonyms*.) It was thus distinguished from both *Hebrew* and
Jew, (*Judæus*,) of which (1) relates rather to language, and (2) to the
national (rather than theocratic) difference between the People and the
Gentiles.

the adoption] See Exod. iv. 22; Hos. xi. 1; also Deut. xiv. 1; Isai.
lxiii. 16. Israel, as a nation, was taken into a relationship with God
altogether peculiar, as to nearness and affection. See Hos. xi. 8 for
some wonderful utterances of the Divine Paternity. This son-ship was
indeed (unlike that in ch. viii.) of the *mass* rather than of *individuals*.
But it was a grant of high privilege and mercy.

the glory] In the special sense of the *Shechinah*, the mysteriously
visible manifestation of the Divine Presence "between the Cherubim"

[1] Rev. H. Moule's *Suggestive Commentary* on this Epistle.

the covenants, and the giving of the law, and the service *of*
5 *God*, and the promises; whose *are* the fathers, and of
whom as concerning the flesh Christ *came*, who is over all,
God blessed for ever. Amen.

on the mercy-seat. See Exod. xxv. 22; Levit. xvi. 2; Psal. lxxx. 1,
xcix. 1; Isai. xxxvii. 16.—It does not appear that this Light was *perpetual;* but anywise it was a pledge of sacred privilege and a means
of communication entirely unique on earth. This *Shechinah* is, in
the Targums, often used as a paraphrase for the Holy Name, and in
Isai. vi. 1 the LXX have the phrase "glory of God" where the Hebrew has the Holy Name.—This special reference of the word "glory"
is more in keeping with the *enumeration* here than any wider reference.

   the covenants] With Abraham, Moses, Levi, David. See Gen. xvii.
4, 11, 19; Exod. xxxi. 16, xxxiv. 28; Mal. ii. 4, 5; Psal. lxxxix. 28, 34.
The reference here is of course *not* (as in Gal. iv. 24) to the *Old and
New Covenants* of Works and Grace respectively.

   the giving of the law] **the Legislation.** The *privilege* of the possession of a Divine Code is dwelt on, Deut. iv. 8; Neh. ix. 13, 14.

   the service] The Gr. specially signifies the Temple-worship. Cp.
Heb. ix. 1. The solemn round of ordinances, all "mysteriously meant,"
under the Old Covenant is specially remarkable in contrast to the com-
parative absence of detailed directions for worship under the New.—
The words "*of God*" are an explanatory addition in E. V.

   the promises] Of the Land, and of the Messiah. The latter promise
was a possession of Israel in the sense that it was to be fulfilled exclusively *through*, though not exclusively *for*, Israel. See John iv. 22. In
Him who is "the Son of David, the Son of Abraham," (Matt. i. 1,)
the great Fulfilment remains for ever a special glory of the ancient
People.—Here, as everywhere, St Paul looks to the Prophecies as a
preeminent reality in the dealings of God with Man. To him they
were no "national aspirations," but voices from eternity.

   5. *the fathers*] Cp. xi. 28. The reference is probably specially to
Abraham, Isaac, and Jacob. But David is also "the *patriarch* David;"
Acts. ii 29.—These sacred Persons are now mentioned, after the previous
sacred Things, so as to usher in the mention of the Christ Himself.

   of whom] **out of whom**; not merely "*whose*," as in previous
clauses; perhaps to keep the thought in view that HE was not exclusively *for* Israel, though wholly *of* Israel.

   as concerning the flesh] In respect of His human Parent's descent
He also was Jewish. His blessed Humanity was indeed, on the Paternal
side, "of God ; " (Meyer;) but this distinction is not in view here, where
the plain meaning is that, by human parentage, He was Jewish.

   who is over all, God blessed for ever] The Gr. may (with more or
less facility) be translated, (1) as in E. V.; or (2) **who is God over
all,** &c.;" or (3) **blessed for ever [be] the God who is over all.**
Between (1) and (2) the practical difference is slight, but (1) is the easier
and safer grammatically: between (3) and the others the difference is,
of course, complete. If we adopt (3) we take the Apostle to be led,

6—13   Limitations of the problem from facts of Divine election

Not as though the word of God hath taken none effect. ⁶

by the mention of the Incarnation, to utter a sudden doxology to the God who gave that crowning mercy.   In favour of this view it is urged, (not only by Socinian commentators and the like, but by some of the orthodox, as Meyer,) that St Paul nowhere else styles the Lord simply "God;" but always rather "the Son of God,"&c.   By this they do not mean to deny or detract from the Lord's Deity, but they maintain that St Paul always so states that Deity, under Divine guidance, as to mark the "Subordination of the Son"—that Subordination which is not a difference of Nature, Power, or Eternity, but of Order; just such as is marked by the simple but profound words FATHER and SON.—But on the other hand there is Tit. ii. 13, where the Gr. is (at least) *perfectly capable* of the rendering "our great God and Saviour Jesus Christ."   And if, as St John is witness, it is divinely true that "the WORD is GOD," it is surely far from wonderful if here and there, in peculiar connexions, an equally inspired Teacher should so speak of Christ, even though guided to keep another side of the truth habitually in view.   Now, beyond all fair question, the Greek here (in view of the usual order of words in ascriptions of praise) is certainly best rendered as in E. V.: had it not been for controversy, probably, no other rendering would have been suggested.   And lastly, the context far rather suggests a *lament* (over the fall of Israel) than an ascription of praise; while it also pointedly suggests *some allusion* to the *super-* human Nature of Christ, by the words "*according to the flesh.*"   But if there is such an allusion, then it must lie in the words "*over all, God.*"—We thus advocate the rendering of the E. V., as clearly the best grammatically, and the best suited to the context.— Observe lastly that while St John (i. 1; xx. 28; and *perhaps* i. 18, where E. V. "Son;") uses the word GOD of Christ, and in xii. 41 distinctly implies that He is JEHOVAH, (Isai. vi. 5,) yet his Gospel is quite as full of the Filial Subordination as of the Filial Deity and Co-equality.   So that the *words* of St Paul here are scarcely more exceptional in him than they would be in St John.

for ever]   Lit. **unto the ages**; the familiar phrase for endless dura- tion, under all possible developements, where God and the other world are in question.

Amen]   The word is properly a Hebrew adverb ("*surely*"), repeat- edly used as here in O. T.   See e.g. Deut. xxvii. 15; Psal. lxxii. 19; Jer. xi. 5 (marg. E. V.).

6—13   LIMITATIONS OF THE PROBLEM FROM FACTS OF DIVINE ELECTION

6.   *Not as though*, &c.]   Here begins a paragraph, and with it the main subject of the rest of this chapter.   St Paul has expressed his intense grief over the failure of the mass of his brethren to "inherit the promises."   He now, in the true manner of the Scripture writers, vin-

7 For they *are* not all Israel, which are of Israel: neither,
because they are the seed of Abraham, *are they* all children:
8 but, In Isaac shall thy seed be called. That is, *They
which are* the children of the flesh, these *are* not the children
of God: but the children of the promise are counted for the
9 seed. For this *is* the word of promise, At this time will

dicates the veracity and majesty of the Faithful Promiser. This he does
by considerations on Divine Sovereignty and Election.

the word of God] The Promise to Abraham, that his seed should be
blessed and a blessing.

hath taken none effect] Lit. **hath fallen out, hath failed**.

Israel—Israel] Probably (1) is the descendants, (2) the forefather,
Jacob. The emphasis of the Gr. is not precisely as in E. V., but
rather (with a slight paraphrase) "*Israel*" (*as intended in the Promise*)
"*is not the total of the descendants of Israel.*"

7. *neither because*, &c.] An illustration from manifest fact, to shew
that an apparently inclusive promise may be limited. We may paraphrase: "Abraham's descendants, again, are not all his '*children*' *in
the sense contemplated*, just because they are his descendants; on the contrary, there is a distinct limitation: 'in *Isaac* and his line are they who
shall bear the title of thy seed.'"—The cases of Israel's and Abraham's
"children" are not here precisely parallel; because *all* Israel's bodily
descendants inherited a Promise, in some sense. But the second case
illustrates the possibility of a limitation in the first.

In Isaac, &c.] The quotation is verbatim from LXX., Gen. xxi. 12,
and literally according to the Hebrew. It is introduced without "It is
written," as being perfectly well known with its context. See on iv. 18.

8. *That is*, &c.] We may paraphrase this verse, after the Gr.;
"That is," (in view of both the vv. 6, 7,) "the children of God" (it
being implied in the Promise that Abraham's children should be also
His,) "are not the mere bodily offspring of Abraham, no more and no
fewer; rather, the children defined by special promise are taken to
be the whole posterity in question."

children of the promise] *Perhaps* in this phrase the Promise is quasi-
personified; so St Chrysostom in Meyer. But see Luke xx. 36 for a
somewhat similar case. There the phrase "children of the resurrection"
must mean "persons who partake resurrection glory;" but the special
form of words is modified by the phrase "children of God" just preceding. So probably here the phrase "children of the promise," for "persons defined by the promise," is suggested by "children of the flesh"
just preceding.

9. *of promise*] Lit. **of the promise**; the promise just referred to
in the illustrative case. The "children of God" among Abraham's
bodily descendants were to be limited within the descendants by *Sarah;*
i.e. within Isaac's line.

At this time] I.e. of the next year. (Gen. xviii. 10.) The quotation

I come, and Sara shall have a son. And not only 10
this ; but when Rebecca also had conceived by one, *even* by
our father Isaac ; (for *the children* being not yet born, neither 11
having done any good or evil, that the purpose of God according to election might stand, not of works, but of him

is nearly literally after the Hebrew, but varies (merely verbally) from
the LXX.

Sara] The name of limitation. Hagar's son was also "Abraham's
seed ;" but not in the intention of the Promise.

10. *And not only this*] Here a still stronger example of sovereign
choice occurs. Isaac and Ishmael had only one parent in common ;
Jacob and Esau had both. In the former case, the choice of Isaac was
declared only after Ishmael's birth and childhood ; in the latter, the
choice of Jacob was declared while both brothers were in the womb.—
The Greek construction in vv. 10—12 is irregular, but perfectly clear.

by one] In contrast to the *divided parentage* of Abraham's sons.

our father Isaac] Here named with emphasis, as shewing that even
within the inner circle of promise ("In *Isaac* shall thy seed, &c.,") there
was still an election.

11. *being not yet born*, &c.] Nothing could go beyond this verse in
stating that the *reasons* of the Divine Choice lie wholly within the
Divine Mind, and not in the works and characters of the chosen.

the purpose of God according to election] So according to the best
order of the Gr. words. Another order, not so well supported, gives
"*the purpose according to God's election.*" The meaning is the same in
either case.—On "*the purpose,*" see last note on viii. 28.—"*According
to election*":—i. e. as determined, or characterized, by the sovereign
Choice of the Divine Mind. In the case of Esau and Jacob, the
"purpose according to election" does not, at least explicitly, mean a
purpose of eternal salvation. But St Paul is evidently here treating the
Divine Choice in the widest and most absolute respects ; and the
sovereign gift to Jacob of sacred privileges, determining his whole course
and that of his posterity, is thus taken as illustrating the fact of an
equally sovereign gift, to "whomsoever God will," of the capacity to
repent, believe, and love. Throughout the argument we must remember
who the "elect" are in the grand special case in hand, viz. the "remnant" who actually (not only potentially) are true believers, under both
the Old and New Dispensations. See especially xi. 2—8.

ELECTION

On the general subject of the Divine Election we may remark,

(1) That "the arguments of the Apostle are founded on two assumptions. The first is, that the Scriptures are the word of God ; and the
second, that whatever God actually does cannot be unrighteous. Consequently, any objection which can be shewn to militate against either an
express declaration of Scripture, or an obvious fact in providence, is fairly
answered." (Dr Hodge, *in loc*.) It is almost needless to add that such

₁₂ that calleth ;) it was said unto her, The elder shall serve

a submission to the Divine Righteousness, while in one sense a surrender of reason, is in another its truest exercise. It is the surrender instinctively yielded by the soul which, *conscious of its own sin*, lies open to the full impression of the overwhelming purity and majesty of its Creator. It is *absolute* trust, under *complete* mystery, in Him who in one respect is truly known, but in another cannot be (by the created being) be "found out unto perfection." See xi. 33—36.

(2) It must be remembered that Divine Election affects a world not of righteous beings, nor even of neutral beings, but of "sinners," "enemies" (ch. v. 8, 9.)[1] We come to face its mystery only when we have first faced, and owned, the unfathomable mystery of SIN. We see it, not making the good evil, nor the evil arbitrarily worse, but judicially leaving the *sinner to himself;* (as we are bound to believe every sinner might righteously have been left; for otherwise Salvation would be our Right, not our Mercy;) save in cases—determined by the Divine Mind by *reasons within Itself*—in which, of mere mercy, a positive and prevailing influence intervenes, producing spiritual life, the life of repentance, faith and love.

(3) This view of the case, which is indeed full of distressing mystery, yet owes what is most distressing in it to the riddle which lies beneath all others connected with it—that of the Existence of Sin at all. But meantime it also assures us that while the will (influenced by sin) is the cause of ruin, it is also the will (influenced by grace) which, acting strictly as the *will*, lays hold on salvation. In neither case is *the will forced*, unless indeed we call *every* influence on the will compulsion, so far as it is successful. The lost *"will not* come;" the saved come as *"whosoever will."* (Joh. v. 40; Rev. xxii. 17.)

(4) The doctrine of Election is, in Scripture, never made the foreground of doctrine ; and it is always so presented as also to assure us, however little we can reconcile the vast range of spiritual truths, that we are in the hands of Righteousness as well as Power, and that our will, affections, and aspirations, are perfectly real. Lastly, the doctrine, if studied in Scripture, is viewed always from the only safe view-point—the foot of the Cross.—See further, Appendix F.

might stand] I.e., continue to act on its necessary principle—"not of works, but of Him that calleth."

of works] Based on, or resulting from, "works;" in the largest sense of "works;" actions whose aggregate is character.

calleth] See on i. 6.

12. *The elder*, &c.] Verbatim as LXX. of Gen. xxv. 23.—Of both Hebrew and Greek the literal rendering is **The greater shall be bondsman to the less.**

shall serve] In the personal history of Esau and Jacob this was not *literally* fulfilled; but it was so in spirit, in the subjection of Esau's interests and privileges to those of Jacob. In the history of their

---

[1] The abstruse questions which have been raised in controversy on this point may be fairly said to "intrude into" what lies wholly outside the *Scripture Revelation*.

the younger. As it is written, Jacob have I loved, 13
but Esau have I hated.

14—33   *Electing Sovereignty: Vindication, Restatement and Application*

What shall we say then? *Is there* unrighteousness with 14
God? God forbid. For he saith to Moses, I will have 15
mercy on whom I will have mercy, and I will have

descendants it was repeatedly fulfilled to the letter; and prophecy (as
in other cases, e.g. that of Abraham,) regarded the ancestor and his
descendants as *solidaire*.

13. *As it is written*] In Mal. i. 2, 3. Nearly verbatim from LXX.—
The prophet is there appealing, in God's name, to the people to remember His distinguishing and unmerited choice of Jacob over Esau to
inherit the land. Not the quotation merely, but the context, is to the
purpose here.

have I loved] Lit., and better, **did I love**; when I gave him the
preference. So below, **did I hate**.

hated] Cp. Gen. xxix. 33 and 30, for proof that this word, in contrast with love, need not imply positive hatred, but the *absence of love*,
or even *less love*. One verse there tells us that Jacob "hated" Leah, the
other that he "loved Rachel more." See too Matt. x. 37; Luke xiv. 26;
John xii. 25.

14—33   ELECTING SOVEREIGNTY : VINDICATION, RESTATEMENT
AND APPLICATION.   (A)   IS GOD UNRIGHTEOUS?

14. *What shall we say then?*] Same words as iii. 5, iv. 1, vi. 1, vii. 7,
viii. 31, ix. 30. St Paul often introduces thus an objection which is to be
solved. The objection here is twofold; (1) "Is God righteous so to
act?" (ver. 14,) and (2) "Is man responsible if He so acts?" (ver. 19.)

Is there unrighteousness with God?] On the Gr. rendered "*with*" see
note on i. 11. The words here, as the words there, may refer to a court
of justice : " Is there injustice *at His bar?*"

God forbid] See on iii. 4.—On the principle of the reply here, see
long Note on ver. 11.

15. *For*] The connexion is ; " The thought of injustice in these
acts of the Eternal Judge is all the more to be rejected because they
follow a principle expressed in His own *words;* for *He says* to Moses,
&c." That the principle, so expressed, is absolutely right, is taken for
granted. To the Apostle, God's word is final and absolute. With Him
nothing indeed can be capricious, but none the less His "judgments"
must, to a vast degree, be "past finding out," just because He is the
Eternal.

I will have mercy, &c.] Exod. xxxiii. 19. Verbatim from LXX.—
The English exactly represents the Hebrew, if it is noted that "*will*"
throughout this verse might equally well be "*shall*." In both Hebrew
and Greek there is no *explicit* reference to "willing," in the sense of

16 compassion on whom I will have compassion. So
then *it is* not of him that willeth, nor of him that runneth,
17 but of God that sheweth mercy. For the scripture saith
unto Pharaoh, Even for this same *purpose* have I
raised thee up, that I might shew my power in

"choosing." However, the general sense plainly is, "In any case,
through human history, wherein I shall be seen to have mercy, the one
account I give of the radical cause is this—*I have mercy.*" It is to be
thankfully remembered, by the way, that close to this awful utterance
occurs that other equally sovereign proclamation, (Exod. xxxiv. 6, &c.)
"The Lord, the Lord God, merciful and gracious, &c."

16. *of him that willeth*] Not that human willing and running are
illusions; but they are not the *cause* of mercy. They follow it ; they
may even be the channel of its present action ; but they are not the
cause. Its origin is not "*of*" them. Cp. Phil. ii. 13.

runneth] The idea is of one actively moving in the path of right.
His energy may tempt him to think that he *originated* the motion; but
he did not.—The word "*runneth*" belongs to St Paul's favourite metaphor of the foot-race. See 1 Cor. ix. 24—26; Gal. ii. 2, v. 7; Phil. ii. 16.

17. *For*] See on ver. 15. In this verse St Paul *recurs* to the question
"Is there unrighteousness, &c.?" and replies to it, by citing not now
a general Divine utterance (as in ver. 15) but a special utterance, to an
individual.

the Scripture saith] For a similar personification of the inspired
word see Gal. iii. 8, 22. Such phrases are a pregnant indication of the
apostolic view of Scripture. (See below, on x. 6.)

unto Pharaoh] Here quoted as an example of Divine Sovereignty. He
appears as one who *might* (in human judgment) have been dealt with
and subdued by a process of grace and mercy, but who was left to his
own evil will. No evil was infused into him; but good influences were
not infused, and his evil took its course.—It is instructive, and a relief
in a certain sense, to read this passage in the light of the history of
Exodus, where it is remarkable that the "hardening" (expressed in
the Hebrew by three different verbs) seems to be attributed in ten
places to the Lord and certainly in ten to Pharaoh himself; and where
the narrative, in its living simplicity, at least shews how perfectly *real*
was the action of the human consciousness and will.—But we must not
think that this *solves the mystery,* nor must we lose sight of St Paul's
object in quoting Pharaoh's case here—viz. to establish the fact of the
sovereignty with which God shews, or does not shew, mercy.

Even for this, &c.] The quotation (Exod. ix. 16) is mainly with
LXX., but the first clause in LXX. runs, "and for this purpose thou
wast preserved," or "maintained."

have I raised, &c.] Or, **did I raise thee up.** Lit. **made thee stand.**
And this is better, for the special meaning seems to be that Pharaoh
was not so much *exalted to be king,* as *raised up and sustained under the
plagues.*—Here the Eternal gives "*His glory*" as a sufficient account of
His action toward this individual soul and will.

thee, and that my name might be declared throughout all the earth.   Therefore hath he mercy on whom 18
he will *have mercy*, and whom he will he hardeneth.   Thou 19
wilt say then unto me, Why doth he yet find fault?   For

18.   *whom he will*]   The emphasis is of course on these words, in
each clause: to us, the *only* account of the differences of His action
is HIS WILL.   The following verses prove beyond fair question that
St Paul means fully to enforce this truth, intensely *trying* as it is to the
human heart.   He lays it down without mitigation or counterpoise :
not that there is *no* mitigation ; but mitigation is far from his purpose
here.—The deepest relief to thought in the matter is just this, that this
sovereign and unaccountable will is HIS WILL ; the Will of the living God,
the Father of our Lord.   But it is none the less *sovereign ;* and that is
the point here.—Observe that the Gr. pronoun rendered *"whom"*
throughout this verse is *singular*.   The application is to individuals.

hardeneth]   Judicially; by "*giving up* to the heart's lusts."

(B)   IS MAN RESPONSIBLE?

19.   *Thou wilt say then*]   St Paul is still, as so often before, writing
as if an opponent were at his side.   How vividly this suggests that he
had *himself* experienced the conflicts of thought which indeed every
earnest mind more or less encounters !   But conflicts do not always end
in further doubts.   Difficulties, often most distressing ones, must meet
us in *any* theory of religion that is not merely evolved from our own
likings; and difficulties are not necessarily impossibilities.   At one point
or another we must be prepared to *submit* to fact and mystery.

yet]   Q. d., "why, *after* such statements of His sovereignty, does
He go on to treat us as free agents?"   Here is the second head of
objection.   God's justice was the first; now it is man's accountability.

who hath resisted]   This is not the place to discuss the profound
problem here suggested.   It must be enough to point out (1) that St
Paul makes no attempt to solve it.   He rests upon the facts (a) that
God declares Himself sovereign in His mercy ; (b) that He treats man's
will as a reality: and he bids us accept those facts, and *trust*, and *act*.
(2) The contradiction to the hint that "*no man hath resisted*" lies, not in
abstruse theory, but in our innermost consciousness.   We know the fact
of our will; we know the reality of moral differences; we know that we
can "resist the Holy Ghost."   On the other hand, the truth of God's
foreknowledge is alone sufficient, on reflection, to assure us that every
movement of will, as being foreseen, could not be otherwise than
in fact it is.   And this is exactly as true of the simplest acts and
tenderest affections of common life, as of things eternal: in each
emotion of pity or joy we move along the line of *prescience*, a line
which thus may be regarded as, for us, irrevocably fixed beforehand.
But meanwhile in these things we feel and act without a moment's misgiving (except artificial misgiving) about our freedom.   Just so in mat-
ters of religion; but the special relations of *sinful* man to God compel

₂₀ who hath resisted his will? Nay but, O man, who art thou
that repliest against God? Shall the thing formed
say to him that formed *it*, Why hast thou made
₂₁ me thus? Hath not the potter power over the clay, of
the same lump to make one vessel unto honour, and an-
₂₂ other unto dishonour? What if God, willing to shew *his*

these plain and even stern statements of the truth of GOD's action in the
matter, even in the midst of arguments and pleadings which all assume
the reality of our will.

(C) THE REPLY: CREATIVE SOVEREIGNTY

20. *Nay but*] Same word as x. 18, and Luke xi. 28; (E.V., "Yea,
rather.") Q.d., "*Rather than* the position of a questioner, take that of
a creature."

man] The word is, of course, emphatic.

the thing formed] Lit. **the thing moulded**; the Potter and the Clay
being in the writer's thought.—Here lies the force of the "*who* art
thou?" The case is not that of yielding to vastly greater power or
subtler intellect, but of yielding to the Origin of your existence; to the
Uncaused CAUSE of your conscience, will, affections, and all. The
Sovereign is the CREATOR; are you, the Creature, really in a position
to judge Him?—This clause is nearly verbatim from Isaiah xxix. 16,
xlv. 9 (LXX.)—"*Why hast thou made me thus?*" is not a quotation.—
In Isai. xlv. 9, the words occur in a context of *mercy*. The mercy of
God, as well as His severity, is sovereign and mysterious.

21. *the potter—the clay*] This is the simile likewise in Isaiah just
quoted, and in Isaiah lxiv. 8. (Cp. Jer. xviii. 1—10.) It gets its force
from the perfect pliability of the material. Certainly the illustration
does not *relieve* the stern utterances it illustrates; nor is it meant to
do so.—It must be remembered that the "clay" moulded by the
Eternal here is not Humanity merely, but Humanity as sinful, and, as
such, void of the least claim to furnish "vessels unto honour." (See
ante, long note on ver. 11.) This, however, is not the main thought
here, but rather the immeasurable difference of position between the
Creator and the Creature.

lump] Lit. **kneaded mass.** Same word as xi. 16; 1 Cor. v. 6, 7;
Gal. v. 9.

one vessel unto honour, &c.] Cp., for similar language, 2 Tim. ii.
20, 21. The connexion there is akin to this, but such as brings out
(what is not in view here) the *moral results* of sovereign grace.
The special imagery of the potter and clay is absent there.

22. *What if God*, &c.] The Gr. construction in vv. 22, 23 is broken
and peculiar. Rendered nearly lit., the verses run: **But if God,
choosing to demonstrate His wrath, and make known what He can
do, bore with much longsuffering vessels of wrath, fitted unto
ruin; and that He might make known the wealth of His glory on
vessels of mercy, which He fore-prepared unto glory?** The general

wrath, and to make his power known, endured with much long-suffering *the* vessels of wrath fitted to destruction : and 23

drift of the passage, though thus grammatically peculiar, is yet clear.— The *"but"* suggests a certain difference between the potter's work and that of the Creator and Judge; q.d., "If the potter's right is so absolute, while the clay is mere matter and so has no *demerit,* the right of God over *guilty* humanity is at least as absolute; and meantime, even so, it is exercised with longsuffering."

willing] **having the will to.** The Gr. verb is frequent of the sovereign Divine will and pleasure. See e.g. Matt. viii. 3; 1 Cor. xii. 18.

to shew] **to demonstrate.** Same word as ver. 17 (*"shew* my power"), and iii. 25 ("to *declare,*" &c.). The justice and energy of His wrath against sin are both demonstrated in the doom of the impenitent.

endured, &c.] The special case of Pharaoh is in St Paul's view, and is to be taken as an example. There we see on the one hand the sovereign will permitting sin to run its course, but on the other hand, in equal reality, warnings and appeals are addressed by God to a human conscience and will, time after time. From our point of view the two things are incompatible; but the Apostle assures us that both are *real,* and therefore compatible.

the vessels] Lit. **vessels.** But the article is rightly supplied. The two classes of "vessels" are exhaustive of mankind.—The word " vessel " is doubtless suggested here by the language of ver. 21. See next note.

of wrath] I.e. *"connected with, devoted to, wrath."* So below, *"connected with, marked out for, mercy."* The genitive need not imply a metaphor, as if the "vessels" were *"filled with"* wrath or mercy; such an explanation would be needlessly remote.—The same word in same construction occurs Acts ix. 15, where lit., "a vessel of choice;" and probably the metaphor does there appear in the next words—"to *bear* my Name." Cp. also 2 Cor. iv. 7; 1 Thess. iv. 4, (where "vessel"= "body";) 1 Pet. iii. 7. In those passages the metaphor is traceable to the idea of the body as the receptacle and casket, as it were, of the spirit. Here, as above said, the *whole* reference appears to be to the imagery of the *potter's work.*

fitted] **Made ready, suitable.** Such indeed every "vessel of wrath" will prove to have been. It is remarkable that St Paul does not say "which *He* fitted." A seemingly rigid logic may say that the lost must be as truly predestined to death as the saved to life; but such logic is faulty in its premisses: *we do not know enough* of the Eternal Mind and the nature of things to reason so[1]. It is at least to be noted that here, while the "preparation" of the saved for glory is expressly ascribed to God, that of the lost for ruin is so stated as to avoid such ascription. Meanwhile the deepest consciousness of human hearts, awakened to eternal realities, acquits God and accuses self.—St Paul, however, does

---

[1] See further, Appendix H.

that he might make known the riches of his glory on the vessels of mercy, which he had afore prepared unto glory, 24 even us, whom he hath called, not of the Jews only, but 25 also of the Gentiles? As he saith also in Osee, I will call

not *dwell* on this. To *relieve mystery* is only a passing aim with him here.

destruction] **Ruin,** perdition, the loss of the soul. See note on ii. 12 (on the word "perish;" where the Gr. is the verb cognate to the noun here).

23. *and that he might*] Some such clause as "so acted," or better, "so had patience," must be mentally supplied. The idea of the patience of God seems to attach here to both parts of the statement: so far from acting in haste, He *bore* both with the persistent rebellion of the lost, and with the once equal rebellion, and then frequent failures, of the saved.

the riches of his glory] Same word as Eph. i. 18, iii. 16; Col. i. 27; (in the last two places, however, the *reference* is different from that here). For comment, see viii. 18. The "glory" of God here is the bliss and exaltation in eternity which He will give to His saints. In that better life His endless "riches" of blessing will be evermore "made known" among the glorified, by being evermore conferred on them. For similar phrases, see ii. 4, xi. 33; Eph. i. 7, ii. 7, iii. 8; Phil. iv. 19.

on] See on viii. 18, last note.

afore prepared] By the Divine process traced viii. 29, 30. See also note above, ver. 22, on "fitted."

24. *even us*] Lit., and better, **whom also he called, us,** &c. The "also" or "even" goes with the verb, and seems to indicate that the "afore-preparation" is rather that of the electing purpose of God than that of personal sanctification (which is, however, the sure sequel of the other). Q. d., "He fore-ordained to glory the vessels of mercy, and then proceeded actually to call them to grace."

hath called] Better, **called.** See on viii. 28.

not of the Jews only] Here St Paul reminds us of the special subject of this discussion; the apparent rejection of *Israel*. By the true heirs of Abraham was all along meant the church of the elect; those who should be "called" and should "love God." In the Mosaic age these were but *some* of the bodily Israel; in the Christian age they were largely found *outside* that Israel. But in both cases the Promise, in its true intention, was fulfilling. He now quotes in proof of that true intention.

(D) QUOTATIONS IN APPLICATION

25. *Osee*] In the Gr., **Oseë** or **Hoseë**; the equivalent of the Heb. *Hoshea*. Here, lit., **in the Oseë**; i. e., probably, "in the writings of Hosea."

I will call, &c.] Hos. ii. 23 (25 in the Heb.). The quotation does not agree with the LXX. The Heb. is, lit., "And I will have pity on the not-pitied-one (fem.), and I will say to the not-my-people, My people

them my people, which were not my people; and
her beloved, which was not beloved. And it shall 26
come to pass, *that* in the place where it was said
unto them, Ye *are* not my people; there shall
they be called the children of the living God.
Esaias also crieth concerning Israel, Though the num- 27
ber of the children of Israel be as the sand of

art thou." St Paul here gives an *equivalent* for "pity;" the Divine
equivalent, *love;* and otherwise quotes nearly with the Heb.—The first
reference of the prophetic word was to the bringing back of the Ten
Tribes to holy allegiance. The Apostle is guided to expound this as a
type of the bringing in of the Gentiles to the chosen Israel of God.—
The same text is quoted by allusion, 1 Pet. i. 10; an important parallel
passage.

her] The familiar personification of a church or nation.

26. *And it shall come to pass,* &c.] A new quotation, linked in one
line with the last. Nearly verbatim with LXX. of Hosea i. 10 (ii. 1 in
the Heb.). For a first and second reference see last note but one.—" *In
the place where :*"—this, in the first reference, may mean the Sanctuary
from which the restored Israelite should no more be excluded ; in the
second, the Church and Family of the Promise, regarded as a *locality*
in the figure. For the doctrine, cp. Eph. ii. 19—22.

the children] For comment, see viii. 14, &c.; John i. 12 ; 1 John iii. 1.

27. *Esaias also*] Better, **But Esaias.** There is a contrast : Hosea
speaks of the bringing in of Gentile believers; Isaiah of the rejection of
all Jews except Jewish believers.

crieth] Perhaps the word refers to the power and intensity of Isaiah's
prophetic manner. So Meyer.

concerning] The Greek preposition is lit. **over**; and *possibly* it may
be rendered so here; as if the Prophet stood lamenting *over* the
fallen. But this meaning is very rare in N.T., and especially in St
Paul.

Though the number, &c.] Lit. **If,** &c. The quotation is from Isaiah
x. 22, 23. The lit. Heb. is "For though thy people Israel (or, O Israel,)
be as the sand of the sea, a remnant shall return thereof; the con-
sumption decreed is overflowing in righteousness; for a final work and a
decisive work doth the Lord execute in the midst of all the earth (or,
land)." The LXX. reads; " Even if the people Israel become as the
sand of the sea; their (or, the) remnant shall be saved. (He is) com-
pleting and cutting short in righteousness; because a work cut short will
the Lord (or, Lord God of Hosts) do in the whole world." St Paul
adopts nearly the words of LXX.; again (as in ver. 25, and very often,)
developing a second and deeper fulfilment where the first fulfilment lay
in past events of Israelite history; e.g. here, in the comparatively *small*
returns of the exiles, under Zerubbabel and Ezra. The "return," in the
Second Fulfilment, is a return to Christ, and thus equivalent to " *salvation.*"

₂₈ the sea, a remnant shall be saved: for he will
finish the work, and cut *it* short in righteousness: because a short work will the Lord make
₂₉ upon the earth. And as Esaias said before, Except
the Lord of sabaoth had left us a seed, we had
been as Sodoma, and been made like unto Go-
₃₀ morrha. What shall we say then? That the Gentiles,
which followed not *after* righteousness, have attained to
₃₁ righteousness, even the righteousness which is of faith. But

the number of] These words are perhaps borrowed and inserted
from Hos. i. 10; a verse close to the last quotation. (Meyer.)

a remnant] Lit. and better, **the remnant**.

shall be saved] In Heb., "*shall return*." See last note but two.

28. *for he will finish*, &c.] These words agree closely with the letter of
the LXX., but not with that of the Heb. They convey the point of the
Heb., however, quite enough for the purpose of the quotation; and St
Paul thus adopts them.—In some important documents the quotation
ends with "cut it short;" but the evidence is not conclusive.—The main
purport of this verse is clear: the Prophet foretells summary and severe
judgments on Israel, such as to leave ere long only a "remnant" able
and willing to "return."—"*In righteousness:*"—i.e. "in righteous
severity."

29. *And*] Q.d., "And again, the small number of Jewish believers
fulfils another prediction."

said before] Lit., and better, **hath said before**; i.e. "as *we have it*
in his book."—"*Before*" refers not to the quotation of an *earlier
chapter*, but to the words as a *prediction*. The quotation is from
Isaiah i. 9, and exactly with LXX., which gives "a seed" where the
Heb. gives the equivalent, "a small remnant." St Paul instructs us
that this passage not only describes a state of distress contemporary
with the Prophets, but also predicts, through this as a *type*, the
spiritual future.—"*Sabaoth*":—the Gr. transliteration of *Ts'vâôth*, the
Heb. word meaning Hosts, Armies.

30. *What shall we say then?*] Same word as ver. 14; where see
note.

followed not after] To them no Revelation had pointed out "righteousness" as a *goal* of efforts.

righteousness] I.e., practically, Justification, which is the admission
to Salvation.

have attained] Lit. and better, **did attain**; at their conversion;
on hearing and receiving the Gospel, previously unsought and un-
imagined.

even] Lit. **but**; and so perhaps better: q.d., "but this righteousness was that which results from faith;" *in contrast* to the Jewish un-
believer's ideal, given in x. 3. The E. V., however, is equally true to
the Greek idiom.

Israel, which followed *after* the law of righteousness, hath
not attained to the law of righteousness. Wherefore? Be- 32
cause *they sought it* not by faith, but as *it were* by the works
of the law. For they stumbled at *that* stumblingstone; as 33
it is written, Behold, I lay in Sion a stumblingstone
and rock of offence: and whosoever believeth on
him shall not be ashamed.

31. *which followed*] Lit. **following**; and so better.

the law of righteousness] Not simply "*righteousness*," as in ver.
30; because Israel had, what the Gentiles had not, the detailed revealed
precepts. These precepts they "followed after," i.e. strove to keep as
a covenant of salvation. For this very reason they "did not attain to"
them, i.e. they failed to reach the true use of the Law—its revelation of
God's will to be followed by His reconciled children, His people
justified by faith.—"*Of righteousness:*"—this phrase may, as often, be
explained to mean "connected with righteousness." So the Law *is*
connected, whether it condemns, acquits, or guides. Israel "followed
after it" as an *acquitting* Law, in vain; and so failed to "attain to it"
as a Law *guiding* in the path of peace. They strove by it to make
themselves just, and so failed to walk by it as the justified.

hath not attained] Better (as in ver. 30) **did not attain.** Their whole
history of effort and failure is summed up in one idea, and viewed as
all past, (though numberless Jews were, and are, still making the same
attempts,) because St Paul's thought is fixed on the *crisis* of the calling
of the Gentiles, after which the case of Israel took a new aspect in
practice.

32. *Wherefore?*] See ch. iv. for the fullest commentary on this
verse.

as it were] Lit. and better, **as**; i.e. "*under the belief* that it could
be so reached."

works of the law] "*Of the law*" should be omitted, on evidence of
documents.

that stumblingstone] Lit. and better, **the stumblingstone**; i.e. the
Stone predicted, in the words now to be quoted.—"*Stumblingstone:*"
—lit. **stone of stumbling**, as in E.V. of 1 Pet. ii. 8, where the same
prophecy is quoted by allusion.

33. *Behold*, &c.] The quotation is a combination of Isai. viii. 14
and xxviii. 16, and is closely after the Heb., but widely differs from the
LXX. of viii. 14. Both passages (q.v.) refer to the great Promise, which
was proposed to Israel of old as a better ground of trust than earthly
policy or religious formalism, but was rejected by the worldly majority.
Here, as so often, St Paul is led to see in a promise which had a present
meaning for Isaiah's time, a revelation of truth for the whole history of
Israel in relation to Him who is the innermost theme of all Scripture
prophecy. In such cases the question "what did the Prophet intend?"
is only subordinate to "what did his Inspirer intend?"— In the
Speaker's Commentary, on Isai. xxviii., the paraphrase of the eminent

Ch. X. 1—21 *Israel has rejected a salvation whose universal intention, and yet partial acceptance, was foretold by the law and the prophets*

10 Brethren, my heart's desire and prayer to God for Israel
2 is, that *they* might be saved. For I bear them record that they have a zeal of God, but not according to knowledge.

Rabbi Rashi is quoted: "Behold I have established *a King, the Messiah,* who shall be in Zion a stone of proof."

a stumblingstone and rock of offence] I.e. Christ, as the Object of humble and absolute confidence and hope. Cp. Psal. cxviii. 22; Matt. xxi. 42; 1 Cor. i. 23; Gal. v. 11; 1 Pet. ii. 6, 7, 8.—"*Offence:*"—in its antique sense of an *obstacle* at which the foot trips.

shall not be ashamed] So too LXX. of Isai. xxviii. 16. The Heb. has "shall not make haste." The idea is the same in both; to "make haste" was to be in the hurry of fear, as when a refuge breaks down before a foe; and so to be "ashamed of," or bitterly disappointed in, the refuge.

In this prophetic passage St Paul is led to find (1) *a prediction* of Israel's stumbling at the truth of Christ our Justification, and thus to re-assure minds disquieted by the sight of Israel's unbelief; (2) a *proclamation* of Faith (reposed on Christ) as the means of salvation. See below, x. 11.

Ch. x. 1—21 Israel has rejected a salvation whose universal intention, and yet partial acceptance, was foretold by the law and the prophets

1. *my heart's desire*] Fully in the Gr., **the preference indeed of my heart.** The "*indeed*" suggests a "*but*" to follow. This does not occur, but is implied: St Paul's choice and prayer contrast with the *present state* of Israel.—The word rendered "*desire*" is elsewhere in N. T. almost always used of the "*good pleasure*" of God. It thus means here not a *longing* but a *choice,* deliberate and decided; St Paul, as far as in him lies, *decides for* Israel's good; a decision coming out in prayer to the Giver.

for Israel] MSS., &c., give simply **for them** as the better reading. The reference of the pronoun is obvious.

that they might be saved] Lit., simply, **unto salvation.** His choice, and consequent petition, *take that direction.*

2. *For*] The connexion is, that they seem to be, but are not, in the way to salvation; and that this stirs up his affectionate and anxious longing that they may find it.

record] **witness**; as one who so intimately knows them and their state of conscience and will.

zeal of God] So lit. The genitive implies that the zeal is in close connexion with, and directed towards, Him. So "faith of God" (Gr. of Mark xi. 22). Jewish jealousy for the Law, Temple, Scriptures, &c.—eagerness to proselytize—hatred of Christian renegades—is all

For they being ignorant of God's righteousness, and going 3
about to establish their own righteousness, have not submitted themselves unto the righteousness of God. For Christ *is* 4
the end of the law for righteousness to every one that be-

implied here; all being connected, rightly or mistakenly, with the true
God, and intended, more or less, to "do Him service."—Observe that
St Paul gives them full credit for sincerity, and yet does not look on
their *sincerity* as a ground of *safety*. His true generosity had in it no
false "liberalism." The Jews (like himself of old, 1 Tim. i. 13,) acted
"ignorantly in unbelief;" but their "ignorance," in face of offered knowledge, was their crime; and so their misguided zeal was indirectly
sinful.

knowledge] Lit. **full knowledge.** (German, *Erkenntniss*.) Same
word as i. 28, iii. 20. The word is appropriate, for it was just the *full*
knowledge of the true God *as God in Christ* which they lacked. Their
knowledge of God impelled them to persecuting zeal exactly because
it was not *full* knowledge. (See Acts xiii. 27.) So it is with all persecution in the name of the true God.

3. *being ignorant of*] **not knowing**: the verb refers back to the
"knowledge" just before mentioned.

God's righteousness] His acceptance of the sinner as righteous, for
Christ's sake. See on i. 17.

going about] **seeking.**

to establish] Same word as Heb. x. 9. They sought to make it
good enough to stand (in the judgment). On Jewish theories of merit,
see Appendix A.

have not submitted themselves] Lit., and better, **did not submit**;
perhaps with reference to the definite ideal occasion of the first appearance of the Gospel amongst them.—The Gr. verb is passive in form,
but may bear a middle meaning; and so probably here, as in E.V.
—For an illustration of this "submission" see 1 Pet. i. 2, where
the election of the Father and the holy influences of the Spirit lead to
"*obedience* and the *sprinkling of the blood* of Jesus Christ." Acceptance
of the one "hope set before us," that of the Cross, is an act of submission as well as of trust. Human pride and human reason both, in
different ways, have to *bow* before the Crucified.

4. *For Christ*, &c.] The connexion is that the conduct of the Jews
was a total mistake of their own Revelation; *for* He whom they rejected
was no accidental or alien intruder, but "the End of the Law."—The
ver. may be closely, and better, rendered: **For the end of the Law is—
Christ, unto righteousness, to everyone that believeth**; the whole idea
conveyed by the words from "Christ" to "believeth" being the "end of
the Law."

the end of the law] Cp. for the phrase 1 Pet. i. 9, "the end of your
faith;" i.e. what your faith leads up to. So here Christ our Justification
was what the Law (the preceptive Revelation by Moses) led up to,
both prophetically by its types and predictions, and preparatively by
its sin-discovering and inexorable demands. (See for the latter respect,

5 lieveth. For Moses describeth the righteousness which is
of the law, That the man which doeth those *things*
6 shall live by them. But the righteousness which is of
faith speaketh on this wise, Say not in thine heart,
Who shall ascend into heaven? (that is, to bring

ch. vii.) The words are capable of the sense "the *close* of the Law,"
i.e. "He who brings it to an end." But this is not the aspect of the
matter in this context, nor in the Epistle as a whole.

for righteousness] **unto righteousness**; in order to be "The Lord
our righteousness" (Jer. xxiii. 6). See on i. 17; &c.

5. *For*] The connexion is that the Law led up to Christ *both* by
prescribing a condemnatory standard as its own, and by mysteriously
suggesting the nearness and freeness of the Gospel.

describeth] Lit. **writeth.**

That the man, &c.] Levit. xviii. 5. Cp. Deut. xxvii. 26; Jerem.
xi. 1—10; and, as a commentary, Gal. iii. 10—13, and the rest of that
chapter.

6. *But the righteousness which is of faith speaketh*] The "righteousness of faith" is here equivalent to "the righteousness of God." So iv.
11, 13.—Here, by a striking personification, not unlike that of the Divine Wisdom in the Proverbs, JUSTIFICATION is said to speak, in the
words of Deuteronomy. In St Paul's view "the Word of God" indeed
"*liveth*," with a life which gives an almost personality to its doctrines.
—Perhaps he avoids the phrase "*Moses* speaketh" because the terms of
the *legal* covenant have just been quoted as uttered by him (ver. 5).

Say not in thine heart] The original of the quotations here is Deut.
xxx. 12—14. The form of the quotation is free; but nevertheless St Paul
really employs the passage as a proof, and does not merely adapt it to
his purpose. For the very point of his argument just here is that, *in
and by the Law*, Christ is suggested and announced; and if he merely
adapted Mosaic words to express his own thought, this point would
be missed. Alford has some admirable remarks on the passage: he
argues that the practical import of the passage in Deuteronomy is
that the Law, as the Revelation of God's will, is not an unintelligible
mystery to man, but a thing that can be known and loved; but that, if
so, then *à fortiori* this is true "of Him who is the end of the law, and
of the commandment to believe in Him, which (1 John iii. 23) is now
God's commandment."—St Paul assumes that the O. T. is full of
Christ (Messiah;) and so it is no wonder to him to see in this Mosaic
passage a *divinely-designed* suggestion of His exaltation, humiliation,
and gospel, under words having another immediate reference.

in thine heart] Words not in Heb. or LXX., but meaning what the
Heb. ("that thou shouldest *say*") means; the "speaking" of *thought*.

Who shall ascend, &c.] This and the next question come of *anxiety
and perplexity:* q. d., "In order to be saved, have I to *bring* the
necessary Manifestation of God's will from Heaven or Hades? Have
I to *procure* Incarnation and Resurrection?" "No; all is now done:

Christ down *from above:*) or, Who shall descend into 7
the deep? (that is, to bring up Christ again from the
dead.) But what saith it? The word is nigh thee, 8
even in thy mouth, and in thy heart: that is, the
word of faith, which we preach; that if thou shalt confess 9
with thy mouth the Lord Jesus, and shalt believe in thine

the Person and the Work are complete, and ready. As at Sinai,
so in the Gospel, God has done His part unasked; and now thy part
is to accept and own His Son as thy Justification."

that is, &c.] The Apostle, guided by the Holy Ghost, explains the
innermost intention of the Holy Ghost as He spoke by Moses. What
was the meaning of Moses, consciously to himself, is only part of the
question.

to bring Christ down] In His Incarnation.

7. *Who shall descend,* &c.] The Heb. has "Who shall go over (or
on) the sea?"; the LXX., "to the other side of the sea?" St Paul takes
the sea, as surely Moses took it, to be the antithesis of "heaven"—the
"great *deep;*" and thus the idea is of exploring depth rather than
breadth. The *Jerusalem Targum* on Deuteronomy has a remarkable
paraphrase: "Neither is the law beyond the great sea, that thou shouldest say, O that we had one like Jonah the prophet, to descend into the
depths of the sea, and bring it to us!" (Etheridge's Translation.) To
Moses, sky and sea were suggestive of heights and depths of supernatural mystery. St Paul finds in this use of them the latent truth of
the special Height of Christ's pre-existent majesty and the special Depth
of His entrance at death into the world of souls; and so sees here an
inspired declaration that this His Descent and Ascent were so "finished"
as to make the means of salvation a prepared and present reality to the
believing soul, which is asked (thanks to Divine mercy) not to elaborate,
but to accept, the "righteousness of God" in the Incarnate and Risen
Christ.

8. *The word*] More precisely, **the utterance**; i.e. of the terms of
the covenant. Alike the elder and later Covenants were not obscure
enigmas, but could be recited by human lips and assented to as "just
and good" by human hearts.

that is, &c.] See last note but one on ver. 6. Here again St Paul
sees in the words of Moses a divinely-meant adaptation to the case of
the New Covenant as well as to that of the Old.

the word of faith] **the utterance of faith**; or, to expand the brief
phrase, "the statement of terms of justification by faith;" the message
whose burden is Faith.

9. *that if thou shalt,* &c.] Here the contents of the "utterance"
are given in more detail.

confess with thy mouth] I.e., practically, "submit to and own Him as
supreme for thee." See, for the demand of such "confession," Matt.
x. 32; Luke xii. 8. For all adult converts, this was an important feature
of Baptism. In all cases, it is to be a test of the intelligence and reality

heart that God hath raised him from the dead, thou shalt be
10 saved. For with the heart *man* believeth unto righteousness ; and with the mouth confession is made unto salva-
11 tion. For the scripture saith, Whosoever believeth on
12 him shall not be ashamed. For there is no difference

of the faith of which it is a fruit.—"*Confession*" is here put before
"believing," because in Deuteronomy "the mouth" had been named
before "the heart." In the order of experience, of course, faith
precedes confession.

the Lord Jesus] Better, **Jesus as Lord**; i.e., as Supreme and
Eternal ; the all-blessed Son. Cp. 1 Cor. xii. 3 ; where light is
thrown on the deep reality and significance of the confession meant
here.—St Paul here refers back to the "who shall ascend?" of ver. 6 :
Jesus, as Lord, is He "who is in Heaven," (John iii. 13,) who came
thence, and is the way thither.

that God hath raised him, &c.] Cp. Heb. xiii. 20 ; where the "bringing
again of the Great Shepherd from the dead," *by the Father*, is the full
and final proof that the Father is the God of Peace; i.e. of Reconciliation, of Justification. See too above, iv. 24, 25, v. 1 ; and 1 Thess.
i. 10.—The belief in the Resurrection here is not merely historical
belief, (which yet is indispensable to all other belief in it,) but "heart"
belief ; the perception and cordial embrace of what the Resurrection
reveals and imports as to the Risen One and His work.—Here,
obviously, the "who shall descend?" of ver. 7 is referred to.

10. *For with the heart*, &c.] The "*for*" introduces a further explanation ; in which the special workings of belief and confession are
noticed.

man believeth] Lit. **it is believed** ; "belief is exercised." So just
below, **it is confessed.**

righteousness] I. e., practically, Justification. See last note but two.

unto salvation] I.e. final salvation ; the "end of our faith, even
the salvation of our souls." (1 Pet. i. 9.) The "confession with the
mouth" represents in fact the whole process by which the Christian, in
his life on earth, owns and obeys Christ as his Lord ; refuses to "deny
Him" in the evil world. It thus stands here for the "narrow path"
along which the justified move to their promised and assured home.
Faith indeed "saves :"—the Christian, in every sense, "*lives* by *faith* in
the Son of God" (Gal. ii. 20). But his "life" is *manifested* in
obedience, which alone (whatever be the influence which leads him to it
and keeps him in it) is the path to heaven.—See Eph. ii. 8—10.

11. *the scripture*] Already quoted, ix. 33; see notes.

believeth] Here faith alone is mentioned, and so through the rest of
the context. Confession of Christ as Lord, the fruit and sequel of faith,
was an incident only in the argument.

12. *For there is no difference*] The same phrase (with precisely
opposite reference) as iii. 22.—The "*for*" here refers to the "whosoever"
of ver. 11 ; and this refers to the truth, suggested through the whole

between the Jew and the Greek: for the same Lord over all *is* rich unto all that call upon him. For whosoever shall 13 call upon the name of the Lord shall be saved. How then shall they call on *him* in whom they have not 14 believed? and how shall they believe *in him* of whom they have not heard? and how shall they hear without a preacher? And how shall they preach, except they be sent? as it is 15 written, How beautiful *are* the feet of them that

passage here, of the "nearness" and freedom of salvation, which, as revealed in Christ, needed no advantage of Jewish privilege in order to reach it. *Belief* and *confession* were as "near" to Greek as to Jewish hearts and lips.—On "*Greek*" see note, i. 16.

for the same Lord, &c.] Better, **for the same Lord is [Lord] of [them] all; abounding in wealth unto all,** &c. Cp. iii. 30, and note.

rich] In "goodness," to pardon and accept. See Isai. lv. 7.—The word "wealth" respects both the splendour of the gift and its sufficiency for "whosoever will," however numerous the suppliants.

call upon him] **appeal to Him.** The Gr. is same word as Acts xxv. 11, 12. See also Acts vii. 59; where Stephen's "appeal" is "Lord Jesus, receive my spirit." The "appeal" here is to the Redeemer as our Justification.

13. *For whosoever*, &c.] "*Whosoever*" refers back to "all" in ver. 12. St Paul here quotes (almost verbatim with LXX.) Joel ii. 32; (Heb., iv. 5;) where the whole prediction is distinctly Messianic, and includes a reference to "the *remnant* whom the Lord calleth." See Acts ii. 21 for a closely parallel use by St Peter of that passage.

14. *How then*, &c.] This is an argument for the evangelization of the heathen, as against the jealous reserve of Pharisaic Judaism. Q. d., "The prophets announce a salvation for all who *turn to Messiah;* but these must first *believe* Him to be able to save; but believers must first be hearers; therefore there must be preachers, missionaries, sent out from the possessors of the true faith." All this proves that a large proclamation of Messiah to the Gentiles, by Jewish missionaries, (as Paul,) was in perfect accord with the prophecies.

15. *except they be sent*] Q. d., "If they be *not* sent, if they are *held back* by misguided jealousy, how can the predicted evangelization take place?" If Rabbinism were right, were in accordance with God's will, in its practical denial of hope to the Gentiles, then missionary work, such as foretold, would be impossible; there could be *no commission* for it.

as it is written] Isai. lii. 7. The quotation varies from LXX., but is nearly with the Heb. The context in Isaiah points rather to "good tidings" *to* Israel than *from* Israel. But (1) the tidings is "Thy God reigneth;" and of this no greater proof could, or can, be given than the universal spread of the kingdom of Messiah; (and see just below, lii. 10, "all nations," "all the ends of the earth;") and (2) it is clear from the drift of many N. T. quotations that a reference to

preach the gospel of peace, and bring glad tidings
16 of good *things!* But they have not all obeyed the
gospel. For Esaias saith, Lord, who hath believed our
17 report? So then faith *cometh* by hearing, and hearing by
18 the word of God. But I say, Have they not heard? Yes

the "Israel of God" (the true Church of Christ) underlies the primary
Jewish reference of very many of Isaiah's prophecies. Thus St Paul
sees here a prediction of the "beauty" of the tidings of that Salvation
which was "of the Jews," and is now for Jew and Gentile alike. See
Eph. ii. 17.—In the Heb. the proclaimer is single; "*him* that bringeth,
&c."

Some editors omit the words "that preach the gospel of peace;"
but without sufficient reason. Probably St Paul had in view the pre-
viously-expounded "*peace* with God," enjoyed by the true Israel.

16. *But they have not all obeyed the gospel*] I.e. the gospel, or
good tidings, just specified; that of "peace."—Here St Paul meets
from prophecy the supposed objection that the message had only partially succeeded. Innumerable Gentiles had rejected it: was not this
an indication that the messengers had *no commission?* No: Isaiah
himself had prophetically deplored just such seeming scantiness of
acceptance for Messiah's message.

have not obeyed] Better, **did not obey.** The apostolic evangelization
of the Gentiles is viewed as ideally past.

Esaias saith] Isai. liii. 1; quoted also, with special reference to
Jewish unbelief, Joh. xii. 38.

17. *So then faith*, &c.] In this verse, which forms a parenthesis of
thought, St Paul uses the quotation just made in a new reference; not
now to the *fact of unbelief*, but to the *means of faith*. Isaiah's words
imply that the "report" of Messiah's messengers was the appointed
means for the conveyance of faith ("who hath *believed?*") in Messiah.
But this faith was (see above, ver. 11,) for Gentiles as well as Jews.
Therefore Gentiles as well as Jews must have the "report" *carried to
them*.

hearing] Same word in Gr. as that rendered **report** just above.
See margin of E. V.

by the word of God] I.e. either "*by His order*," or "*by* (the
delivery of) *His message;*" "by the utterance of truth from and about
Him." The latter is on the whole more likely, both grammatically and
by the context, where the necessity of evangelization is the main
point.—A various reading, but not decisively supported, is "by the
word of *Christ*."

18. *But I say*] Here the connexion recurs to ver. 16, after the
parenthetic inference from the quotation there made. Isaiah had said
"Who hath believed?" St Paul now quotes again to shew that this
means anything but "Who hath *heard?*" Prophecy contemplated a
world-wide *preaching*, whatever might be the limits of *believing*.

Have they not heard?] Better, **Did they not hear?** See on ver. 16.

verily, their sound went into all the earth, and
their words unto the ends of the world. But I say, 19
Did not Israel know? First Moses saith, I will provoke
you to jealousy by *them that are* no people, *and* by
a foolish nation I will anger you. But Esaias is very 20
bold, and saith, I was found of them that sought me

Yes verily] Same word in Gr. as that rendered **Nay but,** ix. 20.
It is corrective; the hearing was not only wide, but world-wide.

their sound, &c.] Here Psal. xix. 4 is quoted, (xviii. 4, LXX.,)
verbatim with the LXX., and closely with the Heb. The Heb.
word rendered *"sound"* means precisely "line" or "chord;" probably
in the sense of a musical note, and specially a key-note—the basis
of the strain.—The words are not formally introduced as a quotation, but no doubt are really such; not merely an adaptation. In
the world-wide message of the stars concerning God, St Paul is led to
see a Divine intimation of the world-wide message of His Gospel.
Natural Religion was but the parable and forerunner of the final
Revelation.—The past tense is the past of prophecy; the purpose is
regarded as fulfilled. Q. d., "Were not all men, in the Divine intention, hearers? Yes, verily: prophecy regarded them as such."—By the
date of this Epistle, vast tracts of the then "world" were penetrated by
the "word of God." But this is not the strict reference of the past
tense in the quotation, which points to the completeness of the Divine
purpose.

19. *But I say*, &c.] Another objection is anticipated and met, (as
indeed it has been already met, less explicitly,) viz., that Israel had no
prophetic warning of the Gentiles' enlightenment and their own unbelief.

know?] I.e. "know the prospect" of the spread of Messiah's Gospel,
and their own rejection of it.

Moses saith] Deut. xxxii. 21; verbatim with LXX. and Heb.,
except that *"you"* is substituted for *"them,"* probably to make the
reference unmistakable. The words occur in the sublime prophetic
Song of Moses, so full of the mysterious future of both judgment and
mercy for Israel. The point of the sentence (see the whole of the verse
in Deut.) clearly is that the God of Israel would *adopt other nations* as
Israel had adopted other gods.—The clause is more strictly rendered
Moses is the first to say. But the difference is not important.

no people...a foolish nation] I.e., probably, *in the opinion of Israel.*
Israel had taken up deities despised of God; He would take up a
people despised of Israel. At the same time the description would be
true of the Gentiles in respect of their lack of previous privilege and
revelation.

20. *But Esaias is very bold*] Moses had not *specified how* the
heathen should be the cause of jealousy and anger to Israel. But
Isaiah says, in so many words, that they shall find and know God, and
so become His people.

I was found, &c.] Isai. lxv. 1; almost verbatim with LXX., but

not; I was made manifest unto them that asked
21 not after me. But to Israel he saith, All day long
have I stretched forth my hands unto a disobedient and gainsaying people.

Ch. XI. 1—10 *Meanwhile the rejection of Israel never was,
nor is, total: a remnant believes, and so abides in covenant*

11 I say then, Hath God cast away his people? God for-

the two clauses are inverted; perhaps to emphasize the decisive word
"I was found." The Heb. is rendered by Kay, "I have let myself be
enquired of by them that asked not; I have let myself be found of
them that sought me not." The rest of the verse in Isaiah is conclusive
for the reference to the Gentiles.—The past tenses both in the Heb. and
Gr. refer to the *Divine view* of the whole experience of Gentiles and
Israel as regards the message of mercy.

21. *to Israel*] Better, **with respect to Israel**.

All day long, &c.] Isai. lxv. 2; verbatim with LXX., but with
slight variation of order of words.—The phrase is parallel to "rising up
early and sending," (Jer. vii. 13, 25, &c.,) and wonderfully describes
the Divine perseverance.

stretched forth my hands] In entreaty and welcome. Cp. Prov.
i. 24.

disobedient and gainsaying] An expansion of the one word "*rebellious*" in the Heb.—It is important to notice, side by side with strong
assertions of Divine Election, these equally strong assertions of human
resistance and Divine kindness.

Ch. XI. **1—10** Meanwhile the rejection of Israel never
was, nor is, total: a remnant believes, and so abides
in covenant

1. *I say then*] **I say therefore.** Thus far St Paul has stated the
adverse side of the case of Israel. He has shewn (1) that the Divine
Promise never pledged eternal light and life to *all* Abraham's descendants; (2) that God is sovereign in His grants of mercy; (3) that the
true work of the elder Dispensation was to prepare for the later;
(4) that both Gentile faith and Jewish unbelief were distinctly foretold
in the Law and the Prophets. And now, true to his main purpose
throughout this argument, he turns to state the happier side; and this
in two main aspects. First he reiterates the truth of the Divine Election,
but now in its *positive* aspect—the existence always of a believing
Israel within the unbelieving mass. Secondly, he predicts a time when
even in the mass Israel should turn to the true Messiah, be restored to
the Church, and become thus an influence of vast good for the world.—
" *Therefore:*"—i.e. as the practical result from my previous account of
sin and judgment in the case of Israel. Q.d., "I have given that
account *in order* the better to give an account of present and coming
mercy; which *therefore* I now do.'

bid.   For I also am an Israelite, of the seed of Abraham, *of* the tribe of Benjamin.   God hath not cast away his 2 people which he foreknew.   Wot ye not what the scripture saith of Elias? how he maketh intercession to God against Israel, saying, Lord, they have killed thy pro- 3

Hath God cast away] Lit. and better, **Did God thrust away?** i.e. when He welcomed the Gentiles into His covenant. (So too ver. 2.)—For the expression cp. 2 Sam. xii. 22; where LXX. uses the same verb and noun.

his people]   Here, obviously, the bodily descendants of Jacob.   St Paul asks whether *all these as such* were now excluded from the covenant.   So immense was the apparent revolution of the admission of Gentiles as such to full covenant, that this fact (along with the fact of the unbelief of millions of Jews) might prompt the thought that the Gentiles were now the *privileged* and the Jews the *aliens*.

God forbid]   See on iii. 4.—The phrase rejects with indignation the suggested thought.   In this intense feeling are combined deep love for his kinsmen, jealousy for his own place in the covenant, and jealousy too for the great principle of the irreversibility of "gifts and calling." See ver. 29.

For I also, &c.]   Q. d., "I am a living proof to the contrary; an Israelite in the strongest and strictest sense of bodily descent; yet a Christian, a child of God, a messenger of His word."

an Israelite]   See on ix. 4.

Benjamin]   Cp. Phil. iii. 5, where St Paul, for a different purpose, dwells on his pedigree.—See Bp. Lightfoot's interesting note on Phil. iii. 5, for the historic dignity and pride of the tribe of Benjamin. (Here, however, such ideas are less clearly in question than there.)

2.   *God hath not cast away his people*]   Lit. **did not cast**, &c. These words are verbatim (save only the change of tense) with LXX. of Psal. xciii. (Heb., xciv.) 14.

which he foreknew]   See on viii. 29.—Two interpretations are possible here.   The "foreknowledge," or sovereign antecedent decision of the Eternal Mind, may be (*a*) that which designated *the nation* for privilege, or (*b*) that which designated *individuals* of it for final glory.   The words of vv. 3, 4, 5 favour the latter view; and thus St Paul would say "God never thrust Israel out of the covenant; for He always had among them a fore-known 'Israel of God'."—The former sense (national designation) would be perfectly legitimate in itself; but it is less in accord with the immediate context, and with the closely kindred reasonings of ch. ix. The question in view here is "Was the *nation* ever so rejected as that *members of it, as such*, were rejected?"   This St Paul negatives by pointing to the "nation within the nation;" the elect faithful.

of Elias]   Lit. **in Elias**; i.e. in the narrative of Elijah's life.

intercession]   On behalf of the Divine Truth and Worship.

3.   *Lord, they have killed*, &c.]   1 Kings xix. 10.   The quotation is not precisely with either LXX. or Heb.; but substantially exact.— The Gr. past verbs here are aorists.

phets, and digged down thine altars; and I am
4 left alone, and they seek my life. But what saith the
answer of God unto him? I have reserved to myself
seven thousand men, who have not bowed the
5 knee to *the image of* Baal. *Even* so then at *this* present time also there is a remnant according to the election of
6 grace. And if by grace, *then is it* no more of works: otherwise grace is no more grace. But if *it be* of works, *then* is

4. *the answer of God*] Lit. **the oracular answer.** The words "*of
God*" are an explanatory addition.

I have reserved, &c.] 1 Kings xix. 18. The Heb. is, "And I have
left in Israel seven thousand; all the knees that have not bowed, &c."
(LXX. has "And *thou shalt leave*, &c.")

5. *at this present time*] In which the mournful phenomenon of
Jewish unbelief occasioned this whole discussion.

there is] Lit. **there hath been**: it was and still is.

a remnant] **a reserve, a leaving.** The noun is cognate to the verb
"I reserved" in ver. 4. This "remnant" at some stages of apostolic
history (Acts vi. 7, xxi. 20,) was in itself very numerous. But it was
always, no doubt, small comparatively; and it became more and more
so the more the distinctive character of the New Kingdom came out,
(as in Stephen's and now in Paul's teaching,) and the nearer the last
crisis of the old order approached.

according to the election of grace] I.e. "on the scale determined by
the Divine choice (to faith and salvation), whose only motive and
reason is grace—the free favour of Him who chooses out His own."—
See on viii. 33.

6. *And if by grace*, &c.] This verse is wholly parenthetical. Not
that its statement is alien to the whole argument, but this is not its
logical place. The argument is continuous between vv. 5 and 7 ; but
St Paul is so desirous to make the truth of Gratuitous Salvation perfectly
clear and familiar that he seizes this passing occasion to re-state it, as it
were in a *note*. The occasion is the quotation (ver. 4) of the words
"*I have reserved*;" in which St Paul sees the sovereign act of Divine
grace, withholding a remnant from the commission of idolatrous sin.
The faithful seven thousand were faithful "not according to their
works, but according to His purpose and the grace given to them."

no more of works] **no longer of works.** I.e. *when once* this
principle is granted, *thenceforth* the thought that it is "of works" is
negatived. So below, "no more grace;" "no more work."—The best
commentary on this verse is the argument of cch. iii. and iv. Nothing
could be clearer than St Paul's anxiety to give an *absolute* denial to the
whole idea of antecedent human merit as a factor among the *causes* of
salvation. Grace, *to be grace*, must be entirely uncaused by anything
of meritorious claim in us.

But if it be, &c.] There is much documentary evidence against the
genuineness of this last half of the verse. It is however not conclusive;

it no more grace : otherwise work is no more work. What 7
then? Israel hath not obtained that which he seeketh for;
but the election hath obtained *it*, and the rest were blinded,
(according as it is written, God hath given them the 8
spirit of slumber, eyes that *they* should not see, and

and slight variations in the Gr. phrases, as compared with those of the
first half, afford an internal argument for retention; for an *imitator*
would probably follow the model exactly. Certainly the reiteration of
the truth in question would be just in keeping here, and it is doubtful
whether that truth is one which was so well grasped in the early
centuries as that copyists would tend to emphasize it by an insertion.

work is no more work] Work, in the sense in question, (i.e. as an
antithesis to grace,) necessarily involves claim. This necessary idea
must be negatived if "works" and "grace" can coincide as causes
of salvation.

7. *What then?*] A phrase of resumption after the digression.

Israel] Here, obviously, the nation. Cp. ix. 6.

hath not obtained] Lit. **did not obtain.** The *crisis* of the offer of
the Gospel to them is in view in the tense. So **did obtain it,** just
below.

that which he seeketh for] I.e. a Righteousness before God; a valid
ground of acceptance. This was the aim of their efforts, as much when
St Paul wrote as ever before; but the method was fatally wrong.
Cp. x. 3.

the election] I.e. the *company* of the chosen. For a similar collective use of singular nouns, cp. the phrases (so frequent in this
Epistle) "the circumcision," "the uncircumcision."

were blinded] Better, **were hardened.** (So **hardening,** ver. 25,
below.) The verb indicates *failure of sensation ;* of which blindness
is only a special instance.—The best commentary is ch. ix. The
verb rendered "harden" there is not the same, but the idea is the
same. Here, as there, St Paul states this dark mystery of the Divine
dealing with sinners with no attempt at explicit clearing up. He does
not try to conjure away the cloud around the throne, but commits the
mystery to "the Judge of all the earth."

8. *according as it is written*] Isai. xxix. 10, and Deut. xxix. 4.
(Heb., 3.) The two passages combined read thus, from the Heb.,
"The Lord hath poured out (or spread) over you the spirit of deep
sleep, and the Lord hath not given to you eyes to see, and ears to hear,
unto this day." The unbelief of Israel of old, traced by Moses and Isaiah
to the mysterious withholding of grace, is here interpreted by St Paul to
be a "prophecy in act" of the unbelief of Israel, and of its cause, in the
days of Messiah.—It will be seen that the words *"unto this day"* are
part of the quotation, and that therefore no brackets should be used in
this verse. As Moses indicated by them a *continuous* "hardening" of
the mass of the nation in his day, so St Paul takes them to foreshadow
the like continuousness in the Gospel age.

9 ears that *they* should not hear;) unto this day. And David saith, Let their table be made a snare, and a trap, and a stumblingblock, and a recompence unto 10 them: let their eyes be darkened, that *they* may not see, and bow down their back alway.

> 11—32 *Moreover, the rejection is not final: it has a provi-dential purpose to serve; but a great reversal of it is in store*

11 I say then, Have they stumbled that they should fall? God forbid: but *rather* through their fall salvation *is come*

9. *And David saith*] Psal. lxix. 22, (LXX. lxviii. 23.) The quotation is nearly (in ver. 10 verbatim) with the LXX.; which in the first of the two verses expands the Hebrew. The Heb. there may be rendered, "May their table before them become a trap, and let it be, when they are at peace, (in security,) a snare." The idea of *requital* lies in the root of the Heb. word for "peace;" and thus the LXX. in-terpreted "unto requitals of them;" assuming another form of the word. —The whole Psalm is full of Messiah.—The point of the quotation is that the Psalm indicates a judicial turning of blessings into curses, and a judi-cial blindness and impotence of the soul, as the way in which retribution would come on Messiah's enemies. "Seeing then that this imprecation remains for all the adversaries of Christ—that their meat should be converted into poison, (as we see that the Gospel is to be the savour of death unto death,)—let us embrace with humility and trembling the grace of God." (Calvin.)

11—32 MOREOVER, THE REJECTION IS NOT FINAL: IT HAS **A** PROVIDENTIAL PURPOSE TO SERVE; BUT **A** GREAT REVERSAL OF IT IS IN STORE

11. *I say then*] Same word as ver. 1. Here begins a new section of the discussion, lasting to the end of the chapter, and of the subject. St Paul has shewn that the rejection of Israel was never total; he now declares that it is not final. A time is to come when the mass of the bodily Israel shall believe, and be restored to the Church.

Have they stumbled] Lit. and better, **Did they stumble**; i.e. when they, as a nation, rejected Messiah. Cp. the figure of the "stumbling-block" to illustrate Jewish unbelief, 1 Cor. i. 23; Gal. v. 11.

that they should fall] Q.d., "Was their stumbling permitted by God *with a view to* their fall?" Evidently here "*fall*" (by contrast with "*stumble*") bears the sense of final and fatal rejection. Was the nation then and there for ever cut off from becoming, on any national scale, *Christian?*

God forbid] For the *spirit* of these words here, see ix. 1—5.

through their fall] Better, **on occasion of their sinful stumbling**. The word rendered "*fall*" is that elsewhere (e.g. iv. 25, v. 15, &c.;

unto the Gentiles, for to provoke them to jealousy. Now if 12
the fall of them *be* the riches of the world, and the diminishing of them the riches of the Gentiles; how much more
their fulness? For I speak to you Gentiles, inasmuch as I 13

Gal. vi. 1; Eph. ii. 1;) rendered "trespass," "fault," "offence," &c.
Literally it is "a falling aside;" and thus nearly approaches the idea
of "stumbling." Since elsewhere in N. T. it always conveys the
idea of *guilt*, we attempt to combine the moral and literal meanings
as above. No doubt the word is chosen by St Paul with reference to
the metaphors, just used, of *stumbling* and *prostration;* and it is
intended to mark a temporary, not final, "false step." The E. V.
fails to keep this point.—The salvation of Gentiles was indeed always
in the Divine purpose; but Jewish unbelief was the *occasion* which
that purpose took for its actual developement.

salvation] Lit. **the salvation**; that salvation which was "of the
Jews;" Messiah's way of peace. Cp. Acts xxviii. 28.

for to provoke them] I. e. the Jews. See x. 19. Here is seen, as
through a veil, a suggestion of mercy conveyed in the warning of
judgment in Deut. xxxii. 21. The "provocation to jealousy" was
indeed in numberless instances to result only in mortification and
hatred; but in numberless other instances (this surely is in view here)
it was to result in an intense desire to regain the blessings of the
covenant side by side with Gentile believers. Cp. perhaps, Rev. iii. 9[1].

12. *the fall*] Same word as in ver. 11. See note there.

the riches] "The unsearchable riches of Messiah," (Eph. iii. 8,)
which "on occasion of" the rejection of Messiah by the Jews were
preached to the "world" of the Gentiles.

the diminishing] The Gr. word, by analogy with cognate words in
the classics, invites the rendering "*defeat*." But it stands here in plain
contrast to that rendered "*fulness;*" and so should be interpreted a
lessening, falling short, in respect of *numbers*. Unbelief in Messiah
reduced to woeful *fewness* the "Israel" which was really in covenant.
More and more it proved to be a mere "remnant." And the causes
which brought this about were also, under God, the causes of the spread
of the Gospel to the Gentiles.

how much more their fulness?] The better cause shall produce a
better effect.—"*Their fulness*."—i. e. the filling up of their numbers.
The true Israel shall at length include a *vastly larger proportion* of
Israel the nation, whether or no the nation shall be literally *all* brought
in. See further below, on vv. 15, 26.

13. *For*] Better, perhaps, **But**, or **Now**; by documentary evidence.
The particle merely calls attention to the fresh and fuller statement.

I speak to you] Immediately. He implies a hope to reach the Jews
through them.

you Gentiles] Evidently the Roman Christians were in the main a
Gentile body, and as such St Paul here speaks to them. The words, **of**

[1] See Abp. Trench's Commentary there.

14 am the apostle of the Gentiles, I magnify mine office : if by
any means I may provoke to emulation *them which are* my
15 flesh, and might save some of them. For if the casting away
of them *be* the reconciling of the world, what *shall* the

course, would be intelligible if he spoke only to a Gentile *section ;* but
the whole drift of cch. ix.—xi. shews that the Gentiles were a very
large majority.

I am the apostle, &c.] " I " is emphatic: his position toward the
Gentiles was distinct among the Apostles. " A noble self-consciousness
here finds expression." (Meyer.)—For the fact of this distinctive
commission see Acts ix. 15; and see below, xv. 15—19; Gal. ii. 7, 8;
Eph. iii. 8. See also 1 Thess. ii. 14—16 for an illustration of his
intense and sympathetic devotion to this his work, and his holy indignation at the sin of Jewish unbelief and persecution.

magnify] Lit. **glorify.** The practical meaning is that he is, and
rejoices to be, the Apostle for the Gentiles; makes much of his commission both in word and deed; discusses with his *Gentile* converts
even those truths which specially concern Jews; and yet, all the while,
not without a longing and design to benefit his Jewish brethren—for he
knows that the more his work prospers among the Gentiles, the more
hope there is that Jews will be roused to attention and enquiry, and
so to the desire to enter the covenant of Messiah. See on ver. 11.

14. *provoke to emulation*] Same word as that rendered "provoke
to jealousy," ver. 11.

save some of them] The phrase implies that he looked for conversions
only one by one, through his own ministry. Probably he suggests the
contrast of results hereafter, when the crisis predicted in ver. 25 should
come. Or again, he may mean that to save *even* some, in any event,
was worth any effort. (A striking commentary on the import of the word
"to save.") Cp. 1 Cor. ix. 22 for this intense desire to "save some,"
whether Jews or Gentiles.—It is instructive to see that St Paul never
allows the promise of a glorious *future* to divert him from practical
efforts in the *present*, however ill-requited such efforts might seem.
And observe that he looks on present and future as in organic connexion : the results were to be vastly different in degree, but the means
was to be *the same* throughout ; the "provocation" of Israel to holy
"jealousy" by the coming of blessing on the Gentiles.—Cp. 2 Cor. iii.
15, 16, for an important parallel. There, in ver. 16, perhaps render
"whensoever it" (i. e. the Jewish heart in any *individual case*) "turneth
to the Lord."

15. *the casting away*] Not the cognate word to that in vv. 1, 2.
But there is no practical difference in the words : it is the *reference* that
differs here. There he denies that *Jews as such* were thrust out of the
covenant; here he asserts the plain fact that the *Jewish nation* was, by
its rejection of Messiah, under (temporary) exclusion.

the reconciling] I. e. the *practical* reconciling. The circumstances
which caused and attended the "casting away" of Israel were the
occasion of the proclamation of the Gospel of Reconciliation to the

receiving *of them be*, but life from the dead? For if the first- 16

world. Thus, in a sense, Israel's unbelief was the *instrumental cause* of the enjoyment of "peace with God" by the host of Gentile believers. On "reconciliation," see on ch. v. 1, 11.

life from the dead] I.e. a vast and intense revival of true religion from a state which, by comparison, was religious death. (For a passage where "life" and "death" are so used, see Rev. iii. 2.) Meyer and some other expositors take the words here to mean *literal* resurrection-life; q.d., "the 'receiving' of the Jews shall usher in the resurrection and the immortal state." But observe (1) that St Paul still has in view a blessing *to the Gentiles* through the Jews: the "*for*" which introduces this verse indicates this. And if so, it is most unlikely that he would mean *resurrection-life* here; a blessing in no way peculiar to Gentiles. Observe (2) that he implies a *causative* connexion, to some extent, between the casting-away of the Jews and the recon-ciliation of the Gentile world; (see last note): analogy leads us then to see a causative connexion also between their "receiving" and this "life from the dead." But how could this be said if the "life" meant here is the literal resurrection? How likely, on the other hand, that its meaning should be just such a spiritual revival of the Gentile church as the conversion of Israel on a great scale would directly tend to awaken!—It is objected that this "life from the dead" must, as forming a climax, be a *greater thing* than the previous "reconciling of the world;" and that no mere revival could be this. No doubt in *some* respects it could not be; but if the revival were really world-wide, and intense, it *would* be a greater thing in respect of *manifest triumph* of Divine truth and life. See further below, on vv. 25, 26.

16. *For*] Lit., and much better, **But**, or **Now**. The word marks transition to a new fact in connexion with the "receiving" of Israel; the fact of the peculiar position of Jews with regard to the Divine Promise. The main effect of the following passage, to ver. 24, is to prove that the restoration of Jews to the Church of Messiah, so far from being unlikely, is in the nature of the case likely. Their peculiar connexion, by lineal descent, with the Fathers, makes it certain that their *return* will be as abundantly welcome to their God as the *admission* of the Gentiles. We might say *more* welcome, but for the fact that *no* welcome can be fuller than that which awaits the true believer of whatever nation. But St Paul wishes to meet the rising prejudice (so strong and stubborn in after ages) of Gentile against Jewish believers, by emphasizing the grand fact that the whole Church springs, so to speak, from a Jewish root; and that thus nothing could be, in a certain sense, more *natural* than the restoration of Jews to the Church. He has also to announce that there is reserved for Israel, in the future, not merely restoration to the Church, but a work of special importance and glory in it for the world.

the firstfruit] The Jewish Patriarchs, but perhaps specially Abraham, who was eminently "holy" in the sense of *consecration to the purposes of God*.—For the figure here cp. Num. xv. 21; "Of the first of your fruit *be* holy, the lump *is* also *holy :* and if the root *be* holy,

dough ye shall offer unto the Lord an heave-offering." The words just below here point to the idea of "firstfruits" not of *grain* but of *bread*.

holy] In the sense indicated in the last note. The Patriarchs were, by the Divine purpose, *separated* to be special recipients of Divine light, in trust for their descendants and the world. In a sense somewhat similar their descendants, viewed as a nation, are still *separated* in the Divine purpose to a special work connected with Divine mercy. The reference is not, of course, to a supposed superior personal sanctity of individual Jews as such, (which would be to contradict the whole reasoning of cch. ii., iii., iv.,) but to the special purpose towards Israel as a nation, in view of which they are reserved (scattered but never vanishing) for a time of grace.

the root] Here again the figure points to the Patriarchs, and especially to Abraham. (Cp. Isai. li. 1, 2, for yet another figure, that of the Quarry, with the same reference.) The "root" and "branches" are here brought in to form the main illustration of the passage following as far as ver. 25. The passage is one of much importance and some difficulty, and calls for a few preliminary remarks.

THE OLIVE TREE; THE ROOT, BRANCHES, AND GRAFTINGS

1. The Olive Tree is the true Israel (cp. Jer. xi. 16,) as the Church, the People of God. Its Root is Abraham and the Patriarchs. Its Stem is the Church of the Old Testament, when in a certain sense (that of external privilege) the Church coincided with the Nation of Israel, and when at least the vast majority of true believers were also physically children of Abraham. Its branches (by a slight modification of metaphor) are potential believers, whether Jewish or Gentile. If Jewish, their faith in Jesus as Messiah is viewed as *retaining* them in the Church; if Gentile, their faith "*grafts*" them into the stem of the covenant-congregation. If, being Jews, they reject the offers of the Gospel, they are thereby "*cut off*" from the stem. If they repent and believe, their faith "*grafts*" them into it *again ;* and this process, says St Paul, is, by the nature of the case, a more likely and *natural* one than the "grafting" of the alien branches—which yet is graciously effected.

2. The whole Olive Tree—its root, branches, and all—is the Church Universal, in which there is "neither Greek nor Jew;" i.e. in which every real part of the organism, every true believer, shares the sap and life of grace in equal reality. But the special imagery is framed to emphasize not this truth, but another truth in harmony with it; viz. that "salvation is of the Jews;"—that with the Hebrew Patriarch began—after a distinct break of continuity—the more definite life and history of the Church; that for ages the saints were all (practically) found among his sons; and that the universal Saviour was of the seed of David.

3. This, and not the evangelical equality of Jew and Gentile, is here in view; with the special object of reminding the Gentile Christian how singular and eminent had been the work of the Jewish Church; how welcome individual Jews must be to return to the Church, which,

so *are* the branches. And if some of the branches be 17
broken off, and thou, being a wild olive tree, wert graffed
in amongst them, and with *them* partakest of the root and

though now universal in *extent*, was, and of course is always, Jewish in
descent; and how natural it was that a special work in that Church
should yet be designed for an aggregate of Jewish believers.

4. It is hardly needful to point out how this metaphorical passage,
like almost every other, secular or sacred, carries its qualifications and
corrections with it. For example, the true Church of God existed ages
before Abraham; it embraced Abel, Enoch, Noah. And no saint, however great, can be the "root" of the rest in the sense of being their
source of life: the Divine Saviour alone can say "Abide *in me*." And
again, the figure here, if taken alone, would leave us with the impression that the Call of the Gentiles was an accident in the history
of the Church, instead of being the great "Purpose of the Ages" (Eph.
iii. 11) to which the privileges and work of the Elder Covenant were
but the mighty prelude. But St Paul writes for those who will read his
revelation in the full light of Gospel-truth; and therefore he securely
leaves the details to self-explanation or self-correction. Carefully so
read, the passage tells us not of a higher level of grace and glory hereafter for Jewish saints as above Gentile saints, but of a gracious work
back, and a special work for God, for repenting and believing Israel.

17. *some of the branches*] A *tender* statement of what, alas, was so
great an amount of unbelief. See below again, ver. 25; "blindness *in
part*."

be broken off] The reference of time is specially to the crisis of the
rejection of Messiah by Israel. It was true, of course, that at no period
of the Church was any *worldly and unbelieving* Jew otherwise than
"broken off" from God's covenant of peace; but not till Messiah was
rejected was it ever possible to think of the Jews, *as a class*, as being so
situated.

thou] The Gentile Christian, who is throughout in view.

a wild olive tree] A scion of a race alien from the special Covenant
of Salvation. This word, from St Paul's pen, implies no Pharisaic contempt of the Gentiles. He merely points to the Divine choice, equally
sovereign for nations and for persons, which had willed that Israel, and
not Greece, Rome, or India, should be the recipient and keeper of
Revelation; the *heaven-cultured* subject of its privileges and ordinances.
Not merit, but grace, made the difference. But a real difference it was,
none the less, and it left the wonder and mercy of the call of the Gentiles
as great as ever.

graffed in] Grafting, as is well known, is always of the good scion
into the inferior stock. St Paul reverses this, no doubt quite consciously.
The mere outline of his language is borrowed from the olive-yard, and
that is enough for him. The union of true believers to the true Church
is vividly illustrated (cp., but with care, the Lord's own great metaphor,
Joh. xv. 5,) by the union of branches to a stem; the bringing of alien

¹⁸ fatness of the olive tree; boast not against the branches:
but if thou boast, thou bearest not the root, but the root
¹⁹ thee.   Thou wilt say then, The branches were broken off,
²⁰ that I might be graffed in.   Well; because of unbelief they
were broken off, and thou standest by faith.   Be not high-
²¹ minded, but fear: for if God spared not the natural
²² branches, *take heed* lest he also spare not thee.   Behold
therefore the goodness and severity of God: on them which
fell, severity; but toward thee, goodness, if thou continue

believers into a Church originally Jewish is vividly illustrated by grafting a piece of one tree into another.   Here the likeness ends.

partakest]   Lit. and better, **didst become a partaker.**

18.   *boast not against*, &c.]   I.e. against the branches that were
broken off; as if in a better position than theirs might have been, and as
if better in yourself, and so (as regards any virtue of your own) better
able to hold your place.—Every insulting thought, word, or act, of professing Christians towards Jews, as Jews, from that day to this, is an
illustration of this verse.   Too often such slights are also offered, in one
form or another, to the re-ingrafted branches—converted Jews.

thou bearest not, &c.]   I.e. Divine mercy has reached thee through
Abraham and his sons, not them through thee.

19.   *then*]   **therefore**; i.e. in order to meet my reasoning.

20.   *Well*]   I.e. **Well said.**   There is, of course, a solemn and earnest
irony in the word.   In *terms*, the Gentile Pharisee (if we may use the
expression) spoke truth; for in the mysterious adjustments of the Divine
Plan the rejection of Messiah by Israel was to precede, and even in a
certain sense to occasion, the call of the Gentiles.   But in the *spirit* of
the words there was deep untruth; for their own sin was the actual
cause of Israel's fall, and Gentile believers were admitted into covenant
on just the same terms of mere mercy as their Jewish brethren—i.e. for
the sole sake of Messiah the Propitiation; "by faith."

because of unbelief—by faith]   The construction in the two phrases
is identical in the Gr.   On the statement of fact here, see last note.

thou standest]   See on ch. v. 2.

21.   *the natural branches*]   Persons who were, without any new
interposition of mercy, born within the scope of the covenant and the
light of revelation.   Not that the *state of human nature* was less fallen
in Jew than in Gentile, but that the *course of nature* led the Jew, as such,
to light and privilege.

22.   *goodness*]   See on ch. ii. 4.

severity]   In the special sense of summary sternness.   The word is
akin to that rendered "*sharply*," Titus i. 13.

on them which fell, &c.]   Better, in view of the best-supported
reading of the Gr., **on them that fell came severity, but on thee came
goodness.**

if thou continue]   On the verb and construction here, see on vi. 1.   The
idea of the word is *adherence*, either rightly resolute or wrongly obstinate

in *his* goodness: otherwise thou also shalt be cut off. And 23
they also, if they bide not still in unbelief, shall be graffed
in: for God is able to graff them in again. For if thou wert 24
cut out of the olive tree which is wild by nature, and wert
graffed contrary to nature into a good olive tree: how much
more shall these, which be the natural *branches*, be graffed
into their own olive tree?

For I would not, brethren, that ye should be ignorant of 25

as the case may be.—Observe that expressions like the present, implying
contingency in man's continuance in the mercy of God, and the reality
of the exertion of man's will in such continuance, are in real *practical*
harmony with the truth, so fully stated in previous chapters, of sovereign
and prevailing Divine grace (viii. 28—30). The *whole reason* of the
harmony is indeed past our finding out, perhaps for ever; but thus much
we can see, that sovereign grace acts on men, not on automatons; that
it acts on them through the human conscience and will; and that these,
in this matter as always, are affected by warnings as truly as by promises.
Grace imparts *perseverance* by imparting and maintaining *faith*, (1 Pet.
i. 5;) and it freely uses *all* means by which such faith is properly
animated and energized. Amongst such means are these *warnings* of
the results that must follow *if* faith loses hold of its object. Cp. Jude
20, 21.

otherwise] The lit. Gr. is simply **since**; but the E.V. expresses
the implied sense.

23. *graff them in again*] Every Jewish convert from the first age
till now has been an example of this statement. St Paul is not yet
dealing with the question of a conversion of Israel *en masse*; he has in
view individual Gentile faith and individual Jewish faith; and he regards each Jew as (ideally) once a branch in the sacred Tree, but cut out
of it, and awaiting a gracious re-ingrafting.

24. *For if thou*, &c.] Cp. on this verse notes on ver. 17.

how much more] I.e. "how much more *easily to our conception.*" *As
a fact*, the Gentile had been grafted in, and no *more* than this could
happen to the Jew. But the latter fact was antecedently much more *likely*
than the former.

25. *For I would not, brethren, that ye should be ignorant*] Same
word as i. 13; 1 Cor. x. 1, xii. 1; 2 Cor. i. 8; 1 Thess. iv. 13.—Here
St Paul leaves the image of the Olive Tree, which he had used to
facilitate to his reader's conception the idea of a restoration of Jews to
the Church of the Messiah, now become the Universal Church. He
now, in plain terms, reveals and predicts a great future Restoration.

"*For:*"—the connexion indicated is somewhat thus: "My parable
of the Olive Tree is no conjecture or peradventure, when it suggests a
brighter future for Israel. *For* such a future is to come, in the purposes
of God."

this mystery, lest ye should be wise in your own conceits;
that blindness in part is happened to Israel, until the fulness
26 of the Gentiles be come in. And so all Israel shall be

ignorant] Whether for want of information, or want of reminders.
Possibly the precise revelation of the future here made had never been
made, in terms, before, though suggestions and intimations of it had often
been heard. (Cp. perhaps Luke xxi. 24.) So in another place, (1 Thess.
iv. 13,) where the Apostle uses the same formula:—the hope of *Resurrection* had been abundantly revealed in a general way, but the *precise
fact* that the buried saints should rise *before* the living saints should be
transfigured was probably then first made known.

mystery] Here, as consistently in N.T., the Gr. word means a truth
undiscoverable by reason, but now revealed. Our use of the words
"mystery" and "mysterious," is often misleading in these connexions,
as it easily suggests the thought of *what cannot be understood.* The Gr.
means, in fact, *a secret*, which, when told, may be found either partially
to transcend the grasp of man's conception, or to be quite within it.
Thus in 1 Cor. xv. 51 we have a "mystery" revealed as a fact which yet
(in detail at least) we cannot clearly conceive: in the present passage
we have a "mystery" revealed which is far more within our reach of
thought, viz. judicial blindness inflicted on the Jews as a body, and
hereafter, at a definite point in the Plan of God, to be removed.

wise in your own conceits] Same word as xii. 16.—"*Conceits:*"—i.e.
opinion. The Gr. is, more literally, **wise,** or **sensible, at your own bar;**
i.e. judged in the court of self-complacency.—The "wisdom" or
"thoughtfulness" here in view is such as that rebuked in ver. 19; that
of a Gentile convert who thought much of his large insight into the
Divine Plan because he saw in the rejection of the Jews not an accident
but a deliberate opening of the door of grace to the world—and *there
dismissed the subject*, careless whether there were, or not, any future
mercy for Israel in the same Divine Plan.

blindness] See on ver. 7, "*were blinded.*" The noun here is cognate
to the verb there. It occurs elsewhere in N.T., Mark iii. 5; Eph.
iv. 18.

in part] This gracious qualification is not necessary to the statement, in which the "blindness" or "hardening" is the emphatic thing.
But St Paul will not omit to remind the Gentile Christian that even in
the dark ages of Israel there ever has been, is, and will be, a "holy
seed," (Isai. vi. 13,) an "election," who behold and welcome the
promised Salvation. Thus the hardening is never total; it is partial,
though, alas, the hardened "*part*" is the large majority, till the great
call of grace.—See further, long note above on ver. 1.

until the fulness of the Gentiles be come in] The Gr. equally allows
the rendering **until the fulness** &c. **come in**. This would not necessitate
(as E. V. does) the inference that the call of grace to Israel was not to
come till the in-coming of the "fulness of the Gentiles" *was over.* In
ver. 15 (q. v.) we have had it intimated that the conversion of Israel
should be a means of immense grace to the world; as indeed it must

saved: as it is written, There shall come out of Sion

be, in the nature of the case. In view of this, it seems best to explain the present verse as predicting that the in-coming of the nations to the Church of Christ shall have largely, but not perfectly, taken place when Israel is restored to grace; so that the closing stages of the in-coming may be directly connected with the promised revival of Israel, and may *follow* it in respect of time.—*"Come in":*—to the Fold, the Refuge, the City, of Messiah's salvation.

the fulness of the Gentiles] Cp. note on "fulness" in ver. 12. The word here plainly means the *full destined number* of the Gentile Church, with the underlying idea of the greatness of that number. Cp. Rev. vii. 9.

26. *And so all Israel shall be saved*] Several interpretations of these words are in themselves legitimate. They may refer (A) to the natural Israel, the Jews; or (B) to the "Israel of God," the true Church of Christ. Again, if the reference (A) is adopted, the prophecy may mean (*a*) that then *all* the *elect of Israel* shall at length be gathered in—the long process shall at length be complete; or (*b*) that every individual of the then generation of Jews shall be brought to Messiah's grace; or (*c*) that "all" bears a less exact reference here, as so often in Scripture, and means "in general;"—"Israel in general, the Jews of that day as a great aggregate, on a scale unknown before, shall be saved."

Of these various possibilities we prefer on the whole (A. *c*,) as the most in accord with the context, and with the analogy of Scripture. The explanation (B) is *in itself* entirely true: the final glory and triumph of the Gospel will surely be, not specially the salvation of the Jews, but that of the Universal Church—the immortal Bride of the King Eternal. And it is extremely important to remember the full recognition in Scripture of *all* its true members as the *"seed of Abraham"* (Gal. iii. 29). But this is not the truth exactly in point here, where St Paul is dealing with the special prospect of a time when "blindness in part" will no longer characterize *Jews as Jews*. And the "Israel" of ver. 25 is probably the Israel of ver. 26, as no distinction is suggested in the interval.—Again, the reference marked (A. *a*), though perfectly true *in itself*, is less likely here because in vv. 15, 25, we have had already a prediction of a restoration of Jews, *en masse*, to grace; whereas the process of gathering in the elect of all ages is continuous, and thus, on the whole, gradual.—Again, the reference marked (A. *b*), though the Divine Plan *may*, of course, intend no less, is far from analogous to the main teaching of Scripture as to the developements (even the largest) of grace in this world.--On the whole, then, we adopt the interpretation which explains the sentence as predicting the conversion of some generation or generations of Jews, a conversion so real and so vastly extensive that unbelief shall be the small exception at the most, and that Jews as such shall everywhere be recognized as true Christians, lights in the world, and salt on the earth.

There shall come out of Sion, &c.] In the following quotation St Paul more or less combines, as often, (see e.g. iii. 10—18,) several O. T. prophecies; with this for the main purport, that one ultimate result of the coming of Messiah should be the gift of grace to the Jews.

the Deliverer, and shall turn away ungodliness
27 from Jacob: for this *is* my covenant unto them,
28 when I shall take away their sins. As concerning the

In Isai. lix. 20, 21, we have in the Heb., "And there shall come a
Redeemer for Zion, and for them that turn from transgression in Jacob,
saith the LORD: As for me, this is my covenant with them." In Isai.
xxvii. 9; "This is all the fruit [of God's dealings, namely] to take away
his [Jacob's] sin." In Psal. xiv. 7 (LXX. xiii. 7); "Oh that the salvation of Israel were come out of Zion!" In Isai. lix. 20 the LXX.
has, "There shall come for Sion's sake the deliverer, and shall turn
away ungodliness from Jacob." In Isai. xxvii. 9 it has, "This is his
blessing, when I shall take away his sin."

St Paul seems to have woven into one Isai. lix. 20 and Psal. xiv. 7,
and to have completed the sentence from Isai. xxvii. 9. In the last
clause of ver. 26 here he adopts the LXX., because, though it represents the Heb. inexactly, the substantial meaning is untouched:—the
Redeemer's coming shall be "for," "for the benefit of," those who
turn from sin, by *being the cause of their so doing;* He shall thus *turn
sin from them*, in the sense of removing its guilt and breaking its power.

shall come out of Sion] Here probably the reference is to the First
Advent. Q. d., "It stands foretold that the Appearance of Messiah,
of the seed of David, shall result in the subdual of the unbelief and
rebellion of Jacob, and the bringing in of a covenant for him of final
pardon and peace. Now Messiah *has* appeared; therefore, how slow
soever the fulfilment be as yet, the remainder of this great promise must
be drawing on: Israel shall yet be saved." The words have been often
explained to foretel a *future* Coming of the Redeemer, whether literal
or figurative, to work the conversion of Israel on a great scale. But
the explanation above is fully sufficient for the argument, and (to say
the least) more in accord with St Paul's general teaching as to the future
Coming of the Lord.

the Deliverer] **the Rescuer;** same word as 1 Thess. i. 10, "who
rescueth us from the wrath to come." Heb. "*Goel*;" the Avenger of a
Kinsman; hence generally the strong friend who rescues the weak.

ungodliness] Lit. **impieties.**—Perhaps omit the "and" before
"shall turn away."

27. *for this is my covenant unto them*] Lit., **and this for them is
the covenant granted by me.** Cp., for the terms of a great "*Covenant*
of Grace," Jer. xxxi. 31—34, with the quotation and inspired comment
in Heb. viii. 8—12, x. 16, 17.

"*This*" refers backward; q.d., "I have covenanted that the Messiah
shall bring Jacob to grace and peace; and this covenant I will carry
out when my time of pardon and renewal comes."

28. *As concerning, &c.*] This ver. and the next form a small detached paragraph: so do vv. 30—32. In both these paragraphs
St Paul adds to his main argument and statement a few closing confirmations.—The phraseology of this verse is very brief in the Gr.; **As to**

gospel, *they are* enemies for your sakes : but as touching the
election, *they are* beloved for the fathers' sakes. For the 29
gifts and calling of God *are* without repentance. For as ye 30

**the Gospel indeed, enemies because of you; but as to the election,
beloved because of the fathers.**

concerning the gospel] The verse may be paraphrased; "With a view
to the spread of the Gospel, which is the message of salvation for *every*
believer, Jew or Gentile, (i. 16,) it pleased God in His sovereign plan
to reject the great majority of the Jews—in order to open His kingdom
wide to you. But with a view to the believing element, the elect
Jews of every age, including the great multitude to be called to grace
hereafter, the Jews are still dear to Him; for His Covenant with
Abraham, Isaac, and Jacob is sovereign and unchangeable."

enemies] See on ch. v. 10. The meaning here is that the Lord was
(judicially) *hostile to them ;* viewed them as hostile, "counted them His
enemies" in the sense of rejecting them from actual participation in His
Gospel. Unbelief cut them off, and was *their own* sin; but it was
judicially and sovereignly permitted to have its way. But meantime, in
another aspect, they were still "beloved;" still included in a plan of
mercy.

the election] The word "election" may mean either *the act of choice,*
or *the chosen persons.* Here it is probably the latter. The word is with
the definite article, as in ver. 7. The reference is to the whole number
of Jews who had obtained, or should obtain, salvation by faith; whether
gathered in one by one, as now, or in multitudes, as hereafter. "With
a view to" these, the Jewish people is still, most emphatically, within
the purposes of Divine Love.

for the fathers' sakes] See Deut. vii. 8, ix. 5, x. 15.

29. *gifts*] Gr. *charismata ;* **gifts of grace.** The word is frequently
used of "*miraculous*" gifts (see on i. 11); but here, obviously, it refers
to all the "innumerable benefits" of Divine Salvation.

calling] See on i. 6, 7, viii. 30.

without repentance] **without change of mind,** i. e. on the part of the
Giver. This profound fact of the Divine Way of Mercy is here applied
to the case of an elect *race.* Elsewhere (see e. g. viii. 30; Joh. x. 28;)
the same mysterious law is plainly indicated with regard to elect *persons.*
The two cases are largely illustrative of each other.

The word rendered "*without repentance*" (same word as 2 Cor. vii.
10; E.V. "not to be repented of,") is strongly emphatic in the Gr.
order.

30. *For as ye,* &c.] A new short paragraph. See on ver. 28.—The
main purpose of this paragraph is to shew, in a new respect, the Divine
"reason why" of the rejection of the Jews; viz., that the salvation of
both Jews and Gentiles might be conspicuously put on the footing of
mere mercy. The Gentile believers had once rejected God (see i.
19, &c.), and mere mercy called them to grace. The Jews were now
rejecting God, and mere mercy would again act in calling them back
to grace.

in times past have not believed God, yet have now obtained
31 mercy through their unbelief: *even* so have these also now
not believed, that through your mercy they also may obtain
32 mercy. For God hath concluded *them* all in unbelief, that
he might have mercy upon all.

have not believed] Better, **did not obey.** For the best commentary, see i. 18—32.

have now obtained mercy] Better, **did obtain mercy.** Lit. **were compassionated.**

through their unbelief] Which was, in a certain sense, the *instrument*, "through," or by, which the covenant was thrown open to the world. Jewish unbelief (1) slew "the Lord of Glory," the Propitiation; and (2) was the *occasion* for the mission of the Apostles "far unto the Gentiles."

31. *have these also now not believed*] Better, **did these disobey.**

through your mercy] Connect these words with "have these not obeyed." The verse will then read ;—**Thus these also now disobeyed through your mercy, that they also**, &c.—The " mercy of the Gentiles " is the mercy of God in Christ to them, not any mercy of theirs to the Jews.—The statement of this verse is the almost exact converse of that of ver. 30. Jewish unbelief was, in a certain sense, the *instrumental cause* of Gentile salvation; so, in a certain sense, Gentile salvation was the *final cause* of Jewish unbelief. In the Divine Plan the call of the Gentiles was to hinge upon the unbelief of the Jews when they should reject Messiah ; and thus the grand act of Jewish unbelief was, in a guarded sense, "*caused*" by the promise of the call of the Gentiles.

that they also may obtain mercy] Q. d., "that their reception again (in single cases, and at length in a mass,) may be as remarkably an act of sovereign compassion as your own call was." The emphatic idea throughout this section is *mercy*.

32. *For God*, &c.] Lit. **For God did shut up the all together into disobedience, that He may compassionate the all.** We give this literal version, though barbarous as English, to elucidate the exact reference of the Greek. "*The all*" are "all the persons in question"; Gentiles and Jews alike, who by turns have occupied the position of aliens from the enjoyment of salvation. The Divine Sovereign has permitted each great class in turn thus to develope its own sin of rebellious unbelief, ("shutting them up into it," as into a cage, or trap, into which they have leapt,) in order to the complete display of mercy, and only mercy, wholly apart from privilege or merit, in the salvation both of Gentiles and of Jews. Here again *mercy* is the emphatic idea.—"*Did shut up:*"—i.e. when He "cut off" the Jews: for this completed, as it were, the process of that developement of unbelief which was to bring out into clear light the equal sovereignty of mercy in all cases.

"*All*" must manifestly be taken here, as so often elsewhere, (see on ch. v. 18,) with limitation. St Paul is contemplating not the whole *race*, but the whole *Church* in its two great elements—Gentile and

33—36   *Doxology to the Eternal Sovereign*

O the depth of the riches both of the wisdom and know- 33
ledge of God! how unsearchable *are* his judgments, and his
ways past finding out! For who hath known the mind 34
of the Lord? or who hath been his counseller? Or 35
who hath first given to him, and it shall be recompensed
unto him *again?* For of him, and through him, and to him, 36
are all *things:* to whom *be* glory for ever.   Amen.

Jewish. See ii. 8, 9, for his distinct warning of a "judgment without
mercy" on the impenitent and unbelieving, Gentiles and Jews alike.

33—36. DOXOLOGY TO THE ETERNAL SOVEREIGN

33.   *O the depth*]   Here, at the close of this discussion of the case of
Israel,—in which he has held up for our submission the unfathomable
mystery of electing sovereignty, and also the strange ways by which
Divine judgment is often made the instrument of Divine mercy,—the
Apostle turns to the Supreme Object of his thought and love, and utters
his ascription of worship and praise to the All-Wise and Almighty. Such
a doxology is perfectly *in the manner* of Scripture, in which the *ultimate*
aim ever is not the glory, nor even the happiness, of Man, (dear as his
happiness is to God and His messengers,) but the GLORY OF GOD.

depth]   Cp. Psal. xxxvi. 6, "Thy judgments are a great deep."

riches]   See on ii. 4.

wisdom and knowledge]   Scarcely, in such a passage as this, to be
minutely distinguished.   They blend into one idea—omniscience acting
in eternal righteousness and love.

unsearchable]   It is well to weigh, and *accept*, this word at the close
of such an argument.   In his very act of praise the Apostle confesses
the inability of even his own inspired thought to *explain* the Divine
mercies and judgments, in the sense of clearing all difficulties.   "Who
art thou that repliest against God?"   "Clouds and darkness are round
about Him;" and, in certain respects, it is only the intelligent but profound *submission of faith* that can say, in view of those clouds, "Righteousness and judgment are the habitation of His throne." (Ps. xcvii. 2.)

past finding out]   Same word as Eph. iii. 8, (E. V. "*unsearchable*,"
lit. "*not to be tracked by footprints*,") an instructive parallel passage.

34.   *For who hath known—counsellor*]   Nearly verbatim from Isaiah
xl. 13. See too Jer. xxiii. 18.—The Gr. verbs are aorists; and the time-
reference is perhaps to creation, or to the eternal decrees "before the
world was."

35.   *hath first given to him*, &c.]   "Who hath laid Him *under obligation?*" (Cp. Job xxxv. 7.) Such is no doubt the special reference here.
It affects not only the discussions of cch. ix.—xi., but also (as does indeed
the whole of this doxology) the whole great doctrinal Argument of the
Epistle. *No merit in man, in the matter of acceptance with God*, is one
of its deep foundation-truths.

CH. XII. 1—8   *Christian practice as the result of Christian truth: self-dedication to the service of God in the Christian Church*

12   I beseech you therefore, brethren, by the mercies of

36. *of him*]   Lit. **out of Him** ; not in the Pantheistic sense, as if all things were evolved from God—phases of God ; but in the Christian sense, that His WILL is the ultimate source of all being, all life and force, all conscience, will, and thought.

through him]   **by means of Him.** He is not the Source only, but the Means. He did not only originate all things, but incessantly sustains and overrules all.   In the special case of the saints, He not only wills their salvation, but—through their regenerated will—gives them power to believe and persevere.   "He keeps them, by His power, through faith, unto salvation."   (1 Pet. i. 5.   See too Phil. ii. 13.)

to him]   To His glory.   He is, to Himself, the Final Cause of all His works.   He is greater, higher, nobler, and more precious, than His whole creation ; and must view Himself as such : what else, then, but Himself could He make His aim and end?

Cp. Col. i. 16, for the same words, "through Him and to Him" used of the Eternal SON ; one of the deepest proofs of His proper Deity.

to whom be glory]   Lit., **to Him [be] the glory** ; the glory due to Him.   Same words as xvi. 27; Gal. i. 5; Phil. iv. 20; 2 Tim. iv. 18; Heb. xiii. 21 ; and nearly the same as 2 Pet. iii. 18; Rev. i. 6.   In the last two passages the ascription is to the Eternal Son.   See Rev. i. 5.

for ever]   Lit., **unto the ages** ; through all future periods and developements of existence.   Same words as ix. 6; where see also note on "*Amen.*"

CH. XII. **1—8**   CHRISTIAN PRACTICE AS THE RESULT OF CHRISTIAN TRUTH : SELF-DEDICATION TO THE SERVICE OF GOD IN THE CHRISTIAN CHURCH.

1. *I beseech you therefore*]   The Doctrinal Part of the Epistle, strictly so to be called, is now closed.   Not that Doctrine, in the special sense of dogmatic revelation, is absent from the remaining chapters; for morality is always in Scripture traced to dogmatic truth, and constantly occasions statements of it.   But the main object, by far, in the remainder of the Epistle is instruction in the application of truth to life —Christian practice.

therefore]   I. e. in view of the whole previous argument, in which gratuitous remission of sin, and acceptance of the guilty, for Christ's sake, has been explained; and the consequent gift and influences of the Holy Spirit ; and the assurance of glory : in which, too, the closing sections have reminded both Gentile and Jewish believers of the special aspects of sovereign *mercy* in their respective cases.

the mercies]   **the compassions** ; His *motions* of tenderness and pity. The same word, or cognates, is used ix. 15; Luke vi. 36; 2 Cor. i. 3; Phil. ii. 1; Col. iii. 12; Heb. x. 28; Jas. v. 11.

God, that *ye* present your bodies a living sacrifice, holy, acceptable unto God, *which is* your reasonable service. And 2 be not conformed to this world : but be ye transformed by

This gracious word is doubly noteworthy here, just after the unqualified assertion of Divine Majesty and Sovereignty in xi. 33—36.

present] Same word as vi. 13, 16, 19 ; where E. V. "yield."

your bodies] I.e., practically, *your energies*. The soul, in the present state, *works* through the body ; so that its action for its Master can take effect only through the dedication of the body to Him—hands, feet, eyes, tongue, and brain.

a living sacrifice] A metaphor used elsewhere of the Christian's tokens of thanksgiving : Phil. iv. 18, (of liberal gifts, for Christ's sake, to the Apostle ;) Heb. xiii. 15, (of praise, the "fruit of the lips ; ") 16, (of beneficence for Christ's sake ;) 1 Pet. ii. 5, (of tokens of thanksgiving of any kind, offered up by believers, who, as such, are "a holy priesthood.") See below on xv. 16 for further sacrificial metaphor.

reasonable] **rational, of the reason.** Same word as 1 Pet. ii. 2, where render "*the rational pure milk ;* " i.e. the pure milk which has to do with the mind not the body. So here :—the "service" which is not of "meats and drinks and washings," but is the dedication of the inmost self with its energies ; spiritual service, not mechanical.

service] Same word as ix. 4. See on i. 9, where the cognate verb occurs. In Heb. xii. 28 the words "service" and "acceptable" reappear, in another but kindred connexion.—Meyer renders the Gr. word here by *Opfer-cultus*.

2. *be not conformed*] Same word as 1 Pet. i. 14; (E. V. "not *fashioning yourselves*.") The Gr. noun (*schema*) on which the verb rendered "*conform*" is based indicates a *form* external rather than internal, transient or unreal rather than solid and lasting :—a " figure." It occurs 1 Cor. vii. 31, (E. V. "the *fashion* of this world,") and Phil. ii. 8, (E. V. "in *fashion* as a man.") In the last passage the reference is to the Lord's Manhood not as *unreal* but as, in a certain sense, *external*, i.e. as distinguished from the real but invisible Deity which lay, as it were, *within the veil or robe* of the real and visible Humanity.—Here the verb indicates that a true Christian's "conformity to this world" could only be (1) conformity to a *transient* thing, a thing doomed to destruction, and (2) *illusory* in itself, because alien from the man's true principles and position.—A similar reference is plainly traceable in 1 Pet. i. 14.

this world] Lit. **this age.** Same word as Matt. xii. 32; Luke xvi. 8; 1 Cor. i. 20, ii. 6, 8, iii. 18; 2 Cor. iv. 4; Gal. i. 4; Eph. i. 21; 1 Tim. vi. 17; 2 Tim. iv. 10; Tit. ii. 12. The antithesis is "the world to come," "the coming age," "that age : " e.g. Matt. xii. 32; Luke xx. 35; Eph. i. 21. The passages quoted (and many might be added) shew that the meaning is rightly conveyed in E. V. "*This age*" is the present order of things, the period of sin and death, and (by a natural transference) the *contents* of that period, the principles and practices of evil. The antithesis is the Eternal Future, the resurrection-

the renewing of your mind, that ye may prove what *is that*

life, (Luke xx. 35, 36,) in which sin and death shall have no place for ever. Thus the exhortation here is, to live as those whose lives are governed by the principles and hopes of a holy eternity in prospect.

be transformed] Same word as Matt. xvii. 2, ("was *transfigured ;*") 2 Cor. iii. 18, ("are *changed*.") The root-noun (*morphè*) is different from the root-noun of "conformed" just above, and forms an antithesis to it. In such antithetical connexions it indicates an essential, permanent, and real form. It is used e.g. Phil. ii. 6, 8 ; in which verses the essential reality of the Lord's Deity and Servitude respectively are emphasized. Here the point of the word is manifest : the Christian, by the Divine "renewal," is to realize an *essential and permanent* change ; to prove himself, as it were, one of a new species ; a "new man," not the "old man" in a new dress.

For masterly discussions of the differences between *Schema* and *Morphè* see Abp Trench's *New Testament Synonyms*, under the word μορφή, and Bp Lightfoot's *Philippians*, detached Note to ch. ii. Abp Trench vividly illustrates the difference thus : "If I were to change a Dutch garden into an Italian, this would be [a change of *schema* ;] but if I were to transform a garden into something wholly different, say a garden into a city, this would be [a change of *morphè*.][1]"

Observe that the Gr. word translated "conformed" in viii. 29 is based not on *schema* but on *morphè*.—This passage is illustrated by that. The predestinating will of God is carried out, as we here see, through the real efforts of the renewed wills of the saints, to which the appeal is here made. See Phil. ii. 12, 13 ; (where render "*for His good pleasure's sake.*")

by the renewing of your mind] As the quasi-*instrument* of the trans-formation. The regenerating power of the Holy Spirit had rectified their intelligence, which they were now to use in "purifying themselves as the Lord was pure." As the Divine change had enabled them to use their intelligence aright, the change is spoken of as if itself the instrument to be used.—The word rendered "*renewing*" occurs Tit. iii. 5 ; and the cognate verb 2 Cor. iv. 16; Col. iii. 10. It may denote, according to context, either the initial "renewing," when man definitely becomes "the child of God through faith in Christ Jesus," and "the Spirit of Christ" takes up His dwelling in the soul; or the progressive "renew-ing" consequent on this, as thought, will, and affections "grow in grace," and the man is (according to the appeal here) progressively "transformed." Such is probably the reference in 2 Cor. iv. 16; Col. iii. 10. Here the other reference is more probable, as we have in-dicated above : the "renewing" here is already a fact, and is *used* in the process of "transformation."

your mind] Here probably, in a strict sense, **your intelligence**, renewed or rectified by Divine grace, so as (in the following words) "to prove

---

[1] We translate the Greek nouns, used by the Abp in this sentence. He para-phrases the present passage: "Do not fall in with the fleeting fashions of this world, but undergo a deep abiding change, by the renewing of your mind, such as the Spirit of God alone can work in you (2 Cor. iii. 18)."

good, and acceptable, and perfect, will of God. For I say, 3
through the grace given unto me, to every *man* that is
among you, not to think *of himself* more highly than he
ought to think ; but to think soberly, according as God hath
dealt to every man the measure of faith. For as we have 4

what is the will of God."—Observe that the "mind," as well as other
parts of the being, is assumed to have *needed* "renewing." Cp. Eph.
iv. 18.

that ye may prove] **may assay**, or **test**. Same word as i. 28, (E. V.,
"like,") ii. 18, xiv. 22 ("allow;"), 1 Cor. iii. 13 ("try;"), 2 Cor. xiii. 5;
Eph. v. 10 (a close parallel;), Phil. i. 10 (where render, "test things
which differ;), &c." Where the context allows, the word often includes
(and sometimes wholly adopts) the idea of *preference*, of *approval;*
e.g. 1 Cor. xvi. 3. Here the meaning is that the Christian's intelligence
has been so "renewed" by grace that he now, by a holy instinct,
can discern, in conflicting cases, the will of God from the will of self or
of the world. And on this perception he is to act.

acceptable] Same word as in ver. 1. His will is "acceptable" to
the saints, because the will of their Father. It is also "acceptable" to
Himself, both in itself, and because *as done by His children* it results in
acts pleasing to Him.

perfect] In wisdom and love, whatever perplexities becloud it.

3. *the grace given unto me*] His qualifications as an Apostle; inspired
authority as the Lord's messenger and interpreter. See i. 5, xv. 15, 16.
Cp. also 1 Cor. iii. 10, xv. 10; Gal. ii. 9; Eph. iii. 2, 7, 8; for parallels
more or less exact to this phrase in this connexion.

not to think—think soberly] In the Gr. there is a forcible "play on
words" here, making an almost epigram. The verbs are, the simple
verb "to think," and two of its compounds meaning respectively "to
overween" and "to be sober-thoughted." Lit. **not to over-think
beyond what it behoves him to think, but to think so as to come to
sober-thinking.** The special direction to be taken by this "sober-
thinking" was the recognition by each Christian of the limits of his
own gifts, the reality of the gifts of others, and the position of the
individual as only a part of the great community; as well as the ever-
important fact that "gifts," whether many or few, are the sovereign
bounty of God.

hath dealt] Lit. **did deal, or distribute**; on the admission of each
soul to His grace and service. Same word as 1 Cor. vii. 17; 2 Cor. x. 13.

the measure of faith] Cp. Eph. iv. 7, where (see ver. 11) the context
is similar to this. There, however, the word "*grace*" is used where
"*faith*" is used here; and "faith" here is not quite easy of explanation.
In this Epistle the special aspect of faith (*trust* in God and His word)
as *justifying* has been consistently in view, rather than its aspect (Heb.
xi. 1) as laying hold upon invisible realities in general. Here, therefore, it seems best to seek for a reference as consistent as possible with
that of the rest of the Epistle, and one also which shall harmonize
with the phrase in ver. 6 below; q. v. We explain the present passage

many members in one body, and all members have not the
5 same office: so we, being many, are one body in Christ,
6 and every one members one of another. Having then gifts
differing according to the grace that is given to us, whether
prophecy, *let us prophesy* according to the proportion of

then as follows:—"*Faith*" here means specially acceptance of Christ,
revealed as the Propitiation: but that acceptance is also, *ipso facto*, the
entrance on *bondservice* to God, (see e.g. vi. 18:) therefore the gift
of faith is *here* mentioned as involving the idea of the allotment of
consequent duties and functions also to the various believers with
their various capacities. Faith, in the Divine plan, is the grand qualification for *service*, (because it is the appointed instrument of reconciliation;) and it is therefore the sphere, so to speak, in which all true service
is to be done.

In this view, we may *paraphrase* the passage before us: "even as
God distributed the sovereign gift of faith, (Eph. ii. 7, 8,) the gift of the
power to 'believe unto justification,' to each of you, with a view in each
case to the various tasks and services of the life of faith."

See further on ver. 6.

4. *For as we have*] Here first (and last) in this Epistle St Paul uses
the simile of the Body and its Limbs, to illustrate the close mutual
connexion of the saints. For parallels, see 1 Cor. x. 17, xii. 12—30;
Eph. i. 23, iv. 4—16, v. 23—30; Col. i. 18, 24, ii. 19, iii. 15. In some
of these passages the Lord appears explicitly as the life-giving *Head* of
the Body; in one as its loving *Bridegroom ;* while in others (as here) He
does not explicitly appear in the imagery; the leading thought being
the connexion of His saints *with each other*, and the diversity of their
functions meanwhile.—The phrase just below, "*in Christ*," does not
strictly belong to the simile, though expressing a truth elsewhere conveyed by the simile of the Head of the Body.

all members] Lit. **the limbs all.**

5. *in Christ*] I. e. by virtue of our union with Him. See on viii. 1.
Cp. also for the profound meaning of the phrase, 2 Cor. v. 17.

and every one] Perhaps better, in view of MSS. &c., **but with
respect to individuality ;** "as concerns our several positions."

6. *whether prophecy*, &c.] The Gr. construction from hence to the
end of ver. 8 is peculiar, because elliptical; but the E. V. well interprets the ellipses.

prophecy] Here probably the *charisma*, or special miraculous gift,
of preaching; of utterance in the Christian assemblies under immediate
Divine impulse and guidance. It is now no longer possible to analyze
minutely this sacred phenomenon; but we gather (from the great
passage on the subject, 1 Cor. xiv.) that up to a certain point the utterances were under the conscious will of the utterer, and (as we see in
the present passage) might be, by negligence or extravagance of will,
distorted and otherwise misused. See next note.

according to the proportion of faith] Lit. **according to the propor-**

faith; or ministry, *let us wait* on *our* ministering : or he 7
that teacheth, on teaching; or he that exhorteth, on ex- 8
hortation : he that giveth, *let him do it* with simplicity; he

tion of the faith, i. e. the faith of the utterer. The meaning "*the
(Christian) faith*" would *in itself* be allowable, but *in this Epistle* (see
note "on measure of faith" above) it is not probable. The Gr. word
rendered "*proportion*" is *analogia*, (whence our *analogy*). It is used
in classical Greek for *arithmetical* proportion, and in its derived meanings closely resembles our word "proportion." Here, accordingly, we
may fairly render **in proportion to his faith**; as regulated by his
faith, in respect of less or more. This may be explained thus :—The
"prophecy" would, above all else, deal with *Christ*, His Person and
Work ; with Christ as made known to the "prophet" as the Object of
his own faith ; a faith which itself (if genuine) was based not on his
own impulses and reveries, but on the solid ground of Divine revelation, verifiable as such. Accordingly the "prophet," in exercising his
gift, was to watch over his utterances, and not to allow them to fluc-
tuate with his own independent thinking or wishing, but to see that
they were steadily adjusted to the eternal Truth concerning his Lord,
already revealed to him as a believer.

7. *ministry—ministering*] Lit. **whether service, in the service.**
The word rendered "*ministry*" is *diaconia ;* (same word as xi. 13, where
it means the *apostolic* service). It is a largely inclusive word ; the main
fixed idea being that of active, "practical," duty in the Church, of whatever kind or degree. Almost any work other than that of inspired
utterance, or miracle-working, may be included in it here.—"*In the
service:*"—i.e. "let us be really *in it ;* devoted to it." So "in the
teaching," "in the exhortation," just below. In 1 Tim. iv. 15, the Gr.
rendered "Give thyself wholly to them," is lit. "*Be in* these things."

he that teacheth] In 1 Cor. xii. 28, 29, (see too Eph. iv. 11,) "teachers"
are mentioned as a class of commissioned workers in the Church.
Perhaps they were specially the *expositors* of revealed truth ; those who
devoted themselves to explaining the application (to belief and practice)
of the Scriptures and of the apostolic preaching.

on teaching] Lit. **in the teaching.** See last note but one.

8. *he that exhorteth*] Here again a special division of Christian work
is alluded to. The "exhortation" was, perhaps, a department of the
speaking-duty of the Church less elaborate than the "teaching ;" more
entirely regarding practice ; and allotted more with a view to physical
qualifications, as of voice, &c.

on exhortation] Lit. **in the exhortation.**

giveth] **distributeth**; "imparteth" of his own possessions to the
needy. Here, of course, no special office, but special opportunity, is
in view. Every Christian would, more or less, be a giver ; but the
wealthier Christians would have peculiar responsibility in the matter.

with simplicity] Lit. **in simplicity.** A derived meaning of the Gr.
word, in connexion with giving, (and so here,) is **liberality, open-
handedness;** the opposite to the *doubled, closed*, hand of the niggard.—

that ruleth, with diligence; he that sheweth mercy, with
cheerfulness.

9—21 *Christian practice: in further detail, with regard to
personal and social duty*

9   *Let* love *be* without dissimulation. Abhor *that which is*
10 evil; cleave to *that which is* good. *Be* kindly affectioned
one to another with brotherly love; in honour preferring one
11 another; not slothful in business; fervent in spirit; serving

Same word as 2 Cor. viii. 2, ix. 11, 13, (where lit. "*liberality of* distri-
bution").

ruleth] Lit. **presideth**; whether in the Church, or over any section
of work, or over his own household.

with diligence] Lit. **in haste**, i.e. **with earnestness:** with laborious
and minute attention to duty.

he that sheweth mercy] Here it is unlikely that a special class,
or duty, is in view; except so far as some Christians, by means or
opportunity, would be specially led to works of love for the sad and the
destitute. Such workers of mercy were to give their work full effect by
a spirit of cheerful, and cheering, kindness; as those who had known
the kindness of God.

9—21 CHRISTIAN PRACTICE : IN FURTHER DETAIL, WITH REGARD
TO PERSONAL AND SOCIAL DUTY

9. *love*] Lit. **the love ;** your love, Christian love.

Abhor, &c.] Lit. **Abhorring the evil, cleaving to the good.** Here
participles, as very frequently through this context, practically stand for
hortative verbs; *describing* in order to *set a standard* for endeavour.—
On the subject here, cp. Ps. xcvii. 10.

10. *Be kindly*, &c.] Lit. **In point of your brotherly love [be]
affectionate to one another.** The word rendered "*kindly-affectioned*"
has special reference to *family* affection; and probably our Translators
had this in view, and used "kindly" in its strict sense; "of the *kind*,"
"of the stock, or family."—For "*brotherly-love*" cp. 1 Thess. iv. 9;
Heb. xiii. 1; 1 Pet. i. 22, iii. 8; 2 Pet. i. 7.—See Isaac Taylor's
Saturday Evening for an admirable Essay on "The Family Affection of
Christianity." We quote a line or two of the summary; "Christian
affection has the *permanence* it derives from an indissoluble bond; the
vigour given it by a participation in sufferings and reproaches; and the
depth it receives from the prospect of an unbounded futurity."

in honour] Lit. **in point of the honour;** the honour due from each
to all.—Cp. Phil. ii. 3; 1 Pet. ii. 17, v. 5.—Spiritual religion is, in its
proper nature, the noblest school of courtesy; habituating the man
to the refining power of the Divine presence, and constantly rebuking
the self-regard which is the essence of discourtesy.

11. *not slothful in business*] Better, **in point of earnest diligence,**

the Lord; rejoicing in hope; patient in tribulation; con- 12
tinuing instant in prayer; distributing to the necessity of 13
saints; given to hospitality. Bless them which persecute 14
you: bless, and curse not. Rejoice with them that do 15

not slothful. The precept *includes* an exhortation to thoroughness in
earthly duty, but much more besides.

fervent in spirit] Better, **as regards the spirit, fervent.** "*The
spirit*" here probably means the human spirit, though the grammar
admits as easily a reference to the Holy Spirit. The context, which
hitherto has referred to the acts of human thought and energy, favours
the reference to *man's* spirit, renewed and animated by grace. Same
words as Acts xviii. 25. Cp. Acts xvii. 16.

serving the Lord] Another reading, but inferior on many grounds,
is **serving the occasion**; the Gr. originals of "*Lord*" and "*occasion*"
being very similar in form.—It is well remarked (by De Wette, in
Alford,) that "the Christian should certainly *employ* the opportunity,
but not *serve* it." He will often have to go apparently counter to it, in
the path of duty.—The special mention of *bondservice to the Lord* here
is perhaps due to the last two clauses: the *diligence* and the *fervour* of
the Christian are to be elevated and regulated by his consciousness
of sacred bondservice.

12. *Rejoicing in hope*] Better, **In respect of the hope, rejoicing.**
Cp. ch. v. 2; where see note. On this holy gladness cp. also 1 Pet. i.
3—9.

patient, &c.] Better, **in respect of the tribulation, enduring.**—
"*The tribulation:*" i.e. that which as Christians you are sure to find,
in one form or another. Cp. Joh. xvi. 33; also ch. v. 3, viii. 35.

continuing, &c.] Better, **in respect of the [duty, or act, of] prayer,
persevering.** Same word as Col. iv. 2. Cp. 1 Thess. v. 16. Prayer
would be either united (Acts xii. 12), or individual (Matt. vi. 6); but in
any case it would be diligent, painstaking, and real.

13. *distributing*] **communicating,** sharing your own with them.
This was almost the first instinct of the Church of Christ; and it was
felt to be connected naturally with the sublimest truths of eternity.
Observe the instant transition from 1 Cor. xv. to 1 Cor. xvi. 1.—Cp.
Gal. ii. 10; Heb. xiii. 16; and below, xv. 25, 26.

given to hospitality] Lit. **pursuing hospitality.** Cp. Heb. xiii. 2,
where lit. "forget not hospitality." The duty of succouring and aiding
fellow-Christians from a distance would be a chief (though by no means
the only) point of the exhortation.

14. *Bless them which persecute you*] According to the Lord's own
express precept; see Luke vi. 28. See also His example, Luke xxiii. 34.—
The Roman Church was not at this time under *special* trial of persecution; so we seem to gather from the general tone of this Epistle. But
soon the Neronian persecution was to break upon it; and meantime, in
one form or another, persecution was always going on, if only on a
private scale. Cp. 2 Tim. iii. 12.

15. *Rejoice,* &c.] On this beautiful and precious precept, cp. 1 Cor.

16 rejoice, and weep with them that weep. *Be* of the same
mind one towards another.   Mind not high *things,* but condescend to *men* of low estate.   Be not wise in your own
17 conceits.   Recompense to no *man* evil for evil.   Provide
18 *things* honest in the sight of all men.   If *it be* possible, as
19 much as lieth in you, live peaceably with all men.   Dearly

---

xii. 26; and see the Lord's example, at Cana and at Bethany. St Paul
himself knew how to practise his own precept. (2 Cor. ii. 2—4.)

16.   *Be of the same mind*] Cp. xv. 5; 1 Pet. iii. 8.—Lit. **Thinking
the same thing towards one another**; "actuated by a common and
well-understood feeling of mutual allowance and kindness." (Alford.)

Mind not]   The verb (on which see on viii. 5) is the same as that
just rendered " Be of the...mind;" and doubtless refers to it : "*Think*
kindly toward one another; and thereto *think not* high things."—The
"*high things*" would be thoughts of personal vanity, or of social, or
perhaps also spiritual, pride.

condescend] Lit. **being led away with**; drawn into sympathy with
them.

men of low estate] So probably, better than "low *things,*" as some
render. To sympathize with *the humble* was the antithesis to the having
"the heart haughty and the eyes lofty." (Psal. cxxxi. 1.)—The "low
estate" in view was no doubt specially that of social inferiority; e.g.
that of the slave.   Wonderful was the work of the Gospel in bringing
home this great and sacred duty, and yet without one note of revolutionary bitterness. See 1 Tim. vi. 1, 2. It is the Gospel alone which
knows the full meaning of *Liberté, Fraternité, Égalité.*

Be not wise, &c.]   Same words as xi. 25.   Obedience to this precept
would be a great help to the fulfilment of those just before and after.

17.   *Recompense to no man,* &c.] Matt. v. 39; 1 Thess. v. 15, (a
pregnant parallel to this context ;) 1 Pet. iii. 9.

Provide things honest]   Lit. **thinking beforehand honourable
things**; using forethought so as to secure the reality and the appearance
of rectitude in your life and its surroundings.

in the sight of all men] I.e. so that all shall see the *results* of the
forethought, in the absence of all fair ground for scandal ; in your well-
ordered household, avoidance of debt, attention to civil duties, &c.—
"*All men :*"—here, no doubt, the "*all*" suggests the duty of avoiding
just reproach from without as well as within the Church.—This watchfulness about the opinion of others is anything but a *slavery to opinion.*
It is an anxiety to "adorn the doctrine of God our Saviour in all things."
(Titus ii. 10.)   It is the very opposite of the tendency to make conces-
sions of *principle,* or to adopt *fashions* of opinion as a standard of duty.

18.   *If it be possible,* &c.] Cp. Heb. xii. 14 ; and see 1 Pet. iii. 9—13.

as much as lieth in you] Lit. **as regards what is on your side ;**
"*you*" being emphatic here: q. d., "Let the peace, if broken, be broken
from *the other* side." The spirit of the Saviour's precepts best illustrates
this verse ; Matt. v. 39—41.—"Peaceable living" would be "*im*possi-

beloved, avenge not yourselves, but *rather* give place unto
wrath : for it is written, Vengeance *is* mine; I will repay, saith the Lord. Therefore if thine enemy hunger, 20
feed him; if he thirst, give him drink: for in so
doing thou shalt heap coals of fire on his head.
Be not overcome of evil, but overcome evil with good. 21

ble," on the Christian's side, only when *duty to others* required him to
withstand or expose wrong-doing.

19. *Dearly beloved*] Words here conveying a singularly beautiful
appeal. The believers are entreated by the voice of love to walk in love.

For a remarkable illustration of the precept see 1 Cor. vi. 7 ; and cp.
1 Pet. ii. 20—23.

wrath] Lit. **the wrath** ; that of the enemy or oppressor.

Vengeance is mine; I will repay] "*Mine*" and "*I*" are, of course,
emphatic.—The quotation is from Deut. xxxii. 35 ; where lit. Heb.,
"To me belongeth vengeance and recompence." The LXX. has
"In the day of vengeance I will repay."—In Heb. x. 30 the same
words are quoted, with another view; namely to warn *Christians* that
their God will visit *their* transgressions, as the chastiser of His people.

20. *Therefore if thine enemy*, &c.] Here again is an O. T. quotation,
(Prov. xxv. 21, 22 ; nearly verbatim with LXX.,) introduced by the
Apostle's "*therefore*," as a practical inference from the previous princi-
ples.

thou shalt heap coals of fire on his head] This phrase has been
explained (1) of burning shame produced by requital of good for evil;
(2) of the melting of the evil-doer's heart by such conduct, as of metal
by fire ; (3) of the result of a spirit of love as producing at length the
"incense" of prayer and praise (as from censer-coals) from the con-
quered heart. (The last is suggested in the *Speaker's Commentary*, on
Prov. xxv.) A simpler, yet more inclusive, explanation is Alford's :
"in thus doing, you will be taking the most effectual vengeance ;" the
idea of vengeance being, in the Christian's view, *transformed*, so as to
become in fact the *victory of love*. Q. d., "You shall thus secure exactly
that sort of vengeance which alone a servant of God can desire."—The
clause "and the Lord shall reward thee," in Prov. xxv., is omitted ; not
as if not true (for the Gospel distinctly teaches that "good works, which
are the fruits of faith, and follow after justification,...are pleasing and
acceptable to God in Christ [1];") but as not pertinent to the context here,
where the ruling *motive* understood throughout is "*the mercies of God.*"

21. *Be not overcome*, &c.] The verbs are in the singular; individual-
izing the appeal. The verse runs, lit., **Be not thou overcome by the
evil, but overcome the evil in the good.**—"*The evil*," "*the good ;*"—
that of the evil-doer and the sufferer respectively. Q. d., "Do not let
his evil principles and acts conquer the better mind that is in thee by
grace, but use 'the good' given to thee—the good of Divine peace and

[1] Art. XII. of the Church of England.

CH. XIII. 1—7 *Christian practice: civil duties: authority and obedience*

13 Let every soul be subject unto the higher powers. For

love shed abroad in thy heart—to subdue the evil in him."—"*In the good:*"=under its influence.

Out of countless examples in Christian history we quote a recent one, from the Native Church in China. In 1878 a small and new Christian community was severely persecuted, and some of the converts, grown-up men, were cruelly ill-used by a petty official, without the least resistance on their part. Some time after, this official was summoned before a superior officer, and sentenced to severe punishment. But one of his former victims, who meanwhile had not been his accusers, inter-posed and procured his pardon; and their enemy was turned forthwith into a grateful and cordial friend. (A. E. Moule's *Story of the Chehkiang Mission*, ed. 2, p. 120.)

CH. XIII. 1—7 CHRISTIAN PRACTICE: CIVIL DUTIES: AUTHORITY AND OBEDIENCE

1. *Let every soul be subject*, &c.] A new subject is here treated—Civil Obedience. It is not isolated, however, from the previous context, in which (from xii. 19) *subjection* to individuals in private life was con-sidered. And it passes in turn into a different but kindred context again, in ver. 8 below. We offer a few general remarks on the subject.

1. In this passage it is stated, as a primary truth of human society, that civil authority is, as such, a Divine institution. Whatever may be the details of error or of wrong in its exercise, it is nevertheless, even at its worst, so vastly better than anarchy, that it forms a main instru-ment and ordinance of the will of God.

2. The passage does not touch on the question of *forms* of govern-ment. "The powers that be" is a phrase which, on the whole, accepts authority *de facto*, irrespective of its theory, or of its circumstances of origin. Just so both human and Divine law, after no long lapse of time, recognize *property de facto*, irrespective of circumstances of acqui-sition.

3. The passage distinctly forbids revolutionary action in a Christian. Action within the limits of the existing constitution he may employ; for the constitution is, in fact, the "power that is," be it good or bad. But he must not *plot* for its demolition, nor indeed *act* for its demolition in any way of "violence;" be it violence of deed or word, violence direct or indirect.

4. The passage by no means forbids Christians to take full advan-tage of existing authority and law; as St Paul himself took advantage of his civil rights. But its unmistakable drift is, what is always the drift of Scripture, (as it is *not* that of human nature), to emphasize the Christian's *duties* far more than his *rights*.

5. As regards the special question of *despotism*, it is treated here not by explicit condemnation, but by the statement of principles which

there is no power but of God: the powers that be are
ordained of God. Whosoever therefore resisteth the power, 2
resisteth the ordinance of God: and they that resist shall

will peacefully undermine its own *distinctive* principles. It is dealt with
precisely as elsewhere the ownership of slaves is dealt with. Just as the
Gospel bids the slave submit to his master, yet meanwhile (above all by
bringing out the value and dignity of every human soul) withers the
root of slavery, so it bids the subject obey the despot, yet withers the
root of despotism.

6. The passage assumes, of course, that where human law, or its
minister, *contradicts Divine precepts*, (as when a Christian is commanded to *do wrong*,) then obedience to the Higher Authority must
take precedence. Christian officials, for instance, under a despot must
not *plot against him*, but also must not *do wrong for him*.

7. This and other considerations combine to assure us that the
principles of the Gospel, so far from favouring tyranny, tend *ultimately*
to make it impossible. A perfectly Christian nation under tyrannic
authority is an inconceivable thing.

8. It is manifest how indispensable to the early growth of the
Christian Church these precepts of obedience were. Though their
truth is for all generations, whatever may be the phases of political
speculation or popular feeling, it was a truth of special and urgent
necessity *then*. But for these principles, humanly speaking, society
would have been convulsed, and then left with its evils intensified; and
the Church would have perished.

See further, Appendix J.

the higher powers] Lit. **supreme (i. e. ruling) authorities.** The
word rendered "higher" is the same as that rendered "supreme,"
1 Pet. ii. 13. The context here shews that the idea is not (as in
1 Pet. ii. 13) *supremacy over other authorities*, but a more general one,
superior position as regards the subject.

there is no power but of God: the powers, &c.] More lit. **there is no
authority except authority derived from God; but the existing authorities have been appointed by God.** The first clause emphasizes
the absolute inalienable Supremacy of God; the second emphasizes the
fact that this Supreme Ruler *actually has* constituted subordinate authorities on earth, and that these authorities are to be known in each
case by their *de facto* existence, and to be obeyed by Christians as God's
present order. It is instructive to remember that Roman imperialism,
under Nero, was God's present order for St Paul and his first readers.

Whosoever—resisteth] Same word as Jas. v. 6; where the possible reference is to the non-resistance of the Just One Himself, when, by an
awful abuse of authority, He was "condemned and killed."

resisteth] **withstandeth**; and so just below, **they that withstand.**
The verb is different from that rendered "resist" just above. The
difference is noteworthy only as shewing the special reference of the
words "they that *withstand*," which thus, plainly, must refer to "the
ordinance *of God*;" and the passage may be thus paraphrased: "those

3 receive to themselves damnation. For rulers are not a
terror to good works, but to the evil. Wilt thou then not
be afraid of the power? do *that which is* good, and thou
4 shalt have praise of the same : for he is the minister of God
to thee for good. But if thou do *that which is* evil, be afraid ;
for he beareth not the sword in vain : for he is the minister

who resist civil authority withstand God's ordinance; and those who
withstand *God's ordinance* will (by inevitable consequence) bring on
themselves *God's condemnation.*"

themselves] Emphatic in the Gr. They will be *their own* victims.

damnation] **judgment.** Same word as ii. 2, 3, iii. 8, v. 16; 1 Cor.
xi. 29. Here the reference is to the *Divine* judgment-seat. See last
note but one.

3. *For rulers, &c.*] St Paul enforces the certainty of "judgment"
in this case by pointing out its manifest justice. "Rulers" (lit. **the rulers,**
rulers as a class,) are, as a fact, an agency on the side of right and order ;
it is justly, then, a sin in the sight of God to resist their authority.—
No doubt the statement here is never *fully* realized save where the rulers
are personally just and the constitution equitable; (and by no means
always, *in detail,* even then). But the statement is not to be limited
to such cases. Civil authority, even in its most distorted forms, never
systematically favours wrong *as wrong* and punishes right *as right.*
Even when a Nero or a Decius persecuted the Church of Christ, the
theory of persecution (apart from personal rancour) was the preservation
of order; and meantime, in the innumerable details of the common life
of the Roman world, the authority of a Nero or a Decius was a necessity
and a providential blessing.

Wilt thou then not be afraid] With the fear of an *enemy ;* the feeling
of a weaker towards a stronger *opponent.*—"*Then*" is lit. **but**; and so
better, perhaps : **But wilt thou not,** &c. Q. d., "But if, as a fact, they
are a terror to thee, and thou willest to shake off that terror- the remedy
is simple ; be a good citizen and subject."

praise] That at least of protection and security; the "good" referred
to in the next clause.

4. *he beareth*] **weareth.** The Cæsars appear to have literally worn
a sword or dagger as an emblem of imperatorial power. But the phrase
here need be no more than figurative.

the sword] A distinct sanction is given by this word here to the
ordinance of capital punishment.—Other and lower punishments are
implied also, of course, in this mention of the highest and severest.—
The word "sword" occurs in this Epistle only here and viii. 35, where
no doubt the execution of martyrs is in view. The two passages are a
suggestive contrast and mutual illustration.

in vain] I.e. **without cause,** without credentials. The Gr. word
may equally mean "without cause" and "without effect;" but the
latter meaning is out of place here. See the next clause, where the
credentials are given : " he is *God's minister.*"

of God, a revenger to *execute* wrath upon him that doeth
evil. Wherefore *ye* must needs be subject, not only for 5
wrath, but also for conscience sake.   For for this cause pay 6
you tribute also : for they are God's ministers, attending
continually upon this very *thing*. Render therefore to all 7
their dues : tribute to whom tribute *is due ;* custom to whom
custom; fear to whom fear; honour to whom honour.

8—10   *Christian practice : Love the best guarantee for the*
rights and interests of others, in general

Owe no *man* any *thing*, but to love one another : for he 8

to execute wrath]   Lit. **unto wrath**; to inflict the consequences of
the displeasure (of the ruler. See next note).
   5.   *Wherefore*] Because of the ruler's *Divine* credentials. The Christian
is accordingly a good subject **not only on account of the wrath**, (so lit. ;
i.e. the ruler's wrath in case of crime,) **but also on account of the**
conscience, (so lit. ; i.e. the Christian's knowledge and sense of the
ruler's *right* to be angry).
   6.   *for this cause*]   I.e. because of "the conscience" that they are
God's appointed agency, and act in *His* name when they demand con-
tributions for the public revenues, which are a vital part of the machinery
of civil order.
   tribute]   **taxes.**
   attending continually]   **persevering in,** "devoting themselves to."
Same word as e. g. xii. 12, ("*continuing instant.*") The word points to
government as the life-work of the governor ; a thing not of pride or
privilege so much as of incessant duty.
   upon this very thing]   Better, **with a view to this very thing**; i.e.,
probably, "with a view to the service of God." The governor may not
consciously "serve God" in his office; but in his office he does a work
which *is* "the ordinance of God," and must be recognized as such by
Christian subjects.—To refer the words "*this very thing*" to taxes, or tax-
gathering, is to limit what is evidently a solemn summary clause, and
greatly to lessen its intended weight.
   7.   *to all*]   To all persons in authority over you. The precept is, of
course, of universal application, but plainly bears this special reference
here : see the next words.
   tribute—custom—fear—honour]   Lit. **the tribute, the custom,** &c. ;
i.e. the tribute, &c. which is in question in each case.—"*Tribute*"—tax
on person and property.   "*Custom :*"—toll on merchandize.   "*Fear :*"
—such as is due to an authorized *avenger* of wrong.   "*Honour :*"—such
as is due to authorized power in general.

8—10   CHRISTIAN PRACTICE : LOVE THE BEST GUARANTEE FOR THE
RIGHTS AND INTERESTS OF OTHERS, IN GENERAL

   8.   *Owe no man any thing*]   The special precept here beautifully
expands into the general.   Not rulers only but all men, (and here

₉ that loveth another hath fulfilled the law. For *this*, Thou shalt not commit adultery, Thou shalt not kill, Thou shalt not steal, Thou shalt not bear false witness, Thou shalt not covet; and if *there be* any other commandment, it is briefly comprehended in this

particularly, no doubt, all Christians; see next note;) are to receive "their dues."

The precept, in its particular application to money-debts, no doubt counsels immediate payment where possible and desirable. Its spirit, however, *obliges* the Christian only to a watchful avoidance of a *state of debt*, by careful restriction of expenses within means; and a thoughtful care for the interests of the *creditor*, to whom deferred payment may be a serious loss. See Prov. iii. 27, 28.—But it is obvious that the "owing" here is not of money only but of every kind of "due" from man to man.

but to love one another] This does not mean that "love" is to be an *unpaid debt* in the sense in which a repudiated or neglected bill is unpaid. It is to be a *perpetual payment;* one which in the nature of things can *never be paid off*, and which will therefore be ever recurring as a new demand for the same happy expenditure.—The phrase "love *one another*" shews that St Paul has the Christian community specially in view here. They were, indeed, quite as truly bound to "love their enemies;" but the love in the two cases was not exactly of the same quality. The love of *benevolence* is not to be confused with the love of *endearment*.—For such special entreaties to *Christian* love see e.g. Joh. xiii. 34, xv. 12, 17; 1 Thess. iv. 9; 1 Pet. i. 22, ii. 17; 1 Joh. iii. 14; and particularly, as a strictly parallel passage here, Gal. v. 13, 14.

loveth another] Lit. **loveth the other;** the other of the two parties necessary to intercourse.

hath fulfilled] The perfect tense conveys the thought that such "love" *at once attains* the fulfilment (as regards principle and will) of the precepts of the "Second Table." It does not move from one to another by laborious steps, but leaps, as it were, to entire obedience. By its very nature "it has obeyed," *ipso facto*, all the demands.

It is obvious that St Paul is not concerned here with the fact of the actual incompleteness of the obedience of even the holiest Christian. He has to state the *principle;* he takes the *ideal*, at which all sincere effort will aim.

It is obvious also that by "the Law" here he means only that part of the Divine Law which affects "the neighbour." The "*first* and great commandment" (see Matt. xxii. 37, 38,) is not here in view.

9. *For this*] Lit. **For the;** each precept being a quasi-substantive with the definite article.

Thou shalt not bear false witness] Perhaps to be omitted, on documentary evidence.

and if there be any other commandment, &c.] The Gr. phrase nearly = **and whatever other commandments there are, all are summed up,** &c.

saying, namely, Thou shalt love thy neighbour as thyself. Love worketh no ill to *his* neighbour: therefore love ₁₀
is the fulfilling of the law.

11—14   *Christian practice: duty enforced by the prospect of
the Lord's Return*

And that, knowing the time, that now *it is* high time to ₁₁

Thou shalt love, &c.] Lev. xix. 18. See the Lord's own quotation
of the words, Matt. xxii. 39. Cp. Jas. ii. 8.
  10. *Love worketh*, &c.] Such is its very nature,—to avoid the kind
of acts which as a fact the Law forbids. Therefore Love ("Charity,"
1 Cor. xiii., &c.), though its action is not, strictly speaking, originated
by the Law, but the necessary result of its being Love, is in perfect
harmony with the Law—which is the precept of Eternal Love; and so
is the surest secret of fulfilling it.
  his neighbour] Lit. **the neighbour:** the neighbour in each case.
  the fulfilling] Better, **the fulfilment.** The Gr. word means not the
process of obedience, but the *result of the process;* obedience as an accomplished fact. For this view of Love, see note on ver. 8; "hath
fulfilled."
  The doctrine of this passage (that to love one another is the true
secret of obedience to the Divine Law,) is in perfect harmony with the
doctrine of the "bondservice" of the Christian, as stated in ch. vi.; for
the true secret of that bondservice is adoring gratitude for emancipa-
tion from the slavery of sin; a gratitude which after all does but joyfully
recognize the unchangeable *fact* of the *lawful claim* of the Creator and
Redeemer to the devotion of the whole man. Thus love to God is
in fact the full acceptance of His will, His law; and love to others for
His sake is therefore the sure way to carry out that law in its special
precepts regarding duty to fellow-Christians and fellow-men.—Manifestly the law is to be the authoritative guide of "love." Love is not
"a law unto itself," but the "fulfilment" of the definite and objective
rule of God's revealed will.

11—14   CHRISTIAN PRACTICE: DUTY ENFORCED BY THE PROSPECT
OF THE LORD'S RETURN

  11. *And that*, &c.] In this last section of the chapter, St Paul
enforces all the preceding precepts (of cch. xii., xiii.) by the solemn
assertion of the approach of the eternal Day of Resurrection and Glory.
Then all that was painful in effort would be over, and the results of
"patient continuance in well-doing" would be realized for ever.
  Language such as that of this passage is often taken to prove that
St Paul expected an imminent return of the Lord, and taught it as a
revealed truth. But the prophetic part of ch. xi. is sufficient to shew
that he looked for an *extended* future. And the expectation here expressed, as a main item of Christian truth, by this great prophet of the

awake out of sleep: for now *is* our salvation nearer than
12 when we believed.   The   night is far spent, the day is at
hand : let us therefore cast off the works of darkness, and
13 let us put on the armour of light.   Let us walk honestly, as

Gospel, has been accepted ever since by successive generations of believers
as the just expression of their own attitude of hope.
It is plain that the Lord Himself both implied and sometimes distinctly foretold a *long* interval.   See Matt. xxv. 19.
the time]   **the occasion**; same word as iii. 26, where see note.   The
"occasion" is, in fact, the "last days;" the times of Messiah.   (See
Acts ii. 16, 17.)
out of sleep]   The sleep of languor and forgetfulness.—The Lord had
used this metaphor in connexion with His Return; Matt. xxiv. 42, xxv.
13.   See elsewhere in St Paul, 1 Thess. v. 6.   Also Rev. iii. 3, xvi. 15.
our salvation]   See note on "salvation," i. 16.   It is here the "salvation" of resurrection-glory.
12.   *The night is far spent*]   Lit. **The night was far spent.**   The Gr.
verb is in the aorist; and the time-reference is, very probably, to the
First Advent, when the Morning Star (Rev. xxii. 16) of the final Day
appeared.—We have here, clearly, a combination of metaphors.   The
"sleep" of ver. 11 was the sleep of *languor;* the "night" of this verse
is not, as we might thus have thought, the night of *ignorance* or *sin,* but
that of *trial;* the "present time" contrasted with the coming glory.
But the combination is most natural and instructive : a period of *trial*
is almost sure, if it does not answer its end, to act directly the other way
—to bring on the *sloth* of *discouragement*.—Cp. on this passage 1 John
ii. 8; where render "the darkness *is passing.*"
the day is at hand]   Lit. **hath drawn near.**—" *The   day:*"—"the
day of Christ;" with the added idea of the *day-light* of eternal peace
and glory which it will bring in.   See 1 Thess. v. 5 for the only exact
parallel: in the many other passages where "the Day" means the
Lord's Return, there is no trace of the special metaphor of *light*, the
contrast of day with *night*.
the works of darkness]   Lit. **of the darkness.**   (Same phrase as Eph.
v. 11.)—Here we recur to the idea of *moral* darkness; not the darkness
of trial or pain; (see last note but one.)   Cp. John iii. 19; Acts xxvi. 18;
2 Cor. vi. 14; Eph. v. 11; 1 Thess. v. 4, 5; 1 Pet. ii. 9; 1 John i. 6.   No
doubt the word suggests also the "*powers* of the darkness," the personal
spiritual "*rulers* of the darkness," who tempt the soul and intensify its
tendencies to evil.   Cp. Luke xxii. 53; Eph. vi. 12; Col. i. 13.—The
habit resulting from these "deeds" is here figured as a *night-robe*, which
is to be put off as the sleeper rises to conflict.   (So Meyer.)
the armour of light]   Lit. **the weapons of the light**.   Not clothing
merely, but arms and armour, must take the place of the night-robe.
The "arms" are Divine grace with its manifold means and workings.
See the elaborate picture in a later Epistle, Eph. vi. 11; a passage full
of illustration for this context.   The earliest use of the metaphor by
St Paul is 1 Thess. v. 8; another close parallel.   See also 2 Cor. vi. 7,

in the day; not in rioting and drunkenness, not in chambering and wantonness, not in strife and envying. But put ye 14
on the Lord Jesus Christ, and make not provision for the
flesh, to *fulfil* the lusts *thereof.*

x. 4; 1 Pet. iv. 1.—" *Of the light:*"—here perhaps the ideas of the *day-
light of sincerity and purity,* and the *day-light of glory* which will end
the conflict, are combined.

Observe how the re-animation of the life of grace is here, as often
elsewhere, (cp. Eph. vi. 11; 1 Pet. iv. 1; and perhaps 2 Cor. v. 20;)
spoken of as if it were the beginning of it. The persons here addressed
had already (on the Apostle's hypothesis) truly "believed," and were
"walking after the Spirit."

13. *honestly*] Margin, **decently, i.e. becomingly;** with the true
decorum of a life of obedience to the will of God.

as in the day] Here again the metaphor slightly varies its point.
The Gr. is, nearly lit., **as by day;** "as men walk by day." The
Christian is thus bidden to think of himself as in the daylight; with
light on him and around him. This is probably here the "light" of
1 John i. 7; the light of the knowledge of the Holy One, and of His
felt presence. (See Psal. cxxxix. 12.) Such "light" is the dawning of
that Day in which "we shall be like Him, for we shall see Him as He
is;" and this accords with the imagery of ver. 12.

rioting] Cp. Gal. v. 21; 1 Pet. iv. 3.

drunkenness] The Gr. (as in Gal. and 1 Pet. just quoted) is plural;
drinking-bouts.

chambering] Again plural: indulgences of lustful pleasure.

wantonness] Again plural: the *varieties* of lascivious sin are suggested.

Such warnings as these, addressed to the justified and believing, not
to a mass of merely conventional Christians, are indications of the immense
force of moral corruption in the heathen world out of which the Christians
had lately come, and which everywhere surrounded them. But they also
indicate the permanent fact that the most sincere Christian, in the
happiest times, is never—in his own strength—invulnerable even by
gross temptation.

not in strife and envying] Sins of the temper are here classed with
lusts of the flesh; as often. See e. g. Gal. v. 19, 20.

14. *But put ye on,* &c.] For similar language see Gal. iii. 27;
(where Baptism is to be viewed in its ideal, as involving and seal-
ing the acceptance and confession of Christ.) Cp. also Eph. iv.
24; Col. iii. 10. Here again (see ver. 12, last note,) observe how
the *new effort* of the life of grace is spoken of as if it were its *beginning.*

the Lord Jesus Christ] Here the Saviour is presented as the soul's
armour and arms. Cp. ver. 12. By means of HIM, beheld by faith,
adored, accepted, and welcomed as the Guest of the soul, sin is to be
resisted and subdued. Grace is to come, above all other means, by
means of personal dealings with HIM.

and make not provision, &c.] Lit. **make not forethought of the flesh.**

Ch. XIV. 1—9   *Christian practice: mutual toleration: each individual directly responsible to the Redeemer*

14   Him that is weak in the faith receive you, *but* not to

The clause, of course, means (under a sort of euphemism) "positively *deny* the flesh;" but it specially suggests the sad thought of the elaborate pains with which so often sin is *planned and sought.*—See the close of 1 Cor. ix. for St Paul's own practical comment on this precept.

to fulfil the lusts thereof] Lit., simply, **unto lusts**; with a view to (evil) desires.

An instructive parallel is Col. ii. 23, where probably render, "*not of any value with a view to* [*resisting the*] *gratification of the flesh.*"   Mere ascetic rules there stand contrasted with the living grace of the personal Saviour here.

This verse is memorable as the turning-point of St Augustine's conversion.   In his *Confessions* (VIII. 12) he records how, at a time of great moral conflict, he was strangely impelled by a voice, perhaps the cry of children at play, ("*Take and read, take and read,*") to open again the Epistles of St Paul (*codicem Apostoli*) which he had recently been reading. "I read in silence the first place on which my eyes fell; *Not in revelling and drunkenness, not in chambering and wantonness, not in strife and envying; but put ye on the Lord Jesus Christ, and make no provision for the flesh in its lusts.*   I neither cared, nor needed, to read further. At the close of the sentence, as if a ray of certainty were poured into my heart, the clouds of hesitation all fled at once."—The following words, *But him that is weak in faith receive ye,* were pointed out to him just after by his friend Alypius, to whom Augustine shewed the present verse.   Augustine was at the time so slightly read in the Scriptures that he was not aware (he says) of this context till Alypius, with an application to himself, drew his attention to it.

Ch. XIV. 1—9   Christian practice: mutual toleration: each individual directly responsible to the Redeemer

1.   *Him that is weak,* &c.] Lit. **But him that is weak,** &c.   The "*but*" marks a slight contrast with the previous passage.   Probably this is q.d., "I have just spoken of vigour and thoroughness in your spiritual life; *but* let this be such as to leave you gentle and sympathetic with imperfectly-enlightened converts.   Be severe with self, gentle with others."

in the faith] So lit.; but render **in his faith.**   See notes on xii. 3, 6. Here, as there, a *subjective* explanation of the word "faith" is better, in view of the usage of this Epistle.

receive you] The Gr. tense is the present, and perhaps indicates (what is otherwise probable) that St Paul means not only the first welcome of a new believer, but the *continued* welcome—a full recognition ever after of his standing as a Christian.   Same word and tense as xv. 7.

doubtful disputations.   For one believeth that *he* may eat ₂

but not to doubtful disputations]   Lit. **not to criticisms of (his) scruples.**   The word *"but"* is not in the Gr., and changes the exact point of the clause, which is q.d., *"receive* him, do not *criticize* him; let him in with a *welcome*, not with a call to *discussion*."—The noun rendered *"criticisms"* (or its cognate verb) is used (e.g. 1 Cor. xii. 10; Heb. v. 14;) for *detection of differences;* and again (e.g. 1 Cor. xi. 31, E.V. *"judge* ourselves,") for *judicial enquiry and sentence,* literal or figurative.   " *Criticism* " thus fairly represents it in a context like this, where needless keenness in balancing varying convictions, and the consequent *sentence* of private or public opinion, is in view. — "His *scruples"*:—same word as i. 21, (E.V. "imaginations,") where see note.   Here it is *the reasoning of the mind with itself;* doubt and perplexity.

Some general remarks are offered on the subject and the teaching of this chapter.

1.   Two passages of St Paul's writings afford striking likenesses or equally striking contrasts to Rom. xiv.; viz. 1 Cor. viii., and the Epistle to the Galatians as a whole.   In all these three places St Paul has in view differences of opinion within the visible Church.   In 1 Cor. viii., as here, he argues for mutual toleration; in Galatians he lays down, with unbending decision, the line between irreconcilables.

2.   This difference may be explained by the different quality and aspect of the controversies.   In Galatia the question was of primary principle; at Rome and Corinth it was, on the whole, of secondary practice.   *How to be justified before God* was the Galatian problem. *How the justified should live* was, at least in the main, the problem at Rome and Corinth.   For there is no proof that the "weak brethren" differed from the "strong" on the great principle of Justification by Faith.   Their error was that the path of duty, laid before the justified, included a moral obligation on the obedient children of God to abstain from certain sorts of food and to keep the Mosaic feasts.   *All* the Roman Christians agreed that the justified *must not* lie nor steal; but the "weak brethren" held that, in the same way, they *must not* taste "unclean" food, nor neglect the festivals.   The error in Galatia affected the very principle of the work and grace of Christ; the error at Rome did not, at all necessarily, do so.   St Paul was thus perfectly consistent in writing Gal. i. 6—9, and Rom. xiv. 1—10.

3.   It is unmistakable, from all the passages in question, on which side apostolic truth lay.   St Paul clearly decides against the *principle* of the "weak brethren;" though he treats it as an error which might lawfully and usefully be met by toleration and the quiet influence of tolerant example.

4.   The question has been much debated whether the observance of the Sabbath was one of the tenets of the "weak brethren," and so whether it is here ruled by St Paul to be not of permanent moral obligation.   (Cp. Col. ii. 16.)   If by "the Sabbath" is meant the last day of the week strictly, the answer to both questions must be *yes*.

3 all *things:* another, who is weak, eateth herbs. Let not him that eateth despise him that eateth not ; and let not him which eateth not judge him that eateth : for God hath
4 received him. Who art thou that judgest another *man's* servant? to his own master he standeth or falleth. Yea, he

But as to the observance of a divinely-consecrated Weekly Rest, it is evident (from Gen. ii. 3 and Exod. xx. 8—11, and cp. such passages of prophetic doctrine as Isai. lviii. 13, 14,) that the institution stands on a very different level from that of the monthly and yearly Mosaic festivals. It is antecedent to all Jewish law, and in the Decalogue of Exodus it is based on strictly universal grounds, and placed among the great elements of moral duty. No doubt it is impossible to trace the whole process of transition from the observance of the Seventh day to that of the First ; but the plain fact remains that the sanctity of the primeval weekly worship-rest was of a kind most unlikely to be *slightingly put aside* by the Apostles; and thus in such places as this and Col. ii. 16 it is far more likely that the wrong opinion in question was that the whole Mosaic code of festivals was still binding in full detail; that therefore the Saturday was the only possible Sabbath; and that it was to be observed by the Rabbinic rules.

How to deal with those who might reject the Weekly Rest altogether might be a difficult question. But all we are here called on to enquire is whether it was likely that St Paul, with the O.T. before him, would treat the Sabbath (the Sabbath apart from its *Rabbinic* aspect) as a thing of the same quality as, for example, the new-moon feast.

2. *believeth that he may eat*] Lit. **believeth to eat**; i. e. *has faith which leads him to* see that sorts of food are no longer a matter of religious scruple.

who is weak] I.e. in his faith. See on ver. 1.

eateth herbs] This is given as an extreme case. Anxious scrupulosity would adopt vegetarianism as the simplest solution of the questions raised by the Mosaic precepts, complicated by the possible "defilement" of animal-food by idol-sacrifices.

3. *God hath received him*] Lit. **God did receive him**; i. e. at the crisis of his conversion; on the sole revealed condition of his accepting and confessing Christ as his Saviour and Lord. Same verb as that in ver. 1.

This clause may probably refer to *both* the two preceding clauses; but its main reference (see next verse) is to the fact that the "*strong*" Christian, in spite of his apparent laxity, had been welcomed by God.

4. *Who art thou that judgest*] The verb "*judge*" connects this with the "judgment" passed by the "eater of herbs" upon the Christianity of his "stronger" brother.—The word "judge" here (as in Matt. vii. 1) manifestly does not forbid the entertainment, nor the right expression, of *opinions*, but the assumption of a tone of *judicial* opinion ; the thinking of others from a level of isolated authority and sanctity.

standeth or falleth] In the sense of acceptance or non-acceptance.

shall be holden up : for God is able to make him stand.
One man esteemeth one day above another : another 5
esteemeth every day *alike*.   Let every man be fully persuaded in his own mind.   He that regardeth the day, re- 6
gardeth *it* unto the Lord ; and he that regardeth not the
day, to the Lord he doth not regard *it*.   He that eateth,
eateth to the Lord, for he giveth God thanks ; and he that
eateth not, to the Lord he eateth not, and giveth God

Yea, he shall be holden up]   Lit. **But he shall be made to stand.**
The " but " points out that of the two alternatives just given ("standing," "falling,") the former, in this case, is certain.

5.   *One man esteemeth*, &c.]   Lit. **One man judgeth day above day,**
but another judgeth every day.   The "*judgeth*" in the second clause
is an echo from the first, without which it would be obscure.   As it
stands, it means not only, as E.V., "esteemeth every day alike," but
"every day *good* alike ;" with a suggestion that the "strong" believer
will be careful to assert his freedom in the spirit of one who wishes not
to *secularize* but to *consecrate* his whole time.

On the question of the Sabbath, see last note on ver. 1.

fully persuaded]   "Quite sure."   Cp. iv. 21.   This word directs individual Christians not to stubborn fixity in their own opinion as such,
but to earnest pains, as in the Lord's presence and by His revealed will,
to form that opinion clearly.   Each man not only has a *right* to " his
own " opinion, but (a very different matter) is *responsible* for it to the
Lord.

6.   *regardeth*]   Lit. **thinketh, mindeth.**   Same word as e. g. viii. 5.

unto the Lord]   I.e. the Lord *Christ*, "the Lord of the dead and
living" (ver. 9).   The word thus used is a good implicit proof of St
Paul's view of the supreme dignity of Messiah ; especially when we find
him just below writing, in the same connexion, "he giveth God
thanks."   It would indeed be unsafe to say that in that clause " *God* "
means specially or exclusively "*Christ*."   But the two words are so
used that no such gulf as that between Creator and Creature can possibly divide them.—"*Unto the Lord* :"—i.e., as one who not only *is*
responsible to Him, but *owns* that he is.   This seems to be required by
the use made of the fact of *thanksgiving* just below.

and he that regardeth not—not regard it]   Documentary evidence
appears to exclude this part of the verse.   But as an explanatory gloss
it is just and valuable.

He that eateth]   Probably read **And** before this clause.

for he giveth God thanks]   And so evidences his sense of subjection
and responsibility.

and giveth God thanks]   Here again, the inward sense of responsibility to "the Lord" is evidenced by the outward act of thanksgiving
to "God."—The thanks given is, of course, for the food (vegetable,
or "clean" meat), which he *does* eat.

₇ thanks. For none of us liveth to himself, and no *man* dieth
₈ to himself. For whether we live, we live unto the Lord;
and whether we die, we die unto the Lord: whether we
₉ live therefore, or die, we are the Lord's. For to this end
Christ both died, and rose, and revived, that he might be
Lord both of the dead and living.

7. *For none of us*] Us the justified, the "sons of God."—Here
(and in vv. 8, 9,) St Paul states the great principle on which the
practice in question is, or should be, based. He takes it for granted
that each Christian owns, and acts upon, a sense of the Lordship
of Christ, because that Lordship is a Divine fact.

liveth to himself] See last note on ver. 4. Here, as in 1 Cor. iv.,
the argument passes from the Christian's independence of man's
judgment to his deep dependence on the Lord's. To "live to himself" is here, manifestly, not so much to live a "*selfish*" life as to
live a life in which the mere dictates of conscience and will are the
supreme rule, irrespective of Christ. Q. d., "none of us believers can
make *anything lower* than Christ and His will the rule of life. Opinions, convictions, conscience itself, must be brought for light and
correction to Him; for we are HIS."

Strictly speaking, this is a digression, as the main purport of
the passage is to insist on the lawful freedom of believers with regard
to *one another*.

8. *we die unto the Lord*] In view of ver. 9, this must mean,
"when we die, we do not pass out of His bondservice, but only
into another mode of it: in the world to come we are still at His
command, responsible to Him." Not so much the act of death as
the *state of the departed* seems to be in question here. (The usage of the
Gr. verb rendered "die" fully admits this: it must occasionally be
rendered "*lie dead*.")

The whole of this passage is deeply significant of the true object
of a Christian's life. We are bound indeed to "live to others;" but
this bond is but a part of the supreme obligation (of which non-
religious philanthropy knows nothing, though it owes to the Gospel
so much of its original impulse,) to "live and die unto the Lord."
There are some excellent remarks on this in *Memorials of a Quiet
Life*, III. 130.

whether we live therefore] "Therefore" gathers up the facts just
stated into one summary expression.

the Lord's] His bondservants. Cp. St Paul's own personal confession, Acts xxvii. 23.

9. *died, and rose, and revived*] Better, probably, **died and came
to life**. The words "*and rose*" appear to be interpolated. The
balance of the clauses is thus made precise:— He *died* and *lived;* He
is Master of the *dead* and *living*.

that he might be Lord] **that He might become the Master**. The
emphasis is on the word Lord, or Master. Here St Paul states

10—23 *The same subject: mutual care and love more important and sacred than eager assertions of liberty*

But why dost thou judge thy brother? or why dost thou 10
set at nought thy brother? for we shall all stand before the
judgment seat of Christ. For it is written, *As* I live, saith 11
the Lord, every knee shall bow to me, and every

one great intended effect of the *mode* of Salvation. It was *Redemption*,
Deliverance by *Purchase;* and thus it made the saved the personal
possession of the Saviour. It was also, specially, through *Death and
Revival;* with a view (among other objects) to the realization by His
servants that He who, to save them, had *dwelt in both worlds*, was
their Master in both.

10—23 THE SAME SUBJECT: MUTUAL CARE AND LOVE MORE IM-
PORTANT AND SACRED THAN EAGER ASSERTIONS OF LIBERTY

10. *But why dost thou*] "*Thou*" is strongly emphatic here, as in
contrast to the Lord. So just below, in the next sentence.—Cp. ver. 4.

thy brother] Here, evidently, "thy brother in Christ;" one of the
"many brethren" who are such as being adopted by the Eternal
Father in the supreme Elder Brother (viii. 29. See also on xii. 10).

all] Strongly emphatic; the critic as well as the criticized will
be there—all on one level.

the judgment seat] Lit. **the bema;** the Gr. equivalent of the Lat.
tribunal. (Same word as e.g. Matt. xxvii. 19; Acts xviii. 16, 17).
The great Session is imaged under the forms of imperial law.

of Christ] The true reading, probably, is **of God.** On the interchange of the words *Christ* and *God* in this context, see on ver. 6.
It is significant that in 2 Cor. v. 10 (the best commentary on this
passage) the undoubted reading is, as in E. V., "*of Christ.*"
The "judgment seat" here is that of the Great Day, when "the
books will be opened." This passage by no means implies that the
Christian must wait till then to know whether he is accepted or not;
a thought which would contradict both the letter and spirit of e. g. ch.
v. 1—11, and viii. (See especially also 2 Tim. iv. 8.) But it does
imply that the judicial declaration of his acceptance, and also of the
Lord's verdict upon his life of new obedience, will be made to him
as to one *at the bar* and *before the Judge.* The Judge will be his
Brother, but yet his Judge, his King.

11. *it is written*] Isai. xlv. 23. The Heb. there runs, "By
myself have I sworn…to me every knee shall bow, every tongue shall
swear." The LXX. runs, "By myself I swear,…that to me every
knee shall bow, and every tongue shall swear (by) God." Here St
Paul substitutes one frequent formula of Divine Oaths for another; and
paraphrases "shall swear to me" by its practical equivalent, "*shall
confess (my sovereignty) before me.*" (Cp. Psal. lxiii. 11; where to "swear
by God" is to take the oath of faithful *allegiance* to Him.)

12 tongue shall confess to God.   So then every one of us
13 shall give account of himself to God.   Let us not therefore
judge one another any more : but judge this rather, that no
man put a stumblingblock or an occasion to fall in *his* bro-
14 ther's way.   I know, and am persuaded by the Lord Jesus,
that *there is* nothing unclean of itself: but to him that

12.   *every one of us*] Because the prediction (finally to be fulfilled
when Messiah finally triumphs) emphatically speaks of *"every* knee,
every tongue."

give account of himself]   *"Himself"* is, of course, emphatic.   The
Christian is dissuaded from "judging" by the remembrance that his
Judge will ask him hereafter for *his own* "peculiar book[1]," not for his
neighbour's.

13.   *judge this rather*]   The verb "to judge" is used elsewhere (e. g.
Acts xx. 16,) in the sense of "to decide, to determine."   Here, of
course, it is so used with epigrammatic emphasis just after the use of it
in the ordinary sense.

that no man put, &c.]   Wonderfully does this passage shew the
harmony of true Christian independence with Christian unselfishness.
The Gospel teaches that man has not merely a *right to his opinion;* a
truth which, taken alone, leads to little save mutual repulsion or indifference.   It teaches that he is *responsible for his opinion* to the Lord ;
and this leads his Christian neighbour to thoughtful watchfulness lest
his own example should lead another astray in this deep matter of
forming the opinions for which account must be given.—See 1 Cor. viii.
throughout for illustrations.

14.   *by the Lord Jesus*]   Lit. **in the Lord Jesus**; i. e. as one who is
both a "member of Christ" and acts under His special influence.

unclean]   Lit. **common** (as margin E. V.) ; i. e. ceremonially unclean. Cp. Acts x. 15.

of itself]   Lit. **by means of itself**; i.e. *per se:* "nothing *makes
itself* unlawful" for food.

but to him, &c.]   Lit. **unless to him**, &c.   But the Gr. idiom is
rightly rendered in E. V.   So Rev. xx. 27, where lit. *"unless they
which are written*, &c."

Here St Paul appeals to the fact that individual conscience, however

---

[1] The phrase is borrowed from Herbert's pregnant little poem, " Judgment :"

> "Almighty Judge! how shall poor wretches brook
> Thy dreadful look,
> Able a heart of iron to appal,
> When thou shalt call
> For every man's peculiar book?
>
> *   *   *   *
>
> "But I resolve, when Thou shalt call for mine,
> *That* to decline;
> And thrust a Testament into Thy hand.
> Let that be scann'd;
> There Thou shalt find my faults are Thine."

esteemeth any *thing* to be unclean, to him *it is* unclean.
But if thy brother be grieved with *thy* meat, now walkest 15
thou not charitably. Destroy not him with thy meat, for
whom Christ died. Let not then your good be evil spoken 16

misguided, must never be violated by its possessor. Mistaken conscience
calls for *correction by better light*, but never for violation. To follow
conscience is, in itself, no security that we are doing what is *per se*
right; but to violate conscience, which is our actual view of right and
wrong, is always wrong. Here, for instance, the "weak brother," so
long as his conscience scrupled about a certain sort of food, would do
wrong to eat it, though his scruple was an error; and the "strong
brother" would be really tempting him to sin by—not patiently explaining the error and leaving him to reflection on it, but—rudely,
sarcastically, or slightingly, inducing him to override his unchanged
convictions.—Cp. the instructive language of 1 Cor. viii. 10.

15. *But*] Another reading is **For**. The documentary evidence is
doubtful; and the evidence of connexion favours **But**. If **For** is
adopted, it must be explained by treating ver. 14 as a parenthesis; and
thus connecting vv. 13, 15 : q. d., "resolve to lay no stumblingblock
for others ; *for you do* lay a stumblingblock, when you neglect their
scruples about food." Reading **But**, the connexion shews it to be a word
not of *contrast* but of *pursuance:* q. d., "But, granting what I have just
urged, it is the opposite of Christian love to neglect your brother's
scruples."

grieved] **put to pain ;** the pain of a conflict with conscience such as
either to lead to its violation, or to harden prejudice.

with thy meat] Lit., and better, **on account of thy food.**—"*Meat*,"
in the E. V., is never exclusively "*flesh*-meat." The word is akin to
French *met;* a thing *put* on the table. In market-language "green
meat" still means vegetables ; and so in some country districts "meat"
alone still does. Here, of course, the word is *inclusive* of flesh.

not charitably] Lit. **no longer according to love :** "Thou forsakest
the rule of Christian love which *hitherto* thou hast followed."

Destroy not him] The natural effect of neglect or contempt of the
mistaken scruple would be to frighten, or embolden, the "weak brother"
so as to become careless of his conscience in general ; to "regard iniquity in
his heart," (Psal. lxvi. 18,) and so to cease to "abide in Christ." Cp. the
language of 1 Cor. viii. 11.—Here the question *what God would do* for
the protection or restoration of the "weak" Christian is manifestly out
of sight, and out of place : not His covenant, but His servants' duty
and responsibility, is before us here. So again in ver. 20.—"*Destroy*"
is the *present* imperative in the Gr., and indicates that a course of
conduct, not an isolated and finished act, is intended.

thy meat] There is a subtle reproof in the word "*thy;*" a suggestion
of the selfishness underlying the conduct in question.

for whom Christ died] The profoundest of all motives for a *Christian's*
tenderness and care.—Here, of course, the reference is to the Lord's

17 of: for the kingdom of God is not meat and drink; but
18 righteousness, and peace, and joy in the Holy Ghost. For
he that in these *things* serveth Christ *is* acceptable to God,

death *for His Church*, (Eph. **v.** 25,) of which the "weak brother" is a
member by faith.

16. *then*] **therefore.** The word sums up and applies the previous
reasonings.

your good] I. e. your Christian light and liberty, in the "kingdom
of God." Misuse of this would be sure to embitter Christian intercourse, and to weaken the tenderness of conscience and so the holiness
of life in the community. Cp. 1 Pet. ii. 12, 15, 16.

17. *the kingdom of God*] This important phrase occurs elsewhere in
St Paul, 1 Cor. iv. 20, vi. 9, 10, xv. 50; Gal. v. 21; Eph. v. 5; Col.
iv. 11; 1 Thess. ii. 12; 2 Thess. i. 5; 2 Tim. iv. 18. In these passages
(as generally in N. T.) the radical meaning of the phrase is always the
same—the Reign of God over Redeemed Man, revealed and effectuated
by the Gospel. This radical meaning branches into different references;
and thus the Kingdom may mean (according to the varying contexts)
(1) the state of grace in this life; (2) the state of glory in the life to
come; (3) the revealed truths which are the laws and charter of the
kingdom; (4) the dignity and privilege (here or hereafter) of the subjects
of the kingdom. This latter is the special meaning here. Q. d., "What
we gain as the subjects of the Kingdom of God is not freedom to eat
what we please, but the possession of righteousness, peace, and joy."

righteousness, and peace, and joy in the Holy Ghost] In view of the
argument of the Epistle it is best to explain these sacred words by
ch. v. 1—5. "*Righteousness*" is the state of the *justified* in the eye of
the Holy Law; "*peace*" is the reconciliation of God and believing
man; "*joy in the Holy Ghost*" is the blissful realization of this state of
peace and mercy, by the hearts in which "the love of God is poured
out by the Holy Ghost given unto us." These Divine gifts stand here
in supreme contrast to the petty gains of temporal and bodily freedom
of choice and pleasure.

18. *For he that in these things*, &c.] The "*for*" indicates a connexion somewhat as follows: "the privileges of the Gospel are above
all things *spiritual: for* the subjects of God's evangelical kingdom
approve themselves as loyal to their King, and worthy of their privileges
in the eyes of men, not so much by insisting on ceremonial freedom, as
by bringing the influence of their spiritual peace and joy to bear on
their service of Christ."—"*In these things:*"—another reading, not so
well supported, is "*in this thing.*" If adopted, the "*this*" must refer
to the whole idea of spiritual privilege.

serveth] The word bears a suppressed emphasis. The assertor of
ceremonial *liberty* is reminded that he is the *bondman* of the Lord, precisely in virtue of his freedom from the doom of the law. See ch. vi.

acceptable to God] As the servant who uses the Master's talent in the
Master's business.

and approved of men. Let us therefore follow *after* the 19
things which make for peace, and *things* wherewith one may
edify another. For meat destroy not the work of God. All 20
things indeed *are* pure; but *it is* evil for *that* man who
eateth with offence. *It is* good neither to eat flesh, nor to 21
drink wine, nor *any thing* whereby thy brother stumbleth, or
is offended, or is *made* weak. Hast thou faith? have *it* to 22

approved of men] As standing the *test* of sincerity and reality. (The
Gr. word suggests the idea of *testing, assaying*.)
Fact abundantly illustrates the Apostle's words. The disciple who
"in *these* things *serveth Christ*" may or may not be *popular* with men
around him; but he is quite sure, on the whole and in the long run, to
be recognized as *real*. No doubt the "strong" Christian is implicitly
warned that punctilious assertions of *liberty* are very likely to have the
opposite result.
19. *the things which make for peace*] Lit. **the things of peace**. So
below, **the things of mutual edification**.—For remarks on the harmony
between St Paul's *eirenicon* here and his stern warnings (e.g. in Gal. i.)
against foundation-error, see long note on ver. 1 above.
edify] Cp. xv. 2.—The metaphor here has its usual (but not invariable) reference to the state and growth not of the individual but of the
community.
20. *destroy not*] Lit. **loosen, dissolve, pull down**. The word is
used in contrast to the idea of *building up* in the previous words.—
Same word as e.g. Matt. xxvi. 61, xxvii. 40; Acts vi. 14; 2 Cor. v. 1;
Gal. ii. 18.
the work of God] I. e. His building, the Church of His redeemed.
All things indeed are pure] As regards eating or abstinence.
with offence] Lit. **by means of a stumbling-block**; i. e. *induced* to
do so by force of mere example, while his conscience is adverse or
undecided.
21. *It is good*] The word is in antithesis to the "*it is evil*" just
before. The "strong" Christian might deem his own exercise of liberty
good *per se;* and his "weak" brother's obedience to scruples evil *per
se*. The Apostle shews him that the exact contrary might be the case.
Not the *principle* of liberty, but its *application*, might be positively
mischievous, and the practical "breach" of the theory might be its
truest "honour."
For a still stronger expression of the noble principle of this verse, see
1 Cor. viii. 12. Never did that principle more need to be remembered
than at the present day.
offended] Here, of course, as throughout this passage, the word
bears its antiquated meaning—"*is made to stumble*."
is made weak] In his obedience to the sense of duty.
22. *Hast thou faith?*] "*Thou*" is emphatic, and marks the contrast
of the persons—the "strong" and the "weak."—"*Faith*" here, as
throughout the Epistle, is (in its radical idea) justifying faith; trustful

thyself before God. Happy *is* he that condemneth not him-
23 self in *that thing* which he alloweth. And he that doubteth
is damned if he eat, because *he eateth* not of faith: for whatsoever *is* not of faith is sin.

acceptance of the Propitiation. But it has here a special reference to
the *results* of that faith in regard of ceremonial restrictions — the
"strong" Christian's decided view that he is wholly above such restrictions, because "justified by faith."

have it to thyself] I.e. **keep it to thyself**. The Gr. verb in this
phrase can be rendered either "*have*" or "*keep*"; and thus affords a
slight "play" on the same word ("*Hast* thou faith?") just before.—St
Paul's meaning is that faith, with its results, is not a matter for personal
display—the use to which many Christians were tempted to put it.—
Admirable is this plain warning in the very Epistle in which the pre-
ciousness and power of justifying faith have been the primary topic.

before God] In the calm, and heartsearching, secrecy of the soul's
intercourse with Him.

Happy is he, &c.] In this clause, and the next verse, we have a
double warning; (1) of the "strong" Christian's risk in the eager
assertion of his liberty; (2) of the "weak" Christian's sin, should he
violate his conscience—the thought of which must check the conduct
of the "strong" in dealing with him.—The present clause may be
paraphrased, "Happy is the man who so understands his liberty as
never to misapply it to sinful indulgence! For the risk is great; *self*-
assertion may easily take the place of the assertion of *free grace*; and
so you may persuade yourself to accept as an act of true freedom what
is really a moral wrong, and thus bring yourself into judgment."

condemneth] Lit. **judgeth**; but the connexion implies the *guilt* of
the party on trial, and thus E.V. is practically right.

23. *And he that doubteth*] This verse, like the last clause, is really
aimed at the "strong" Christian's mistaken conduct. He is reminded
of the real sin he may occasion in his "weak" fellow-Christian. See
last note but one.

doubteth] He whose conscience is *not at ease* on the question of
"meats."

is damned] Lit. **hath been condemned**. The perfect gives the
thought that *ipso facto*, then and there, he passes under God's sentence
of displeasure, as a rebellious child.

The idea of eternal doom is not, of course, at all *inherent* in the
words; the sentence may be only one of merciful chastening. But
even thus, this verse is a suggestive comment on the Divine view of the
sinfulness of the *lightest* transgressions.

not of faith] I.e. he "takes a liberty," not on the right principle
but on the wrong; not from clear conviction that it is authorized
by his acceptance in Christ by faith, but from neglect of conscience.
And all such acts, as being results of a known wrong principle, are
sins.

CH. XV. 1—7   *The same subject: the Lord's example in the*
matter

We then that are strong ought to bear the infirmities of **15**
the weak, and not to please ourselves. Let every one of 2
us please *his* neighbour for *his* good to edification. For 3

It is plain from the context that St Paul does not assert that *every
act* is sinful which is not directly based on conscious faith in Christ; but
that *every act of "liberty" of the kind in question*, not so based, is
sinful; for it can be based only on neglect of conscience.

for] Lit. **but**, or **now**; the argumentative word.

At the close of this chapter many MSS. place the Great Doxology,
xvi. 25—27. See on this question, *Introduction*, ii. § 3.

CH. XV. 1—7   THE SAME SUBJECT: THE LORD'S EXAMPLE IN
THE MATTER

1. *We then*, &c.] This chapter and the next have been suspected and
discussed by some foreign critics, as either (*a*) out of place—written by
St Paul, but not originally for Roman Christians; or (*b*) as being, in
whole or part, later additions to the Epistle. It is not too much to say
of these theories, (as Meyer says of one of them, in his long prefatory
note to this chapter), that "they result from assumptions and combina-
tions which are either purely arbitrary, or lack, in the exposition of details,
all solid ground and support." The connexions of thought between
cch. xiv. and xv., and between passage and passage to the close of the
Epistle, are either so obviously or so minutely *natural*, that the most
difficult of all literary theories is that which accounts for them by
designing imitation or accidental addition. Such things, seventeen or
eighteen centuries ago, not to speak of the present day, were practically sure to betray themselves by *manifest and startling* incon-
gruities. —See further, *Introduction*, ii. § 3.

We then that are strong] Lit. **We then [that are] the able.** The
word rendered "able" is the same word as that rendered "mighty" in
E.V. of e.g. Luke xxiv. 19; Acts xviii. 24; 1 Cor. i. 26; and "strong"
in E.V. of 2 Cor. xii. 10. It seems to convey the thought of *strength
and something more;* the resources and opportunities of strength.
Able thus best represents it. Bp Lightfoot (on Phil. ii. 15) suggests
that it may have been a favourite title for themselves amongst the
persons here contemplated; and so that there is irony in its use here.—
"*Then:*"—lit. **but**, or **now**. The word marks an added fact or argument. The connexion of thought with the close of ch. xiv. is
manifest.

ought] We *owe* it to Him who has set us free.

to bear] Lit. **to carry**; i.e. as a burthen, a trial, which needs
patience. Same word as Rev. ii. 2, 3.

the weak] Lit. **the unable**; in contrast to "the able" just above.
Same word as Acts. xiv. 8, (E.V. "impotent.")

2. *for his good to edification*] These words taken together perfectly

even Christ pleased not himself; but, as it is written, The
reproaches of them that reproached thee fell on
4 me. For whatsoever *things* were written aforetime were
written for our learning, that we through patience and

define the principle of Christian *complaisance.* Cp. 1 Cor. x. 33, and
contrast Gal. i. 10, where St Paul treats the case of radically false
doctrine, not, as here, a question of secondary practice.—"*Edification:*"
—see on xiv. 19. The Christian's aim in "pleasing his neighbour "
was to be the harmony, advance, and strength, of the "blessed company
of the faithful " as a united aggregate.

3. *For even Christ*] Here first in the Epistle St Paul explicitly
quotes the Lord's EXAMPLE. He soon repeats the reference, ver. 7.
The main burthen of the Epistle has been His SACRIFICE ; but the more
the Sacrifice is apprehended, the more powerful will the Example
be felt to be. It will emphatically be "not merely a model, but a
motive."

pleased not himself] " Not My will, but Thine be done."
To Messiah Himself, as to His people, suffering was in itself "not
joyous, but grievous;" and, in that sense, it was *against His will.*
The doing of His Father's will involved sufferings; and in those
sufferings He "pleased not Himself," while yet He unutterably "de-
lighted to do the will of Him that sent Him." (Psal. xl. 8; John
iv. 34.)

as it is written] Psal. lxix. (LXX. lxviii.) 9. The quotation is verbatim with LXX.—It has been doubted whether we are meant in this
passage to view the Saviour as preferring *the Father's pleasure,* or *Man's
salvation,* to His "own will." The context (vv. 1, 2) favours the
latter ; the words of the quotation favour the former. But as the two
objects were inseparable in our Lord's work, *both* may well be in view
here. His "bearing reproach" was the necessary path, alike to "finish-
ing His Father's work," and to saving the lost.

Does not St Paul here allude specially to the conflict of Gethsemane,
and to the outrages which our Lord patiently bore just afterwards ?
He had scarcely said " *Thy will be done,*" when the awful "reproaches"
of His night of shame and insult began.

reproached thee] God was "reproached" in effect, by those who,
while claiming to act *in His Name,* were teaching and practising all
that was alien to His love and holiness.—Such persons, when they
beheld His *true* Likeness in His Son, inevitably hated and rejected it.

4. *For whatsoever things,* &c.] St Paul takes occasion from his last
quotation to state a great principle; namely, that the O.T. was throughout designed for the instruction and establishment of N.T. believers.
"*Our,*" just below, is emphatic.

On the principle, cp. 2 Tim. iii. 15—17. It is almost needless to
remark on the witness borne to the O.T. in such passages as this.

aforetime] Before *our* time; under the Elder Dispensation.
learning] I.e. **teaching**. Cp. Prayer-Book Version of Psal. xxv. 8 ;

comfort of the scriptures might have hope. Now the God 5 of patience and consolation grant you to be likeminded one towards another according to Christ Jesus: that ye may 6 with one mind *and* one mouth glorify God, even the Father of our Lord Jesus Christ. Wherefore receive ye one 7 another, as Christ also received us, to the glory of God.

8—13 *The Lord's example enforced by a view of the equal bearing of His work on Jewish and Gentile believers*

Now I say that Jesus Christ was a minister of the 8

"them shall He *learn* His way;" and the present use of "learnèd" as an adjective.

through patience, &c.] Lit. **through the patience and the comfort of the Scriptures may have the hope.**—"*The hope*" is not hope in general, but the special hope of glory through Christ. (ch. v. 2.)—"*The patience, &c. of the Scriptures*" is the patience and comfort taught by the Scriptures, whether in precept or example. Here, for instance, the Lord's blessed " patience," His unwearied bearing of the burthen He had undertaken, forms, both in itself and as an example, a part of the " *comfort* " of His followers. (Cp. 1 Pet. ii. 19—21, iv. 13.) It cheers them on to tread in His track; to "gird up the loins of their mind;" to "*hope* to the end."

On the word "patience," see on ch. v. 3.

5. *Now the God of patience*, &c.] Lit. **of the patience**, &c.; i.e. that now in question.—Here is a subtle and beautiful sequence of thought. From patience and comfort, and the hope of glory, St Paul passes at once to the duty of affectionate unanimity. The stronger was the sense of peace and hope in each individual believer, the more would the believing community be lifted above the bitterness and littleness of secondary controversies. Cp. perhaps Col. i. 4, 5; "*the love* which ye have to all the saints, *by reason of the hope* laid up for you in heaven."

according to Christ Jesus] As taught by His precept and example.

6. *that ye may—glorify God*] Whose praise is the ultimate aim of all His gifts to His people. Cp. on xi. 33—36.—See, on the holy unanimity enjoined here, Phil. iii. 15, 16.

God, even the Father] Far better, **the God and Father**. Same words as 2 Cor. i. 3; Eph. i. 3; 1 Pet. i. 3. See Joh. xx. 17; Heb. i. 8, 9.

7. *receive ye*, &c.] See on xiv. i. Cp. Col. iii. 13.

as Christ also received us] " He receiveth sinners," to be His "brethren."—Better, perhaps, **received you**.

to the glory of God] Christ received us "to the praise of the glory of His Father's grace;" Eph. i. 6. But possibly a comma should stand after "received us:" q. d., "receive one another, (as Christ received us;) for this will, by its holy effects, bring praise to God." This certainly fits the context somewhat more closely; see ver. 6.

circumcision for the truth of God, to confirm the promises
9 made unto the fathers: and that the Gentiles might glorify
God for *his* mercy; as it is written, For this cause
I will confess to thee among the Gentiles, and
10 sing unto thy name. And again *he* saith, Rejoice, *ye*
11 Gentiles, with his people. And again, Praise the

8—13 THE LORD'S EXAMPLE ENFORCED BY A VIEW OF THE EQUAL BEARING OF HIS WORK ON JEWISH AND GENTILE BELIEVERS

8. *Now I say*] Better, on documentary evidence, **For I say**. St Paul here expounds the words "Christ received you," by shewing the bearing of the Lord's Work on the salvation alike of Jewish and Gentile believers. And in so doing he reminds the two Sections of the holy Bond in which they stood united.

Jesus Christ] Better, simply, **Christ**.

a minister of the circumcision] I. e. One who came to *serve the circumcision;* to labour for Israel. See His own words, Matt. xv. 24.

St Paul mentions first the Lord's work for Israel, then His work for the Gentiles. Cp. i. 16.

for the truth of God] **for the sake of** it; to secure its vindication. "The Truth" had foretold that the Redeemer should be of the seed of Abraham, Judah, David.

to confirm] By being their Fulfilment.

9. *and*] Lit. **but**. A slight contrast or correction is implied; "to confirm indeed the promise given to Israel, *but also* to bring in mercy for the Gentiles."

for his mercy] Lit. **for mercy**. The word "mercy" is here used, perhaps, with reference to the previous position of the *Gentiles* as "strangers from" an explicit "covenant of promise." (Eph. ii. 12.)— Cp. however xi. 32 for the real equality of mercy in *all* cases of salvation.

For this cause, &c.] Psal. xviii. (LXX. xvii.) 49. Verbatim with LXX., only omitting the word "*Lord*."

St Paul interprets the ver. as ultimately fulfilled in Messiah, and as foretelling that He, as Saviour, shall rejoice among the Gentiles as the saved.

10. *he saith*] Or, better, **it saith**; i.e. the Scripture.

Rejoice, &c.] Deut. xxxii. 43. Verbatim with LXX. The word "*with*" is not in the Hebrew Received Text; which may be rendered either "Praise His people, ye nations," (i.e. congratulate them on His saving goodness;) or "Rejoice, ye nations, who are His people." In either case the prophecy indicates, (what is the Apostle's meaning here,) that the "nations" shall have cause for sacred gladness in connexion with the Covenant of Israel.

11. *Praise the Lord*, &c.] Psal. cxvii. (LXX. cxvi.) 1. Nearly verbatim with LXX. See ver. 2 of the Psalm, where the steadfastness of

Lord, all ye Gentiles; and laud him, all ye people.
And again Esaias saith, There shall be a root of Jesse, 12
and he that *shall* rise to reign over the Gentiles;
in him shall the Gentiles trust.   Now the God of hope 13
fill you with all joy and peace in believing, that ye may
abound in hope, through the power of the Holy Ghost.

14—21   *Commendation of the Christian maturity of the
Roman believers : yet St Paul writes to them with the
authority of the commissioned and laborious Apostle of the
Gentiles*

And I myself also am persuaded of you, my brethren, 14

the "*mercy*" and the "*truth*" of God is given as the cause of the
praise.
laud him, &c.]   Perhaps better, (with another reading,) **let all the
peoples laud Him.**
12.   *a root*]   Lit. **the root.**   The quotation is from Isai. xi. 10:
verbatim with LXX.   The Heb. reads, "It shall come to pass...the
root of Jesse, which standeth for an ensign of the peoples, unto it
(or Him) shall the Gentiles seek."   Here the LXX. forms a sufficient
rendering of the substance of the Heb.
trust]   Lit. **hope.**
13.   *the God of hope*]   Lit. **of the hope;** i.e. of *our* hope, the special hope in question; the Christian's hope of glory.   So just below,
that ye may abound in the hope.
St Paul takes up the last word of the last quotation, and applies it
in this expression of holy and loving desire.   He ceases now to speak
of controversy, and looks joyfully heavenward.   On the whole ver., cp.
ch. v. 1—5.
in believing]   The word seems to sum up the great argument of the
Epistle.   Here closes its course of explicit Instruction, whether concerning Doctrine or Practice.   The remainder is devoted to personal
and other incidental topics.   Meyer calls the passage, xv. 14—33, the
"Epilogue" of the Epistle.

**14—21   COMMENDATION OF THE CHRISTIAN MATURITY OF THE
ROMAN BELIEVERS: YET ST PAUL WRITES TO THEM WITH
THE AUTHORITY OF THE COMMISSIONED AND LABORIOUS
APOSTLE OF THE GENTILES**

14.   *And*]   Lit., and better, **Now;** the word of transition.
I myself also]   I.e. as well as others, by whom "your faith is
spoken of throughout the whole world;" (i. 8).
In this verse and the next we have an echo, as it were, of i. 8, 11,
12, 15.   What St Paul says here is in no insincere diplomatic compliment, but the well-grounded conviction of his mind as to the Roman
Christians *as a body.*   And it is quite in harmony with the substance

that ye also are full of goodness, filled with all knowledge,
15 able also to admonish one another. Nevertheless, brethren,
I have written the more boldly unto you in some sort, as
putting you in mind, because of the grace that is given to
16 me of God, that I should be the minister of Jesus Christ to

and tone of the Epistle, which is evidently written for those who were
no novices in Christian doctrine, and who were also comparatively free
from such faults of Christian practice as defiled, for instance, the
Corinthian Church. He wrote to them as he had written just because
they were in a state of spiritual vigour and maturity. Perhaps too,
he instinctively *expresses* this conviction the more strongly, because he is
writing to the Church of the imperial Metropolis, the mighty Centre of
influence. See on i. 15.

ye also] As truly as your Teacher can be.

full] Lit. **brimful**. Same word as i. 29.

goodness] Same word as Gal. v. 22; Eph. v. 9; 2 Thess. i. 11. It
is "*excellence*" in a wide sense.

15. *I have written*] Lit. **I wrote**; the "epistolary past."

the more boldly] Lit. **more boldly**; i.e., in our idiom, **somewhat
boldly.**

in some sort] More lit., and better, **in part**; i.e. ,**here and there.**
He refers to occasional passages such as vi. 17—21, ix. 19, 20, xi.
19—21, xiv.

as putting you in mind] Of what, as regards substance and principle, they already knew. Such is evidently the tone of both the doctrinal and practical passages of the Epistle, taken as a whole. Cp.
2 Pet. i. 12, 13, iii. 1.

the grace] I.e. the loving favour which had made him an Apostle.
Cp. i. 5, and especially Eph. iii. 2, 3, 7, 8. St Paul's deep and beautiful personal humility is in sincere harmony with his distinct knowledge and firm assertion of his Divine commission.

16. *the minister*] The Gr. word (not the same as that in e.g. ver.
8,) is the original of our word *liturgy;* and is the same as in xiii. 6;
Phil. ii. 25; Heb. i. 7, viii. 2; &c. The word in Biblical Greek has
a frequent sacerdotal reference; which is certainly present here, as
the rest of the verse shews. For the word rendered "ministering" just
below is lit. "*doing priest's-work with;*" and it is followed, in the next
clause, by "the *offering-up* of the Gentiles." The whole passage is
strikingly pictorial and figurative; representing the Gospel as the *sacerdotal rule;* the Apostle as the *sacrificing priest;* and the converts from
heathenism as the *victims* of the sacrifice. A passage of somewhat
similar imagery is Phil. ii. 17, where the Gr. of "service" is kindred
to the Gr. of "minister" here. There (in Bp Lightfoot's words) "the
Philippians are the priests; their faith (or their good works springing
from their faith) is the sacrifice; St Paul's life-blood the accompanying
libation."

It is clear that the Apostle here speaks of himself as a Sacrificer in a

the Gentiles, ministering the gospel of God, that the offering up of the Gentiles might be acceptable, being sanctified
by the Holy Ghost. I have therefore whereof *I* may glory 17
through Jesus Christ *in those things* which pertain to God.
For I will not dare to speak of any of *those things* which 18
Christ hath not wrought by me, to make the Gentiles obedient, by word and deed, through mighty signs and won- 19

sense wholly figurative; and this passage and i. 9 (where see note,)
are the only examples of his application of the sacrificial idea, in even a
figurative sense, to himself. Dr Hodge remarks that we here see the
true nature of the priesthood which belongs to the Christian ministry:
"It is by the preaching of the Gospel to bring men to *offer themselves*
as a living sacrifice, holy and acceptable to God." See xii. 1.

the offering up of the Gentiles] I.e. the offering which consists of the
Gentiles; the Gentiles, as "yielding themselves to God" to be His dedicated servants. For the phraseology, cp. Heb. x. 10.

being sanctified by the Holy Ghost] Lit. **having been sanctified in
the Holy Ghost.** His Divine grace was, so to speak, the water in
which the sacrifice was washed; it alone made the self-dedication *real*,
and therefore *acceptable*.

17. *I have therefore*, &c.] Lit., with the best reading, **I have therefore my exultation in Christ Jesus as to things God-ward.** The
words "*I have*" are slightly emphatic, indicating the reality of his
commission, labours, and success; and so the reality of his right to
speak as a Teacher to the Roman Christians.

glory] He exults in the "grace given to him," (vv. 15, 16), and in
its results (ver. 19).

through] Lit., and better, **in.** It is as in union with Christ that he
labours, and so his exultation is "in Christ."

18. *For I will not dare*, &c.] This ver. may be paraphrased, "To
justify this exultation, I *need not presumptuously intrude* on the work
of others, putting in a false claim to credit for that work: I need only
speak of what Christ has done through my personal efforts, both of
preaching and miracle, in bringing Gentile converts to Him, &c." The
sentence evidently glides from the negative to the positive in the course
of this verse.

which Christ hath—wrought] St Paul recognizes the Saviour as
the personal and present Worker. Cp. Matt. xxviii. 20, and the suggestive words (Acts i. 1) "all that Jesus *began* to do and teach"—as
if His doing and teaching continued in the work of His messengers.
Cp. also 1 Cor. xv. 10; Gal. ii. 20.

me] Emphatic in the Greek.

obedient] To the Gospel. See on x. 3.

deed] Specially (see next verse) deeds of miracle. Cp. Acts xiii.
9—12, xiv. 8—10, xv. 12, xvi. 18, xix. 11, 12, xx. 10—12, xxviii.
3—9. St Paul elsewhere distinctly claims miraculous gifts, 1 Cor.
xiv. 18; 2 Cor. xii. 12. In his life and teaching, as in the whole

ders, by the power of the Spirit of God; so that from Jerusalem, and round about unto Illyricum, I have fully
20 preached the gospel of Christ. Yea, so have I strived to

of Scripture, the natural and the supernatural are inextricably interwoven: the strongest reality of practical plans and efforts, and the
most vigorous reasonings, stand linked with open references to, and
cogent proofs of, the special presence around him of "the powers
of the world to come."

19. *through mighty signs*, &c.] Lit., and better, **in the might of
signs and wonders, in the might of the Spirit of God.** The second
clause seems to explain the first; q. d., "and that might was not
mine, but of the Spirit."—The "might *of signs*, &c." is the might
(of influence and effect) resulting from the display of miracle.

signs and wonders] Same words as Matt. xxiv. 24; Mark xiii.
22; John iv. 48; Acts ii. 19, 22, xv. 12, &c.; 2 Cor. xii. 12; 2 Thess.
ii. 9; Heb. ii. 4. There is, no doubt, a difference of precise meaning
between the two words; but taken together they are a summary phrase
for supernatural works of all kinds.

from Jerusalem, and round about unto Illyricum] These words
are interpreted by some, "from Jerusalem, and thence *in a circuitous
track* to Illyricum." But the Gr. more properly means, "from Jerusalem *and its surroundings* even to Illyricum." The "surroundings"
of Jerusalem would be (1) Judæa, where St Paul did a work known
only from Acts xxvi. 20; and (2) neighbouring regions, as Syria, and
perhaps "Arabia;" (Gal. i. 17: but see *Introduction*, i. § 8 *note*). St
Paul's work really began at Damascus; but Jerusalem was his *most
distant* centre of operations.—Acts xiii.—xix. forms the best comment
on this verse.

Illyricum] The Acts contains no mention of Illyricum; and some
commentators doubt whether St Paul did more than approach it. But
Meyer rightly says that, if so, this verse would be tainted with just
that boastfulness (*Grossthuerei*) which was so earnestly renounced in
ver. 18. The narrative of the Acts is manifestly a *selection ;* and see
Acts xx. 1—2 for a suggestion of the *possible* time of this visit. (See
Introduction i. § 22).

Illyricum was "an extensive district lying along the E. coast of
the Adriatic, from the boundary of Italy on the N. to Epirus on the
S., and contiguous to Mœsia and Macedonia on the East." It was
divided "into two portions, Illyris Barbara, the northern, and Illyris
Græca, the southern. Within these limits was included Dalmatia."
(Smith's *Dict. Bibl.*) Illyricum thus included the whole or parts of the
modern Croatia, Dalmatia, Bosnia, Montenegro, and Albania.

fully preached] Lit. **fulfilled.** Meyer well compares Acts vi. 7,
&c., "the word of God *increased;*" i.e. in extent of influence. So here,
St Paul "fulfilled" the whole possible scope of the Gospel-message,
in point of geographical space, in the direction taken by his work.
A fair paraphrase would thus be, "I have carried the Gospel everywhere."—The idea of unreserved *doctrinal faithfulness* (for which see

preach the gospel, not where Christ was named, lest I should build upon another *man*'s foundation : but as it is 21 written, To whom he was not spoken of, they shall see: and they that have not heard shall understand.

22—33 *His work has hitherto kept him from personal visits to Rome: now it will lead him to the city: but first he must go to Jerusalem, on business of the Church. He requests prayer*

For which cause also I have been much hindered 22 from coming to you. But now having no more place in 23

Acts xx. 20, 27), is not suggested by the context here, where the emphasis is on *extent of area.*

20. *Yea, so have I strived*] Better, **But jealously striving so, &c.** The "but" adds a qualifying additional fact ; that his line and area of action were determined, in a measure, by his aim to work only in untouched regions. This is partly to explain why, with all his vast range of travel, he had not yet visited Rome.—" *Jealously striving:* "— the Gr. verb indicates an effort in which personal desires and principles are kept in view. St Paul made it a *point of honour* to be a *pioneer* in his missionary work; not with a selfish love of *éclat*, but because his devotion to his Master took this peculiar line, very probably under Divine suggestions.

lest I should build, &c.] He avoided this, probably, both from consciousness of the vastness of untouched heathendom, and from scrupulous avoidance of needless discord on secondary points.—For similar imagery, see 1 Cor. iii. 10.

21. *but as it is written*, &c.] There is, obviously, an ellipsis. Q. d., " I have made it my principle to preach, not where Christ was named, but where that prediction would be verified—' To whom He was not spoken of, &c.' " The quotation is from Isai. lii. 15, verbatim with LXX., which paraphrases the Heb. The whole passage refers to the great Servant of the Lord, and to the effects of His work, and of the " report " of Him, on " nations " and "kings."

22—33 HIS WORK HAS HITHERTO KEPT HIM FROM PERSONAL VISITS TO ROME : NOW IT WILL LEAD HIM TO THE CITY : BUT FIRST HE MUST GO TO JERUSALEM, ON BUSINESS OF THE CHURCH. HE REQUESTS PRAYER.

22. *I have been much hindered*] Better, **I was hindered for the most part** ; i. e. hindrances outweighed facilities : he was more hindered than furthered by his active movements.

from coming to you] See Acts xix. 21 for St Paul's fixed purpose to visit Rome.

these parts, and having a great desire these many years to
24 come unto you ; whensoever I take my journey into Spain,
I will come to you : for I trust to see you in my journey,
and to be brought on my way thitherward by you, if first I
25 be somewhat filled with your *company*. But now I go unto
26 Jerusalem to minister unto the saints. For it hath pleased

23. *place*] Evidently in the sense of *opportunity*.

parts] **regions.** Same word as 2 Cor. xi. 10 ; Gal. i. 21. He
means, probably, in a large sense, Roman Europe east of the Adriatic ;
in which he had now "fulfilled" the Gospel.

a great desire] The Gr. is the word that would be used of home-
sickness, or the like affectionate longings. See i. 11.

24. *take my journey*] Lit., simply, **travel.** The Gr. does not,
as the E. V. ("*my* journey") may seem to do, imply that this was a
journey previously expected at Rome. But on the other hand it is
almost certain that it was more or less definitely expected, considering
that St Paul had such intimate friends (and no doubt correspondents) at
Rome as Aquila and Priscilla.

into Spain] Gr. **Spania.** The form *Hispania* is also found in
Greek ; *Spania* never in Latin. The far commoner Greek name of the
Peninsula is *Iberia*.

On the question whether this journey ever took place, see *Introduction*, i. § 31. See also on i. 10, 13.

I will come to you] There is much documentary evidence against
this clause, though it is not absolutely conclusive. The words are
needful to the sense ; and, if they are interpolated, we have here a
strong example of St Paul's elliptical style : he leaves the statement of
his intention to be *inferred* from the words of ver. 22.

to see you] The Gr. verb naturally implies a deliberate **beholding,**
as of one admitted to a spectacle. Cp. Col. ii. 5.

in my journey] Lit. **travelling through.** He would not make a
long stay at Rome, because there "Christ had been already named."
He little anticipated the "two years in his private lodging." (Acts
xxviii. 30.)

to be brought on my way] Perhaps some of the Roman Christians
might accompany him to Spain.

by you] A better reading gives, **from you.**

somewhat] Lit. **in part.** He affectionately implies that the intercourse must be far shorter than his wishes ; but that what enjoyment of
it he can secure, he will.

filled] As a faint and hungry traveller with welcome food, which
sends him on refreshed. "Ch. i. 12 furnishes the commentary to this
word." (Meyer.)

with your company] Lit. **with you.**

25. *I go unto Jerusalem*] See Acts xix. 21, xxiv. 17.

to minister] I. e. to carry temporal relief. He gives a good, because
wholly unselfish, reason for the new delay of his visit to Rome.—This

them of Macedonia and Achaia to make a certain contribution for the poor saints which are at Jerusalem. It hath ₂₇ pleased them verily; and their debtors they are. For if the Gentiles have been made partakers of their spiritual *things*, their duty is also to minister unto them in carnal *things*. When therefore I have performed this, and have sealed to ₂₈

very journey to Jerusalem was in fact, in God's purpose, his way to Rome.

26. *For it hath pleased*, &c.] Lit. **For Macedonia and Achaia were pleased.** (The tense is aor., perhaps here an "epistolary past.") The verb rendered "were pleased" implies, as E. V. also does, not only a voluntary act but the act of a superior; in the sense in which the giver of bounty is the superior party. It is no doubt chosen as a word of gentle irony, to be used further in the next sentence.

"*Macedonia and Achaia*" are the personification of the Churches of Greece, North and South.

a contribution] Lit. **a communion.** The giver *communicates*, or shares his store, with the receiver.—The word is kindred to the Gr. of "distributing," xii. 13.

For this same Collection, see 1 Cor. xvi. 1—4, where incidentally we see the Apostle's own influence, methodical care, and high sense of honour, at work in the matter. See too 2 Cor. viii. 1—14, ix. 1—15, for beautiful examples of appeal in this same matter to "Achaia" and to "Macedonia" respectively.

On this passage as a note of chronology, see *Introduction*, ii. § 1.

for the poor saints] Lit., and better, **for the poor among the saints.** The Christians at Jerusalem were not all poor, but included an unusually large proportion of poor, apparently, among them. Doubtless the special influences of the Capital of Pharisaism kept Christian artizans at a great disadvantage in matter of employment.

27. *It hath pleased them verily*] Lit. **For they were pleased**; an exact repetition of the first words of ver. 26; a note of kindly irony. St Paul was far from thinking with *real* coldness of these gifts of Christian love: see 2 Cor. viii., ix.

and their debtors they are] "*Debtors*" is emphatic. The two reasons stand side by side; the givers' *goodwill*, and their *duty*.

For if the Gentiles, &c.] Lit. **For if** (or **as**) **the Gentiles shared in their spiritual things, they are bound even in fleshly things to serve them.**—"*Even in fleshly things :*"—i. e., as well as in spiritual things. Such should be their gratitude as to think no service, however earthly its guise, beneath them.—"*To serve them :*"—the verb is cognate with the Gr. of "minister," ver. 16; where see note. It is significant here : the Gentiles should look on their charitable gifts as a solemn and *sacred* service, as at an altar.

28. *sealed*] The metaphor is from a solemn ratification. St Paul, handing over to the Church at Jerusalem the "fruit," or proceeds, of the Macedonian and Achaian collections, would thereby finally *attest*

₂₉ them this fruit, I will come by you into Spain.   And I am
sure that, when I come unto you, I shall come in the fulness
₃₀ of the blessing of the gospel of Christ.   Now I beseech you,
brethren, for the Lord Jesus Christ's sake, and for the love
of the Spirit, that *ye* strive together with me in *your* prayers
₃₁ to God for me; that I may be delivered from them that do
not believe in Judea; and that my service which I have for
₃₂ Jerusalem may be accepted of the saints; that I may come

it to be now the full property of the receivers : he would put the *seal
of their ownership* upon it.—Meyer suggests that the word indicates
also the solemn close of his apostolic work in the East.   It is not clear,
however, that he would view the transition from the E. to the W. of
the Adriatic as a wholly peculiar crisis.

29.   *And I am sure*]   Lit. **But,** or **now, I know.**—This "knowledge"
was abundantly justified by the event.

in the fulness of the blessing of the Gospel of Christ]   The words "*of
the Gospel*" must be omitted.—He is sure that he will come attended
by the "fulness," the full range and variety, of "Christ's benediction;"
which would so rest on the visit as to make it *in every way* happy and
helpful both to the Romans and the Apostle.

30.   *Now I beseech you*, &c.]   For similar requests for prayer, see
2 Cor. i. 11 ; Eph. vi. 19; Col. iv. 3, 4; 1 Thess. v. 25 ; 2 Thess.
iii. 1, 2.   For the language of the request ("*strive* together, &c.") cp.
Col. ii. 1, 2, iv. 12.

the love of the Spirit]   I.e. the love of saints for saints, awakened
by the Divine Spirit who "sheds abroad the *love of God* in their
hearts."—The words admit the explanation : "the love which the
Spirit bears to us;" but the want of a distinct Scripture parallel for
such language makes it the less probable explanation.   For a similar
appeal at once to the Saviour's Name and to holy spiritual affections,
cp. Phil. ii. 1, 5.

31.   *that I may be delivered*, &c.]   This prayer was granted, though
not in the way expected.   See Acts xxi. 31, 32, xxiii. 12—24, xxv.
2—4, 12.—The words here (cp. 2 Thess. iii. 1, 2,) are among the many
proofs of St Paul's naturally anxious and sensitive character, and that
his faith and zeal had always this secret obstacle to struggle with.   His
life-long victory is the more admirable, and the more illustrates Divine
grace.

accepted of the saints]   This seems to indicate his consciousness that
some of the Christians of Jerusalem bore a prejudice against his person.
(Cp. Acts xxi. 20, 21.)   Otherwise, this would scarcely be named as a
matter for "*striving*" prayer.

32.   *that I may come unto you*, &c.]   His coming might be hindered
either by violence from "the unbelieving," or by revivals of controversy
and prejudice among "the saints;" and the latter would also grievously
mar the "joy" of his visit to Rome when at length that visit was
made.—Here again the event forms a remarkable commentary.   St

unto you with joy by the will of God, and may with you be refreshed. Now the God of peace *be* with you all. Amen. ₃₃

Cᴴ. XVI. 1—16   *A commendation, and many salutations*

I commend unto you Phebe our sister, which is a **16** servant of the church which is at Cenchrea : that ye re- ₂

Paul *was* permitted to come "with joy" (see Acts xxviii. 15, 16, and cp. Phil. i. 12, 18,) to Rome, and to spend there a time of even unusual opportunity and influence; but the unforeseen circumstances of his *imprisonment* were to lead to this.

> "Thus God grants prayer, but in His love
> Makes times and ways His own."

by the will of God]   As exercised in answer to your prayer.

may with you be refreshed]   Lit. **may with you repose** ; (same word as 1 Cor. xvi. 18; 2 Cor. vii. 13;) a beautiful metaphor for the refreshment of holy intercourse in the midst of toil and care.—Cp. i. 12.—The "repose" would come in "the mutual communication of faith, inner experiences, love, hope, &c." (Meyer.)

33.   *the God of peace*]   So also xvi. 20; 1 Cor. xiv. 33; 2 Cor. xiii. 11; Phil. iv. 9; 1 Thess. v. 23; Heb. xiii. 20.   In some of these passages, the Sacred Title indicates the peace of reconciliation (ch. v. 1) with which God regards His people; in others, the peace of outward quiet or inward concord which He grants to them.   Here, probably, we have the latter meaning.   St Paul is led to think of the precious gift of *rest and calm* both by the dangers he is about to face in Judæa, and by the loving intercourse for which he looks at Rome.

It is quite needless to take this verse as an *intended close* to the Epistle.   We may be sure that some personal greetings must have been all along in St Paul's intention; and none have yet been written.   The wish here expressed quite naturally follows the previous context, (see this note, just above,) and also marks the pause before the commendation and salutations now to follow.

Cʜ. XVI. **1—16**   A ᴄᴏᴍᴍᴇɴᴅᴀᴛɪᴏɴ, ᴀɴᴅ ᴍᴀɴʏ sᴀʟᴜᴛᴀᴛɪᴏɴs

1.   *I commend*]   Lit. **But,** or **now, I commend.**   The particle marks transition to a new subject.

Phebe]   Strictly, **Phœbe.**—Nothing is known of Phœbe beyond the information in this passage.   It is probable that she was the bearer of the Epistle to Rome; for no other bearer is mentioned, and the prominence of this notice of her suggests a special connexion with the writing.   See further below.—The early Christian converts seem to have had no scruple in retaining a pre-baptismal name even when the name (as in this case) was that of a heathen deity.   Cp. *Hermes,* (ver. 14); *Nereus,* (ver. 15); and such derivative names as *Demetrius* (3 Joh. 12).

a servant of the church]   Plainly the word "servant" here bears more than a menial reference: Phœbe was in some sense a *dedicated* helper of the community at Cenchreæ, and very probably a person

ceive her in the Lord, as becometh saints, and *that* ye assist
her in whatsoever business she hath need of you: for she
3 hath been a succourer of many, and of myself *also*.   Greet
4 Priscilla and Aquila my helpers in Christ Jesus: who have

of substance and influence.—There is good evidence of the existence
in the Apostles' time of an organized class of female helpers in
sacred work; for see especially 1 Tim. v. 3—16.   Just after the
apostolic age the famous Letter of Pliny to Trajan indicates that
such female helpers (*ministræ*) were known in the Bithynian Churches;
and for two centuries from the time of Tertullian (cir. A.D. 210)
allusions to them are frequent, and shew that they were largely employed
both in the relief of temporal distress, chiefly among women, and also in
the elementary teaching of female catechumens.   They were regularly
set apart by imposition of hands.   As a rule, they were required to
be of mature age, (rarely of less than 40 years,) and in most cases they
appear to have been widows and mothers.   By the 12th century the Order
had been everywhere abolished.   (See Bingham's *Antiquities*, Bk. II.
ch. xxii.)—We must not *assume* that Phœbe was a deaconess in the full
later sense of the word; but that her position was analogous to that of
the later deaconesses seems at least most probable.

"*The church:*"—here in the very frequent sense of a local community
of Christians.

Cenchrěa]   In the Gr. **Cenchreæ**: the Eastern port of Corinth.   Cp.
Acts xviii. 18.—See *Introduction*, ii. § 1.

2.   *in the Lord, as becometh saints*]   With all the attention and
delicacy due from Christians to a Christian woman.

assist her]   Lit. (in the lit. sense of "*assist*,") **stand by her.**   What
Phœbe's business at Rome was, is quite unknown to us.   It may have
concerned property, and involved enquiries and directions about law.
Or it may have been (though less probably) religious business.

a succourer]   Lit. **a champion**; one who *stands before* another.
The word conveys a graceful allusion to the request that they would
"stand *by*" Phœbe: she had "stood *before*" many a needing and suffering Christian.

of myself also]   Very probably at some time of illness, such as that
other time which apparently delayed him in Galatia, on his first visit
there, and called out the sympathetic love of the Galatians.   (Gal. iv.
13—15; where read, "*on account of weakness of the flesh;*" i.e. "*because
of illness*").

3.   *Priscilla and Aquila*]   Better, **Prisca and Aquila**; so 2 Tim.
iv. 19.—See Acts xviii. 2, 18, 26, for the whole known history of these
two eminent Christians, (except the references to them here, and in
1 Cor. xvi. 19, and 2 Tim. iv.).   Aquila (whose name in its Greek form is
Akulas) was born in Pontus—as was another well-known Aquila, a
translator of the O.T. into Greek.   He and his wife, Prisca or Priscilla, first met St Paul at Corinth; then, 18 months later, went with
him to Ephesus, where they both took part in the instruction of Apollos:
here we find them again at Rome; and in St Paul's last days they are

for my life laid down their own necks: unto whom not only I give thanks, but also all the churches of the Gentiles. Likewise *greet* the church that is in their house. Salute my 5 wellbeloved Epenetus, who is the firstfruits of Achaia unto

probably again at Ephesus. (2 Tim. iv.) Their after-history is quite unknown. Whether or no they were converts of St Paul is uncertain. (See *Introduction*, i. § 17, 23; ii. § 2.)—"Priscilla is an example of what a married woman may do, for the general service of the Church, in conjunction with home-duties, just as Phœbe is the type of the un-married servant of the Church, or deaconess." (Dr Howson, in Smith's *Dict. Bibl.*)—The variation in the *form* of Prisca's name has many parallels in Roman nomenclature.

4. *who have for my life*, &c.] Lit., and better, **who did for my life lay down their own neck**, (not **necks**). An entirely unknown occasion, on which Aquila and his wife had risked their lives for St Paul's.—"*Laid down:*"—the figure is of presenting the neck, or throat, to the executioner. Whether the word is *only* figurative here, we cannot determine.

all the churches of the Gentiles] To whom they had, by their self-devotion, preserved their Apostle.

5. *the church that is in their house*] Their house at Rome, like their house at Corinth, (1 Cor. xvi. 19,) probably contained a large room (like the "Upper Room" at Jerusalem) which was devoted to Divine worship, and used by the Christians of the neighbouring district, who thus formed a "Church," or assembly, which itself was an organic part of the main "Church at Rome." No doubt the whole Roman community had a central meeting-chamber, probably of the same kind, (indeed Aquila's may have been this central chamber,) in which e.g. this Epistle would be read.—Bingham (*Antiquities*, Bk. VIII. ch. i.) collects the allusions to Christian places of assembly in the first century. He makes it clear that special *chambers* were set apart for holy uses, but does *not* make it clear that *whole buildings* were, in those first days, built for, or devoted to, worship. No doubt the circumstances of society and the inexpediency of *obtruding* Christian worship on the view of the heathen, made this a natural and wise practice at first. But the ex-istence of Jewish synagogues alone would make it equally natural, in due time, to dedicate whole buildings. By the third century, at latest, this was common.

For similar allusions to church-assemblies under private roofs, see 1 Cor. xvi. 19; Col. iv. 15; Philem. 2, and perhaps below, vv. 14, 15.

Epenĕtus] Strictly, **Epænetus** : known only from this verse. We may suppose that he was not only the "*firstling of Asia*" (see below) but St Paul's *own* convert, and thus specially "*well-beloved*" by the Apostle.—Cp. 1 Cor. xvi. 15.

Achaia] The better reading is **Asia**; i. e. Asia in the strict sense, the Roman province of which Ephesus was the capital. See Acts xix. 10, 22, 26, 27, 31.

6 Christ. Greet Mary, who bestowed much labour on us.
7 Salute Andronicus and Junia, my kinsmen, and my fellowprisoners, who are of note among the apostles, who also
8 were in Christ before me. Greet Amplias my beloved in the

unto Christ] I.e. as a *convert to* Him.

6. *Mary*] **Mariam** or **Maria**. Both forms represent the Heb.
Miriam. In the Gospels, the Holy Mother is always, or nearly always,
called *Mariam* in the Greek text; the other Maries, *Maria*.—This is
the only Hebrew name in this chapter.

bestowed much labour] Lit. **toiled**; the strongest word for pains and
efforts.

on us] The better reading is, **on you**. We do not know the occasion
or occasions of these "labours." The verb is aorist, and refers to a
definite past period or crisis.

7. *Andronicus and Junia*] Or, perhaps, **Junias**, i.e. **Junianus** (in
a contracted form, as *Lucas* for *Lucanus*, *Silas* for *Silvanus*, &c.). There
is no various reading, but the Gr. accusative may belong to either *Junia*
(feminine) or *Junias* (masculine). It is impossible to decide, but
perhaps the following expressions favour the view that we have here
two Christian *men*.

my kinsmen] Of course in a literal sense, which alone can be *distinctive* here. Their names are Greek and Latin (respectively); but this
was continually the case with Jews, (cp. *Paulus, Crispus, Apollos*, &c.).
They were, we may assume, Benjamites at least, if not near relatives of
St Paul's.—Of his "kinsmen" we elsewhere (outside this chapter) hear
only where his *nephew* is mentioned, Acts xxiii. 16.

fellowprisoners] Strictly, **fellowprisoners-of-war**. Same word as
Col. iv. 10; Philem. 23. The word indicates that these Christians
had once been in prison with St Paul (a glorious reminiscence) in the
course of the *warfare* of Christian duty and suffering.

See 2 Cor. vi. 5, xi. 23, for hints of the many (to us) unknown im-
prisonments of the Apostle. The last passage is specially instructive as
proving that the Acts is a narrative of *selection* only.

of note among the apostles] The words may mean either (1) "*distinguished Apostles*," or (2) "*well known to, and honoured by, the
Apostles*." If (1) is right, the word "Apostle" is used (as in the Gr. of
2 Cor. viii. 23; Phil. ii. 25;) in its literal and wider sense of a
messenger, and here probably (if so) a messenger of the Gospel, a
missionary. The context, however, in 2 Cor. viii. and Phil. ii., is of a
kind which *explains*, and so justifies, such a reference more distinctly
than the context here. We may suppose that St Paul would more
naturally have written here, had (1) been his meaning, "of note among
the apostles of the churches." We incline, then, to the explanation (2):—
these two Christians, possibly because of special deeds of love and
help to others of the Apostles besides St Paul, were particularly
honoured by the apostolic body.

in Christ before me] A beautiful and affecting tribute to these his
"senior saints."

Lord. Salute Urban our helper in Christ, and Stachys my 9
beloved. Salute Apelles approved in Christ. Salute them 10
which are of Aristobulus' *household*. Salute Herodion my 11
kinsman. Greet them that be of the *household* of Narcissus,
which are in the Lord. Salute Tryphena and Tryphosa, 12
who labour in the Lord. Salute the beloved Persis, which
laboured much in the Lord. Salute Rufus chosen in the 13

8. *Amplias*] A name probably contracted from **Ampliātus**, which
appears in some documents. The name is Latin.
9. *Urban*] Strictly, **Urbānus**. (The letter *-e* in the E.V. form is
not to be pronounced : it is like the final *-e* of *Constantine*, and has
nothing to do with *feminine* terminations. It would have been better
to write **Urban** in E.V.) The name is Latin.
Stachys] A Greek name, and masculine.
10. *Apelles*] A Greek name. It is used by Horace, in a well-known
passage, (*Satires*, I. v. 100,) as a name common among Jews.
approved in Christ] I.e. one who has been *tested* and *found true*, as
a "member of Christ." Perhaps he had borne special suffering or
sorrow with strong faith.
them which are of Aristobulus' household] Lit. **those from amongst
Aristobulus'**.—Aristobulus' name is Greek: we know no more of him. He
may, or may not, have been a Christian; and the latter is slightly the
more likely alternative. See next verse, and cp. Phil. iv. 22.—"*Those
from amongst his*" household*, or *people*, are probably the converts in
his *familia*, or establishment, of slaves and freedmen.
11. *Herodion my kinsman*] See on ver. 7. The name is Greek.
them that be of the household of Narcissus] Lit., as just above, **those
from amongst Narcissus'**. There was one notorious Narcissus, a freedman of Claudius; and another, one of Nero's bad favourites. Either
of these *may* have been the master of the Christian dependents here
saluted ; but the name was a common one. The freedman of Claudius
was probably by this time dead, but his household may have been subsist-
ing still.
12. *Tryphēna and Tryphōsa*] Greek names. These Christian
women are otherwise unknown to us. They were very probably, like
Phœbe, "servants of the Church."
labour in the Lord] **toil** (same word as that rendered "*bestow much
labour*," ver. 6,) **in the Lord** ; as being "in Him," and working under
His presence and influence.
the beloved Persis] A Greek name. It is noticeable, as a sign of
St Paul's faultless Christian delicacy, that he does not call this Christian
woman "*my* beloved."
laboured] **toiled**. The aorist may point to some special occasion in
the past. Or possibly Persis was an aged believer, whose day of toil,
being over, was now viewed as *one act* of loving work for Christ.
13. *Rufus*] A Latin name. Possibly this was the Rufus of Mark xv. 21,
brother of Alexander and son of Simon the Cyrenian. Alexander and

¹⁴ Lord, and his mother and mine. Salute Asyncritus, Phlegon,
Hermas, Patrobas, Hermes, and the brethren which are
¹⁵ with them. Salute Philologus, and Julia, Nereus, and his
sister, and Olympas, and all the saints which are with them.

Rufus are apparently named by St Mark as well known in the Christian
Church, and it is observable that his Gospel was probably written at
Rome. But the name is a common one.

chosen in the Lord] Lit. **the chosen one,** &c. All true Christians
might be so described, (viii. 33,) but this, as Meyer remarks, would not
forbid a special and emphatic use of the word, in the case of a Christian
remarkable for character or usefulness.

his mother and mine] Evidently, the mother of Rufus (possibly the
wife of Simon the Cyrenian,) had endeared herself to St Paul by
special Christian kindness; the sweeter to him as his own parents, probably, were long departed.

14. *Asyncrĭtus, Phlegon, Hermas, Patrŏbas, Hermes*] All otherwise,
unknown. The names are Greek.—*Hermas* was the name of the author of
"The Shepherd," a celebrated religious romance, sometimes compared
as such to the Pilgrim's Progress. But it is at least probable that " The
Shepherd " belongs to a later generation than that of the Hermas here
named.—On *Hermes,* see second note on ver. 1.

the brethren which are with them] Perhaps forming with them a
"church" such as that of ver. 5; where see note. If so, the next verse
may similarly be a greeting to a similar district "church," meeting
under another roof.

15. *Philolŏgus*] A Greek name.

Julia] Possibly the wife of Philologus.—The name *may* (as in the
case of *Junia:* see note on ver. 7;) be really *Julias,* i.e., *Julianus;*
a masculine name. But the mention just after of " Nereus and his
sister " weighs, however lightly, in the other direction. So Meyer.

Nereus] A Greek name; that of a minor sea-god, tutelar of the Medi-
terranean under Poseidon. See second note on ver. 1.

Olympas] A Greek masculine name.

the saints which are with them] See last note on ver. 14.

At the close of this long roll of names we cannot but remark on it as
a noble and beautiful illustration of the "family-affection of Christianity." It is often observed that a peculiar charm attaches to succes-
sions of names,

" Lancelot, or Pelleas, or Pellenore;"

and such a rhythmical charm is not absent here. But far above it is
the charm of the pure intense spiritual intimacy of hearts, an intimacy
created by the possession of "one Lord, one Hope," and which with the
advent of the Gospel touched the weary world as a new and unknown
visitor from heaven. We might quote many parallels from later Christian literature; but one will be enough—the dying farewell to his flock
of a man who had no small measure of the holy love and zeal of St Paul
—Felix Neff, the "Apostle of the Hautes Alpes." Two days before

Salute one another with a holy kiss. The churches of ¹⁶
Christ salute you.

17—20   *Special warning against certain teachers of error*

Now I beseech you, brethren, mark them which cause ¹⁷

his death (April, 1829,) "being scarcely able to see, he traced the following lines at different intervals, in large and irregular characters,
which filled a page: 'Adieu, dear friend André Blanc; Antoine Blanc;
the Pelissiers, whom I dearly love; François Dumont and his wife;
Isaac and his wife; Aimé Deslois; Emilie Bonnet, &c., &c., Alexandrine, and their mother—all, all the brethren and sisters at Mens—
Adieu, adieu. I am departing to our Father (*je monte vers notre Père*)
in perfect peace.—Victory, victory, victory, by Jesus Christ.—FELIX
NEFF.'" (*Vie*, Toulouse, 1875.)

16. *Salute one another*] As if to respond to the example set them in
the Apostle's loving greetings.

a holy kiss] So 1 Cor. xvi. 20; 2 Cor. xiii. 12; 1 Thess. v. 26; 1
Pet. v. 14. See also Acts xx. 37.—The kiss, as a mark both of friendship and of reverence, is still almost as usual as ever in the East.—In
the early offices for Baptism the kiss is given to the newly-baptized.
(Bingham, Bk. XII. ch. iv.).

The churches] A better reading gives, **All the churches.** He assumes this universal greeting, from the fact of the universal good-report
of the Roman Christians. (See i. 8.) And he offers it as a seemly
message to the Christians of the mighty Capital.

17—20   SPECIAL WARNING AGAINST CERTAIN TEACHERS
OF ERROR

17. *Now I beseech you*, &c.] From this ver. to ver. 20, inclusive,
we have a paragraph or section by itself. It contains a brief but
earnest warning against an evil which everywhere beset and en-
countered the Apostle—the bold or subtle efforts of perverted and
perverting teachers, Christians in name. We may gather that this evil
was only just beginning at Rome; otherwise more of the Epistle would
be given to it.

Bp Lightfoot, in his note on Phil. iii. 18, gives good reason to think
that the teachers specially in view here are not Judaizers, but their
antipodes—Antinomians. "They (the persons in this passage) are described as......holding plausible language, (ver. 18,) as professing to be
wise beyond others, (ver. 19,) and yet not innocent in their wisdom.
They appear therefore to belong to the same party to which the passages
vi. 1—23, xiv. 1—xv. 6, of that Epistle [to the Romans] are chiefly
addressed." [1]

---

[1] We think, however, that the opinions refuted in ch. vi. are not identical with
those corrected in cch. xiv, xv. In the former case, St Paul makes no compromise;
in the latter, as regards *abstract principle*, he almost identifies himself with those
whom he reproves. In the present verse, accordingly, we take the Antinomians
whom the Romans are to avoid to be Antinomians in the fullest sense: rejecters of

divisions and offences contrary to the doctrine which ye
18 have learned; and avoid them. For *they that are* such
serve not our Lord Jesus Christ, but their own belly; and
by good words and fair speeches deceive the hearts of the
19 simple. For your obedience is come abroad unto all *men*.

mark] **watch**; so as to *avoid* them. Cp. Phil. iii. 17, where the
same word is used with an opposite reference—"watch, so as to *follow*
with them."

divisions and offences] Strictly, and better, **the divisions and the
stumblingblocks.** He refers to circumstances already well-known in
various Churches, and beginning to be felt at Rome.

contrary to the doctrine which ye have learned] Lit. **beyond the
teaching which you** (emphatic) **did learn.** ("*Contrary*," however,
rightly represents the Gr.)—The emphasis on "*you*" seems to indicate
that the erring teachers were, or would be, visitors to Rome, not
original members of the Roman Church. — "*Did learn:*"—at the time of
their evangelization. On the question, when that time was, see *Introduction*, i. § 17, 23.

"The teaching they had learned" could admit no real compromise,
just because it was, in its origin, "not the word of men, but the word
of God." 1 Thess. ii. 13. Cp. Gal. i. 6—10.

avoid them] A peaceable but effective way of resistance.—Cp. 2
Tim. iii. 5; 2 Joh. 10. But these parallels are not *exact;* for the
present passage seems to be specially a caution to individual Christians,
not to go as *learners* to the erring teachers.

18. *serve not*] Perhaps these words (lit. **do not bondservice to,**)
allude to the professed "*liberty*" of the erring teachers. Q. d., "they
decline, indeed, the bondage of Christ, but they are in bondage to their
own appetites all the while." Cp. 2 Pet. ii. 19.—With a similar
emphasis, probably, he writes "our *Lord* (*Master*) Jesus Christ."

their own belly] Cp. Phil. iii. 19. The words indicate sensual self-
indulgence generally, whether grosser or lighter.

by good words, &c.] Lit. **by their sweet-speech and fair-speech.** The
first word denotes the seeming piety, the second the seeming reason-
ableness, of their doctrine.

the simple] Lit. **the evil-less**; people unconscious of bad intentions,
and hence unsuspicious of them.

Meyer remarks that St Paul did not write thus severely till after
long and full experience.

19. *For your obedience*, &c.] This verse is sometimes explained q.d.,
"You are known to be singularly *docile;* a good thing in itself, but
which may be abused by these false teachers: therefore see that your
simplicity is in the right place, and be on the watch." But this is

the moral (as well as ceremonial) law *in all respects;* heretics, in fact, of the type
afterwards developed in some forms of Gnosticism,—holding, probably, that the acts
of the body were indifferent to the soul. They thus may have coincided with the
persons in view in ch. vi, but hardly with those in view in cch. xiv, xv.

I am glad therefore on your behalf: but *yet* I would have you wise unto *that which is* good, and simple concerning evil. And the God of peace shall bruise Satan under your 20 feet shortly. The grace of our Lord Jesus Christ *be* with you. Amen.

unlikely. For (1) St Paul would scarcely commend, even passingly, the spirit which listens deferentially ("*obedience*") to *any teacher whoever he may be;* (2) this Epistle alone proves that, as a fact, the Roman Christians were "in understanding, *men ;*" (3) the word rendered "obedience" is always, elsewhere in N. T., a word of pure good; (4) the closing words of this verse do not agree with the suggested explanation, which would rather demand "simple (in listening) to good, but wise (in watching) against evil." Far more probably the ver. may be paraphrased : "These sectaries deceive the simple. I do not say they deceive *you;* for your heartfelt acceptance of the Truth is known everywhere ; and I rejoice to think of *you* in this light, whatever I may have to mourn over in others. But a caution, even for you, may be in season : do not be led astray by tempting baits of fancied *wisdom.* Be deep in the wisdom of humble faith; be content to be untainted by acquaintance with a wisdom which at its root is evil."

is come abroad] Lit. **did come.** Probably the occasion of their first definite acceptance of the Gospel is referred to. Their strong and deep *allegiance to the Truth,* ("obedience,") was at that time famous everywhere.

on your behalf] Lit. **as to what concerns you.** The word "*you*" is emphatic, with a reference to others who might give St Paul less cause for joy.

but yet I would; &c.] See the paraphrase above, in the last note but two. Cp. Rev. ii. 24, where probably the words imply that the false teachers at Thyatira tempted the believers to listen to them by promising to reveal "depths" of wisdom ; depths which were really, says the Lord, "*depths of Satan.*"

simple] Lit. **untainted.** Same word as Matt. x. 16; Phil. ii. 15; (E. V., "harmless"). The original idea (freedom from *alloy,*) passes into that of freedom from ill motives, or (as here) from defiling knowledge.

20. *the God of peace*] See on xv. 33. Here the sacred Title seems to refer to the miseries of the strife ("divisions and offences") attendant on false doctrine. The God of Peace would be with those who, by clinging to the holy Truth once delivered, held fast to true unity.

shall bruise Satan, &c.] The very first promise of Redemption (Gen. iii. 15,) is doubtless here referred to.—The "Enemy who soweth tares" had been already "bruised" by the Redeemer, in His triumphant work; and that victory would be, in due time, realized in the personal ("under *your* feet,") triumph over sin and death, and final deliverance from all trial, of each of His followers.

shortly] In the eternal "Day," so near at hand, (xiii. 11, 12,) when

21—24 *Salutations*

21 Timotheus my workfellow, and Lucius, and Jason, and
22 Sosipater, my kinsmen, salute you. I Tertius, who wrote
23 *this* epistle, salute you in the Lord. Gaius mine host, and

all "enemies shall be made the footstool" of Messiah, and of His
saints through Him.

The grace of our Lord Jesus Christ, &c.] It may be that St Paul
was about to close the Epistle here. If so, we may suppose that the
request of the Christians round him to add their greetings gave him
occasion to add the few remaining sentences. But may not this benediction be specially connected with the immediate context? Q. d.,
"You have a battle to fight against the assaults of error. It will soon
be over; and meantime may your Lord's grace be with you in the
strife."—The "*Amen*" should be omitted.

21—24 SALUTATIONS

21. *Timotheus my workfellow*] Cp. especially Phil. ii. 19—22 with
this brief allusion to this singularly beloved and honoured friend and
helper of the Apostle. His name appears in eleven Epistles; Rom.,
1 and 2 Cor., Phil., Col., 1 and 2 Thess., 1 and 2 Tim., Philem., Hebr.

Lucius] Perhaps the same person as Lucius of Cyrene, (Acts xiii. 1).
He is sometimes identified with St Luke (Lucas); but there is no good
evidence for this. The names *Lucius* and *Lucas* (*Lucanus*) are quite
distinct.

Jason] Perhaps the same as Jason the Thessalonian; Acts xvii.
5, 6, 7, 9.

Sosipater] Perhaps the same as Sopater the Berœan; Acts xx. 4.
That Sopater perhaps started from *Corinth* with St Paul on the journey
to Asia there mentioned.

my kinsmen] See on ver. 7. Lucius bore a Roman name; Jason
and Sosipater, Greek names.

22. *I Tertius,* &c.] This ver. may be read, **I Tertius greet you,**
who wrote the Epistle in the Lord; i.e., who wrote it, (as the
Apostle's amanuensis,) in the spirit of a Christian, as a work of holy
privilege and love. But the E. V. is also justified by the Greek, and is
the more probable on the whole.

Tertius had a Latin name, and was perhaps a Roman, personally
known to the Church at Rome. There is something strangely real and
life-like in this sudden interposition of the amanuensis, with his own
personal greeting.

who wrote this epistle] Letter-writing by amanuensis was very common in the days of St Paul; and if St Paul suffered in his eyes, as
is not unlikely[1], he would be doubly sure to use such help. It was his
custom (in his earliest Epistles, at least,) to write a few words at the close
with his own hand. See 2 Thess. iii. 17.—Cp. Gal. vi. 11; where render,
"*See in what large letters I write to you, with my own hand.*"

23. *Gaius*] The same Latin name as **Caius.** This Gaius may be

[1] See *Introduction*, i. § 32.

of the whole church, saluteth you. Erastus the chamberlain of the city saluteth you, and Quartus a brother. The 24
grace of our Lord Jesus Christ *be* with you all. Amen.

25—27 *Final Doxology to the Giver and Revealer of the universal Gospel of Salvation by Faith*

Now to him that is of power to stablish you according 25

the same as Gaius of Macedonia, (Acts xix. 29,) or as Gaius of Derbe,
(Acts xx. 4;) and again the Gaius of 2 John may be identical with
either of these. But the name was exceedingly common.

We may be fairly sure that the Gaius here and the Gaius of 1 Cor.
i. 14 are the same. In this Christian's house St Paul seems to have
lodged on this visit to Corinth; and it was a house ever open to
Christian guests. Perhaps the words "*and of the whole church*" mean
that St Paul's stay with Gaius led to a large concourse of other Christian
visitors there, whether Corinthian residents or not.

Erastus] A Greek name. This was probably not the Erastus of
Acts xix. 22, (and probably also of 2 Tim. iv. 20,) who was an assistant
to St Paul, like Timotheus.

chamberlain] Better, **treasurer.** Erastus stands almost alone in the
apostolic history as a convert from the dignified ranks. Cp. Acts
xvii. 34, and perhaps Acts xiii. 12. See 1 Cor. i. 26.

the city] Corinth. The brief phrase indicates the eminence of the
place whence the letter is written.—See *Introduction*, ii. § 1.

Quartus] A Latin name; (in its Greek form here, *Kouartos*.)
Possibly Quartus, like Tertius, was a Roman. We know him only
from this verse.

a brother] Lit. **the brother**; i.e. "our fellow-Christian."

24. *The grace*, &c.] Cp. 2 Thess. iii. 16, for a similar adieu before
the actual close.

We venture to suggest that thus far the amanuensis wrote; that St
Paul then in some sense reviewed his great Epistle; and then, perhaps
with his own hand, added the rapturous Doxology with which it now
ends, and which sums up with such pregnant force so much of the
mighty argument[1].

25—27 FINAL DOXOLOGY TO THE GIVER AND REVEALER OF THE UNIVERSAL GOSPEL OF SALVATION BY FAITH

25. *Now to him*, &c.] The construction of this Doxology is irregular;
for in ver. 27 the lit. Gr. is, **To God only wise, through Jesus Christ,
to whom be glory for ever. Amen**; and the relative pronoun "*to
whom*" is redundant. (See further on that verse.) The practical
meaning, however, is clear. The whole is a Doxology to the Eternal
Father, through the Son, for the gift and manifestation of the world-

---

[1] Alford quotes the same suggestion from Fritzsche, and points out that the
diction of the Doxology resembles passages elsewhere which are known to have been
written with St Paul's *own hand.*

to my gospel, and the preaching of Jesus Christ, according
to the revelation of the mystery, which was kept secret
26 since the world began, but now is made manifest, and by

wide Salvation by Faith, which prophets had foretold and which was
now at last fully proclaimed.—On the questions raised about this
Doxology, see *Introduction*, ii. § 3.

to stablish you] Cp. i. 11; 1 Thess. iii. 13; 2 Thess. ii. 17, iii. 3;
1 Pet. v. 10. See also Acts xiv. 23, xx. 32.

according to my gospel] I. e. in the way revealed and promised in the
Gospel as taught by St Paul; the Gospel which offers justification to
the believer, and with it the gift of the Divine Spirit and His aid.—
"*My Gospel*:"—same words as ii. 16, (where see note;) 2 Tim. ii. 8.
Cp. 1 Tim. i. 11.

the preaching of Jesus Christ] This may grammatically mean either
(1) "the preaching which *speaks of Him*;" (in which case it would be
a phrase explanatory of "my Gospel;") or (2) "the preaching which
He Himself delivers." In the latter case again the reference may be
either (*a*) to the Lord's utterances when on earth (as e.g. Joh. iii., vi.);
or (*b*) to His after work through St Paul and the other Apostles; cp.
xv. 18, and note there. On the whole, the last reference seems the
most likely. St Paul thus both qualifies the thought that the Gospel
he preached was "his," and enforces the thought of its absolute truth.—
"*Preaching*:"—the Gr. word (same as 1 Cor. i. 21,) means the *contents
of the message*, not the *act of preaching*.

according to the revelation, &c.] St Paul's Gospel and the Lord's
Proclamation were "*according to,*" in harmony with, this "*unveiling*"
of the great hidden Truth. The unveiling of the Truth occasioned the
proclamation, and was the substance of it. The unveiling and the
proclamation were thus coincident and harmonious.

the mystery] On the word "*mystery*," see note on xi. 25.—The
great Secret here is that of Salvation by Faith for all, of whatever
nation, who come with "the obedience of faith" to Christ the Propitiation. See especially Eph. iii. 3—9. Here, however, more than
there, the emphasis seems to be on the freedom of the WAY of
Acceptance as well as on the world-wide largeness of the offer;—on
the "obedience of FAITH" as well as on the "making of it known to
all nations." Not that Salvation by Faith was a secret unheard of till
the Christian age; (for see ch. iv.;) but that its Divine manifestation in
the Cross, and consequent unreserved proclamation as the central truth
of Redeeming Love, were new.

which was kept secret since the world began] Lit. **which had been
reserved in silence during æonian times**, or **periods of ages**. The
"ages" here probably refer to the whole lapse of periods before the
Gospel "age," perhaps including not only human time with its patri-
archal and Mosaic "ages," and its ranges of pagan history, but the
"age" of angelic life. For we gather (cp. Eph. iii. 10) that even to
angels the Incarnation and its results in believing mankind formed a

the scriptures of the prophets, according to the commandment of the everlasting God, made known to all nations for
the obedience of faith: to God only wise, *be* glory through 27
Jesus Christ for ever.   Amen.

¶ Written to the Romans from Corinthus, *and sent* by Phebe servant
of the church at Cenchrea.

new manifestation of the Divine wisdom.—The E. V. thus well represents the Gr. as a paraphrase.—Cp. again Eph. iii. 3—9.

26.   *now*] In the days of Messiah, and in Him as the Propitiation.
Cp. Col. i. 26.

by the scriptures, &c.] Lit. **by means of (the) prophetic scriptures**.
This Epistle, and e.g. Acts xiii., are the best commentary on these
words.   The O. T., as the great prediction of Messiah and preparation
for Him, was the text and the warrant of His Apostles wherever they
went, and that for Gentiles as much as for Jews.   When the Gentiles
previously knew nothing of the O. T. the preaching would, of course,
not take the O. T. as its starting-point; (see St Paul's discourse at
Athens;) but even in such cases it would bring forward the Prophecies as soon as possible, both as its credentials and its text.—We
have heard this verse unintentionally illustrated by a distinguished
Hindoo convert, of great intellectual power; who attributed his ultimate escape from the maze of Brahminic pantheism to the attentive
study of the Messianic prophecies side by side with the Gospel history.

the everlasting God] The Gr. word (*aionios*) rendered **everlasting** perhaps refers back to the "*æons*" or "ages" of ver. 25.   Q. d.,
"The Gospel is now revealed and proclaimed according to the will of
Him who appoints and adjusts all the developements of His providence, alike past, present and to come."   He who rules all duration
knows when to keep silence and when to break it.—This adjective is
nowhere else in the N.T. attached to the word GOD.—On the adjective,
see further on ii. 7.

to all nations] Lit. **to** (or perhaps better, **for**) **all the nations**.   The
special reference is, of course, to the *Gentiles*.

for the obedience of faith] I. e. to invite that obedience which, in
fact, faith implies; that trustful acceptance of the terms of Salvation
which may be described, in one aspect, as "*submission* to the righteousness of God."   (See note on x. 3.)   The thought is not so much of
the course of moral obedience to which faith leads, as of the element of
submission in the act of faith.

In this brief phrase the great Theme of the Epistle is heard for the
last time.

27.   *to God only wise*] So certainly; though the Gr. equally allows
the rendering **to the only wise God**.   But the assertion of His glory as
the Only (absolutely) Wise *Being* is far more in harmony with the
height and fulness of the language here, than the assertion that among
all *Divinities*, real or supposed, He only is wise.—The eternal *Wisdom*

is here emphasized because the Gospel is its supreme expression. See especially the profound words of Eph. iii. 10, and 1 Tim. i. 17 (with its connexion). Cp. also "Christ...the wisdom of God," 1 Cor. i. 24. —In Jude 25, the word "wise" is probably to be omitted.

be glory, &c.] The lit. order and rendering of the remaining words is—**through Jesus Christ, to whom be the glory for ever. Amen.** Here the construction becomes involved by the use of the relative, "*to whom ;*" and this is equally so whether the relative refers to God or to Christ. That it refers to God seems to be proved, (1) by the opening words of ver. 25, which lead us to expect, through the whole passage, an ascription of praise to the *Father;* (2) by the name of Christ occurring in a phrase (see next note) which indicates His *mediatorial* work, as the Channel through which praise rises to the Father.

through Jesus Christ] Meyer connects these words closely with the phrase "to God only wise," and explains them to mean that the absolute Wisdom of God *acts and is revealed through Jesus Christ.* But this, though in itself eternally true, involves a grammatical construction sufficiently peculiar to recommend the more obvious one which takes the words "through Jesus Christ" to refer to the Son of God as *our Channel of thanks and praise.* Cp. ch. i. 8.—We now explain the abrupt construction (see last note) as if St Paul had fully written, "Now to Him that is of power to stablish you, &c., *we give thanks;* even to God Only Wise, through Jesus Christ; to whom (i.e. to God) be the glory for ever."

The construction of this Doxology is remarkable not only in itself, but in the fact that it was evidently left unaltered by St Paul and his friends. No various reading of the least importance occurs throughout it.

for ever. Amen] See on i. 25, and on xi. 33, &c. Justly does the great Epistle end with the highest of all thoughts, the GLORY OF GOD everlastingly manifested and confessed. AMEN, SO BE IT.

THE SUBSCRIPTION

Written to the Romans, &c.] Lit. **To the Romans [i.e. The Epistle to the Romans] was written from Corinth, by means of Phœbe the servant of the Cenchrean church.** This ancient "Subscription" is no doubt true to fact. In this it differs from those appended to 1 Cor., Galat., 1 Tim., which are contradictory to the contents of the respective Epistles ; and from those appended to Thess. and Titus, which are difficult to be reconciled with the contents.

These "Subscriptions" (to St Paul's Epistles) are said to be the work of Euthalius, a Bishop of the fifth century. They thus possess an antiquarian interest, but no historical authority. (See Scrivener's *Introduction to the Criticism of the N. T.*, ed. 1874, p. 60.)

APPENDICES

A. RABBINIC DOCTRINES ; MERIT, PRIVILEGE
(Cch. II., III.)

THE following extracts from the Talmud are from the late Dr A. M‘Caul's *Old Paths*. The original Rabbinic, as well as the reference, is there given in each case.

(On the Talmud as evidence to opinion in St Paul's day, see just below, Appendix B.)

" Every one of the children of men has merits and sins. If his merits exceed his sins, he is righteous. If his sins exceed his merits, he is wicked. If they be half and half, he is an intermediate person, בינוני."
p. 125.—" Circumcision is equivalent to all the commandments that are in the Law." p. 230.—" The wise men have said, that Abraham our father sits at the door of hell (Gehinnom), and does not suffer any one that is circumcised to be cast into it." p. 229.—" Amongst all the commandments, there is not one that is equivalent to the study of the Law. Whereas the study of the Law is equivalent to all the commandments ; for study leads to practice. Therefore, study always goes before good deeds." p. 131.—" What is a sojourning proselyte? A Gentile, who has taken upon himself the commandments given to the sons of Noah, but is not circumcised nor baptized. Such a one is received, and is of the pious of the nations of the world. And why is he called *a sojourner?* Because it is lawful for us to let him dwell among us in the land of Israel. ...But a sojourning proselyte *is*

not received except during the celebration of the year of jubilee" (p. 34);
i.e., during one year in fifty. But elsewhere the Talmud says that
there *has been no jubilee* since the Captivity of the Ten Tribes (p. 35).
Full proselytism is thus the only real hope for a Gentile.—"What
constitutes a *Stranger* (i.e. a full proselyte)? Sacrifice, circumcision,
and baptism. At the present time, when there is no sacrifice, circumcision and baptism are necessary; and when the Temple is rebuilt, he
must bring a sacrifice. A *Ger* (Stranger) is not a *Ger* until he is both
circumcised and baptized." p. 154.

These extracts may aid us, in some measure, in estimating the kind of
prejudice against which St Paul aims in Rom. ii. &c.

The work from which the extracts are taken, *The Old Paths*,
(נתיבות עולם), is itself no mean illustration of the prophecies of Rom.
xi. It was originally a serial, circulated (1836—7) among the Jews of
London, as "a comparison of Modern Judaism with the religion of
Moses and the Prophets;" and it is a deeply earnest while most
temperate appeal by a Gentile *Messianist* to Jews.

B. THE EXAMPLE OF ABRAHAM (Ch. IV.)

Bp Lightfoot (*Ep. to the Galatians*, detached note to ch. iii.)
makes it very probable that "at the time of the Christian era the
passage in Genesis relating to Abraham's faith had become a standard
text in the Jewish schools...and that the interest thus concentrated
upon it prepared the way for the fuller and more spiritual teaching
of the Apostles." By Philo, the great representative of Alexandria,
Gen. xv. 6 "is quoted or referred to at least ten times." And in the
Talmud, which reflects "fairly, though with some exceptions, the
Jewish teaching at the Christian era," "the significance attached to
Abraham's example may be inferred from the following passage in
the *Mechilta* on Exod. xiv. 31: 'Great is faith, whereby Israel
believed on Him that spake and the world was. For as a reward
for Israel's having believed in the Lord, the Holy Spirit dwelt on
them. ... Abraham our father inherited this world and the world to
come solely by the merit of faith whereby he believed in the Lord;
for it is said, *and he believed in the Lord, and it was counted &c.* ......
So...Habakkuk, *The righteous liveth of his faith*...Great is faith!'"[1]
Bp Lightfoot adds in a note, that some later Jewish writers, "anxious,
it would appear, to cut the ground from under St Paul's inference
of 'righteousness by faith,' interpreted the latter clause [of Gen. xv. 6],
'and Abraham counted on God's righteousness,' i.e. on His strict
fulfilment of His promise. ... Such a rendering is as harsh in itself
as it is devoid of traditional support."

[1] Observe that the idea of *merit*, visible in the above passages, is carefully excluded by St Paul.

C. ST PAUL AND ST JAMES ON JUSTIFICATION. MEANING OF THE WORD FAITH

THE facts given in Appendix B. help to clear up the verbal discrepancy[1] between St Paul's explicit teaching that "a man is justified by faith *without works*" and St James' equally explicit teaching that "*by works* a man is justified, and *not by faith only*" (Epistle, ii. 24). With only the N. T. before us it is hard not to assume that the one Apostle has in view some distortion of the doctrine of *the other*. But the fact that Abraham's faith was a staple Rabbinic text alters the case, by making it perfectly possible that St James (writing to members of the Jewish Dispersion, i. 1,) had not apostolic but *Rabbinic* teaching in view. And the line such teaching took is indicated clearly by Jas ii. 19, where an *example* is given of the faith in question; and that example is concerned wholly with the grand Point of *strictly Jewish orthodoxy*—GOD IS ONE. This is doubly instructive; for it suggests (1) that the persons addressed were still almost as much Judaic as Christian; and (2) that, however that might be, their idea of faith was not *trustful acceptance*, a belief of the heart, but *orthodox adherence*, a belief of the head. And St James may very justly have taken these persons strictly on their own ground, and assumed, for his argument, their own very faulty account of faith to be correct.

He would thus be proving the point, equally dear to St Paul, that mere theoretic orthodoxy, apart from effects on the will, is valueless. He would not, in the remotest degree, be disputing the Pauline doctrine that the guilty soul is put into a position of acceptance with the FATHER only by vital connexion with the SON, and that this connexion is effectuated, *absolutely and alone*, not by personal merit, but by trustful acceptance of the Propitiation and its all-sufficient vicarious merit. From such trustful acceptance "works" (in the profoundest sense) will inevitably follow ; not as antecedents but as consequents of Justification. And thus, to quote again words quoted in the notes, (p. 137,) "It is faith alone which justifies; but the faith which justifies can never be alone."

See further Bp O'Brien's *Nature and Effects of Faith*, Note V. p. 145.

It may be well here to make a few remarks on the meaning of the word "Faith" in connexion with the main doctrine of the Epistle to the Romans.

"FAITH," on the whole, i. e. in cases where an *exceptional* meaning[2] is not traceable, is explained in Scripture (and this is only in harmony with human language) to be, as to its essence, TRUST. It will be enough

---

[1] Even should that discrepancy be still perplexing, the believer in the Divine plan of Scripture, as he looks at the relative fulness and detail of the passages in the two Apostles, will feel that the right order is to explain St James by St Paul, and not *vice versâ*.

[2] E.g. that of *trustworthiness*, (as in Rom. iii. 3,) or that of the *standard* of belief, or that of *a trust*.

to say that in every case where our Lord Himself inculcates Faith, the idea of Trust as the essence of Faith gives the one satisfactory account of the word. Faith is not reverence, nor credence of historic fact or evidence ; nor is it zeal, nor even affection. It is personal and acting *Trust*[1].

Such trust may be rightly or wrongly *placed;* and in its *placing*[2] lies all its efficacy or inefficacy in respect of putting guilty man into a position of acceptance with God. Even the persons rebuked in Jas. ii. *trusted;* but they *were not justified;* for their trust was, in effect, reposed not on God and His Promise, but on their own correct conception of His Unity. The man described in Rom. iv. 5 *trusts*, and *is justified;* not because it is in itself meritorious to trust, but because trust "in HIM that justifieth the ungodly" is trust placed precisely aright, on a sinner's part, in view of the Promise and the Propitiation, and of his own guilt.

In Heb. xi. 1, it must be remembered, by the way, we have not a *definition* but a *description* of faith : we there see not what it essentially is, but what it is found, when really applied to God and His promises, to be able to do ; even to grasp and anticipate the invisible Future. Faith has many directions of exercise *besides* trustful acceptance of the Propitiation ; but it is with this latter work, which is also its perfectly *characteristic* work, that we have to do in Rom. iii.—viii. ; where certainly St Paul labours on every side of the subject to shut off extraneous ideas, and to give his reader not a vague but most definite view of the correlative facts of the *all*-sufficiency of Christ the Propitiation and the *all*-efficacy, for justification, of trustful acceptance of Him as such.

D. IMPUTED GUILT OF THE FIRST SIN   (Ch. V.)

WE make no attempt (beyond what is said in the notes) to *clear up* this Doctrine, which approaches as nearly as well can be to *complete* mystery, and leans upon relations between the Head of an intelligent Race and that Race which are probably "knowable" by the Eternal alone.   All that we do here is to clear up the *statement* of the Doctrine ; which means not that the Omniscient Judge is to be held to *think of every individual man as having done Adam's sin*, but to hold every individual man (because of the mysterious link between him and the Head of his Race) liable to penalty because Adam sinned.

---

[1] It is not too much to say that this account of Faith is given in the Documents (Confessions, Articles, or Homilies,) of *all* the Churches of the Reformation, and by *all* the great Protestant teachers of that age. See O'Brien, *Nature &c. of Faith*, p. 291 &c.

[2] That justifying faith is "the gift of God" is certain, not only from Eph. ii. 8, (where we hold the E. V. to be the *true* rendering,) but from the general testimony of Scripture and the reason of the case.   But this means not that something is given us which is different from absolute trust as exercised in other cases, but that such trust is divinely guided and fixed upon the Right Object.

Exactly thus, we are not asked to believe that the Omniscient *thinks of the justified as having personally satisfied His justice*, but that He holds them (because of their connexion with the Head of the New Race) accepted because Christ obeyed.

E. THE STATE DESCRIBED IN Ch. VII. 14—24

THE controversy over this profound passage is far too wide to allow of full treatment here. It is scarcely needful to say that conclusions very different from those in the notes have been drawn by many most able and most devout expositors, ancient and modern. Very earnest convictions, mainly based on St Paul's *general* teaching, and that of Scripture, alone could justify us in the positive statement of another view.

Here we offer only a few further general remarks.

(1) On the question *what St Paul here meant* very little certain light is thrown by quotations from pagan writers describing an inner conflict. For in the great majority of such passages the language manifestly describes the conflict of *conscience* and will; and the confusion of the voice of *conscience* with the far different voice of personal *will* is so easy,—and no wonder, if Scripture truly describes the state of the human *mind* (cp. Eph. ii. 3, iv. 17, 18) as to spiritual truth,—that we believe that even the grandest utterances of pagan thought on this subject must yet be explained of a conflict not so much of *will* with *will*, as of *will* with *conscience*.

A careful collection of such passages (from Thucydides, Xenophon, Euripides, Epictetus, Plautus, both the Senecas, and Ovid) is given by Tholuck[1], on Rom. vii. 15. And our conviction on the whole, from these and similar passages, is that either they do not mean to describe a conflict of will with will, or that they betray the illusions to which the mind, unvisited by special grace, must surely be liable regarding the conditions of the soul's action; illusions which this chapter, among other passages of Revelation, tends to dispel.

(2) Suppose the person described in ch. vii. 14—25 to be not re-generate, not a recipient of the Holy Spirit; and compare the case thus supposed with the language of ch. viii. 5—9. The consequence must be that one who is "*in the flesh*," (for St Paul recognizes neither here nor elsewhere an intermediate or semi-spiritual condition,) and who as such "*cannot please God*," can yet truly say, "It is no more I that do it, but sin that dwelleth in me;" and, "I delight in the law of God after the inward man;" and, "With the mind I myself serve the law of God."

Now is this possible, *from the point of view of St Paul's teaching?* For consider what he means by the LAW : not man's subjective view of

[1] Whose conclusions are very different from ours.

moral truth and right, but the absolute and profoundly spiritual demands of the TRUE GOD upon not the approval of man but his WHOLE WILL.

Surely when Divine grace makes plain to the man the width and depth of *those* demands, he needs a "renewing of the *mind*" (Rom. xii. 2) if he is to say with truth, "I *delight*[1] in the Law;" "I myself *with my mind* serve it."

(3) The supposed impossibility of assigning the language of this passage to one who is meanwhile "in Christ" and "has peace with God" will at least seem less impossible if we remember St Paul's manner of *isolating* a special aspect of truth. May he not, out of his profound, intense, and subtle spiritual experience, have chosen for a special purpose to look on one aspect only as if it were the whole? on his consciousness of the element which still called for "mortification," hanging on "a cross," "buffeting," "groans," "fear and trembling," (viii. 13, 23; 1 Cor. ix. 27; Col. iii. 5; Phil. ii. 12, &c.;) almost as if he had no other consciousness?

(4) It is often assumed that ch. viii. is an express contrast to ch. vii. 14—25. But it is far more likely that it is written to sum up the whole previous Epistle. (See note on viii. 1.) If it is designed as a contrast to ch. vii., surely such words as those of viii. 13, 23, are out of place.

With this view of ch. viii. there is less likelihood of our taking ch. vii. to describe a state antecedent to the experience of ch. viii. But however, if we are right in our remarks in (3), *any* view of ch. viii. still leaves ch. vii. quite free to be a description of (one side of) regenerate experience.

(5) Tholuck (on vii. 15) quotes from Grotius the remark that "it would be a sad thing, indeed, if the Christian, *as such*, could apply these sayings" (those of the pagan writers who describe an inner conflict) "to himself." But those who interpret ch. vii. of the experience of a Christian take it to describe not his experience *as a Christian*, but his experience as *a man still in the body, but who, as a Christian, has been illuminated* truly to apprehend that infinite Holiness which can only cease to conflict with a part of his condition when at length his trial-time is over.

F. ELECTION   (Cch. VIII., IX.—XI.)

IT is almost needless to say that the Election spoken of in ch. viii. &c. is variously explained. A large and important school of Theology (the Arminian) interprets it as a *personal* election, but *contingent* upon foreseen faith and perseverance. Another school[2] interprets it as an election not personal at all, but (so to speak) *social;* an election, like

---

[1] A word which it is impossible to explain away.
[2] Or, more properly, other schools, with important differences among themselves in other respects.

the election of the Jewish Nation, not to life eternal but to a vantage-ground for attaining it.

Without forgetting for a moment the awful mysteries of the subject, we yet feel that both these theories, with all (and it is very much) that can be said for them, *do not fit the language of ch. viii.* and of St Paul's (not to quote St John's) general teaching. "NOT according to OUR WORKS" is surely the tone of this chapter and of the whole previous epistle, and of the next three chapters. And it seems to us impossible, on any other theory than that of a Personal Election to Life, antecedent to "our works" and mercifully prevailing in its purpose, *quite naturally to explain the tone of rapturous joy* which marks the closing passages of the chapter.

In the Seventeenth English Article, a masterpiece of careful expression, this result of the humble belief in an Election personal and effectual (but, observe, taking effect through moral means,) is strongly stated:—"The godly consideration of Predestination, and our Election in Christ, is *full of sweet, pleasant, and unspeakable comfort*, to godly persons, &c."

See the whole Article; and especially the closing paragraph, in which the word "*generally*" is technical, and means "with regard to *the genus;*"—i.e. probably, *mankind.* The Article warns us to begin with faith in the promises to man as man, not with the question of personal election.

G. PREDESTINATION (CH. IX.)

SEE note on chap. viii. 30, on the original word.

On this great mystery, brought up with such stern force in ch. ix., we quote a few sentences from one who certainly spoke from no cold or unsympathetic heart—Martin Luther. His *Præfatio in Ep. ad Romanos* (translated into Latin from Luther's German by his friend Justus Jonas) is indeed, as Tholuck describes it, "admirable, and breathing the very spirit of St Paul." There is a very noble contemporary English paraphrase of it, by Tyndale, from which we take the following passage (Tyndale's *Doctrinal Treatises*, Parker Soc. Edition, p. 505):—

"In the ninth, tenth, and eleventh chapters he (Paul) treateth of God's predestination, whence it springeth altogether whether we shall believe or not believe...By which predestination our justifying and salvation are clean taken out of our hands, and put in the hands of God only. For we are so weak and so uncertain, that, if it stood in us, there would of a truth be no man saved; the devil, no doubt, would deceive us. But now is God sure, that His predestination cannot deceive Him, neither can any man withstand or let Him; and therefore have we hope and trust against sin.

"But here must a mark be set to those unquiet, busy, and high-climbing spirits which begin first from an high (*sic*) to search the bottomless secrets of God's predestination, whether they be predestinate or not. These must needs either cast themselves down headlong into desperation, or else commit themselves to free chance, careless.

But follow thou the order of this Epistle, and noosel thyself[1] *with Christ,* and learn to understand what the Law and the Gospel mean, and the office of both the two; that thou mayest in the one know thyself, and how thou hast of thyself no strength but to sin, and in the other the grace of Christ; and then see thou fight against sin and the flesh, as the seven first chapters teach thee. After that, when thou art come to the eighth chapter, and *art under the cross and suffering of tribulation,* the necessity[2] of predestination will wax sweet, and thou shalt well feel how precious a thing it is. For except thou have borne the cross of adversity and temptation, and hast felt thyself brought into the very brim of desperation, yea, and unto hell-gates, thou canst never meddle with the sentence of predestination without thine own harm, and without secret wrath and grudging inwardly against God; for otherwise it shall not be possible for thee to think that God is righteous and just... Take heed therefore unto thyself, that thou drink not wine, while thou art yet but a suckling. For...in Christ there is a certain childhood, in which a man must be content with milk for a season, until he wax strong and grow up unto a perfect man in Christ, and be able to eat of more strong meat."

And to the last, surely, the dark problems that gather round the central and insoluble mystery of SIN will be safely approached only when the remembrance that "the JUDGE of all the earth" will "do right;" that He is the ETERNAL, and that His "ways" must therefore be "past finding out;" and that He "so loved the world that He gave His Only-begotten SON."

H. REPROBATION (Ch. IX.)

IN the last note but one on ix. 22 we have alluded to the tenet that the lost are personally and positively fore-doomed to ruin.   To this tenet Calvin was led, not by a passionless rigidity, from which his deep and sensitive temperament, and truly ample mind, were far removed; but by the conviction that it was inexorably demanded by Scripture and reason.   But St Augustine, the great patristic teacher of Predestination, carefully avoided such a tenet; teaching that, however little we can fathom the mystery, man's sin, running its proper course, is the only cause of man's ruin; while yet special grace is the only cause of his salvation.

J. SUBJECTION TO "THE POWERS THAT BE" (Ch. XIII.)

THE following extract from Thomas Scott's remarks on Rom. xiii. is full of strong sense and clear statement:—

---

[1] I.e. *find shelter, as a child with a nurse.* This striking clause is not in the Latin of the *Præfatio.*

[2] *Necessitas,* fixed certainty.

"Perhaps nothing involves greater difficulties, in very many instances, than to ascertain to whom, either individually or collectively, the authority *justly* belongs...If then, the most learned and intelligent men find insuperable difficulties...respecting this subject, how shall the bulk of the people be able to decide it? And if Christians are first to determine concerning the *right* by which their rulers possess and exercise authority, before they think themselves bound to obedience, they must very commonly indeed be engaged in opposition to 'the existing authorities.' But the Apostle's design was to mark out the plain path of duty to Christians, however circumstanced. ... Submission in all things lawful [i.e., not forbidden by the Supreme Divine Authority] to 'the existing authorities' is our duty at all times and in all cases; though in civil convulsions, and amid great revolutions, or sudden changes in governments, there may frequently, for a season, be a difficulty in determining which are ...'the existing authorities.'"

K. RESEMBLANCES BETWEEN THE ROMAN AND THE CORINTHIAN EPISTLES

IN the Introduction, ch. v., we have collected and analyzed the main resemblances between the *Romans* and *Galatians;* resemblances so marked and peculiar that they fairly constitute an independent proof that the two Epistles stand nearly together in point of time. The case is rather different with the resemblances between *Romans* and *Corinthians.* These (except the resemblance of *quotation* noticed below) are scarcely sufficient to afford independent proof of date; for resemblances nearly as considerable in proportion might be traced, e. g., between *Romans* and *Philippians.* But since other and external evidence fairly establishes the nearness in date of *Romans* and *Corinthians,* it becomes an interesting enquiry in the way of illustration, how far their topics and expression run in similar lines. We subjoin some of the *chief* instances; giving references to the Corinthian Epistles only, and leaving the reader to supply the parallel (and sometimes the contrast) from his own study of the Epistle to the Romans.

a. I. COR. i. 29, ("that no flesh should glory in His presence;") ii. 10, ("The Spirit searcheth all things, &c.";) iii. 22, ("all things are yours...things present, or things to come;") vi. 11, ("Ye are justified;") viii., (Principles of toleration for the guidance of "the strong;") ix. 27, (Conflict with the body;) xii., (Diversity of Christian gifts;) xv. 21, 22, 45, (The Second Adam;) 56, ("The strength of sin is the Law.")

β. II. COR. i. 24, ("By faith ye stand;") iii. 16, (The "vail" on Jewish hearts;) iv. 17, (Contrast of present suffering and coming glory;) v. 2, (The "groaning" of the saints;) 10, ("The judgment-seat;") 14, (Vicarious death;) 19, (Imputation;) 21, (Christ made sin for us; cp. Gal. iii. 13;) ibidem, ("The righteousness of God;) x. 13—16, (Paul will take no credit for labours not his own;) xi. 2, (Christ the mystic

Husband;) 22, ("Are they Hebrews? so am I; are they Israelites? so am I.")

Perhaps the most striking general sign of relationship between the Epistles to Corinth, Galatia, and Rome, is their abundance of Old Testament quotation. An examination of any other Epistle of St Paul's (putting the *Hebrews* apart) will make this plain. The only Epistles of the N.T. which in this respect can be compared to the Four now in question are the Epistle to the Hebrews, and the First Epistle of St Peter.

POSTSCRIPT

AFTER an interval of some years, the Editor adds a few words of qualification to his notes on the opening of ch. vi. and the close of ch. vii.

(1) Ch. vi. 1—11. The explanation of this passage as a whole still seems to the Editor to be right, particularly in respect of vv. 2, 7, 10, 14. But in the whole interpretation more prominence should be given to the Union of the Christian with his Lord, not only in *acceptance* or *justification*, with its great moral results upon the will, but also in *life* by the Holy Spirit. The new creation is such that the member and Head are "one Spirit" (1 Cor. vi. 17), and the member derives from the Head spiritual force and faculty profoundly altering the conditions and possibilities of deliverance from sin's "reign" (ver. 12), and so of holy obedience.

(2) Ch. vii. 7—25. Here again the explanation as a whole still seems sound. But one great feature of the passage needs to be noticed; its silence about the Holy Spirit. In view of this the Editor adds the following remarks (from his *Outlines of Christian Doctrine*, pp. 196, 197): "[We have in Rom. vii. 7—25] the inner experience of the fully regenerate, but presented for study under peculiar conditions —isolated from the Divine factor of the Holy Spirit's conquering work, and observed as in view of the absolute holiness of the law of God (ver. 12), and the constant presence (ver. 18) of 'the flesh,' and the insight of the renewed reason (vv. 22, 23, 25) into the glory of the will of God and the hatefulness of the least sin....The regenerate man, assailed by temptation through 'the flesh' (in its moral...sense), meets the attack with his highest regenerate powers, but without actively calling in the Divine force of the Comforter, by whom he is in Christ and Christ in him. And the conflict continues in partial but serious failure, at the best. It is otherwise when (viii. 13) we '*through the Spirit* mortify the deeds of the body.' Rom. vii. thus describes a real element in the regenerate life, liable to be experienced at any... moment. And in the mystery of the Fall it *is* experienced, in the light of the absolute holiness of the law (ver. 12), brought home by the Spirit as enlightener."

INDEX